W9-CDM-518

Applications in Basic Marketing

Clippings from the Popular Business Press

1998-1999 Edition

Applications in Basic Marketing

Clippings from the Popular Business Press

1998-1999 Edition

William D. Perreault, Jr.
University of North Carolina

and

E. Jerome McCarthy
Michigan State University

Boston   Burr Ridge, IL   Dubuque, IA   Madison, WI   New York   San Francisco   St. Louis
Bangkok   Bogotá   Caracas   Lisbon   London   Madrid
Mexico City   Milan   New Delhi   Seoul   Singapore   Sydney   Taipei   Toronto

Irwin/McGraw-Hill

A Division of The **McGraw·Hill** *Companies*

APPLICATIONS IN BASIC MARKETING: CLIPPINGS FROM
THE POPULAR BUSINESS PRESS, 1998-1999 EDITION

Copyright © 1999 by The McGraw-Hill Companies, Inc. All rights reserved. Previous edition ©
1998. Copyright © 1993, 1996, and 1997 by Richard D. Irwin, a Times Mirror Higher Education
Group, Inc. Printed in the United States of America. Except as permitted under the United States
Copyright Act of 1976, no part of this publication may be reproduced or distributed in any form
or by any means, or stored in a data base or retrieval system, without the prior written permission
of the publisher.

This book is printed on acid-free paper.

international   1 2 3 4 5 6 7 8 9 0 QPD/QPD 9 3 2 1 0 9 8
domestic   1 2 3 4 5 6 7 8 9 0 QPD/QPD 9 3 2 1 0 9 8

ISBN 0-07-561028-0

Vice president and editorial director: *Michael W. Junior*
Publisher: *Gary Burke*
Executive editor: *Stephen M. Patterson*
Coordinating editor: *Linda G. Davis*
Senior developmental editor: *Nancy Barbour*
Senior marketing manager: *Colleen J. Suljic*
Project manager: *Kari Geltemeyer*
Senior production supervisor: *Melonie Salvati*
Director of design BR/DBQ: *Keith J. McPherson*
Compositor: *Electronic Publishing Services, Inc.*
Printer: *Quebecor Printing Book Group/Dubuque*

INTERNATIONAL EDITION
Copyright © 1999. Exclusive rights by The McGraw-Hill Companies, Inc. for manufacture and export.
This book cannot be re-exported from the country to which it is consigned by McGraw-Hill.
The International Edition is not available in North America.

• When ordering the title, use ISBN 0-07-115841-3

http://www.mhhe.com

Preface

This is the ninth annual edition of *Applications in Basic Marketing*. We developed this set of marketing "clippings" from popular business publications to accompany our texts—*Basic Marketing* and *Essentials of Marketing*. All of these clippings report interesting case studies and current issues that relate to topics covered in our texts and in the first marketing course. We will continue to publish a new edition of this book *every year*. That means that we can include the most current and interesting clippings. Each new copy of our texts will come shrink-wrapped with a free copy of the newest (annual) edition of this book. However, it can also be ordered from the publisher separately for use in other courses or with other texts.

Our objective is for this book to provide a flexible and helpful set of teaching and learning materials. We have included clippings (articles) on a wide variety of topics. The clippings deal with consumer products and business products, goods and services, new developments in marketing as well as traditional issues, and large well-known companies as well as new, small ones. They cover important issues related to marketing strategy planning for both domestic and global markets. The readings can be used for independent study, as a basis for class assignments, or as a focus of in-class discussions. Some instructors might want to assign all of the clippings, but we have provided an ample selection so that it is easy to focus on a subset which is especially relevant to specific learning/teaching objectives. A separate set of teaching notes discusses points related to each article. We have put special emphasis on selecting short, highly readable articles—ones which can be read and understood in 10 or 15 minutes—so that they can be used in combination with other readings and assignments for the course. For example, they might be used in combination with assignments from *Basic Marketing,* exercises from the *Learning Aid for Use with Basic Marketing,* or *The Marketing Game!* micro-computer strategy simulation.

All of the articles are reproduced here in basically the same style and format as they originally appeared. This gives the reader a better sense of the popular business publications from which they are drawn, and stimulates an interest in ongoing learning beyond the time frame for a specific course.

We have added this component to our complete set of **P**rofessional **L**earning **U**nits **S**ystems (our **P.L.U.S.**) to provide even more alternatives for effective teaching and learning in the first marketing course. It has been an interesting job to research and select the readings for this new book, and we hope that our readers find it of value in developing a better understanding of the opportunities and challenges of marketing in our contemporary society.

William D. Perreault, Jr. and E. Jerome McCarthy

Acknowledgments

We would like to thank all of the publications that have granted us permission to reprint the articles in this book. Similarly, we value and appreciate the work and skill of the many writers who prepared the original materials.

Linda G. Davis played an important role in this project. She helped us research thousands of different publications to sort down to the final set, and she also contributed many fine ideas on how best to organize the selections that appear here.

The ideas for this book evolve from and build on previous editions of *Readings and Cases in Basic Marketing*. John F. Grashof and Andrew A. Brogowicz were coauthors of that book. We gratefully recognize the expertise and creativity that they shared over the years on that project. Their fine ideas carry forward here and have had a profound effect on our thinking in selecting articles that will meet the needs of marketing instructors and students alike.

We would also like to thank the many marketing professors and students whose input have helped shape the concept of this book. Their ideas—shared in personal conversations, in focus group interviews, and in responses to marketing research surveys—helped us to clearly define the needs that this book should meet.

Finally, we would like to thank the people at Irwin/McGraw-Hill, our publisher, who have helped turn this idea into a reality. We are grateful for their commitment to making these materials widely available

W.D.P. and E.J.M.

Contents

Marketing's Role in the Global Economy and in the Firm

Trade Is Bustling Again In the Old East Bloc, Thanks to Free Market

---

Competition, Quality Goods And Foreign Companies Are Engines of Enterprise

---

Computers, Crystal and Cars

By Robert Frank
Staff Reporter of The Wall Street Journal

WYSZKOW, Poland — When communism crumbled, so did Route E12, a wooded highway that cuts through northeast Poland to the former Soviet Union. Trucks that once hauled wheat and cement from Poland — and oil and tank engines from Russia — vanished. Hotels closed. Even the *babushkas* selling mushrooms to passing motorists disappeared.

Now, the two-lane E12 is humming again, this time with the freight of the free market — computer parts, steel and pharmaceuticals. Crews are repaving the road, and hotel parking lots are filled with Russian truckers. The babushkas are returning, along with glistening BP gas-and-convenience stores selling Cokes and kielbasa. "It's like old times," says a Polish trucker buying pretzels, "except the traffic moves faster."

Opportunity Zone

Trade among the former East Bloc countries is roaring back to life. Seven years after smashing their command economy links like a Stalin statue and embracing business with the West, Eastern Europe is rediscovering the value of old ties. Some companies, beaten back by tough competition and sluggish economies in Western Europe, see the East as a safe — and profitable — harbor. Others are simply looking to diversify and take advantage of a consumer boom in the region.

Leciva AS, a big Czech pharmaceuticals company that lost almost all its Eastern business after communism, will rack up 34% of its $150 million in sales this year from Slo-

vakia, Belarus, Georgia, Russia and other Eastern markets. Staropramen, a sweet Czech beer, is flowing in Polish pubs with distribution help from Britain's Bass PLC, and Hungarian sausage is a new treat in Prague. MOL, the Hungarian oil giant, is charging into Romania and Ukraine with new filling stations. Polish and Czech banks are chasing one another into the Baltics and Central Asia. On the streets of Warsaw, Skoda cars are a new status symbol; just a few years ago (before Volkswagen AG took over), consumers were leaving the Czech-built clunkers for scrap metal. "I vowed in 1990 never to buy another Skoda," says Marek Michalczyk, an engineer in Warsaw, shining his new Skoda Felicia. "What can I say? It's a totally different car."

Indeed, the new trade is nothing like the old. Competition, quality and foreign companies, not central planning, are the drivers. It has taken years for businesses to retool and restructure — and they still have far to go — but the resurgence in trade means they are finally making goods their former comrades actually want to buy. Shiny red Zelmer vacuum cleaners, made at a state-owned plant in Poland, now sell alongside comparable Hoovers at the Europa store in downtown Warsaw, for half the price.

Products of a New Sort

Computers, consumer electronics and advanced building materials unobtainable under communism are being sold by startups or newly arrived foreign companies. A recent World Bank study found that about 80% of Central Europe's exports to the West weren't sold under communism, and analysts estimate the figure may be equally high for trade within the region.

American companies are fueling much of the cross-border activity. Because East European countries are small and close to one another, U.S. giants prefer to use one market to serve the rest. Colgate-Palmolive Co. makes Mennen deodorant and shower-gel in a plant in Budapest but ships more than 80% of it outside Hungary mostly to the former East Bloc. General Motors Corp.'s Adam Opel AG unit welds and paints car bodies in Hungary before sending them to Poland to make the hotselling Astra.

"We like to balance our purchases and sales throughout the region," says a GM spokesman, adding that some of the parts for its engine-block plant in Hungary come from Poland.

EU Fitness Test

Under communism, trade among the East Bloc countries flourished because it was mandatory. More than 70% of their trade was among themselves, particularly with the Soviet Union. In the early 1990s, the backlash against communism caused an equally artificial shift west: Companies were hungry for dollars and German marks, and consumers were hungry for products with Western labels. Economists say the drift back to the East is one of the strongest signs yet of the

region's long-term fitness and stability. The European Union sees local trade as a crucial test of whether Poland, the Czech Republic and Hungary will be competitive enough to join the EU in 2001.

No one suggests trade within the East Bloc will return to Communist-era levels. And recent turmoil in the Czech Republic reflects how fragile the region's economies remain.

In addition, Western Europe will always be the region's main market and supplier. Hungary's exports to its Eastern neighbors jumped 52% last year, compared with growth of only 2% with the West. Yet the West — mainly Germany — still accounts for more than 70% of Hungary's trade. What's more, many of the less-developed countries in the former East Bloc — Romania, Bulgaria and Belarus, for instance — are only now beginning to build trade economies. Still, the return of neighborly trade is giving a strong boost to a number of companies. Poland, the biggest trade force in the region, has seen some of the most remarkable gains.

Cows and Computers

On the dirt road to Nowy Sacz, in the far southwest corner of Poland, peasants amble home with small herds of cows or carts loaded with onions. Children bundle hay for winter feed, and women harvest the last of the year's carrots and beets. It is a town the free-market might have forgotten were it not for Optimus SA and the computers Roman Kluska started building in his attic nine years ago.

The mild-mannered manager had been fired from his job at a Communist bus factory in the late 1980s, for trying, he says, to maximize profits and performance. He was picking raspberries on a farming collective when communism fell, and he dropped his spade to join the ranks of new entrepreneurs. Today, he is the largest single shareholder of Optimus, which went public in 1994. He owns 30% of the publicly traded company and has 51% voting control. Merrill Lynch Co. owns a 24% capital share and has an 11% voting interest.

Now, in its modern white headquarters complex, Optimus builds 30% of the personal-computers sold in Poland. A recent deal with Microsoft Corp. allows the company to sell its computers under a "Microsoft PC" label.

Mr. Kluska's original plan, like many in Poland, was to sell to Western European markets. But the venture was a disaster. Competition was brutal, with International Business Machines Corp., Compaq Computer Corp. and Hewlett Packard Co. going after the market. Advertising costs were high and Optimus unknown. The company sold only 100 computers in Holland in 1991, the year it entered and left that market. (It continues to sell a few computers in Greece, Cyprus and Portugal.)

"We weren't selling computers," Mr. Kluska says. "We were just spending our money competing."

(Cont.)

Common Culture

"In 1995, he headed back east, where there was less competition and where he shared a culture with his customers. They all spoke Russian. They finished deals with vodka toasts, rather than with contracts. "I wouldn't say it was like the old days, exactly," he says. "But there's a historical bond there that makes it easier." He made two big deals worth $6 million with the Ukrainian government and is in negotiations for more in Russia. Last month, Mr. Kluska was surprised to get his first call from a Czech company. For years, the Czechs wouldn't even consider buying a computer from Poland.

Companies like Optimus have caused Poland's exports to the region to surge. Though he won't give exact figures, Mr. Kluska says his company's sales to the East are growing at more than three times sales to the West. Last year, the country's eastern exports grew 16%, to $1.5 billion — more than twice the growth to the West. Polish imports from the region grew 31%, compared with 26% from the West.

Optimus, though, has had to grapple with the unusual business practices that come with the Wild East. Just after Optimus got a large order from Ukraine last year, the Ukrainian government passed a heavy tariff on imported computers. So Optimus took apart the 300 PCs it had just built, shipped the parts to Ukraine and set up a team to rebuild them there. Earlier this year, a private Ukrainian company didn't have the cash to make a $300,000 payment, but another Ukrainian company that supplied Optimus with raw materials agreed to cover it.

"A lot of Western companies wouldn't tolerate this," he says. "But we're used to it. It's the way business here works. And it's profitable." Optimus's profit last year was $765,000, on sales of $16 million. Former state-owned companies, though, have often had a tougher time reinventing their image for old customers. Irena SA, Poland's largest manufacturer of quality hand-cut crystal, was once one of the prides of communist craftsmanship. The Communists decided that crystal — once a luxury — would be made for the masses. Irena built a hulking complex of furnaces and workshops in the 1970s to expand, and flowery cut crystal flooded Polish homes, rich and poor. It became ubiquitous and therefore banal, and the masses quickly grew sick of the limited number of designs available.

Drug on the Market

"Crystal became an eyesore," says Anna Bogucka, marketing director at Irena, sitting in a giant storeroom of glass kitsch. "It's like the joke of communism."

Now, Irena is making low-cost tableware and is trying to reinvent crystal as a luxury by coming up with new more modern designs that are simpler, more colorful and more utilitarian than the glass baskets and candy bowls that were its stock in trade. The company is doing some business with the West — including a contract to make decanters designed by Ralph Lauren and Christian Dior for the U.S.— but import quotas and fierce competition in Germany and the rest of Europe have chased its sales force back east. It has cut costs by using more molds and created new designs with more fashionable art-deco patterns. This year the company plans to infiltrate Ukraine, Kazakstan and Latvia, where sales are still limited. The good news: Irena sent a shipment to Russia last month, its first in 10 years.

Still, most of its sales in the region are low-cost wine glasses stamped out on a fully automated machine. "Crystal is not high on people's lists right now," Mr. Bogucka says with a sigh.

But furniture is. Forte SA, Poland's largest furniture company, gleaned about 25% of its $87 million in sales from the East last year, up from 5% in the early 1990s. More and more Russians are showing up in the company's showroom in Ostrow Mazowiecka. "We can spot them because they're always carrying a stack of dollars and want to take the furniture home right away," a saleswoman says.

Popular Polish Furniture

To boost sales, the company recently hired a crew versed in the culture and economies of Ukraine and the former Soviet Union. Forte's new line of budget futons and Formica cabinets are especially attractive to the cost-conscious East. Variety is an added bonus: Under communism, the Forte plant produced seven kinds of cabinets. Now, it makes more than 1,800.

"We're finding the Eastern markets can be very profitable, sometimes even better than the West," says Maciej Formanowicz, the company's founder and president. "That wasn't our attitude five years ago."

Mr. Formanowicz, a veteran of communist business, says nostalgia and cultural ties are nice, but they don't buy you sales in the new Eastern markets. "None of the old sales networks exist anymore," he said. "It's totally different people involved — everyone's young now. The competition is tough and customers sometimes expect more than those in the West."

Still, some of the old rules still apply. On a recent trip to Ukraine, Mr. Formanowicz had to stay in a hotel with no heat or hot water, and it took him more than an hour to check out.

"I looked around and thought 'What's changed?'" he recalls. "For a moment, it was like doing business in the old days."

Reprinted by permission of *The Wall Street Journal,* © 1997 Dow Jones & Company, Inc. All Rights Reserved Worldwide.

Tea and Tropicana? Seagram Wants Juice To Be Chinese Staple

Yield on $55 Million Venture To Produce O.J. Locally Is Hardly Certain, Though

By Kathy Chen

Staff Reporter of The Wall Street Journal

ZHONGXIAN, China — As Edgar Bronfman Sr. disembarks from the five-decker cruise liner that has brought him to this dusty settlement on the banks of the Yangtze, school-children armed with flowers chant a greeting while a band strikes up "Yankee Doodle."

Tens of thousands of people cram the narrow streets and building rooftops. Before stepping into a waiting car, complete with police escort, the 68-year-old Seagram Co. chairman waves to the crowds. "This feels fantastic," he says.

Why all the fanfare? Mr. Bronfman is bringing Tropicana orange juice to China, with grand plans to produce and sell the stuff in the world's biggest market.

China is no stranger to orange juice. Oranges, after all, have been a staple fruit of China for more than four millennia, though the juice is mostly quaffed at banquets and by children. Today, the country ranks as the world's No. 3 producer of citrus after Brazil and the U.S., growing eight million tons of oranges each year. Seagram's Tropicana Beverage Group estimates sales in China of pure juices is a relatively minuscule $100 million annually, but that number is growing by one-third each year.

Yet plenty of roadblocks loom, as the company grapples with China's poor transportation system, inefficient distribution networks and the challenges of converting thousands of traditional, small-time farmers to growing citrus the Tropicana way.

Such hurdles have kept many agricultural investors out of China. Utilized foreign investment — those investments that have actually been channeled into a project — in agriculture totaled $152 million for the first nine months of 1997, accounting for just 1% of all utilized overseas investment in China. While those projects include a handful of large ventures, like Minneapolis-based Cargill Inc.'s animal-feed mills or the chicken farms of Thailand's CP Group, most remain small in scale.

But Mr. Bronfman is dreaming big: His is a $55 million joint venture with the Chongqing Three Gorges Construction Group to squeeze orange juice in southwestern China. Under the agreement signed in November, Seagram will build a technology center, seedling nursery and demonstration grove, providing technical assistance to help farmers design groves, raise trees and do soil analysis; the Chinese group will oversee and help finance as many as 40,000 farm families to plant more than one million orange trees. Both sides will share the costs of constructing a juice-processing factory.

Even with the current financial crisis rocking Asia, Mr. Bronfman is determined to push ahead with the orange-juice project. "Everyone will have a real hard time and China will go through some difficulties in the short term," he says. But "my father always taught us to think in terms of generations. In 20 years, this will be the most fantastic country in the world."

Seagram already sells orange juice from concentrate in China under the Dole juice brand, which it acquired in 1995. Next summer, it will introduce the Tropicana brand in three Chinese cities, including in Beijing at an entertainment and retail center called "The Universal Experience" that Seagram's Universal Studios unit is opening. But because the beverage will be shipped from Florida in pure-juice form, it will be sold for a hefty $5 a liter, triple U.S. prices, and will be marketed mainly to expatriates, hotels and nightclubs. The hope is that once orange-juice production is up and running in China, Tropicana can lower the price of its product by at least half.

Mr. Bronfman started thinking about producing orange juice in China in 1992, when he first tasted a China-made version of the beverage during lunch with a Chinese official and proclaimed it "fabulous," he says. "I was determined that Tropicana would find a great future in China."

Unfortunately for him, executives at Tropicana didn't share his enthusiasm. Wary of international expansion, especially into a business morass like China, they resisted. Tropicana, which Montreal-based Seagram acquired in 1988, had $2.1 billion in global sales in 1997 and boasts a 41% share of the U.S. market for fresh juice, but its business has remained focused largely on the U.S. The Brandenton, Fla., company rings up three-quarters of its beverage sales in North America and sources virtually all of its oranges in its own backyard in Florida.

"Initially, there was no other support for this," says Roger Knight, managing director of Tropicana Asia Pacific. Every year when Mr. Bronfman visited China, he would ask if Tropicana had come up with a project. "Everyone would stare at his shoes," says one Seagram executive.

Fed Up

By 1995, Mr. Bronfman was fed up with the inaction. And after sending Seagram associates on a dozen scouting trips to find the perfect site in China for an orange project, the company settled on Zhongxian.

Situated high above the muddy waters of the Yangtze, the region's lush mountains slope at a gentle incline and offer good drainage. The sun rarely shines here, but temperatures are mild, as in Florida. Just as important, the area has been included in China's Three Gorges Dam project, a gargantuan undertaking to harness the Yangtze. More than one million peasants, many from Zhongxian, face resettlement because of the damming, and authorities eagerly welcome any job-generating investments.

The realities of investing in China's agriculture sector are on harsh display here. Tucked high in the hills, the project site is a day's travel by boat and car from the central city of Chongqing. Peasants live and farm as they have for centuries, lugging buckets of water using shoulder poles and terracing small squares of rice paddy that drape the mountains like patchwork. "There's a lot to do," sighs Steven Schafer, general manager of Tropicana Beverages Greater China Ltd. Phone lines are few. Modern toilet facilities were nonexistent until local officials erected a porta-potty in honor of Mr. Bronfman's arrival.

Winning Over Farmers

Seagram is betting that multilane highways will proliferate by the time the processing plant is operational in 2005, to allow for easy transport of the juice out to cities on the coast. But "it's basically a crap shoot," warns Harold Pollack, director of agricultural sciences at Tropicana Products Inc. in Florida. "There was a lot of concern then, and still some now, over the remoteness of the area."

The biggest challenge will be winning over the Chinese farm families who will grow the oranges Tropicana plans to squeeze. Like 25-year-old Chen Shimeng, many of the farmers have planted *jincheng,* a local type of orange, for years as a cheap side crop — "without fertilizer or watering either," he says. Such neglect has resulted in diseased trees and yields of one-fifth to one-tenth of those in Florida. Tropicana will have to persuade the farmers not only to switch to growing Valencia and Hamlin oranges (the base for Tropicana orange juice), but also to water, fertilize and otherwise tend the trees regularly, an expensive proposition that won't see any returns for up to five years.

"Farmers are very risk-averse," says Mr. Schafer. "All we can do is show people it works, provide the resources and hope they will believe us and do it."

Mr. Chen, the farmer, is game. Sort of. "Will the seedlings cost money?" he asks. "If not, of course I'll grow them."

Reprinted by permission of *The Wall Street Journal,* © 1998 Dow Jones & Company, Inc. All Rights Reserved Worldwide.

Why Foreign Distillers Find It So Hard to Sell Vodka to the Russians

The Market Seemed Ripe, But Cost Matters a Lot, And So Does Patriotism

No 'Drink-the-Label Market'

By ERNEST BECK
Staff Reporter of THE WALL STREET JOURNAL

MOSCOW — Roman Drenovich marches down the cluttered liquor aisle of his neighborhood supermarket and discovers that in today's Russia, all vodkas are not created equal.

Picking his way along the shelves, Mr. Drenovich fingers a fancy frosted-glass bottle of Absolut, selling for $25. He scrutinizes the sleek reindeer on an equally expensive bottle of Finlandia. He moves past a $12 bottle of Smirnoff. Squinting at prices, the 58-year-old finally reaches for a local brand called Komdiv. Made by Moscow's Cristall Distillery, it has a flimsy twist-off cap and a picture on the label of a famous Russian actor. The price: $3.

"I buy only Russian vodka," declares Mr. Drenovich, with patriotic fervor. "It is the purest, the smoothest, the best."

Grandiose Plans

In 1990, when Western companies — like Smirnoff's owner Diageo PLC of Britain and Absolut's V&S Vin & Spirit AB of Sweden — first eyed the vast vodka market here, they believed Russia's voracious drinkers could be lured to their products. With famous brand names and well-honed selling skills, the companies reasoned, they could carry coals to Newcastle, as it were, and overpower stodgy, Communistera products. The goal was to capture consumers eager to trade up to Western brands.

But in a surprising role reversal, Russia's private and state vodka producers are challenging Western marketers and even beating them at their own game — pouring new niche brands onto the market and hawking them with clever, eye-catching packaging and advertising campaigns. After nearly a decade, the newcomers have little to show for their efforts — except a bad hangover and a combined market share estimated at less than 1%.

The setback is frustrating because Russia is by far the world's largest vodka market:

Consumption reached an estimated 250 million cases in 1996, industry watchers say, though exact figures aren't available. That compares with 33.4 million cases in the U.S., the largest market outside Eastern Europe, according to Impact International, a trade-research company. While vodka sales are declining world-wide, about 80% of Russians drink vodka on a regular basis, surveys indicate, and consumption is increasing. Russian drinkers could help power much-needed growth for distillers and their distributors in a crowded, global spirits sector.

Humbled, foreign companies now concede that it may be years before they can grab a big share of the market, but they insist that they aren't giving up. "We're not here to make a profit now — that might only come in five, maybe 10, years," says John Kamviselis, country manager of Seagram Co., which distributes Absolut in Russia. "This is a strategic market, and we're still in the early stages of the game."

'Strategic' Industry

To be fair, not all the problems of the Western companies are of their own making. In many ways, what went wrong in Russia is a classic tale of a risky emerging market, with the usual problems of creaky infrastructure, economic turmoil, low incomes, a poor distribution network and quickly shifting consumer tastes. Yet Russia posed other obstacles: a government determined to protect the "strategic" vodka industry by imposing high taxes and import duties. Another blow came in 1994, when alcohol-advertising restrictions — including a ban on television ads — began to be phased in, in a bid by health authorities to cut the high rate of alcoholism.

What's more, organized crime infiltrated the vodka trade and today is said to control the market for cheap, illicit hooch. About 50% of the Russian vodka market is said to be "illegal," that is, untaxed, counterfeit or bootleg, according to industry officials. While police have cracked down on moonshine merchants, sales still flourish in alleys. One winter night in Moscow, an elderly woman in a threadbare coat plies her wares on an upturned banana box. "Real Russian vodka!" she screams in a raspy voice, offering a suspicious bottle with an unsealed cap to a group of men standing nearby. They fork over rubles worth about $1 and swill the stuff while swaying down the street.

Drinking Objectives

"Russia isn't a drink-the-label market yet," remarks Leon Stelmach, an analyst at Canadean, an alcohol-industry research company in London. "Russians aren't fussy: The goal is to get drunk."

Selling any foreign vodka to Russians was never going to be easy. Most Russians believe vodka, a colorless spirit distilled from grain or beets and potatoes, originated here in the 12th century — although the Poles dispute that. So for many Russians,

vodka is like mother's milk — a native drink from the sacred Russian soil that makes you feel warm in winter, bonds friends, enlivens family celebrations, and nourishes the legendary Russian soul. "Vodka is a *Russian* product," notes Vladimir Korovkin, planning director at Smart-Communications, a Moscow marketing consultant. "Just try selling whisky to the Scots."

But in the early 1990s, the market seemed ripe for the taking. Trade liberalization had opened the borders to importers. And vodka was vodka, a basically generic product. Few real brands — in the Western sense — existed here, though Russians knew names like Cristall, a distillery, and Stolichnaya. (Five distilleries make the popular Stolichnaya for export.) Sensing a great opportunity, popular brands like Smirnoff — the world's best-selling Western vodka — and Absolut arrived, hoping to capitalize on the rage for Western products — from Mars bars to Tide laundry detergent. Initially, they proved popular as bribes or trophy gifts, kept on display in the buyer's home, or as status symbols for the brash, free-spending new Russian rich.

For the most part, though, marketing strategies that worked well in London or New York were simply plunked down in Moscow, with only minor tinkering.

Absolut, trying to communicate directly with Russians, adapted its famous global ad campaign to include Absolut *dacha* and Absolut Bolshoi, but it kept its high prices. "We aim for the rich, and aspiring middle classes," explains Andreas Berggren, vice president of Russian operations for Absolut. Indeed, less than 2% of the population can afford to buy a bottle of Absolut, the company estimates. It is Absolut's policy never to produce outside Sweden, officials insist, and even Russia's mind-boggling potential didn't change that.

Smirnoff had a rough ride in Russia, too, after an initial surge of interest as a status brand. At first, it was available only in foreign-currency shops. But by 1993, consumerism was booming and Smirnoff felt emboldened to import and sell via a joint venture on the retail level. However, the company didn't carefully consider important factors like income levels, distribution and a swing away from pricey, foreign-branded goods, says a company insider who didn't want to be identified. A move to become more Russian — by launching an inexpensive brand, called Bread Vodka — was rejected because the low end of the market was overcrowded. Ads weren't customized to the local market; instead, global campaigns were deployed.

Limited-Success Story

While Smirnoff and Absolut struggled with their high-priced products, one company went after the mass market and — at first — did reasonably well.

White Eagle, a brand owned by American United Distilled Products Co., in Minneapolis, Minn., in a joint venture with Archer-

(Cont.)

Daniels-Midland Co. of Decatur, Ill., launched a big advertising and marketing campaign in 1992. Ads were geared to Russian tastes, featuring a stumbling, drunken American Indian that Russian consumers considered funny, says a company official. "We couldn't do that in America," he adds. Lightweight plastic bottles were used to cut shipping costs. A large variety of vodkas — including cranberry and lemon-flavored ones — were introduced, creating a family of related products. The strategy worked: Sales of White Eagle soared to between three million and four million cases annually, according to the company.

But in 1994, the government started raising import duties to help local vodka producers compete with imports from the West and former Soviet republics. Further tax increases followed, as well as strict rules requiring that all duties be paid in advance. For White Eagle, that meant adding about $9 in costs to a liter bottle of vodka that cost 60 cents to produce in the U.S. White Eagle subsequently pulled out of direct sales and marketing in Russia.

"Russia is a wonderful market, and we were making money, but basically, the government prohibited us," grumbles Douglas Mangine, chief executive of American United. The company also looked into building a production site in Russia but backed away. "You can't invest in bricks and mortar when laws change every day," Mr. Mangine says.

Something for Everyone

Meanwhile, Russian marketers grew savvier and began outmaneuvering the Westerners. Maverick businessman Vladimir Dovgan jumped into the value-for-money vodka sector and backed the launch of myriad midprice vodka brands with packaging and advertising featuring the chubby entrepreneur as pitchman.

His food-and-spirits company currently markets 25 brands — each with his picture on the label. "The foreigners fight for the money of the wealthy, and I flood the market and let the people choose," boasts Mr. Dovgan, a self-styled consumer populist. Bolting around his modern Moscow office, Mr. Dovgan shows off a glass case crammed with bottles of Dovgan vodka. Among the offerings are a mild-tasting Lady brand, a robust Imperial variety and a hardy Winterone. Retail prices are from $5 to $10.

Such saturation marketing, which cuts across price points and niche categories, appears to be working. After two years, Mr. Dovgan claims he will have sold 2.5 million cases in 1997. The Western companies refuse to disclose sales figures, but their shares are estimated to be significantly lower than Dovgan's.

For consumers, the market is awash with vodkas, known here as the "water of life." At a small, well-kept store in a Moscow suburb, vodkas of all shapes and sizes, labels and prices can be found next to a deli counter stuffed with sliced meats and slabs of smoked fish. On the shelves are odd, local brands like Sibirskaya, in a bullet-shaped bottle, and Narkom, short for People's Commissar. "This probably appeals to crazy old Communist drunks," scoffs Leonid Tarasov, director of Ansdell Russia, a consultant to United Distillers & Vinters, the new Diageo beverage unit, in Russia.

New Brand Loyalty

Despite the wide selection, Irina Maximova, the store manager, says Russians are sticking to brands — mostly Russian ones — and closely comparing prices. In other words, they are evolving from being "buyers and users," in marketing-speak, to brand-loyal consumers. "Five years ago, customers would wander around and didn't know what to buy. Now, nobody is confused," Mrs. Maximova explains. According to Gallup Media in Russia, leading Russian brands like Moskovskaya and Russkaya score over 70% in brand awareness surveys, while Smirnoff is at 28.7%. White Eagle scores an impressive 43.7%.

With few self-service retail stores, clever packaging is essential, and Russian distillers like Cristall are learning from their Western competitors. State-owned Cristall's new range includes Priviet, which sports bold black lettering and silver foil wrapping over the cap. "Made with water from Russia's icy glacial lakes that are perfectly clean," attests the label, in an appeal to Russian fears of pollution. And then there's a premium range for around $13 — roughly on a par with Smirnoff — with bold black-and-gold labels. The Cristall name is daubed in elegant script.

"Russians are coming back to Russian vodka, and we're helping with attractive new brands," says Edward Kusmitsky, deputy director of Cristall. He shows off a limited edition Cristall vodka to commemorate Moscow's 850th anniversary.

The explosion of vodka brands — there are more than 400 now — took Westerners by surprise. (Even Vladimir Zhiranovsky, the right-wing politician, launched his own vodka.) But for Smirnoff, there was another woe: Boris Smirnov, a Russian namesake, launched a vodka and sued Smirnoff for trademark infringement.

Going Local

While the case is still tied up in the courts, Smirnoff is implementing a new marketing gambit: After years of turbulence as an importer, it has gone local. Since March 1997, the brand has been produced in Russia at a St. Petersburg distillery.

"This should make Smirnoff seem more Russian," suggests a Smirnoff official, who asked not to be named because of security and legal concerns. Indeed, the revised strategy — which includes made-in-Russia labels, a Smirnoff telephone hot line and ads that underline the brand's "international quality" and Russian roots — is an attempt to convince consumers that Smirnoff is indeed a Russian brand. "We want Russians to realize that Smirnoff came to Russia to produce for Russians," adds the official. New print and poster ads highlight the double "ff" in Smirnoff, to mirror the way the rulers of Imperial Russia, the Romanoff family, spelled their name.

So far, though, Smirnoff's gamble hasn't paid off: The company says sales volumes haven't budged, although its price has fallen 15%, to around $11 a bottle, because of lower costs.

Sergey Koptev, chairman of ad agency DMB&B in Moscow, which has the Cristall premium account, believes foreign brands will eventually find a niche in the huge market but will never capture a major share of it — or the Russian soul. "Vodka was, and is, a matter of love and trust for us. It's our national brand," says Mr. Koptev.

Reprinted by permission of *The Wall Street Journal*, © 1998 Dow Jones & Company, Inc. All Rights Reserved Worldwide.

Capitalism spawns a new breed

By Bill Montague
USA TODAY

MOSCOW — If anyone illustrates the puzzling contradictions of Russian capitalism, it's Vladimir Bryntsalov: avowed socialist, politician and millionaire Russian businessman.

Bryntsalov (pronounced Brint-SAL-off) is chairman of Ferane, one of Russia's largest pharmaceutical companies. His business also generates substantial cash flow by selling a cheap brand of vodka. Bryntsalov, 49, is a member of Russia's emerging business elite — known here as the *Novye Russkie*, or "New Russians."

> **'You can do anything in this country now'**

From the rubble of Soviet communism, the *Novye Russkie* are building a rough-and-ready capitalism in which knowing how to deal with corrupt government officials or underworld bosses can be a more vital business skill than understanding a quarterly financial statement. It's a Darwinian world in which the fittest not only survive but can accumulate vast wealth. Moscow is home to an estimated 10,000 to 20,000 millionaires.

The *Novye Russkie* thrive in a chaotic post-Soviet world where an estimated 40% of the population lives in poverty. They show few inhibitions about flaunting their new-found wealth, creating a nation of stark social contrasts — and a certain degree of animosity.

"Everyone hates the Novye Russkie" because the average citizen is skeptical about how someone can accumulate vast wealth in a short time, says Oleg Bogomolov, director of the Institute of International Economics and Political Studies.

Boutiques and bodyguards

Across Red Square from Lenin's tomb, GUM — once a dreary Soviet department store — has been turned into a shopping arcade filled with trendy boutiques selling the latest fashions from Paris and Rome. During the week, Moscow's businessmen can drink vodka and talk shop at $200-a-night sauna clubs. On weekends, they can gamble or dance until dawn in a growing number of discos and casinos or retire to their palatial *dachas,* or country homes, on the outskirts of town.

Business is conducted under the shadow of underworld hits and contract killings. Each day, Moscow newspapers carry reports of the latest mob hits. There have been nearly 500 contract killings so far this year in Russia, up from 100 in 1992, according to the Interior Ministry. Among the victims: At least 35 Russian bankers, three members of Russia's parliament and one prominent journalist.

"It's clear that organized crime controls large parts of the Russian economy," says Peter Charow, executive director of the American Chamber of Commerce in Russia. "It's a real problem."

The environment has led some Russian businessmen to travel like heads of state, surrounded by bodyguards.

"It's not comfortable to live in this country, even if you are rich," Bryntsalov complains during an interview at Ferane's heavily protected compound in the suburbs of Moscow.

Getting to the top

The *Novye Russkie* do not easily fit into normal Western models of business executives. For many, the climb to the top followed one of two paths. Some were political insiders who gained control of factories and other assets privatized by the Russian government following the collapse of the Soviet Union. That's particularly common in the oil and gas industries, by far the most profitable sector of the ramshackle Russian economy.

Secrecy surrounded many of the privatization deals hastily negotiated by the Russian government in 1993 and 1994. That veil has reinforced a common suspicion that capitalism is just another device to enrich the *nomenklatura* — the old Soviet bureaucratic elite.

Others, such as Bryntsalov, jumped at the opportunities for moneymaking that opened up in former Soviet president Mikhail Gorbachev's era, when cooperatives and youth clubs first were allowed to operate for-profit businesses.

Bryntsalov's official biography is a Russian Horatio Alger story. A big, square-shouldered man, Bryntsalov was a coal miner who rose to head a state construction firm in Stavropol province. But he was ejected from the Communist Party in 1980, supposedly for building himself a house thought too grand by local party leaders.

Unemployed, Bryntsalov turned to raising bees and foxes. He used the profits from the sale of honey and furs to turn his one-man operation into a cooperative in 1988. In 1990, he bought his way into a deal to lease the factory of an insolvent Soviet drug company.

By 1992, he was president and owner of 98% of the firm, which he renamed Ferane.

Bryntsalov claims to have turned Ferane into a world-class pharmaceutical maker, with about 30% of the Russian market and roughly $600 million in annual revenue. But a big chunk of the profit comes from distilling a cheap brand of vodka popular in Russia's working-class neighborhoods. Bryntsalov's picture peers from the back of every bottle.

How does Bryntsalov reconcile his achievements as a capitalist with socialist ideals he still admires? "It's natural for capitalists to seek big profits, just as it's natural for workers to demand big wages," he explains. "We need to get rich together."

Bryntsalov tested the political scene earlier this year when he used his fortune to run for president as head of the Russian Socialist Party. His platform called for higher wages for Russian workers and steep tariffs to shield Russian manufacturers from foreign competition. But he diluted this populist message by repeatedly boasting of his own wealth. His favorite campaign slogan: "Money is mankind's greatest invention."

Bryntsalov finished dead last in the election's first round, with less than 0.2% of the vote. He scandalized official Moscow with his eccentric campaign behavior. Appearing with his 29-year-old wife, Natasha, on Russia's most popular TV interview show, Bryntsalov urged her to display her Spandex-clad posterior to the viewers, then gave the body part in question an approving slap.

Growing political power

Bryntsalov's presidential bid flopped, but wealth has brought a more subtle form of political power to the *Novye Russkie*. Russian business owners donated generously to President Boris Yeltsin's successful June re-election campaign. NTV, Russia's private TV network, openly promoted Yeltsin's campaign. Other media firms did the same.

"It was a very difficult decision for us," says Alexander Lapshin, 43, general director of Kosmos TV, Moscow's private wireless cable network. Kosmos donated thousands of dollars in air time and advertising to the Yeltsin campaign — a heavy financial burden for the company. Lapshin decided to spend the money, concluding: "After all, if the Communists had won they would have shut us down anyway."

Yeltsin, 65, took the oath of office last week to begin his second term.

Lapshin shatters the stereotype of the Russian businessman as crude hustler or retooled Soviet bureaucrat. Polished, articulate, fluent in English and Japanese, he shares a cramped office in an old vocational school with the company's chief financial officer. Originally an environmental activist, Lapshin was the first Russian director of the Moscow Greenpeace office.

He says he dreamed up the idea of launching an independent cable network in 1986 at the dawn of *glasnost*, Gorbachev's policy of allowing limited free speech and freedom of the press. Despite the new party line, Lapshin says his early efforts to obtain permission for his cable venture "led to some interesting conversations in some not-so-interesting places," such as the headquarters of the KGB, the Soviet secret police.

The collapse of the Soviet Union created a more favorable climate, and Kosmos began operating in 1991. In 1994, Lapshin sold a controlling interest to a subsidiary of Metromedia, the U.S. media conglomerate.

Now, with Metromedia's financial muscle behind him, Lapshin speaks eagerly of turning Kosmos into a diversified entertainment company, producing its own Russian-language programming. He wants to beef up his modest news division and add to the list of 34 former Soviet cities already served by Kosmos' corporate parent, International Telcell. He wants to expand into Southeast Asia.

"You can do anything in this country now," Lapshin says. "I want to do something big."

Copyright 1995, *USA Today*. Reprinted with permission.

THE NEW LATIN CORPORATION
These savvy companies are
moving beyond national borders

Miguel Gómez Mont Urueta has put roofs over the heads of half a million of Mexico's working poor. As chief executive of Corporacion GEO, the country's largest low-income housing developer, he expects to put up many more. Mexico needs at least 5 million more houses and apartments. This year, GEO is building 19,000 two-bedroom homes in attractive developments that cluster houses and apartments with schools, shops, and cultural centers. Since the houses are modular, purchasers can easily upgrade them as their family's fortunes improve. "We want to do for housing what Henry Ford did for the automobile," says Gómez Mont.

And profit from it. GEO, long a contractor for Mexico's public housing authority, has tripled its sales since 1993, when the government got out of the housing business, to $246 million last year. Its stock has risen to $25.80 from $17.50 when it went public in 1994. Now, GEO is taking its low-cost formula to Chile and to poor southern U.S. communities. "We can compete with anybody," says the 44-year-old Gómez Mont, who runs the company with six other directors in a collegial style that is rare for Latin America.

GEO is one of Latin America's corporate stars. A decade after most governments in the region began opening their markets to trade, competition, and investment, a new breed of Latin American company is making its mark. Many are niche operators building a booming business as they serve a rising consumer class. Run by a generation of relatively young and internationally savvy managers, they are expanding rapidly not just at home but throughout the region.

Others are long established groups that had been written off as dinosaurs. Mexico's Alfa, for instance, has turned itself from a bloated conglomerate into a focused, profitable maker of steel and auto parts. Technology-driven groups such as Mexican software developer Softtek are exploiting low costs and NAFTA connections to supplant Asian suppliers to U.S. companies. Indeed, the region's corporate strength contrasts sharply with the problems in Southeast Asia, where heavy debt has caused widespread distress among companies.

BUSINESS WEEK has taken a close-up look at the new Latin American corporation. Based on scores of interviews with CEOs, fund managers, and business consultants, we have identified companies that stand out as leaders in the region. They include new Latin multinationals whose clout is expanding as trade barriers fall. Others are companies that are zeroing in on the region's new consumer class (tables). Innovators and entrepreneurs, meanwhile, are tapping a nascent flow of risk capital, while blue chips reinvent themselves to match foreign competition. As state companies have privatized, billions of dollars of assets have landed in private hands.

BIG PLAYERS. What all these companies share is the conviction that they must equal their global rivals in technology, productivity, and entrepreneurial drive. With multinational heavyweights encroaching fast, Latin companies know that in many sectors, they must grow or perish. In electric utilities, where foreign competition is fierce, "Latin America is for big players now," says Ricardo Alvial Munoz, director of investor relations for Chilean energy conglomerate Enersis, which supplies electricity to 32 million people throughout the region.

While few Latin companies are well-known beyond the region's borders, that's starting to change. Mexico's Cemex recently bought a stake in a Philippine cement maker, extending its earlier march into Europe and the U.S. Smaller, but no less competitive, is Brazilian textile maker Coteminas, whose state-of-the-art factories are turning out garments that undersell even Chinese rivals. "A number of Latin American companies have figured out how to be world-class competitors," says Monterrey-based Roberto Batres, head of consultant Arthur D. Little Inc.'s Latin American division. "They have done everything possible to lower their costs, become more efficient and productive, and export all they can."

What shaped many of these winners—and wiped out thousands of others—was the financial squeeze of the 1982 debt crisis and the ensuing free-market reforms that stripped away trade barriers and subsidies in many countries. The survivors ditched products in which they had no chance of competing, plowed all available resources into cutting-edge technology, and sent promising young executives abroad for MBAs. Many went public and learned how to communicate with investors. With the return of corporate financing to the region, these companies are thriving.

Nowhere is this new Latin dynamism more evident than in those companies chasing opportunities for cross-border invest-

ments. Economic opening has let companies leverage the strengths they've developed at home by taking them abroad. Chilean companies led the way, cashing in on the business knowhow they accumulated since they pioneered open markets in the mid-1970s. Flush with cash from fast growth and a buoyant stock market, they have plowed more than $8 billion in the past five years into cross-border investments from supermarkets to banking.

Chile's pension fund managers have been among the most aggressive emissaries, offering expertise they gained setting up the region's first privatized pension system. Countries from Argentina to Mexico have copied the model, and Chilean companies are front-runners. Provida, Chile's biggest fund, with $5.4 billion in assets under management, has already captured 30% of the market in Colombia and 25% in Peru. Last year, it started a Mexican pension fund with local and Spanish partners.

Other companies are border-hopping with new factories and distribution systems. Mexico's Grupo Industrial Bimbo has for decades baked and delivered bread and cakes to thousands of mom-and-pop stores. Its 13,000 trucks travel unpaved roads to towns and villages all over the country. Now, Bimbo vans are carting locally baked bread throughout 11 countries, from Guatemala to Argentina. "Globalization pushed us to go abroad—we had no choice, even though it's a risky proposition," says President Rafael Velez Valadez. He first started investing abroad in 1990. Now, Bimbo earns 16% of its annual $1.9 billion in sales outside Mexico.

Argentine candymaker Arcor has adopted the same strategy. This year, it expects to top $1 billion in sales to 75 countries. Arcor started eyeing foreign markets in the 1970s, when Argentina was still a protected backwater. "We brought in good technology and became very efficient in order to compete with the rest of the world from inside a closed country," says Daniel Feraud, general manager of the international division. "We were investing not for the Argentina that was but for the Argentina that would one day be."

The ability to round up new customers is a skill the best of the new Latin companies are honing. As growth has taken off and inflation slowed, the region's 470 million consumers are demanding products and services that were once beyond their reach. To be sure, there are big gaps in income across the region's 23 countries. While Argentina

(Cont.)

boasts a per capita income of over $6,000, Nicaragua's is less than $500.

But incomes have been rising, often quickly. In Chile, incomes are up over 5% a year since 1990. Just to stroll the shopping malls of Lima or Sao Paulo is to see that millions of people are slowly moving up the income ladder from grinding poverty toward the middle class. Latin America's new business class is tuned in to the new opportunities. Sales are booming as they develop products for lower-income families. Others are offering more sophisticated goods and services to richer consumers.

Retailer Elektra is targeting Mexicans eager for a first taste of the consumer society. The company has built a half-billion-dollar business selling everything from washing machines to VCRs to the nine out of 10 Mexicans who make less than $5,900 a year. "We sell poor people goods on credit when nobody else will," says Elektra's chief financial officer, Luis J. Echarte.

To keep customers coming back, Elektra is constantly rolling out new schemes. The latest is a savings account launched in August with Mexico's third-largest lender, Banca Serfin. Customers unable to make the minimum deposit that most banks require can begin earning interest with as little as one peso—12 cents—on deposit. To keep the cash flowing, Elektra is in the business of electronic money transfers sent home by Mexicans working in the U.S. This year, it will handle about $600 million worth, up from $100 million in 1993.

In Peru, retailer Carsa has taken Elektra's approach a step further: It not only sells poor consumers home appliances but also helps finance materials for construction of barebones shanties. Carsa's goal is to win loyal customers early, as they take their first steps up the path to prosperity.

Further up the income scale, Banco Excel Economico, known as Brazil's "populist bank," is catering to a growing middle class. It allows interest-free overdrafts for 12 days or more on some checking accounts—a bid to hook clients who may later bring in higher fees with investment accounts. Excel also struck a deal with Sao Paulo cinemas to reserve 20% of seats for the bank's credit-card customers until 10 minutes before show time—a perk that's prized in the traffic-plagued city of 18 million.

Leisure activities such as movies and concerts were the first items cut from family budgets when inflation was soaring a few years ago. Now, Latins are spending more of their reals and pesos on entertainment. Enter Mexican mogul Alejandro Soberon Kuri: Ten years ago, the former movie producer launched Corporacion Interamericana de Entretenimiento (CIE) to promote international music concerts in Mexico. Soberon, now 37, figured that, with 34% of Latins under age 15, he had a ripe venue for rock concerts, sports events, and theater.

SMART SET. CIE shook up the live-entertainment business by introducing telephone ticket sales in a joint venture with Ticketmaster. CIE also manages sports stadiums, industrial expositions, and theaters, handles 50% of all soccer stadium advertising, and does telemarketing for business clients—grabbing a big chunk of each entertainment dollar spent in Mexico. Soberon plans to take his formula to other Latin countries, starting with productions of Walt Disney Co. theatrical shows throughout the region.

Latin America's smart set is also the target of Saraiva Livreiros Editores, Brazil's leading publisher and Latin America's No.1 bookstore chain. Book sales are up 60% since Brazil tamed triple-digit inflation in 1994. Now, Saraiva is pioneering the megabookstore format in Latin America with stores featuring Internet cafes. Five dollars buys 30 minutes on the Net and a snack of *pao de queijo*, a Brazilian cheese-filled bread.

Saraiva's chief operating officer, Ruy Mendes Goncalves, wanted to build a chain of megastores after spotting a giant outlet in France 15 years ago. But "it was too early for Brazil," he says. He waited until after the country lifted its ban on imported software and video games in 1992. In the meantime, Goncalves was almost arrested in Madrid in 1994 as he videotaped a megastore to show his colleagues in Brazil.

Such enthusiasm is the stuff of many of the managers running Latin America's hottest companies. Bright and hard-working, these often U.S.-trained executives are now

Cross-Border Pacesetters

For 20 additional company listings visit www.businessweek.com or America Online: Keyword: B

COMPANY/COUNTRY INDUSTRY	EMPLOYEES	1996 SALES* MILLIONS	NET PROFIT MILLIONS	SALES ■ FOREIGN ▨ DOMESTIC	MAJOR SHAREHOLDERS	STRATEGY
ARCOR / Argentina Candy and foods, packaging CEO: Luis A. Pagani	10,000	$914 +3%	$40 −20%**		Pagani, Maranzana, Seveso, and Brizio families, 100%	Lower costs to compete globally by investing 90% of profits in technology and integrating vertically
•**BIMBO** / Mexico Baked goods CEO: Daniel Servitje Montull	45,000	$1,920 +16%	$108 +165%		Servitje and Mata families, 13 other families	Use homegrown distribution expertise to expand throughout Latin America
•**CEMEX** / Mexico Cement CEO: Lorenzo Zambrano	20,500	$3,390 +5%	$981 +3%		Zambrano family, 30%	Adapt world class technology to manufacturing in diverse markets from U.S. to Philippines
•**ENERSIS** / Chile Electricity distribution CEO: José Yuraszeck	14,300	$2,700 +48%	$240 +2%		Chilean Pension funds, 33.4%; Endesa (Spain), 26%	Win 20% of regional electricity market by aggressive acquisitions with partners
•**PROVIDA** / Chile Private pension fund CEO: Gustavo Alcalde	5,100	5,400‡ +13%	$23.8 −5%‡‡		CorpGroup, 38%; Bank of New York, 35.3%	Earn 35% of profits from abroad within 5 years by launching funds in other Latin countries

• Publicly traded   *Current market exchange rates. Mexican data at yearend 1996 rate.   **Large investments required in 1996 to meet rising competition in Argentina; expect 12% profit gain in 1997
‡Funds under management   ‡‡One-time rebates under pension law raised 1995 profit

(Cont.)

COMPANY/COUNTRY INDUSTRY	EMPLOYEES	1996 SALES* MILLIONS	NET PROFIT MILLIONS	SALES ■ FOREIGN ▨ DOMESTIC	MAJOR SHAREHOLDERS	STRATEGY
CARSA / Peru Sales of appliances & homebuilding materials CEO: Guido Lucioni Chirinos	4,500	$433 +19%	−$6** −		Lucioni family, 100%	Win lifelong customers by selling on credit to the poor
•**ELEKTRA** / Mexico Appliances, home furnishings, money transfers CEO: Pedro Padilla Longoria	10,300	$557 +20%	$78 +58%		Salinas Price and Salinas Pliego families, 80%	Use knowhow in retailing to poor to tap other markets such as insurance; expand abroad
•**GEO** / Mexico Low-income housing CEO: Miguel Gómez Mont	2,380	$174 +27%	$18 +40%		Luis Orvananos Lascurain, Miguel Gómez Mont, and 5 other directors, 45%	Use innovative design and low costs to expand into other Latin countries and the southern U.S.
•**INTERAMERICANA DE ENTRETENIMIENTO (CIE)** / Mexico Live entertainment, advertising, telemarketing CEO: Alejandro Soberón Kuri	2,500	$47 +2%	$8 +81%		Group of 16 investors led by Soberón, 60%	Integrate all levels of business from operating stadiums to telemarketing; do same with partners abroad
•**SARAIVA** / Brazil Publishing, bookstore chain CEO: Jorge Eduardo Saraiva	1,650	$145 +23%	$16 +58%		Saraiva family, 96% of voting shares	Cash in on rising literacy; attract young customers to bookstores with Internet cafes

*Current market exchange rates. Mexican data at yearend 1996 rate.   **Loss due to startup costs in Colombia and Bolivia

in charge at many top companies. They are skilled at using technology and freer trade to expand their companies.

Josue Christiano Gomes da Silva is one of Brazil's new-style managers. With an MBA from Vanderbilt University, the 33-year-old CEO runs Coteminas, one of the world's lowest-cost textile producers. By investing in the best technology, Gomes da Silva can manufacture even more cheaply than rivals from Asia. He cranks out T-shirts for a wholesale price of 75 cents, while a similar shirt from China goes for 90 cents.

His strategy is to boost the company's margins by moving beyond his textile base into clothing. After just two years in the business, he is Brazil's largest T-shirt manufacturer. The company wants to get two-thirds of its sales through higher-ticket clothing by 1999, up from 15% now. Coteminas earned $70 million on sales of $223 million last year, with revenues rising at a 16% pace. Analysts expect sales to top $1 billion early in the next century.

Fast-moving companies such as Coteminas are getting a closer look from global investors, making it possible for them to raise capital outside of the region. Analysts say Gomes da Silva is hoping to raise $100 million from an issue of American depositary receipts later this year. Other entrepreneurial companies, such as Mexico's Softtek, are also looking overseas for capital, largely because the region's banks still lend mainly to traditional blue-chip customers.

Even many of Latin America's establishment companies are starting to step lively. Blessed with considerable resources from years of protected markets, the better companies are remaking themselves. "They wield a lot of political clout and have strong financial leverage, which gives them access to low-cost capital," says Mexico City-based Carlos Lukac of consultant Bain Co. These conglomerates, many of them family-owned, are shedding businesses, bringing in new managers, and tapping outside markets.

In Argentina, for example, the Perez Companc conglomerate is dumping real estate and other businesses to focus on energy. It's investing $900 million this year in oil, gas, electricity, and petrochemicals from Venezuela to Chile, often in partnership with heavyweights such as Exxon Corp. "Our idea is to become one of the world's major energy companies," says Daniel Rennis, manager of corporate financial planning.

CORRUPTION. Despite the hard-won gains, Latin companies still face many challenges. They still operate in an underdeveloped region, with legal systems that are politicized and often corrupt and with thin capital markets and low savings levels. While many companies are giving multinationals a fight, the assault from outside is intensifying as Latin markets prove more promising. Even for deep-pocketed Latin blue chips, the new competition rules out going it alone in many businesses. To fortify themselves, many are taking on foreign partners in joint ventures and alliances.

Such infusions of foreign equity aren't bad, of course. And they may mean a much faster transfer of top management knowhow. Meanwhile, day by day, success by success, Latin America's corporate pacesetters are consolidating the region's free-market reforms. By ignoring national boundaries they're creating a close-knit regional economy out of a continent long fragmented by economic nationalism. The next step is for Latin America's biggest and best players to join the ranks of America's, Europe's, and Asia's best companies. That's still a stretch, but for Latin America's new bosses and citizens alike, it's a hopeful prospect.

Reprinted from October 27, 1997 issue of *Business Week* by special permission, copyright © 1997 by McGraw-Hill, Inc.

Grads say shoe doesn't fit

Industry left holding the bag

by Chris Woodyard
USA TODAY

CHICAGO — She manages 15 employees, runs one of the busiest shoe departments in the Windy City and aims for the fast track in a $38 billion company.

Yet Harvard graduate Hannah Schott, 23, says, "I get asked almost every day why I'm working at Sears."

Once, working as a junior executive in a department store chain carried a certain prestige. Now, the retail industry fears picky college grads view store careers as one step ahead of running the Slurpee machine at the local 7-Eleven.

The image problem exploded in the faces of recruiters for major retail chains this year.

Sears has filled only 77 of its 175 management-trainee positions. Only about half the students extended offers by the giant retailer were accepting them, "lower than it's ever been," says Robert Wery, Sears' college relations director.

While other chains aren't as specific about the numbers, they report a similarly tough recruiting atmosphere. "It's a problem," says John Gremer, hustling to find enough qualified candidates for the fast-growing Walgreen drugstore chain.

The shortfall comes at a difficult time. After a decade of restructuring and store closings, many chains are expanding in an industry that traditionally has a voracious appetite for talent. About a third of all store managers' jobs turn over every year.

Recruiters and academics say they're not entirely to blame for the hiring sinkhole. A strong economy and a drop in the number of college-age workers shrank the pool of potential recruits. But they also acknowledge that they haven't done enough to sell the business of selling.

"The industry has done a horrible job of marketing the opportunities," says Barton Weitz, director of the University of Florida's Center for Retailing.

IMAGE PROBLEMS

Observers attribute much of the retail industry's troubles to image: Movies such as 1994's *Clerks* portrayed stores as being inhabited by listless, low-paid slackers.

The truth, recruiters say, is otherwise.

Executive trainees generally start in the $25,000 to $30,000 range and can expect steady raises and promotions for good performance, recruiters say.

Retailing management careers place enormous responsibility into a young college grad's hands. The hardware or menswear department of a large department store can generate revenue of $2 million a year and requires supervision of a staff of 10 or more employees.

Quick studies can rise to store manager within a few years. A veteran department store manager can earn up to $100,000 a year, although the range is quite wide. The average manager of a specialty store, the smaller stores that sell dishes, women's clothing, sporting equipment or similar goods, earns an average of about $29,000, reports the National Retail Federation, a Washington-based trade group.

And running a store has its pleasures.

"You can put on a finance hat one day and a marketing hat the next," says Tom Holmes, who at 25 is second-in-charge of the Sears store in Woodfield Mall in Schaumburg, Ill., flagship of the 823-store chain. With a bonus, he says he hopes to make $50,000 this year.

After working in a store, some young managers opt to go into a speciality.

Laura Farris, 23, is scheduled to take her fourth trip to South Korea and Hong Kong this week as a toy buyer for Wal-Mart. The University of Florida graduate says she chose retailing after working as a summer intern in a Wal-Mart store in Johnson City, Tenn., and the home office in Bentonville, Ark.

"I think most of my friends, when I told them I was going to work for Wal-Mart, envisioned me in a blue smock greeting people," she says.

ODD HOURS, FREQUENT MOVES

But so much for the recruiting poster. The downside is that budding execs can expect to work lots of night and weekend shifts that significantly cut into social life.

"They have to work when their friends and peers are off. That's a hard pill to swallow," says Wal-Mart recruiter Joey Jones.

Initial management assignments require postings to small towns, such as Gun Barrel City, Texas, and frequent moves thereafter.

Bill Abrams, 48, has bought and sold seven houses since starting with Sears in Florissant, Mo., in 1971.

(Cont.)

"I always said I wanted to move around a bit," says Abrams, a former store manager who now is operations manager for direct delivery of Sears appliances in the Midwest.

Before this year, recruiters didn't have much trouble filling their quotas. A number of universities have undergraduate retail programs that produce a supply of fresh blood, besides the usual collection of business grads and liberal arts students.

Then came the fickle Class of 1997, and the recruiters are left wondering who will mind the store. Here are some of the reasons that experts list as they try to decipher why retailing has lost it appeal:

▲ No hero CEOs. Microsoft's Bill Gates, Southwest Airline's Herb Kelleher and General Electric's John Welch all rate high on the boardroom recognition scale. Wal-Mart's Sam Walton is dead. Quick, name a living retailing giant.

▲ Fewer prestigious programs. Macy's, Gimbel's and other large department store chains used to be known for top-flight training programs. But when some major chains became playing chips in the leveraged buyout wars of the 1980s, training programs fell by the wayside.

▲ Competition from other fields. Retailers are feeling the competitive heat for top talent from such fun-filled occupations as accountancy. Accounting firm recruiters have been showing a flashy video on some campuses loaded with images of easy money and mingling with movie stars to counter the profession's green-eyeshade image.

▲ Mundane work. Nancy Elich, who has been trying to find a few good computer programmers for the Crate & Barrel specialty chain, says "these kids want to be on the cutting edge." Problem is, most retailers don't need computer systems on the cutting edge — just good, solid systems that work.

So it's no wonder that recruiters say they're coming up short this year.

HIGH-LEVEL CONCERN

The situation has become dire enough that Sears CEO Arthur Martinez, in a talk to recruiters, asked, "How do we think of these students as our customers?" And observed, "We are speaking to them too often like it was the 1950s. . . . We need to communicate with them in their terms."

He addresses the image issue directly. "It is not the kind of mindless work that some of them think it is," Martinez says.

But the outside world apparently isn't convinced.

Shoe department manager Schott says that when she went job hunting last year after earning her history degree at Harvard, some industry recruiters were thunderstruck that she was considering a retail career.

She recalled telling one recruiter she was turning them down to work at Sears. "They were dumbfounded. They said, 'Corporate?' 'No,' I said, 'It's a job in the store.'"

With too few recent graduates like Schott to choose from, retail recruiters are scrounging for ways to make retail appear more glamorous.

They are dismayed at a Sears survey of retailers and academics that found 78% listed lack of prestige as a barrier to enticing students into retail careers.

At a gathering last month among competing retail recruiters, they threw around phrases that describe what they like about retailing: exciting, hip, happening, trendy. They eventually arrived at a slogan: "Retailing, the heartbeat of business."

"It's like changing a bad reputation," says Ellen Goldsberry, director of the Southwest Retail Center at the University of Arizona.

But perhaps the answer rests with the more mundane. Retailing is a universe, from jetting around Europe as a buyer for high fashion or working the counter at McDonald's. "Somewhere in between lies an aurora borealis of opportunity that most people don't realize," says Eric Segal, president of the executive search firm Kenzer in New York.

Copyright 1997, *USA Today.* Reprinted with permission.

Top Toilet Makers From U.S. and Japan Vie for Chinese Market

Toto Finds There's No Place Like Home; U.S. Rival Leads in the Cheap Seats

The Ping-Pong Ball Test

By Steve Glain

Staff Reporter of The Wall Street Journal

SHANGHAI, China — "These are the trenches," says Horace Whittlesey, looking out over Shanxi Road, a seemingly placid tree-lined street in this city's commercial district. "This is where we compete head-on."

Well put. Mr. Whittlesey is a top commander on the American side of an intense and instructive skirmish in the trade war between the U.S. and Japan. The commodity at stake: commodes.

Here on what locals call Plumbers' Row, Chinese builders and homeowners browse through a collection of dusty shops displaying new toilets from around the globe. More often than not, customers shopping for imported commodes choose between the products of the world's two top bathroom-equipment makers: American Standard Inc., of Piscataway, N.J., where Mr. Whittlesey is the general manager for China, and Toto Ltd., its archrival from Kitakyushu, in southern Japan.

The clash of these toilet titans offers a vivid example of how two global companies compete in today's borderless economy, and how U.S. companies can gain the upper hand when they aren't fighting in protectionist economies against home-turf competitors.

A Market Worth Billions

China, where American Standard and Toto are in many ways an even match, is a perfect proving ground. As it is for the producers of many modern conveniences, China is the world's fastest-growing and potentially most profitable market for toilet manufacturers, who face marginal growth in developed countries. Until recently, China's toilet market was limited to an unenticing demand for more primitive "squat" facilities. But now Western-style sit-down fixtures, which are easier to keep clean and use less water, have become the standard in thousands of new apartment complexes, office buildings and department stores. The Chinese likely will spend billions of dollars annually on foreign-made toilets in the coming years.

The two top competitors, meanwhile, offer Chinese consumers similar flagship models — two-piece, vacuum-rinse, self-cleaning toilets, mostly in light pastels. Both design their products at home and manufacture in Thailand and other developing countries where labor is cheap and then ship them to China for sale. "A water closet is a water closet," says Koichi Noda, president of Toto's China unit. "The trick is in setting up the best distribution system and marketing campaign."

'We Must Change'

If that's the case, Toto needs to learn some new tricks, for American Standard has gained the upper hand for now by outmaneuvering its rival at several key junctures in the process that brings a toilet from design concept to showroom sale. The U.S. company estimates that it sells about 30% to 40% of all bathroom fixtures imported into China. Toto has a 10% to 15% share, its officials say.

To be sure, American Standard has been marketing in China since before World War II, while Toto didn't start until 1979. But American Standard's success also reflects the competitive advantage U.S. companies are reaping in the aftermath of the turbulent 1980s, often at the expense of Japanese rivals. American Standard, like much of corporate America, went through a wrenching restructuring in the 1980s that left it lean, flexible and aggressive overseas.

Toto, on the other hand, is typical of many firms cultivated in the greenhouse of Japan's protected economy. It has only recently been forced by a saturated domestic market to pursue significant business opportunities overseas. But it must first come to grips with a rigid business style that works at home but not abroad. "Toto's problems are the same as most Japanese companies'," one Toto manager says. "We know we must change, but it won't happen overnight."

The Christian Dior of Toilets

The commode competition begins, literally, on the drawing board, where American Standard overcomes a technological advantage by Toto with a more malleable design process. At Toto's design studio in Chigasaki, an hour outside of Tokyo, designers conceive new toilets with computers that automatically mill models out of blocks of foam. Blueprints can be in factory engineers' hands in four weeks. American Standard's process takes two months, on average. Near Lexington, Ky., Jack Kaiser and six associates sketch designs and craft models by hand. There aren't any computers.

But Mr. Kaiser is the Christian Dior of water-closet couture, having designed the legendary Cadet, an oft-copied compact commode introduced in 1965. He and his designers have broad leeway in developing new models, working closely with the marketing department. Toto's designers have little say because the engineers who tailor products for production dominate the process, limiting creativity and neglecting overseas consumer tastes. This limits Toto's ability to break into new markets, one of its senior designers says.

For example, while Toto dominates the luxury bathroom market in China, its biggest handicap is that it has been slow to adapt to the largest and fastest growing Chinese market — the low-end. The company's China operations are geared largely to the kind of flawless, high-quality product lines that Japanese users demand, such as cast-iron tubs or the Washlet, Toto's revolutionary toilet with a strategically located bidet-like water-jet.

Because developers tend to buy their sinks, bathtubs and toilets in sets, American Standard is in a better position to undercut Toto when gunning for subluxury projects. The U.S. company recently beat out Toto for a big contract to outfit the headquarters of the Agriculture Bank of China and China Tobacco Industry (Group) Corp., largely because it could offer less-expensive products. Five-star hotels can afford pricey cast-iron tubs, but most consumers want simple steel tubs that cost less than half as much. Toto doesn't make a steel tub; American Standard does.

"To ask a Japanese engineer to make something cheaper is harder than to ask him to make something better," says Thibault Danjou, a Toto marketing manager. "We have to learn to make products cheaper so Chinese consumers can afford them."

American Standard deploys another important tactical advantage once the blueprints and models are sent by air to factories for production overseas. Their Thailand plants appear similar at first glance. Smock-clad artisans build plaster casts, which workers fill with liquid clay. The dried bowls go into gas-fired kilns. Both companies boast of cutting-edge production technology, which they jealously guard by barring photography at their plants. Finished units go through the same rigorous flushing test at both factories: Each toilet must successfully digest numerous sponges, ping-pong balls or rags.

The real difference emerges from a simple inventory statistic: American Standard only stocks enough toilets to last 14 days; Toto keeps two-months' worth on hand. American Standard's production process is flexible enough to fill most orders by making new toilets, instead of by drawing from inventory. "We're producing constantly based on sales expectation," says Norman Livingstone, the Thai unit's managing director. "Then we adapt that to actual demand."

Nibondh Theeranartsin, managing director of Toto's joint-venture factory, Siam Sanitary Ware Co., concedes American Standard's advantage: "They can sell every piece they make."

American Standard wasn't always so flexible. A decade ago, it was as complacent as any other company with a comfortable domestic market share. But in 1988, it was targeted in a hostile takeover bid by Black & Decker Corp. of Towson, Md., and took evasive action: It went private, buying back all of its stock by borrowing $3.2 billion. That stopped Black & Decker from buying enough stock on the open market to take control, but left American Standard with staggering debt.

So American Standard pursued business more aggressively in less-mature markets overseas and adopted a made-to-order manufacturing system known as Demand Flow, moving inventory as quickly as possible to reduce overhead — and to help pay off the loans. The company estimates that it has saved up to $500 million in inventory costs since 1989.

American Standard's Thai factory also can quickly fill odd-sized orders that Toto says can be difficult to fill at all. A recent morning at the American Standard factory finds Shusri Phothisri taking an order for 500 Cadets in bone and tan. As with many orders from China, the toilets must be custom-built because they will replace old-fashioned squat toilets, which have outlet ports that aren't in a standard place. Replacements must be customized to line up with existing sewage pipes.

"We can special-order a Cadet with those specs. Piece of cake," American Standard's Mr. Whittlesey says of such orders.

Toto isn't so accommodating, in part because it never faced the kind of reckoning American Standard did. Like most Japanese construction-industry companies, Toto's domestic sales boomed in the late 1980s, when real-estate development reached a frenzy. Foreign competition was nil, and Japanese customers didn't demand customized products.

Toto never felt much need to venture into more competitive overseas markets in a big way — until Japan's building boom went bust five years ago and competitors at home began eating into its comfortable domestic market share. Unfortunately for Toto, "They can't seem to find their niche overseas, while their home market is becoming increasingly very competitive," says Mark Berman, an analyst at Jardine Fleming Securities Ltd. in Tokyo.

Exports accounted for less than 3% of Toto's 213 billion yen ($1.9 billion) in sales in the latest six-month reporting period, compared with 69% of American Standard's $1.3 billion in plumbing sales for all of last year. American Standard has 79 overseas factories, including nine in China, compared with Toto's 17 overseas factories, with four in China. (Both companies have begun shifting some of their manufacturing capabilities to China.)

Once the toilets are manufactured, they flow into a cutthroat distribution system. Both companies use dozens of authorized distributors that sell through hundreds of dealers, such as the ones on Plumbers' Row. American Standard once tried to bury Toto in sales by offering its toilets to distributors on credit, but the strategy failed because they rarely paid. (American Standard's distributors are so cashstrapped that its premier showroom in Shanghai lacks its own working toilet.)

Toto, meanwhile, poached one of American Standard's longtime distributors. Sun Xing Ming, general manager of the Shanghai-based East-China General Agency/Xing Ming Sanitaryware Co., is a second-generation American Standard toilet merchant. But he left in a huff after the U.S. company cut him out of negotiations with a hotel contractor. Toto's China sales chief, who already had been wooing him, immediately signed him up. He is now Toto's top distributor in Shanghai.

Mr. Sun and Toto plan to give American Standard a run for its money in coming years. The company doesn't intend to "follow American Standard down market," Toto's Mr. Noda says.

Though he concedes his company is abandoning an important market to American Standard for now, Toto is betting that Chinese toilet tastes will mature, egged on by a planned $1 million television campaign.

"Toto is looking toward the next century," Mr. Sun says. "It's not in a hurry to make money."

Reprinted by permission of *The Wall Street Journal,* © 1996 Dow Jones & Company, Inc. All Rights Reserved Worldwide.

Hospitals Court Foreign Patients to Fill Beds

By Lucette Lagnado
Staff Reporter of The Wall Street Journal

When Johns Hopkins medical center in Baltimore heard about a remote border war between Peru and Ecuador last year, it geared up for battle. The mission: to treat the wounded — and, not incidentally, negotiate a lucrative contract. Using a network of carefully cultivated diplomatic and military contacts, the medical center persuaded the Ecuadorian government to send more than 45 wounded soldiers to Johns Hopkins for artificial limbs. The price: about $35,000 per casualty.

"There are wars all over the world, bombs all over the world," says John Hutchins, director of international services at Hopkins. "Casualty patients," he says, are a new and enriching "market niche." Hopkins hopes to treat Peru's wounded, too, and maybe casual ties from Bosnia and Turkey. It is even talking with Argentina about new prostheses for soldiers maimed in the Falklands Islands almost 15 years ago.

Soliciting patients from areas of violence and warfare — "a delicate business," says Mr. Hutchins — is but one element in U.S. hospitals' push to attract more patients of all kinds from overseas. Driven by the pressures of managed care and empty beds, medical centers and clinics of all sizes cross oceans and deserts seeking the business of ailing Saudi royals, Asian tycoons and potentates from around the globe.

Some hospitals are hiring translators fluent in Arabic or Swahili and offering package deals on, say, coronary bypass. Hospitals in Florida lure affluent South American clientele to stay at resorts for "health vacations" that combine golf and tennis with EKGs and blood tests. Other institutions run satellite offices staffed by locals who stimulate patient referrals. In Chile, the Mayo Clinic relies on a local advisory board whose members include the publisher of the nation's leading daily newspaper, the former interior minister of Gen. Augusto Pinochet and other establishment figures. The Mayo Clinic's foreign business is up 10%.

Critics of these foreign forays argue that if U.S. hospitals were better run they wouldn't need to scour the globe for new patients. Medical centers "shouldn't be running around the world looking for people to do heart surgery on," says Michael Servais, an executive at Universal Health Services, a for-profit hospital company. "It seems a little strange to go out and recruit patients because you have an operating room and a surgeon and need to keep them busy. I say shut that program down."

Stanford Medical Center's president, Peter Van Etten, counters: "Industry has certainly approached international markets as a normal part of their operations, and so why shouldn't hospitals?" Stanford is building an imaging center in Singapore to provide on-site CAT scans and mammograms and refer patients to Palo Alto, Calif., for treatment.

Providing some of the best medical care in the world, U.S. hospitals have always attracted wealthy foreigners. Though no one seems to track exact numbers, hospitals believe the total each year is already in the tens of thousands and could grow exponentially. Latin America's growing affluent class is in-creasingly a source of patients; and rising prosperity in Asia, particularly Singapore, India and the Philippines, is adding to the pool of people who can afford to seek treatment abroad. The Persian Gulf's vast wealth and inadequate care make it an especially inviting target for the U.S. hospitals.

Most foreign visitors plunk down heavy deposits before they are even admitted to a U.S. hospital, sparing the institution the hassles of insurance plans and managed-care gatekeepers. "This past week, I got a wire for $75,000 for a deposit toward a kidney transplant. The patient isn't even here, yet I have money in the bank," says Regina Grisales, international-business coordinator at Florida's Tampa General Hospital, which courts prospective patients in the Cayman Islands and Guatemala.

An added advantage: many foreign patients pay the balance of their bills in cash. "They come to us with money in a suitcase," says Jose Nunez, who directs international marketing at Methodist Hospital in Houston.

Methodist set its sights on Mecca — literally — when it embarked on a new venture to woo Arab patients. It built a 700-square-foot mosque in a storage area, positioning a special prayer wall decorated with passages from the Koran so that Muslims would face precisely 40 degrees northeast to pray to Mecca. A Saudi donor paid for the construction, and "the hospital is very happy," says Abdus Saleem, the pathologist who oversaw the project. Foreign business is up 12% from last year.

Among the hospitals marketing abroad, poaching one another's patients is common — often on the basis of price. Renowned medical centers such as Houston's Methodist Hospital, the Cleveland Clinic and Johns Hopkins charge about $25,000 for a bypass

The Multifaceted Global Medical Market

Region	Key Medical Issues	Market
Latin America and Mexico	Many infectious and digestive diseases; lung, stomach, prostate cancer in men; breast cancer in women; sexually transmitted diseases	Growing affluent class can afford to travel abroad and pay cash for medical treatment.
Middle East	Genetic diseases (congenital malformations), especially among royal families; heart disease; cancer, lymphoma; asthma; cystic fibrosis; childhood leukemia	Persian Gulf governments guarantee medical care for every citizen. As medical infrastructure collapses, government prefers to send patients abroad for treatment. Sizable wealthy population can afford to pay for best care in the world.
Asia	Cancer; coronary diseases; childhood asthma (Malaysia); geriatric diseases	Somewhat limited as countries try to create their own medical infrastructures. Patients seeking services abroad typically do not get past California. But wealthy populations in India, Singapore, Malaysia and Japan could be tapped.
Europe	Mental illness; lung, breast and cervical cancer; sexually transmitted diseases, especially AIDS; heart disease	Has some great medical facilities, but some Europeans still turn to U.S. for treatment of complex ailments. Several insurance policies cover treatment in this country.

Source: N. J. Pierce & Associates, Houston

(Cont.)

operation "package," covering surgery, hospitalization, anesthesia and doctors' fees (complications are extra, as is catheterization); but the Miami Heart Institute in Miami Beach says it can price the procedure 10% cheaper, and nearby Mercy Hospital says it can do it for 20% less.

"We are very competitive," says Mercy's Eugene Bajorinas, who runs its budding international program. "A lot of people who have landed in Miami and gone on to Houston [Methodist] or the Mayo Clinic don't have to do that anymore." Mercy has teamed up with Fisher Island, the luxury resort island near Miami Beach, to offer a $5,000 visit: The patient gets picked up at the airport by limousine, undergoes a battery of tests the next day, and is escorted back to Fisher Island to unwind with a game of golf or tennis.

"We call this health tourism," says a rival, Bob Jimenez of Florida Hospital in Orlando, which offers a family vacation package — a physical for Mom or Dad, while spouse and the kids tool around Disney World.

To better implement its overseas ambitions, Johns Hopkins has opened a marketing office near Washington's Embassy Row that concentrates on wining and dining ambassadors and attaches. The hospital also recently held a luncheon for United Nations diplomats in New York. Guest speaker: a famed Hopkins doctor who told his listeners — most of them male, middle-aged envoys — how he can treat prostate cancer without causing impotence.

Such tactics pay off. Hopkins treated 610 foreign patients in 1994, doubled the overseas traffic last year and will almost triple it this year to more than 4,400. "War is a business, and hospitals are like Switzerland — neutral territory," says Maureen Ryan, whom Hopkins hired to open the Embassy Row office.

In fact, Hopkins wooed both sides of the Peru-Ecuador border dispute — successfully; during a truce in the fighting, a Peruvian general and an Ecuadorian colonel arrived at the same time for a checkup. Ending up in the same waiting room, the officers saluted one another and avoided hostilities.

Reprinted by permission of The Wall Street Journal, © 1996 Dow Jones & Company, Inc. All Rights Reserved Worldwide.

Love My Brand

Marketers today are trying to foster true relationships between their brands and their customers. At the center of the process are direct marketers that have left "junk mail" behind on the scrap heap. *By Daniel Hill*

Brian Evans is a 43-year-old investment counselor, living in Worcester, Mass., and he commutes to his office in Boston every day. In the car, when he isn't on his hands-free cell phone, he is listening to opera CDs, not the radio. At home, he says, he spends maybe three hours a week watching TV, and when he does, he is usually multi-tasking, making out bills or leafing through catalogs or a business magazine. The rest of the time is spent "doing stuff" with his wife, Amanda, and their 5-year-old daughter, Anna. He also spends about six hours a week online, doing research, checking email and general surfing.

"I think I must be hard to reach for companies," says Evans. "I get so much stuff via the mail and email that has nothing to do with my needs or wants that my reflex has become to shut *all* of it out."

Evans, with his six-figure salary and family, and others like him, are becoming maddeningly difficult to reach for marketers in all categories. Just reaching them, and getting the Brians and Amandas of the world to open a piece of direct (i.e., junk) mail used to be the goal. Today, the objective for companies like Radio Shack, Saturn, Sears and Gateway is not merely to sell, but to have a "relationship" with their customers. And that puts direct marketing agencies at the center of the storm, trying to figure out not only how to tickle a customer into a date, but how to keep them interested for the long haul. It's no longer, "What do you have to sell me?" but "What can you do for me?"

"It's not like 25 years ago when you bought a spot on *Bonanza* and hoped people went to the showroom the next day," says Jim Julow, Chrysler's executive director of corporate marketing.

The drift toward relationship marketing (RM) is in the numbers. Direct advertising in the U.S. grew by an annual rate of 8% (versus 7% for total advertising growth) from 1992-97, reaching $153 billion last year. That was 57.8% of total U.S. advertising expenditures. From 1997-2002, the Direct Marketing Association projects, expenditures for direct marketing will increase by 6.9% annually. The DMA also estimates U.S. sales attributable to direct to be $1.2 trillion in 1997. And what it refers to as direct marketing employment reached almost 23 million workers in 1997.

Not all Americans, though, welcome these figures as good news. Don Peppers, president of marketing 1:1 in Stamford, Conn., complains that, "I get 10 catalogs a day, and I've never bought anything from any of them." Meanwhile, Julie Highsmith, a New York designer, gets numerous, lavish stock photography catalogs (some a couple of times a year) that she pegs at costing five or six bucks a pop. They've never gotten a dime from her. That's an extremely wasteful use of wood pulp. But no one ever got fired for doing what they've done in the past.

As more consumers resist traffic jams down at the mall, and more surfers yawn at their televisions or forsake it for games or the Net, big money is available to companies who develop (and more crucially, manage) cost-effective databases that indicate who to contact and, rather than why, *how* they should be contacted and when.

Pamela Larrick, executive vp of McCann Relationship Marketing Worldwide, cites numbers from Strategic Marketing Institute, Cambridge, Mass. showing a high commitment to RM yields a return on sales 12 times greater than low RM, and an ROI that's six times greater.

That may be, because, as Wendy Riches, North American chairman of OgilvyOne Worldwide, notes, it has traditionally cost six times as much to acquire a customer as to retain one. The trick, says Peppers, is to con-

> **"The frequent flyer model is one that tries to achieve economic loyalty," says agency boss Bob Lieber. "Relationship marketing strives for emotional loyalty. If you got 'em first with coupons, you'll probably have to continue with coupons."**

sider customers' lifetime value and to start a cost-efficient dialogue, so that, based on past purchases, a book store cashier, for example, can steer someone to the new Elmore Leonard novel. That may sound creepy to some—that a stranger would know what authors they like—but companies right now are struggling with this issue of where the line between the "creeps" and helpful customer handling is.

(Cont.)

"It can't be a faux intimacy," says Peppers, who quips that he is still looking for a dry cleaner he can call his own, one that will store the little swatches of spare material for his suits. Just playing back things they've said, or repeating their name, he says, is a poor way to begin. That was the strategy of Blockbuster Video last year, which, at some of its stores, instructed store workers to say, "hello" to everyone who came in the store, and then address each customer by name when they came up on the computer, as in, "Mr. Hill, that will be $3.99. Enjoy the movie Mr. Hill. That's not due back until Monday night Mr. Hill."

A few companies at the forefront of RM are Dell Computers and Radio Shack. Scott Nelson, research director at the GartnerGroup, says from the very start Dell used surveys and ordering contacts and re-contacts to go beyond capturing names and addresses to asking why customers chose particular configurations, what other systems they looked at and what they might have paid elsewhere. Dell concentrates on what its customers look like over time, so it can upgrade them to multiple usage.

Since over 99% of customer households have purchased something at Radio Shack over the last three years, "We don't need new customers, we need to increase the frequency of our existing customers," says David Edmondson, senior vp of marketing & advertising at Radio Shack. That's understandable when you have 119 million customers in 89 million households. The company, the butt of jokes on occasion for its compulsive quizzing of customers, captures copious data on over 80% of its in-store transactions. It started its current database around three years ago, but using archival data, took only 30 months to achieve historical data on five years of behavior. Radio Shack, says Dennis Duffy, president of

MINING THE DATABASE

Perhaps you've seen the Saturn TV commercial that humorously touts its database, to the point of showing a customer profile on a computer screen: a guy who drives from dealer to dealer with various fabricated complaints just to nab the free jelly donuts.

Now part of the zeitgeist, databases have been key to relationship marketing since the outset. Seemingly dozens of vendors are pushing new products, all with their own bells and whistles. Marketing database software sales in 1997 were just over $1 billion, up from $100 million in 1993. David Raab of Raab Associates outside Philadelphia notes an explosion of software offerings, perhaps a dozen in the past year alone. He published a guidebook in April, and laments that it was obsolete by August.

Vernon Tirey, president of DiaLogos, Boston, cites the decidedly biased claim of the Data Warehousing Institute that a successful data operation can increase a company's customer base by well over 200% within two years of implementation. Less that sound too fantastical, the equally-biased Tirey thinks less than 30% of all data warehousing efforts are successful. Tirey figures 10–15% of the data collectd usually answers 80% of the questions. He recommends companies concentrate more on product attribute information that's easy to get, but often ignored.

The nex big thing, says Scott Nelson, research director at the GartnerGroup, is a third-generational, enterprise-wide model that captures on a single platform information from all points of customer contact, be it from the Internet, call centers, blow-back cards or store questionnaires. Say, for instance, someone calls in complaining your shampoo has left his hair oily. Rather than just send him a free sample, the operator can use his age, profile information and past dealings with the company to craft a specific response.

Ideally, says Nelson, such systems will allow companies to focus on issues broader than direct marketing, i.e., "channel management," where—no matter the time or place of contact—the customer receives a consistent message and response. Only about 2% or 3% of all companies are even thinking this way, according to Nelson, and less are up and running. He maintains there's not one off-the-shelf, third-generational system available. Companies pursuing them turn to systems integrators such as DiaLogos, Naviant in Philadelphia or Tessera in Boston. Most companies won't tackle them until they've solved their year 2000 problem and dealt with any snafus associated with the European Monetary Union's common currency, he concludes. Raab feels some computer and financial service firms are taking baby steps in this direction, but no one's really doing it.

The cost? Raab figures it takes $1 million for any sizable firm to buy, modify and get these latest programs flying. And that's if you don't need front-end modifications to your call center, which can cost $5,000 a seat. Tirey puts the cost at up to $3 million. Nelson prices it differently: a typical marketing database costs around 5% of the overall marketing budget; an aggressive program clocks in at 7–10%, he says. —D.H.

Cadmus Communications, N.Y., is better positioned than virtually any other company in the category for direct relationship marketing. "What Radio Shack has been doing for years, you couldn't get anyone to start that today," Duffy said.

Consumers exercise tremendous control over how they want to shop, says Chrysler's Julow. They shop at their own speed, at the location they want, in an information-friendly manner, with the right amount of information, he says. Along with rivals Ford and General Motors, Chrysler is building a massive database with new "black-box" artificial intelligence to make the carmaker less reliant on mass media advertising and to make its direct efforts more productive. Right now, most of the direct efforts done by each carmaker are little more than mailed ads, or perhaps an invitation to a special event. But the company has no way of knowing where a recipient is in the car buying cycle or what he or she has responded to in the past. They may be inviting someone to a regatta who is only one month into a 36-month lease on a competing make. Julow has been managing his data internally for around three years. "When it crashes in a year, we'll know we have too many fields," he says. As to his database, he figures he's still perhaps a year-and-a-half from knowing "how high up is up."

Many marketing executives are chary with the details of exactly what RM has achieved. But you get a few gleanings. Julow says RM has enabled Chrysler to raise response rates from 1% or 2% "up into the teens," in some cases, for a corporate or dealer initiative. Lifecycle marketing is in full force in autos, he says, whether it employs a free oil change or free wiper blades for folks with older cars. Three years ago, a customer might have gotten a card from one dealer one week, another from a second dealer the following week and then a catalog from Chrysler. Now the company is hooked up by satellite to all its dealers to prevent this sort of annoying overkill.

Another big-ticket company that is well underway with RM is Mercedes-Benz of North America, which has had a program up and running for 18 months. One initiative was an old-fashioned multi-vehicle launch event, involving food and wine and a dramatic undraping of new models. In Los Angeles, they sent out 100,000 invitations to customers and prospects, and they had to close the highway down. In another instance, Mercedes and its dealers invited customers to the symphony, with 2% of the invitees attending. Last fall, Mercedes sent out one million invitations for customers and prospects to attend one of an array of events at dealerships. Called the "Fall in Love" event, it was supported by a national ad with the same theme. And, two years before the introduction of the

> **"Relationship marketing allows companies to minimize the spiral of price cutting, an inevitable war of attrition," says OgilvyOne's Wendy Riches.**

M-class sport utility vehicle last fall, Mercedes began polling luxury car owners on what they were looking for in a SUV. The company achieved its goal of a dialogue with 100,000 potential customers and sales of 25,000. It's commitment to RM is in the company's numbers. In 1996, Mercedes' RM budget, which included creative, production, lists, postage, etc., was 8.2% of Mercedes marketing budget for the year. With 800,000 pieces mailed, the response rate (leads) was 225% over 1995's controls and the conversion rate (sales) was 65% better than the controls. Incremental sales were between 30% to 40% higher than those who would have bought anyway.

One tool that companies are using today to make their RM programs more efficient is more powerful and often cheaper computerized capabilities to segment their prospects and tailor their message.

Bob Lieber, chairman and CEO of Lieber Levett Koenig Farese Babcock, New York, describes four criteria for "actionable" segmentation. Consumer segments have to be: "Groupable" (sharing "like attitudinal, behavioral, and/or demographic characteristics"); "Influence-able" (their behavior changeable by communications); "Reachable" (targeted by existing media); and "Measurable" (as to the communication's impact).

One of Lieber's clients, *Readers Digest,* will implement a value-added, segmentation strategy starting this spring. Subscribers will have identified particular health issues of interest, basically "inviting us into their home," says Lieber. Their copy of the magazine will include an advertorial section with news regarding specific maladies.

Jim Ramaley, vp of circulation systems at Ziff-Davis Publishing, which puts out *PC Week* and *Computer Life,* among others, segments his subscribers by whether they paid a discounted or full price initially, whether they subscribe to any related Z-D publications or attend trade shows, hit the company's Web site or avail themselves of any of its online "courses." This enables him to identify different price breaks and change the offer as time elapses. Most importantly, it enables him to drop poor prospects sooner. To similarly keep an eye on her ROI, Denise Tarantino, vice president of marketing for Repp's Big & Tall Stores (a catalog and retail outfit with 200 units

(Cont.)

nationwide), slices her customers into 12 segments, according to response rates, average sales and the like. Some get 6-to-8 pieces a year, some 3-to-5, some only 1-to-3. Repp tries to steer low-volume catalog shoppers into a nearby store they may not even know existed. And infrequent store shoppers might be offered an extra incentive, such as 15% off, for a particular weekend. Repp also has a Web site that gathers data, and its enrollees get short emails from time to time advising them of sales and discounts.

Tarantino gets a 6% response rate to her mailings, far superior to what she describes as a typical, huge non-RM mailing of maybe 750,000 pieces that might get a 0.5% response rate. She also boasts a whopping 30-40% response rate for VIP special events that feature appointments and wardrobe consultations and steep discounts of 20% off a $200 purchase and 30% off $300 tallies.

Some companies mine their transactional data better than others. Barry Blau, chairman of Barry Blau & Partners in Fairfield, Conn., says that though Blockbuster Video Stores has huge amounts of transactional data, "They sent a promotion on a new Nintendo game to every customer they had, though 10% of kids buy 90% of the computer games."

Likewise, some financial services are still sold by simple zip code data. Along with affluence and number of adults in a household, long-distance phone companies look at things like "foreign" surnames or recent immigration to indicate likely high-volume prospects. By not going beyond traditional geodemographic data, says Blau, marketers don't capture what stage people are at in their lives and how that affects their income and spending.

As companies establish relationships, they're able to retreat somewhat from the rewards, coupons and discounts that erode margins. Companies like hotels, airlines and telecommunication firms with high fixed and low variable costs can earn big profits from incremental increases in business. The frequent flier model works for airlines, and they go to great lengths not to fly with empty seats. But it's a model that tries to achieve "economic loyalty," says Lieber. But RM strives for emotional loyalty; getting a customer for life. "If you got 'em first with coupons, you'll probably have to continue with coupons," he says. And even the airlines are now offering some upgraded seats and special boarding lines rather than freebies. Riches at OgilvyOne asserts that RM "allows companies to minimize the spiral of price cutting, an inevitable war of attrition."

Cadmus' Duffy declares, "AT&T threw money away with its True Rewards program. Points and prizes are a fad whose time has passed." He also figures people buy Eddie Bauer for the quality, not some 2% reward program, and that the preferred shopper program launched by Waldenbooks and copied by B. Dalton "is just a margin erosion."

But how do you manage RM, and what the heck does it all cost? It has to emanate from the CEO, say the experts. "You can't have a random act of marketing," says Duffy. "A lot of companies want a quick behavior hit, like you get with a promotion or a sales drive. But that's not RM."

Another reason it has to come from the top is the dedicated personnel to analyze all this data don't come cheap. "You can't just pile this onto the circulation managers who are already up to their necks in alligators," says Ziff-Davis's Ramaley. He sees a particular challenge in asking the right questions, since even with the most sophisticated data mining, the answers don't leap off the page. He'll have hired between 5 to 10 new people by the time he's through.

© 1998 ASM Communications, Inc. Used with permission from *Brandweek* magazine.

Finding Target Market Opportunities

If It Looks Like a Truck but Rides Like a Car, It's Hot

BY JOSEPH B. WHITE

Staff Reporter of THE WALL STREET JOURNAL

The RX 300 — a splashy new luxury sport-utility vehicle from Lexus — has a front end that says dirt roads and a back end that says carpools.

Call it a hybrid, a crossover vehicle or an "urban SUV," as Jim Press, the Lexus division general manager, does. Or label it a "mall cruiser," as **General Motors** Corp. Chairman John F. Smith Jr. does.

Whatever the name, most industry executives at the big Detroit Auto Show this week agree the RX 300 and other vehicles that look like sport-utility vehicles but ride and maneuver like cars are the industry's next big thing.

As sales of rugged looking sport-utility vehicles have surged in recent years, auto makers have touted the off-road stamina of their four-wheel-drive trucks. All the while, car makers knew that few customers actually took their Jeeps, Ford Explorers or Chevrolet Suburbans off pavement and that most didn't like the kidney-jarring rides and stiff handling that came with the macho looks and big cargo spaces.

Now, auto makers are rushing to bring out off-road vehicles aimed squarely at the on-road-only driver. If that sounds confusing, it only points up the often contradictory motivations of the well-heeled consumers who have made these products a mainstay for auto makers in the U.S.

"The key issues for people leaving SUVs are ride and price, in that order," says Coopers Lybrand partner William R. Pochiluk. By the year 2000, he estimates, sales of car/truck hybrids like the RX 300 could grow to 500,000 to one million vehicles a year. Americans bought more than 2.3 million sport-utility vehicles last year, most of them midsize and large models.

If the Jeep Cherokee and the Ford Explorer launched the sport-utility craze in the early 1990s, industry executives say vehicles like the RX 300 will define the next generation, particularly in the luxury end of the market where the big profits are.

The RX 300, built in Japan, is scheduled to go on sale in March, with a base price of $31,500 for a front-wheel-drive-only model. A well-equipped four-wheel-drive model will sell for about $35,305, Lexus officials say. That is roughly $2,000 less than the asking price for a comparable Mercedes M-Class sport utility. Lexus officials clearly see the hot-selling Mercedes as their main foe, and at least initially they are keeping sales goals for the RX 300 modest, forecasting annual sales of 20,000 vehicles, well below expectations for the Mercedes.

When Toyota engineers began developing the RX 300 hybrid three to four years ago, Toyota's marketing people in the U.S. and Japan balked, says Akihiro Wada, Toyota's executive vice president of research and development. But he insisted that "much more riding comfort was needed" than Toyota's truck-based sport utilities provided, he says, and about two years ago, marketing officials began to agree.

Rivals agree as well. "It's definitely a market that interests us," says Thomas Elliott, executive vice president of **Honda Motor** Co.'s U.S. sales operations, as he sizes up an RX 300 at Lexus's auto show display.

While they wouldn't disclose specifics, executives at **Chrysler** Corp. — owner of the granddaddy of sport-utility vehicle brands, Jeep — made it clear during auto-show interviews that they have vehicles similar to the RX 300 in the works. Similar hints came from GM executives.

If concern about global warming translates into tougher government restrictions on emissions, the pressure to move away from less efficient truck designs will become even greater. By using car chassis and engines, auto makers can design lighter, more fuel efficient vehicles.

The RX 300 is expected to average 19 miles per gallon of gasoline in the city and 22 miles per gallon on the highway with a three-liter V-6 engine. That compares with 15 miles per gallon in the city and 20 miles on the highway for a V-6 powered, four-wheel-drive Jeep Grand Cherokee.

"The crossover market is the SUV market of the future," says John Smith, the GM vice president in charge of the Cadillac luxury division. Mr. Smith makes no secret of his desire to get a vehicle like the RX 300 in Cadillac's lineup. "Relative to Lexus, we'll be playing catchup," he concedes.

The Lexus RX 300 isn't the first four-wheel-drive hybrid to spring from a car chassis. **Subaru of America** Inc. in July introduced a hybrid called the Forester, based on a small-car design, as a companion to the Outback version of its Legacy station wagon, introduced in 1996. Honda's CR-V and Toyota's RAV4 small sport-utility vehicles also ride on small-car underpinnings.

But Lexus officials argue, and some rivals agree, that the RX 300 breaks new ground with its combination of generous size and luxury amenities.

Mercedes-Benz and **Ford Motor** Co., meanwhile, are scoring hits by engineering four-wheel-drive trucks that offer substantially smoother rides than previous models. Ford's Lincoln Navigator was outfitted with a suspension that borrowed heavily from the plush Lincoln Town car limousine. Mercedes' hot-selling ML 320 also offers a more car-like ride than older models. But both vehicles are still trucks at heart — heavy and greedy for gas.

Other car makers are trying to inject some off-road vehicle macho into their cars or minivans. Sweden's **Volvo** AB, for example, last fall launched a new line of all-wheel-drive station wagons, including one called the V70 XC Cross Country. With a price that starts at about $38,000, the Cross Country sits an inch higher off the road than a regular V70 wagon and puts the driver two inches higher, thus delivering some of the sense of command that attracts many people to sport-utility trucks.

Volvo stresses that the V70 also offers a full array of safety features, such as airbags mounted in the front seats designed to protect

Lots of room for packages for a day off road at the mall

Macho grille and hood design says truck

Four-wheel-drive system is for snowy pavement. No heavy-duty mode for off-road use

Floor is 7.7 inches off the ground —lower than rival sport-utility trucks for easier entry

Suspension based on front-wheel-drive car design

passengers in a side-on crash. Many trucks don't yet offer such amenities.

It probably won't be long before consumers have many more car/truck crossovers to choose from, if the direction of the cars on display at the Auto Show is any indication. Ford has two hybrid prototypes on display, one a small off-road wagon called the Alpe built on the chassis of a subcompact Escort.

And Chrysler raised eyebrows with a prototype model called the "Jeepster" that merged its signature Jeep grill and fat off-road tires with a low-slung sports-car body. Tom Gale, Chrysler executive vice president for product strategy, won't say when Chrysler will field a hybrid vehicle for real. But he makes it clear the question is when, not if. Hybrids are "a natural progression," he says.

Reprinted by permission of *The Wall Street Journal*, © 1998 Dow Jones & Company, Inc. All Rights Reserved Worldwide.

Minoxidil Tries to Grow Women's Market

By Tara Parker-Pope
Staff Reporter of The Wall Street Journal

After years of pitching to anxious men with shiny pates, makers of baldness remedies are hoping sales will sprout in a risky new market: women.

"They say you can never be too thin—unless you have thinning hair," trumpets a new television ad for **Pharmacia & Upjohn's** Rogaine. The campaign, developed by **Grey Advertising,** also includes ads in women's magazines such as Cooking Light and Weight Watchers telling women to "give yourself the chance to grow."

Marketers of minoxidil, the generic version of Rogaine, are reaching out to women, too. **Bausch & Lomb's** U.S. pharmaceutical unit, which markets the drug under its Healthguard label, has begun selling the stuff in pink boxes with special applicators for women's hair. **Copley Pharmaceuticals** is seeking approval from the Food and Drug Administration to package a minoxidil product for women, and other pharmacutical companies are expected to follow suit.

Minoxidil, the only FDA-approved baldness remedy, became available without a prescription in April. Sales totaled $111.6 million through Dec. 1, according to Information Resources Inc., in Chicago. Rogaine accounts for 87% of the market.

Dermatologists estimate that about 40 million men and 20 million women suffer from hereditary hair loss. But women may present the real growth opportunity. Most men eventually come to terms with hair loss, making them bad long-term prospects for hair-growth products. Pharmacia's survey show only about half the nation's balding men are really worried about their plight, while nearly every woman with thinning hair is concerned. And women are more likely than men to put up with the twice-a-day treatment and prolonged use requirements of hair-growth products.

"We see some indication that women would be more loyal customers," says Richard A. Spangler, product manager for Rogaine. "They're used to going through all the extra steps to prepare their hair in the morning."

Some analysts think the focus on women could help with another prickly problem for marketers of minoxidil — the fact that it doesn't seem to do much for the vast majority of users. According to the FDA, the drug spurs "meaningful" hair growth in only 25% of men and 20% of women after several months of use. (Rogaine also claims to arrest hair loss in 80% of users.) Rogaine ads promise only that the drug *can* grow hair and carry a disclaimer that it doesn't work for everyone.

Some experts say that the drug may be more effective for women than men because women are more likely to be looking to stop hair loss than regrow it. Such customers also may be more likely to experience a placebo effect, says Hemant K. Shah, a health-care analyst with HKS & Co. in Warren, N.J. "If you're bald, you'll know immediately if the product is working," he says. If your hair is merely thinning, "how do you really know if you're losing fewer hairs?"

Rogaine's Mr. Spangler says women, more than men, want the information and educational support the company offers. To that end, Rogaine has set up a free telephone service and soon plans to launch a new women's magazine for its customers. Its tentative title, Women's Living, delicately sidesteps its true focus: hair loss. The magazine will also feature general-interest articles from **Time Warner.** During the first 10 months of 1996, the company spent $50 million to advertise Rogaine, according to Competitive Media Reporting.

No one knows exactly how minoxidil works on the human head — it began as a blood pressure medication with the unwelcome side-effect of excessive hair growth. But dermatologists say the drug appears to prolong the growth phase of the hair cycle in some users. Most people lose an average of 100 to 150 hairs a day, a small percentage of the 100,000 hairs that grow on the average head. People who suffer from genetic baldness problems don't replenish that hair at a normal rate, says dermatologist Arthur P. Bertolino, director of the hair consultation unit at the New York University Medical Center.

One woman who is sold on minoxidil is 40-year-old Tracy Pattin of San Francisco. Ms. Pattin started losing her hair in her 20s and began using Rogaine during clinical trials in 1991. Today she's writing a book about her own hair-loss and sometimes works with Pharmacia as a spokeswoman for Rogaine.

For Pharmacia & Upjohn, the focus on women appears to be increasing sales. When the product was available only by prescription, women accounted for about 20% of Rogaine users. Now that it is available without a prescription, about 30% of sales are to women, according to Mr. Spangler.

For Rogaine, spiking interest in the drug is particularly important to stave off growing generic competition. Although most drug companies get a three-year monopoly when a product is converted to over-the-counter use, that didn't happen with Rogaine. In an unusual move, the FDA decided Pharmacia failed to meet the criteria for the exclusive status and immediately approved several generic versions of the drug, which are now being sold at about half the $30 cost for a bottle of Rogaine.

Reprinted by permission of *The Wall Street Journal,* © 1997 Dow Jones & Company, Inc. All Rights Reserved Worldwide.

Sneaker Company Targets Out-of-Breath Baby Boomers

BY JOSEPH PEREIRA

Staff Reporter of THE WALL STREET JOURNAL

BOSTON — **New Balance** Inc. has been spending a scant $4 million a year to advertise its athletic shoes. Its best-known endorser is a marathoner named Mark Coogan, who placed 41st in the last Olympics. Its logo is a prosaic NB.

And its shoes are jumping off retailers' shelves.

While **Nike** Inc. and other sneaker makers struggle to eke out gains in shoe sales, New Balance is riding a boom — specifically, the baby boom. Using a flashless formula that includes moderate prices, links to podiatrists and an expansive range of widths tailored to an aging population's expanding heft, the company gobbled up market share last year while recording a 16% gain in sales to $560 million.

President Clinton wears New Balance. So do Steve Jobs, Dustin Hoffman and Richard Templeton, who puffs as he works out on a StairMaster at the YMCA in Quincy, Mass. "My doctor told me to do something about my weight," says the 44-year-old insurance adjuster. "So I got myself a pair of New Balances for Christmas, and here I am."

New Balance "is becoming the Nike of the baby-boom generation," says Mike Kormas, president of Footwear Market Insights, a research firm based in Nashville, Tenn. Mr. Kormas, whose firm polls 25,000 households every four months on footwear-purchasing preferences, reckons that "the average age of a Nike consumer is 25, the average age of a Reebok consumer is 33 and the average age of a New Balance consumer is 42."

New Balance's gains come at a time when manufacturers' U.S. athletic footwear sales climbed less than 3%, to $7.7 billion, in 1997. The industry sales forecast for 1998 is for more of the same, as the inventory-laden retailers are expected to unload some poor sellers at deep discounts. New Balance,

meanwhile, is projecting sales of $700 million, up 25%.

It's a triumph of demographics over razzle-dazzle. While industry leaders like Nike, **Reebok International** Ltd. and **Fila Holdings** SpA jump through expensive hoops to court youngsters, New Balance is quietly tracking America's changing population. U.S. Census figures show that while the number of 20-to-34-year-olds in the country has declined by 5.3 million in the past seven years, the population of 35-to-59-year-olds has jumped by 16.5 million.

Although a youngster tends to buy more sneakers than a middle-ager, New Balance's older-age niche has some potent marketing virtues. Customers are less fickle, so the company doesn't worry as much about fashion swings.

Thus, while competitors come out with new models about every six weeks, New Balance introduces one about every 17 weeks. That lets retailers hold onto inventory longer without needing to discount it to free up space. And with fewer models and fewer expensive updates, the company believes it can risk skimping on marketing and big-name endorsers.

"You won't find a poster of Michael Jordan hanging in the bedroom of a New Balance customer," says Jim Davis, New Balance's president and chief executive. The $4 million the company spends on advertising and promotions is less than 1% of Nike's $750 million or Reebok's $425 million.

Another tactic: While most companies offer shoes in two widths — medium and wide — New Balance offers consumers five choices, ranging from a narrow AA to an expansive EEEE. About 20% to 30% of the population has narrower, or wider, than average feet, and retailers say that they sell more EE and EEEE New Balances than any other widths offered under the brand.

Now the company wants to stretch its appeal to include younger consumers. As it is now, New Balance loyalty pretty much ends with the baby boom. Among Gen-Xers and younger age groups, awareness of the brand plummets, according to New Balance market studies. This year, the company will more than triple its marketing budget to $13 million and venture into television advertising for the first time.

It's a calculated risk: The company has courted youth before, without much success.

In the 1980s, when sales were stuck at about $100 million a year, New Balance made a full-court press into the teen-basketball market, hiring former Los Angeles Laker James Worthy as its marquee endorser. Efforts were disappointing, partly because Mr. Worthy was arrested for soliciting prostitution in 1990. (He pleaded no contest to two misdemeanor charges.)

"We learned our lesson," says Mr. Davis. "We chose not to be in a position where we live and die by basketball. We'd just as soon pass the $10 to $15 a pair we need in superstar endorsement to the customer." New Balance shoes generally carry a moderate price tag, behind Nike, Reebok and Fila, though overlapping price ranges muddy the comparison.

For now, the company maintains a small stable of athletic endorsers, most of whom are runners with contracts ranging from $2,000 to $50,000 a year. But they are used mostly for product research, Mr. Davis says. None appear in the company's advertisements.

Instead, New Balance has a less glamorous but powerful way of promoting its sneakers. Just as toothbrush companies work with dentists, New Balance frequently networks with podiatrists, who use the roominess of the wide models to insert foot-support devices.

The Eneslow Foot Comfort Center, a shoe store in New York that specializes in "pedorthics," or therapeutic shoes, carries only New Balance among its sneaker selections. Its chief executive, Robert Schwartz, is the former president of the Pedorthic Footwear Association.

Many New Balance wearers buy the same models again and again and go into stores knowing exactly which pair they're looking for. Last month, President Clinton entered a Foot Locker store in the Pier 17 mall in downtown New York seeking a walking/running New Balance model. When informed that the store didn't have that particular model, the president turned to leave. The store manager, Stacey Lighty, refused to let the president leave empty-handed and pressed a pair of New Balance running shoes into his hand as he exited the store.

Reprinted by permission of *The Wall Street Journal*, © 1998 Dow Jones & Company, Inc. All Rights Reserved Worldwide.

Lenders woo car buyers with bad credit records

By Earle Eldridge
USA TODAY

When Levi and Yuvetta Staples of Renton, Wash., went looking for a car this summer, they were resigned to buying a 1991 or older car.

They knew their past credit problems would not qualify them to buy a late model or new car. Surgery in 1994 put Levi Staples out of work for more than a month. With only one income, and with an 11-year-old son, the Stapleses got behind on bills.

"It doesn't take long to get behind on one income," says Yuvetta Staples, 37.

To their surprise, they were able to get a loan for a $14,995 1996 Buick Regal from Curt Warner Buick/Pontiac/GMC in Bellevue, Wash.

"When they brought out the Regal, I never expected this," Yuvetta Staples says.

The Stapleses are benefiting from the recent surge in subprime auto lending or what the auto industry prefers to call specialty financing.

Pressed by new car dealers and eager to sell more cars, automakers, banks and other lenders are pursuing customers whose past credit problems prevented them from getting a loan at a dealership.

New car dealers and automakers are desperate to sell cars. New car sales have been stagnant at about 15 million annually for the past two years. And automakers have more cars and trucks coming off two-year lease deals that they want their dealers to sell.

Now, the former credit-risk customers are bombarded by promotional ads, direct mailers and dealer calls aimed at getting them in a new car.

"This has been an explosive industry because the investment community realized that this is profitable business," says James Ziegler, whose firm, Ziegler Supersystems, helps dealers with subprime loans. Analysts say subprime lending is a $60 billion to $100 billion annual business and growing.

And the industry is active:

In 1991, there were about 25 subprime lending companies. Today, there are about 170, according to analysts.

Both Ford Motor Credit and General Motors Acceptance Corp. (GMAC) established separate subprime auto finance companies in 1997.

Automakers say they are responding to demands from car dealers, who were tired of turning away potential customers. Profit margins for new car dealers are getting squeezed. Through the first eight months of 1997, dealer profits from new car sales fell 30% and used car sales fell 20% vs. from the 1996 period, the National Automobile Dealers Association says.

Dealers say they are responding to the stories they hear in the showroom. Downsizing hit many high-wage earners in the pocketbook. With less income, their credit suffered. Others, like the Staples family, suffered medical problems that hurt them financially.

About 40% of consumers don't qualify for an auto loan through conventional banks or credit unions.

The number of personal bankruptcies is expected to top 1.3 million in 1997, up 30% from 1 million in 1996, the first year bankruptcies hit a million.

But the strong economy and low unemployment give large lenders, such as Ford and General Motors, the confidence to enter subprime lending. And unlike smaller lenders, they have enough capital to weather bad loans.

In August, GMAC acquired LSI Holdings and converted some of the assets into a new subprime lending company called Nuvell Credit. Nuvell currently works with GM dealers in Georgia and Illinois but plans to expand to six other states in the first quarter of 1998.

"We want our customers to move from Nuvell to GMAC for financing," says Terry Sullivan, a GMAC spokesman.

Auto loans are profit makers for companies. GMAC accounted for $1 billion of GM's $4.9 billion in profit in 1996.

Ford Motor Credit contributed $1.4 billion of Ford's $3 billion in profit in 1996.

Last July, Ford created Fairlane Credit in response to demands from Ford dealers. Fairlane currently operates in Colorado and will expand to California next month.

THE PREMIUM PROBLEM

Specialty finance customers usually pay an interest rate of at least 18% and up to 24%, depending on the interest rate cap in their state. Customers with good credit can get interest rates as low as 1.9% from automakers and about 8% from banks.

That can mean a big difference in the monthly payment.

At an interest rate of 24% annually, for a $15,000

(Cont.)

car with a 20% or $3,000 down payment, a borrower would pay $391.22 a month for 48 months. For the same price car, at an interest rate of 8% and the same down payment and 48-month term, the monthly payment would be $292.96 a month.

It's mainly because of those high interest rates that credit representatives recommend consumers try instead to re-establish their credit.

"It would make sense for borrowers to look at their overall financial situation to see if there's anything they can do short of taking out credit at those high rates," says Durant Abernethy, president of the National Foundation for Consumer Credit, an umbrella organization for more than 1,400 non-profit credit-counseling services across the USA.

"I urge consumers to make sure their credit reports are accurate before they presume they only qualify for these higher cost loans," says Ed Mierzwinski, consumer program director at U.S. Public Interest Research Group. "You may, in fact, get a better deal at a credit union or even at another bank if you first improve your credit report by correcting mistakes."

"I'd stay away from these loans," Mierzwinski says. "It's a secured loan, and if you can't pay the high rates, they'll take the car and it will make your credit even worse. So try to fix any mistakes in your credit report or improve it over time. And if possible, avoid subprime loans.

"But Jerry Heimlicher, president of Fairlane Credit, says high interest rates reflect the high costs required to service specialty finance loans.

Heimlicher says Fairlane Credit needs five more customer service representatives per 1,000 borrowers to handle specialty finance loans. Specialty finance customers will get a call much more quickly if they miss a payment date.

To get a loan, specialty finance customers must provide more details about their credit than other borrowers. They must show lenders utility bills; apartment-rental contracts; the names, addresses and telephone numbers of at least six relatives instead of one; W-2 tax forms; and recent pay stubs. They likely will need at least a 10% cash down payment. Lenders say more people are needed to check loan applications, and that drives up costs.

"These customers don't believe they are financeable," Heimlicher says. "They are, but it takes additional attention and additional work."

CHAPTER 11 MAY NOT BE A PROBLEM

Ironically, some of the best potential subprime customers are people who recently declared bankruptcy.

Their debts have been cleared and they can't declare bankruptcy again for seven years, which is attractive to lenders.

Car dealers are using all sorts of marketing pitches to lure specialty finance customers.

Bob Cockerham, general manager at Quality Jeep ChryslerPlymouth in Albuquerque, N.M., bought a list of consumers from the major credit reporting bureaus, and working with a finance company narrowed it to about 1,000 people likely to be approved for a car loan.

Quality guaranteed customers $100 if the dealership couldn't get them a loan on a new or used car worth $500 to $17,500. Instead of the typical 1% to 2% response rate from a mailer, Quality got about 4%. "A lot of people didn't think they could get financing," Cockerham says.

The surge in subprime lending has sparked a cottage industry to serve dealer needs. Several companies help dealers produce TV infomercials.

One of the most popular is Auto Credit 2000 Telethon, developed by Tech-Tronix. The show features a host, co-host, commercials, testimonials from customers, a live call-in phone set complete with ringing phones and operators seen on any other live telethon.

In two years, John Palmer's ProMax system has gone from working with 20 dealers to servicing more than 300 and expect to have 1,000 dealers by the end of 1998.

ProMax computer software determines all the requirements of subprime lenders and lets the dealer know in 15 minutes, which subprime lender will approve the loan.

The surge in specialty financing is not without risk. Dealers have been beat by shady subprime companies that promise to finance a car loan but don't pay for several weeks or not at all.

But analysts say they don't expect a repeat of the problems that hit Mercury Finance and Jayhawk Acceptance in 1997. Mercury has been close to bankruptcy since January 1997, when it said it found phony bookkeeping records that caused it to overstate earnings. The report caused Mercury's access to capital to finance car loans to begin to dry up.

Jayhawk sought bankruptcy after its bad loans caused banks to cut its credit line.

"Subprime can be a win for all parties," says John Palmer of ProMax. "It's a win for dealers because they get to sell more cars. It's a win for customers because they can buy a nice car with a warranty, and it's a win for lenders because they get to make money."

Copyright 1998, *USA Today*. Reprinted with permission.

Motorola Is Getting the Signal on Pager Use by Blacks

"More Power to You," declares the magazine ad, featuring a stylish black woman next to a pager and a cellular phone emblazoned with the word "ELITE."

With this come-on, electronics giant **Motorola** is recognizing a fact that other advertisers aren't capitalizing on: African-Americans have become a disproportionately big piece of the market for pagers.

Black adults 35 years old and younger are more than twice as likely to have bought a pager last year than the average U.S. adult, according to Simmons Market Research Bureau's 1996 Study of Media and Markets. For black adults 24 years old and younger, the likelihood is even greater — more than triple that of the overall adult population. And although blacks make up only 12% of the U.S. population, they represent 18% of the nation's 24.2 million adult pager owners, according to Simmons data collected last year. Industry researchers say there were more than 34 million pagers in service in the U.S. at the end of 1995.

Signs of the popularity are visible in cities across the country, where pagers have become snugly woven into urban hiphop culture. In downtown Brooklyn, a four-block stretch features at least five pager retailers, selling models with handpainted sports-team logos, snakeskin patterns and colors such as Vanilla Swirl and Bimini Blue. In Cleveland, you can pick up a pager at a convenience store. In Detroit, there are "party stores" that sell beer, cigarettes, snacks and pagers, competing with each other across the same street.

In some cities, kids can even buy Bubble Beepers, pager-shaped packages of bubble gum, with messages on each stick, such as "See you later!" "I'll call you!" and "Meet me at . . . ."

Suppliers have long known that pagers have a huge black following and have suspected some of the complex and revealing reasons: They confer a visible mark of status and success, they offer an inexpensive way for working parents to keep tabs on their kids, and they've even become a fashionable way to socialize. Plus part of the appeal, especially for teenagers, may be the rebellious thrill of using a product that some people still associate with drug dealers.

But Motorola is the first pager maker to court blacks explicitly. Black consumers "are more disposed to buy the bells and whistles of telecommunications," says Rachelle Franklin, a promotions manager at Motorola, the world's biggest supplier of pagers and cell phones. Its campaign, running through the end of the month, aims to reach African-Americans between 21 and 54 years old with ads in Ebony, Essence and Black Enterprise magazines, as well as radio spots in Cleveland and Dallas.

Motorola has been looking for new advertising strategies as consumer-market growth for pagers has eclipsed growth in the company's traditional business sector. Meanwhile, Motorola's companywide sales growth has slowed in recent quarters. The Schaumburg, Ill.-based company concluded that it had to begin segmented marketing to consumers to meet ambitious sales goals. And others in the industry may follow suit. "Many people are looking very seriously at ethnic marketing," says Matt Wisk, director of marketing for the U.S. at Motorola's big pager rival **Nokia** of Finland.

Motorola's campaign, designed by black-owned Chicago ad agency **Burrell Communications Group,** offers a '90s yuppie version of the image of black "power," using that charged word in its print ad. Chuck M. McClellan, vice president and client-services director at Burrell, says the agency found through focus groups that "status, image and self-enhancement" are priorities to black adults.

Take Laurent Jarrett, a 33-year-old, black consumer-electronics salesman in New York. Mr. Jarrett says he bought a pager in the early 1990s and recently got a cell phone because he "wanted to be a big shot."

"It fills your ego a little bit," agrees Barry Smalley, a 31-year-old black administrative employee for a securities firm in New York. He adds: "As a black man, I have to be an extra step-and-a-half ahead. If you miss the call, you don't get a second chance."

Moreover, he says, "All my friends had them," explaining that in his largely black social circle, a pager is considered "a necessity."

Kim Ling, a 27-year-old black nurse, shares this view. "For my mother, who calls me all the time, I give her my pager number," Ms. Ling says. She also depends on her pager to keep tabs on her two small children in school and day care as she runs from work to her part-time college studies.

For some teens, pagers offer a touch of rebellion. The devices are strictly prohibited in many public schools. Malik Wilson, an 18-year-old black student at the University of Pennsylvania, says he carried a pager in high school in Maryland, even though being caught with it could have gotten him expelled. "I think defiance comes into play somewhat," he says, adding that the popularity also has a lot to do with "a desire to have the playthings of the rich."

People who study consumer behavior and attitudes say the ballooning popularity of pagers and cell phones among black consumers makes economic sense. "Groups in the United States who are most rapidly finding new affluence tend to spend more discretionary income on visible signs of success," says Dick Tobin, president of Strategy Research, a Miami-based market-research company.

According to Burrell, 26% of African-American households had income between $25,000 and $49,999 in 1993, up from 15% in 1980. That compares with an increase to 31% from 27% for the U.S. overall during that period.

Pagers also suit jobs and lifestyles that draw a greater number of blacks. The Simmons survey found that black consumers most likely to own pagers work in technical, clerical or sales positions. Those sectors have a heavy demand for pagers and a disproportionate number of black workers.

Last year 17% of service jobs in the civilian work force — from babysitters to medical assistants, to security guards and police — were held by blacks, according to the U.S. Bureau of Labor Statistics. "Every plumber and every service person that I know has got a pager," Mr. Tobin says.

Reprinted by permission of The Wall Street Journal, © 1996 Dow Jones & Company, Inc. All Rights Reserved Worldwide.

A Bit of Prosperity And Some Fast Food Fatten Zimbabweans

Weight Watchers Sees a Niche Serving Nation's Blacks; Hazel Millar Perseveres

By Matt Murray

Staff Reporter of The Wall Street Journal

HARARE, Zimbabwe — Nearly a dozen women have already weighed themselves and settled into their chairs when Shumi Shava arrives.

She grabs a plastic chair in the back row of the Highlands Anglican Church, just in time to hear Hazel Millar, a slim woman, 60 years old, dispense the following nuggets of advice:

"The Cokes!" warns Ms. Millar, putting space between her words. "You must cut down on the Cokes." The women nod. "Keep away from the spreadable cheeses. Make your own cottage cheese. We are losing weight on it."

Mrs. Millar then points to Mrs. Shava. "Look at Shumi! She has coped, and it hasn't been easy, has it?" Mrs. Shava shakes her head. She has been dieting for a year and has lost 22 pounds.

This is one of Weight Watchers' most unlikely outposts. While dieting in Africa might sound about as necessary as sailboats in Iowa, people here and in other developing countries are getting fatter, and are seeing incidents of obesity-related diseases like hypertension and diabetes rise with the influx of processed foods and fast-food places.

Outlets selling fried chicken, steak subs and hot dogs have proliferated in the congested streets of downtown Harare, where workers and homeless people jostle at lunch time. Two KFC franchises are in operation here alongside South African chains, and four more KFC locations will open by the end of the year. McDonald's, a presence in South Africa, says it is exploring possibilities here.

Grocery shelves are filling with new brands of cookies, fried cheese curls and ice cream. Few food products have nutrition labeling. Cola has become a staple in Zimbabwe, where water is scarce and wells are limited. Billboards with Coke logos proclaim: "Save water. It's precious."

Most nonwhites here still eat a traditional diet, the main ingredient of which is *sadza*, a

white cornmeal porridge tasting something like grits. Sadza, eaten with greens or meat, is cheap and filling. Zimbabweans who like the taste of fast food and are accustomed to the filled-up feeling of traditional sadza are apt to overeat.

To be overweight is seen here as a sign of prosperity, and therefore desirable. The new prosperity that is thickening midsections is, for now, limited to a minority of urban residents. The country still has a shaky economy; the inflation rate exceeds 20%. Growth has been just 1.8% annually over the last decade; unemployment and wildcat strikes are rampant.

Weight Watchers sees a niche opening here and believes its marketing to black Africans in Zimbabwe could establish a beachhead for efforts in other parts of Africa.

Weight Watchers has been in Zimbabwe before, when war and sanctions didn't intrude. But then, "it was solely a white organization," says Kat de Beer, managing director of Weight Watchers' South African operation. "Now a major emphasis will be placed into the black markets."

Twenty-four years ago, when Mrs. Millar joined Weight Watchers in what was then Rhodesia, dieting was largely a luxury for wealthy white women who were colonizers' descendants.

Mrs. Millar, who says she was "always plumpy, all my life," lost 40 pounds in six months. Her enthusiasm won her a job as a lecturer, and in the late 1970s, even as the nation's civil war intensified, she toured the country leading weight-loss classes.

One day in 1980, the company's auditor phoned Mrs. Millar at her home outside of town to say Weight Watchers was pulling out of the war-torn country. "Everything must be destroyed," he told her. "Close the office."

She sped into Harare to retrieve material from the office and spent a day feeding a bonfire in her backyard with membership books, financial records and index cards on which members record their weight. She kept a few newsletters and recipe books, as well as the little scales used to weigh food portions. She stashed them in a back closet in her house, hoping the program would return someday.

Seven years later, with the postwar country stabilizing, she was notified that Weight Watchers wanted to restart its Zimbabwe organization. Mrs. Millar drove to her son's home in Johannesburg, where Weight Watchers had continued operating, to gather updated pamphlets and recipes. Fearing government restrictions on outside "propaganda," she hid them under the seats and floor mats of her car, but border guards found and seized the contraband.

Back home, Mrs. Millar gamely forged ahead, advertising meetings in local papers. Then in 1989, Weight Watchers and its parent company, H.J. Heinz Co. of Pittsburgh, pulled out of South Africa as part of sanctions against apartheid. This time though, she

continued on her own, in relative anonymity. "I just carried on as best as I could," she says.

Out of Africa, Heinz was unaware that she had kept the program going. But when Weight Watchers returned to South Africa last November, Mr. de Beer, the managing director, heard about Mrs. Millar. Soon after, Al Lippert, a Weight Watchers cofounder and the South African franchisee, told Mr. de Beer that he wanted to bring the program back to Zimbabwe.

Weight Watchers is in Zimbabwe, Mr. de Beer told him.

"That's impossible," Mr. Lippert responded.

When Mrs. Millar's operation was revealed to Mr. Lippert, he called her up to introduce himself.

"Thank God," she told him. "I've been waiting for you for years." She then delivered a second surprise: She had built up a bank account for Weight Watchers of several thousand U.S. dollars, having religiously collected and deposited dues from those attending the meetings over the years.

Now, Weight Watchers is promising Mrs. Millar an influx of materials and money; until that arrives, she will continue using and improving dated material. Basic membership materials from the 1970s have been copied so many times, they are faded. The battered recipe books she brings to meetings are 15 or 20 years old. Recipes for Chicken Teriyaki and Chicken Greek Style are copied and handed out, with members agreeing among themselves which local ingredients might best be substituted for those that aren't available in Zimbabwe. Often it has been challenging: Even with all the new foods here, sugar and salt substitutes, "lite" salad dressings and other diet foods aren't on shelves.

Today, about 115 members attend Mrs. Millar's weekly meetings, and still, most of them are white. She charges members $4.55 to join and less than $2 a month. Meetings are simple affairs, with weigh-ins, a brief lecture and a discussion before members head back to work.

Reaching Out to Blacks

If Mrs. Millar has her way, the program will soon hold classes aimed at and led by black and multiracial Africans, and launch operations in smaller cities and towns across Zimbabwe.

Of particular concern are the country's youth. "We get kids in here weighing 220 pounds," says Elizabeth Small, a nutritionist near the city center. "They're living on fatty things, sugary things and lack of exercise."

On the outskirts of town, teens hang out at Westgate, a new shopping mall. Customers at the food court can choose from a dozen outlets. Flame Diners — "Food you'll be back for!" — offers a T-bone steak, fries and a salad for $3.40, while spending less than $1 at a place called Piefect gets you a greasy, flaky pie filled with fatty chicken in a gooey cream sauce.

"When I first came here, people said, 'What are you doing, spending $2 million setting up a store? These people haven't got money,'" says Ritch Gilliam, who runs Chicken Licken, a fast-food chain packed at lunch time on a recent Wednesday. "I can tell you: Collectively, these people have heaps of money."

Lynda Lemming, who attends Mrs. Millar's Weight Watchers class, worries about her two sons, ages 18 and 5. "They want to try all the new stuff," she frets. She began attending Weight Watchers after seeing a video of herself and "getting a shock."

The Thin Look

Not only is Western food sweeping Zimbabwe, but Western obsession about weight, too, is hitting young girls. "At 12, they all talk about their weight. I never thought about it when I was their age," says Mary Nyandoro, at a recent Weight Watchers meeting.

Weight Watchers' Mrs. Millar lives in an affluent suburb called Chisipite and has shopped at the Bon Marche supermarket for eight years. Not long ago, it was frequented only by whites and offered a narrow range of goods. These days, more blacks can afford the store, and the selection is wider. "We don't want for anything," Mrs. Millar says.

There are now four breads. Cheese-and-onion flavor potato chips line the second aisle, next to Fritos corn chips and Zimbabwe's home-grown brand, Willards, which a few years ago was the only brand available here. Nearby are five cooking oils. "Everything's oil," Mrs. Millar sighs. "Chicken, fish, vegetables — they cook it all in oil."

All of which makes her task of helping members lose weight increasingly difficult. "We have everything we want now," she says. "But we still don't know how to eat well."

Reprinted by permission of *The Wall Street Journal,* © 1997 Dow Jones & Company, Inc. All Rights Reserved Worldwide.

MEDICAL LESSONS FROM THE BIG MAC

Startups thrive by treating specific illnesses or conditions

On two leased floors of St. Francis Hospital in Beech Grove, Ind., Intensiva HealthCare takes on patients that most hospitals can't afford to keep. Ray Liggett, for one, has been hospitalized for a month with Guillain-Barre syndrome, a neurological disorder. St. Francis lost money every day he took up one of its beds. But because Intensiva accepts only long-term acute cases and operates independently—though within St. Francis' walls, often using its staff—an insurance quirk allows it to collect higher reimbursement. Its costs, meanwhile, are 50% lower than those of a typical intensive-care ward.

Intensiva opened the first of its 10 centers only in 1995 and still loses money. But its model is drawing attention across the health-care field. The key is focus: Its hospitals-within-hospitals handle only certain patients in strictly defined settings and markets. "We treat them more aggressively and get them out of the hospital quicker," says Intensiva Chief Executive David W. Cross. And, Intensiva says, more patients leave in better health.

Steelmakers, carmakers, and burger joints long have understood that mass specialization can pump up productivity. Volume, standardization, and focus drove the success of Nucor's minimills, General Motors' Saturn venture, and McDonald's Big Mac. Now, the health-care industry is catching on. Doctors, hospitals, and insurers are pursuing strategies that depend on caring for a narrow range of patients or on mastering a small slice of treatments.

It's the latest step in health care's rapid evolution, promising to alter once more the way Americans are treated for a broad range of medical conditions. In Boca Raton, Fla., Orthopedic Medical Networks of America is organizing teams of orthopedists, occupational therapists, chiropractors, and other specialists to provide soup-to-nuts back care. Sheridan Healthcare Inc. emphasizes management of in-hospital physician services, such as anesthesiology and neonatology.

MONEY MAGNETS. A raft of specialty startups, in fact, is attracting investments from top-drawer venture firms such as Mayfield Fund, TA Associates, and Morgenthaler Ventures. Meanwhile, Columbia/HCA Healthcare Corp., the nation's biggest hospital chain, is creating "centers of excellence" within some of its general-purpose institutions to compete for contracts for coronary and cancer care,

much as the Mayo Clinic has long done.

Regina Herzlinger, professor of health-care management at Harvard business school, calls these new specialized entities "focused factories." Such organizations, she says, "get economies of scale from horizontal integration and from doing the same thing over and over." With professional management and close coordination of services, she says, such companies can lower costs and produce better medical results.

It's a straightforward notion, but one that fights decades of health-industry tradition. Managed-care advocates long have viewed medical specialists as the enemy. Most still prefer to see generalist "gatekeepers" control treatment decisions, limiting access to expensive cardiologists and podiatrists. That has helped slow medical inflation, but HMOs generally haven't changed the way those physicians actually practice medicine, so overtreatment and waste persist. Patients, meanwhile, hate the inconvenience the gatekeeper model imposes.

Increasingly, insurers are addressing such failings by creating "carve-outs"—awarding specialist groups portions of patients' premiums for the care of discrete disease categories. An HMO pays a provider group a fixed monthly sum to take responsibility for all physician, hospital, and other services related to, say, cardiac care, no matter what treatment patients require.

On Feb. 3, Oxford Health Plans, a managed-care insurer, will go one step further, unveiling a plan to pay groups of doctors and hospitals for specific medical cases. A neurologist, for example, could join with a hospital, therapists, and other professionals to bid on care for stroke victims. The team would be responsible for consultations, lab tests, surgery, and post-operative care, receiving a flat rate for the packaged services.

INTEGRATION. Oxford plans to contract out 120 of its most expensive cases by the end of 1998. Executive Vice-President David B. Snow Jr. says the resulting integration of providers, and adherence to its care guidelines, could reduce medical costs by 20%. Ultimately, the insurer could restructure itself into several operating companies, each focusing on a disease group. "This model really gets to the point of care," Snow says.

Focused providers can survive on flat, per-patient compensation because their operations are standardized and thus predictable. HealthSouth Corp., based in Birmingham,

Ala., operates 1000 centers dedicated to outpatient orthopedic surgery and rehabilitation, producing revenues last year of $2.4 billion. With patient records from thousands of operations over 10 years, it has created medical protocols for 54 different diagnoses, such as a sprained ankle. "We're no longer in learning mode," says CEO Richard M. Scrushy. "It's proven, and that's why we're so cost-efficient." Liberty Mutual Insurance Co. says 86% of its worker-compensation patients treated by HealthSouth eventually return to work; Liberty Mutual's average is 47%.

> **FOCUS** It may not be long before "department store" medical centers offer brand-name "boutiques" operated by specialty vendors

The trend toward specialization could take on many forms. Rather than working with insurers, some focused providers are taking on subcontracts from primary-care groups. Consultant Michael Sachs sees the possibility of "department-store" medical centers containing branded "boutiques" operated or franchised by specialty companies. Joslin Diabetes Center, for example, licenses its name and treatment protocols to 12 affiliates nationwide; M.D. Anderson Cancer Center has similar arrangements with four hospitals and dozens of doctors.

As such models proliferate, critics predict that care will increasingly grow less personal and more regimented—"cookbook medicine," as some call it. Doctors and hospitals will win more autonomy from insurers but also will be obliged to adopt protocols that carefully orchestrate their practices. It's a trade-off that they and their patients may resist, even in the name of higher quality. But soon, they may not have a choice.

By Keith H. Hammonds in New York and Nicole Harris in Atlanta, with Bill Koenig in Beech Grove, Ind.

Reprinted from February 10, 1997 issue of *Business Week* by special permission, copyright © 1997 by McGraw-Hill, Inc.

Evaluating Opportunities in the Changing Marketing Environment

Siphoning U.S. companies' knowledge

By James Cox
USA TODAY

HONG KONG—Outside a Beijing boiler factory at closing time one day, Bob Donovan stared into the faces of the workers streaming home. His thought: Who would be the next to vanish?

"Every so often somebody doesn't show up for work. You go to his apartment and there's not a trace," says Donovan, head of the U.S. arm of ABB, a European engineering giant.

In time, the mystery is often solved. "You'll be walking down the hall at a design institute or at one of your Chinese competitors, and there's old Mr. Li working in a new job," Donovan says. "That's when I wonder, what did he walk away with? What's in his head?"

Donovan isn't the only western executive asking such questions these days.

China's remarkable modernization drive is being powered by one of the largest transfers of technology and technical knowledge in history. Much of the critical equipment and know-how is coming from the USA and U.S. companies.

U.S. firms are walking a tightrope in China: Without bringing their hardware and know-how, they can't get into the world's largest market. But without the ability to protect what is theirs, they risk being overtaken later by Chinese rivals they helped equip and train.

They wonder if China's hunger for technology and trade secrets in the fields of aerospace and aviation, telecommunications, semiconductors, software, computer-aided design and power generation, to name a few, poses a long-term threat to U.S. jobs and competitiveness.

"If someone's knocking off Mariah Carey CDs in China, it's unfortunate for Ms. Carey," Donovan says. "But (many) patents represent 230 years of accumulated knowledge and work. If lesser countries can make a 230-year leap and pay nothing, that will alter the course of industrial development in the world."

Chinese officials downplay the issue. "We're doing our best to change the situation. We have changed a lot," says Mei Jian-Ping, a former State Science & Technology Commission official. "Four or five years ago, you could have worried about this situation, but I don't think so today."

Some western executives say they have no complaints about Chinese tactics. "They negotiate hard, but once the deal is done the agreement is honored—more so than by the Japanese and Koreans," says Don St. Pierre, a Beijing-based executive who has run several auto-parts ventures in China. "I don't see how anyone could expect to enter the market without agreeing to help them develop the local industry."

THE PUSH FOR TECHNOLOGY

China pressures U.S. investors for their most advanced products, plant equipment and manufacturing processes. It educates its brightest science and engineering students at U.S. universities. It scours U.S. government archives and technical journals for vital information. It taps the vast network of overseas Chinese, some of whom are willing to buy or steal trade secrets. And it sometimes infiltrates the factory floors and office suites of U.S. firms operating in China, western executives say.

Firms lured by potential profits risk partners becoming rivals

As a result, a nation with only one telephone line for every 34 of its citizens (vs. one for every 1.8 people in the USA) has managed to build a supercomputer.

China makes no secret of its appetite for technology — the springboard it's using to vault into the ranks of developed nations.

Chinese authorities vow to squash joint ventures with foreign partners if the foreigners aren't willing to share their secrets and hardware. "The foreign party in a joint venture is required to ensure a continuous technology transfer," is how a Chinese news service summarized the rules set out last year by China's Ministry of Electronics Industry.

THE PRICE OF ADMISSION

Firms from the USA, Europe, Japan and South Korea are tripping over each other to supply equipment and expertise for China's Three Gorges Dam project, expected to cost at least $18 billion. But Premier Li Peng has warned that the foreigners can take part only "in the form of technology transfer or cooperation."

In telecommunications, AT&T competes with France's Alcatel, Germany's Siemens, Sweden's Ericsson, Canada's Nortel, and Japan's NEC and Fujitsu. All are vying to be chief architect of China's first advanced, nationwide telephone system.

The big payday is years off, but already the price of admission is steep: AT&T agreed last fall to train a state-owned electronics firm to process and design integrated circuits. It also pledged to build its flagship switching system in partnership with five Chinese companies, giving them a chance to learn in a few months a process that took AT&T years to develop and refine.

Chinese officials pressed Motorola in 1991 for a commitment to build a semiconductor plant in China. The company will open its new $720 million chip-fabrication plant in Tianjin in 1998. But partly as a result of Chinese pressure, it will make a more sophisticated chip there than it originally had planned. "This is a higher level of technology than we had envisioned," says Rick Younts, executive vice president at Motorola. "But it's an overstatement to say that we were badgered or forced. It was a fairly cordial negotiation."

China's state-controlled auto industry is no different.

General Motors got government approval in October to start talks on a $1 billion passenger-car venture in Shanghai. The go-ahead came after GM offered to fund a technical center where it will train Chinese engineers in state-of-the-art automotive design techniques.

In contrast, Chrysler, which was favored to win a deal to build minivans in China, lost out to Mercedes last summer. Months before, Chrysler President Robert Lutz had openly expressed reservations about sharing Chrysler's latest technology with two Chinese automakers involved in the minivan project.

Aircraft manufacturers are not immune either. Boeing and McDonnell Douglas of the USA are battling with Europe's Airbus and Daimler Aerospace for a contract to design and build a 100-passenger airliner.

The competition "is all about how much technology you're going to give. Everything else is a facade," says Jim Eckes, an aviation industry consultant in Hong Kong. "China wants the technology to develop good airframes."

ANOTHER JAPAN?

The Clinton administration says it wants to prevent China from becoming another Japan. The Japanese rebuilt after World War II by plucking manufacturing know-how from the west, eliminating foreign rivals from their home market, then taking on the world with subsidized exports.

U.S. officials say they want to open Chinese markets as wide as possible before China develops sophisticated, large-scale manufacturing across a range of industries. That is at least a decade away, they say.

In the meantime, joint ventures—contractual marriages between foreign companies and Chinese enterprises — are China's main pipeline for outside technology.

China's modernization drive is being powered by one of the largest transfers of technology and technical knowledge in history. And much of the critical equipment and know-how is coming from the USA and U.S. companies—often without their knowledge or approval.

Too often, the Chinese partner has a "hidden agenda," says Norman Givant, a lawyer who advises western investors in China.

The foreign investor schools its Chinese partner in modern manufacturing and dreams of big profits in the world's largest market. But the Chinese partner often is biding its time until, armed with new knowledge, it can break free and compete on its own, Givant says.

"The Chinese have a saying for it —'Sleeping in the same bed, dreaming different dreams,'" he says.

A frequent negotiating ploy used by China's state-sector firms and private companies is to accuse prospective foreign investors of withholding technology. U.S. firms say they come under assault even when they can prove their best technology can't be made or used in China.

"There are always continuous accusations that the foreign partner is not sharing. That's standard these days," says Diane Long, a Shanghai-based consultant.

China's drive to acquire technology doesn't stop at joint ventures.

EG&G, a Wellesly, Mass.-based company that makes a range of industrial products, believes that a Chinese research institute somehow copied one of its oilfield measuring devices. The company found out about the bogus instrument when firms that bought it began calling EG&G to request spare parts.

When DuPont wanted to make a rice herbicide, it found its U.S. patent was not enforceable in China. Still, it pressed ahead with plans to make Londax after getting assurances from government authorities. They told DuPont that its only Chinese competition would come from three or four companies authorized to make generic versions of Londax. But before DuPont could start production, more than 20 versions were on the market.

The world's chemical makers, in fact, are alarmed by new procedures imposed by China's Ministry of Chemical Industry. In some cases, the ministry, which owns it own chemical companies, requires foreign producers to disclose the exact chemical makeup of their products.

(Cont.)

FOR OTHERS, NO TROUBLE

On the other hand, many U.S. companies report they've never had any problems in China.

Says Bob Yeager of Rockwell International in Hong Kong: "We've never had even an inkling of any fooling around or any attempt to steal or divert our technology."

Rockwell licenses the manufacture of its avionics in China and makes printing presses, car parts, industrial controls and truck axles there. Its ties to China are among the oldest in Corporate America.

TURNING THE TABLES

There is little doubt Chinese enterprises intend to take on their foreign rivals — at home and abroad — once they acquire the machinery and expertise to do it.

In at least one case, they've been brazen enough to demand help in doing so. Before a division of China's national oil company would buy an oil-well-analysis kit from Houston-based Baker Hughes, it wanted the company to find jobs outside China for Chinese well teams, which would compete with Baker's own oilfield servicing business.

Baker balked at the demand.

"As I explained to them in the two-hour Business 101 course I had to give them," says Larry Williams of Baker Hughes, "we're not in business to put competitors into business."

Copyright 1996, *USA Today*. Reprinted with permission.

A WAY OUT OF THE WEB MAZE

It's called Webcasting, and it promises to deliver the info you want, straight to your PC

By AMY CORTESE

Since the World Wide Web burst into the mainstream two years ago, it has seized the popular imagination with a vengeance. The number of Web sites has exploded as companies and individuals have jumped eagerly into cyberspace. Today, hundreds of thousands of sites offer everything from government documents to financial data to pure whimsy. Internet terminology—Web page, hyperlink, anything.com—are part of the everyday lexicon. And being wired has become a measure of status among Gen-Xers and business leaders alike.

The Web is hip. The Web is way cool. And increasingly, the Web is way frustrating.

The Web, it seems, is a victim of its success. The volume of information on it is staggering, and search engines and other devices bring little order to the chaos. "It's a little like taking a farm boy from the Midwest, putting him in the middle of Manhattan, and telling him to go have the time of his life," says Ariel Sella, an Internet software entrepreneur. Then there are those endless waits to see Web pages. These days, when you log on, don't forget to bring a book.

The noise and congestion is making it hard for Web sites to attract visitors—and keep them coming back. Without steady traffic, Web sites have a hard time selling advertising, which, despite meager sales today, remains the most promising way to make money. As reality sets in, dozens of sites are scaling back or shutting down. At this rate, the Web could collapse under its own weight.

Even the Web's biggest promoters are sounding the alarm. "The Net for the first time is causing information overload," says Marc Andreessen, who helped write the Navigator browser at Netscape Communications Corp. Adds Eric Schmidt, chief technologist at Sun Microsystems Inc.: "Manually searching the Web is not a sustainable model, long term."

So, software entrepreneurs are borrowing from another medium—TV—to take the work out of the Web. "People want their computers to be as easy as their television," says Kim Polese, former Java product manager at Sun and now chief executive of Marimba Inc., a Palo Alto (Calif.) software startup. "They want just a few channels that they can turn to."

Computers won't get as simple as TVs anytime soon. But a new crop of programs will cut through Web clutter for you by using the same principle as broadcasting. Instead of having to spend hours scouring the Web, news, entertainment, and other Web fare is

---

The Web Gets Pushy

1. A person downloads Webcasting software. She is asked to fill out a profile specifying what type of information she'd like to receive—for example weather, computer industry news, and selected stock prices.

2. The profile is submitted to the Webcasting service and stored on a database.

3. Special software programs then search a pool of content—in most cases a selection of content "channels" and Web sites. The software retrieves the requested information and sends it out.

---

delivered automatically to your desktop. These new software programs also can deliver rich visual images and animation that approach TV quality.

Internet-style broadcasting has some unique advantages, too. TV features one-size-fits-millions programming. On the Net, digital programming can be targeted to a particular group or individual. It can even be delivered to your pager or cell phone. That ability to "narrowcast" is transforming the Net into a personal broadcast system. "The combination of broadcast and personalization is really a new world," says Schmidt.

And it comes with a whole new lexicon. Companies such as Marimba call their programs "tuners" and "transmitters." Information is organized into "channels," and "push delivery" gets it out to "viewers." Such familiar concepts promise to tame the Web, enhance corporate communication, spur digital commerce, and provide one more jolt to the software Establishment.

Welcome to the world of Webcasting. "Just as the browser opened the door to the Internet, 'push' will bring another fundamental way of communicating to the Net," says Christopher R. Hassett, chief executive of Webcasting pioneer PointCast Inc. Adds J. Neil Weintraut, a partner with 21st Century Venture Partners: "It makes the Web relevant to the masses."

The new Net software is not just for couch potatoes, either. Companies such as Amoco and Fruit of the Loom are pushing industry news and other data to employees' desktops. They're also setting up in-house channels on their own networks, or intranets, to make sure employees get the latest announcements and corporate communiqués. And because any digital information can be Webcast, the new approach is a natural for distributing software programs, applets, and updates—saving time and money. "This kind of push technology is going to be a big thing," says William Stewart, co-chairman of the Chicago Board of Trade's Internet Advisory Committee, which is looking at push delivery to reach its 4,000 members.

HOT BUTTONS. As with any new technological shift, Webcasting is creating fresh opportunities for software and media entrepreneurs. The ferment has already produced dozens of PointCast challengers, from Marimba to BackWeb Technologies to IFusion Com. They're all taking different tacks. But one of them could hit on the right formula and become the next Internet powerhouse.

Or maybe not. Both Microsoft Corp. and Netscape are scurrying to bring out later this year their own software to display Webcasting information on your desktop. When they do, your PC screen might consist of half a dozen channel buttons: one for news, one for company information, one or two for entertainment, and—someday—a "productivity" channel that you'll switch to when you need spreadsheets and word processing programs. "It fundamentally changes the whole concept of software," says Weintraut. The line between software programs and content begins to blur.

For such a fundamental innovation, Webcasting is almost deceptively simple. In most cases, it works like this: When you register for a service, you specify the channels you want and the specific topics you're interested in. You also choose how often you would like updates, which can arrive continuously and seamlessly on corporate networks.

Behind the scenes, Webcasting is more complex. Software programs diligently monitor Web sites and other information sources on your behalf. Upon finding news of interest to you, most will send an alert that pops up on your screen or scrolls across a ticker. When you click for more details, you might be launched to the Web site.

Other Webcasting programs, including PointCast, take the liberty of sending full articles, Web pages, and animations to your PC. You may not realize it, but when you pause to look at a Web page, which leaves the line free, these Webcasting programs grab

(Cont.)

Who's Who in Webcasting

AOL: Its 8 million members will be able to have AOL and Web content sent to them automatically when the online service launches Driveway this spring.

BACKWEB: Sells software tools so content providers and corporations can create their own Webcast channels.

BERKELEY SYSTEMS: The screen-saver veteran is getting into Webcasting with After Dark Online, which delivers content from *Sports Illustrated* and others to consumers.

IFUSION: This startup has a service similar to PointCast, but it can handle more TV-like animation and video.

MARIMBA: Founded by former members of Sun's Java development team, Marimba's Castanet software can send programs and applets along with content.

MICROSOFT: The company will make its foray into Webcasting midyear with a new version of Windows merged with the Internet Explorer browser and organized into channels.

NETSCAPE: Today, Netscape E-mails articles to users of its browser with In-Box Direct. In the spring, it will come out with Constellation, a browser and user interface that will display Webcast content.

POINTCAST: The Webcasting pioneer. Content from partners, including CNN, *The New York Times*, and *Wired* magazine is displayed, along with ads, on a screen saver.

WAYFARER: Its software is intended for use by companies that want to Webcast corporate information over their intranets.

the line and start downloading files onto your hard drive. When you click on a sports score for more detail, there's no World Wide Wait: The full story and a video clip can appear on your screen instantly.

Push delivery is as old as E-mail. But PointCast took things one step further. Hassett and his brother, Greg, launched their first product in 1992. Journalist, a custom news service for CompuServe Inc. and Prodigy Services Co. members, was difficult to use, though, and never caught on. By early 1995, when the Web took off, the brothers tried again. This time, they would pump out continuously updated information and, in a novel twist, display it on a screen saver when a PC was idle. Flying toasters gave way to scrolling news headlines, stock quotes, and weather updates.

"DIFFERENT." PointCast released a test version of its software last February and a finished version in May. By early fall, a million people had downloaded it. Today, PointCast has more than 1 million regular viewers—mostly within businesses—and some 15,000 people register for the service each day. At 30 million to 50 million viewer hours a month, the PointCast Network is comparable to a midsize TV network. "I see push creating almost a second Internet," says Halsey Minor, CEO of CNET Inc., a Web news service. "The model is really different."

Indeed, Webcasting offers the best hope yet to build a business on the Net through advertising and delivering customized content that people might finally pay for. "We're huge believers," says Time Inc. New Media General Manager Bruce Judson. The Internet is already a direct-marketer's dream. Now, instead of waiting for Web surfers to stumble onto their sites and banner ads, marketers can send animated ads directly to the desktops of target customers. Retailers such as Lands' End Inc. and Virtual Vineyards are dabbling with such in-your-face methods to notify subscribers of promotions and even send them order forms. Merchants can approach live sales prospects and not just couch potatoes. "It's not about cost per thousand, but cost per lead," says J.G. Sandom, director of Ogilvy & Mather Worldwide Inc.'s Interactive business.

How do they identify leads? Webcasters have a unique ability to track viewers' actions. They do that two ways. First, when you sign up for a Web service, you're asked to give some basic demographic information along with your interests. Then, once the receiver software is downloaded onto your PC, Webcasters can track when you tune in and what you click on for more detail. That provides a level of accountability that TV and print can't touch.

PointCast offers still more: access to the corporate market. "It's the first medium to ever reach people at work in a meaningful way," says John Nardone, director of media and research services at Modem Media, an interactive ad agency in Westport, Conn. "You can literally say, 'We had 3,000 people

from Microsoft looking at your ad yesterday,'" crows Nardone.

MISSTEPS. For these reasons, Webcasting could quickly grab a sizable chunk of the Internet economy. By 2000, Webcasting and related push technology will generate a third of the $14 billion in Net advertising, subscriptions, and retail revenues, projects Yankee Group Inc.

If Webcasters aren't careful, though, they could spark a backlash. "There's a fine line between adding value and the consumer feeling that you're being intrusive," warns Evan Neufeld, an analyst with market researcher Jupiter Communications Inc. People are already inundated with junk mail and now junk E-mail. Webcasting, if misused, could become one more avenue for unwanted solicitations and irrelevant material. "It's bad enough to pull garbage, but you don't want it pushed," says Joe Firmage, CEO of USWeb Corp., a Web-site builder.

There are potentially more serious problems. Webcasting programs can tie up networks and load up hard drives. Most of the programs do regular garbage collection, deleting ads and files from your PC after a certain amount of time has elapsed. But dangers still lurk. A lot of programs, including PointCast, automatically download the latest versions of their software; when you're ready to update, it's already on your PC. That saves you time, but there's a downside: "If it's buggy, you've just hosed a million people," says Sun's Schmidt.

These concerns resonate with corporate managers. PointCast's early missteps don't help assuage their fears. When the PointCast software came out last February, it quickly spread throughout corporations. Before long, some sites had thousands of people running PointCast—and soaking up as much as 30% of network capacity. Companies began banning it.

Last November, PointCast came out with a fix. With a new program called I-Server, companies can have PointCast content sent once, then rebroadcast it to employees. That cuts down on Net traffic going through the corporate security firewall. Another plus: Companies can set up their own channels to broadcast internal news. So far, Hassett says, more than 1,000 orders have been placed for the $1,000 package.

Still, companies remain wary. Hewlett-Packard Co., for one, discourages the use of PointCast, although it isn't banned outright. Robert R. Walker, HP's chief information officer, says push programs can help cut through information clutter, but for now, the benefits don't outweigh the risks. "We don't view this as a panacea," he says.

Potential problems are eclipsed for now by an all-too-familiar burst of Netmania, with startups galore. At this early stage, there is plenty of opportunity—and money. "The venture-capital community is fully engaged and fully lathered," says Andreessen. Some $80 million in venture funding has been lined

(Cont.)

up by just five startups, according to Venture-One Corp. Some investors can't wait to harvest some profits.

The startups are all over the map, both in terms of technology and business model. PointCast provides a collection of brand-name channels in a one-stop service—sort of a Webcast version of America Online. Point-Cast reformats the content, and the company's giant broadcast center handles the transmission. Unlike AOL, the PointCast Network is free. It makes its money by selling ads on its network, which has four dozen advertisers, and shares ad revenues from its partners' channels. So far, the PointCast Network is delivering. After Pfizer Inc. started promoting an allergy site and its Zyrtec drug on PointCast last August, "traffic on our site increased tenfold," says Mark L. Linver, an information technology director at Pfizer.

A number of upstarts spot a chink in PointCast's model. They figure that, just as with Web sites, companies are going to want to offer their content directly to customers. BackWeb Technologies, IFusion, Marimba, and others offer software tools that let any company create its own channel. They also offer more flexibility than PointCast. Marimba's Castanet software, for example, allows software programs to be linked to content. That makes it possible for subscribers to play a game on an entertainment channel or analyze a stock portfolio on a financial channel. And IFusion has an edge in delivering sophisticated multimedia.

Companies are embracing the idea of do-it-yourself channels. General Motors and ZDNet have BackWeb channels. And *The Wall Street Journal* Interactive Edition is testing one for subscribers to its Personal Edition. When news stories are updated, a tiny front page containing headlines will appear on their screen. "It's kind of like being paged," says Tom Baker, business director for the Interactive Edition, which has increased its paying subscriber base to 70,000 from 30,000.

In Korea, Samsung Group's New Media Group is preparing to launch a series of information and entertainment channels for the Korean market, using software from IFusion. And The Weather Channel is experimenting with Webcasting software from IFusion, BackWeb, and NETdelivery. "Push technology allows us to be more proactive," explains Kathleen Daly, director of new business development for The Weather Channel.

Weather, sports, and news are all obvious applications for Webcasting. The less obvious possibilities are only starting to open up. Rent Net's Web site provides constantly updated apartment-rental listings and relocation help for 1,000 cities. IFusion's ArrIve software will run a new Rent Net channel that will alert people to listings that meet their specific criteria. Subscribers can then look at floor plans and do 3-D virtual walk-throughs. "It brings the information right to you," says Rent Net Vice-President Jed Katz.

For all the activity, the hottest market right now for push programs is not Web sites but corporate intranets. It makes sense. Business professionals rely on up-to-date information, and they typically have high-speed, full-time connections to the Net. "It helps raise the corporate I.Q.," says Patrick Flynn, vice-president for systems development at Fruit of the Loom, which has PointCast installed on 250 employees' desks.

FOCUS. After spending last year putting up intranets, corporations are finding that they are becoming as cluttered as the public Web. By setting up their own channels, they can make sure that important company news and announcements get out to employees. Nations-Bank, for example, is developing a system it calls NationsCast, using software from Wayfarer Communications. It will broadcast corporate news, product information, and the bank's stock price (a keen interest since the bank recently granted employee stock options) to 23,000 headquarters staff. Mitch Hadley, vice-president of NationsBank's Strategic Technology Group, says someday such technology could even be used to push information to customers at kiosks or ATMs.

What's more, these systems can be tied to corporate databases and programmed to Webcast alerts automatically. Ben & Jerry's Homemade Inc. is evaluating Wayfarer's software for a system that would alert managers when the company's perishable inventories drop below a certain level. Companies are just beginning to explore the possibilities. "We're drinking from a fire hose," says Kelsey Selander, vice-president for marketing at BackWeb.

The consumer market may be slower to develop. But that isn't stopping companies from targeting news and entertainment junkies. Berkeley Systems has turned its famous flying toaster screen saver into a Point-Cast-like service called After Dark Online. It culls information from such sources as *Sports Illustrated* and *The Wall Street Journal* Interactive (for paid subscribers) and displays it on the screen saver. Cambridge (Mass.)-based My Way Inc. has launched a service that will deliver personalized Web fare and Web site reviews to home users it figures are too busy to surf.

This spring, Paul Allen's Starwave Corp. will begin testing a PointCast competitor called Starwave Direct. It will pull together content from various Web sites the company has set up, including ESPNET SportsZone and Mr. Showbiz, along with personal-finance information and news, probably from ABC.

BATTLE ROYAL. The competition is jolting established players into action. This spring, AOL's 8 million members will get their first taste of Webcasting. AOL plans to add a feature called Driveway that will periodically go out and fetch AOL content, Web pages, and E-mail based on members' preferences and download it onto their PCs. By letting members view information offline, AOL could ease the network jams that have plagued its service.

AOL, PointCast, Starwave, Microsoft—any one could become a media powerhouse of the emerging Internet broadcast medium. And they'll have plenty of competition as the distinctions between traditional media disappear in this digital melting pot. "What matters is having viewers' eyeballs," says Weintraut.

Ultimately, this is a battle for the desktop, and the two companies with the most to lose—Microsoft and Netscape—are quickly trying to rope it all in. As Webcasting transforms the way we consume business and entertainment information and even software, controlling the delivery platform will be even more critical. So in the coming year, the two rivals will each try to define what the desktop of the future will look like.

Netscape will be first out. This spring, the company will introduce Constellation, a software interface written in Sun's Java language and designed to run on top of any desktop operating system. Netscape hopes Constellation will become the main way people view information, whether it is stored on their PC, on a Web site, or Webcast to their screen.

Microsoft will make its move this summer, with a version of Windows that folds in the Internet Explorer browser and will display Webcast information in windows. Microsoft's name for the technology, Active Desktop, says a lot about the shape of things to come: The new Windows will be organized into half a dozen or more channels—including one for Microsoft's MSN and others featuring brand names such as PointCast.

The two giants have similar visions for how the Net will merge with the desktop, but their agendas diverge sharply. Microsoft wants to pull the Web into Windows and all of its software. Netscape is trying to break its rival's hammerlock by creating software that will work on any PC or gadget. To do so, it's enlisting the help of Marimba. The company's Castanet software will be included in Constellation so it will be able to store Java applets. That could help accelerate the move toward software components delivered off the Net—and it could put Microsoft at a disadvantage. Companies such as Lotus Development Corp. and Corel Corp. are creating software applets that could be distributed that way.

There's nothing to stop Microsoft from doing the same. But for now, its big sellers, such as Microsoft Office, are way too big for that kind of delivery. And the Net is moving so fast that both companies are scrambling. "You're catching us right in the eye of the tornado. A lot of this hasn't been decided yet," says Brad Chase, a vice-president in Microsoft's Application & Internet Client Group. Either way, the battle promises to keep viewers riveted to their seats. So don't touch that mouse.

With Robert D. Hof in San Mateo, Calif., and bureau reports

Reprinted from February 24, 1997 issue of *Business Week* by special permission, copyright © 1997 by McGraw-Hill, Inc.

19

Kiosks, PCs take borrowing out of banks

By Christine Dugas
USA TODAY

Critics caution against impulse loans and unfair credit evaulations

When Harmony Woodyard wanted to apply for a credit card last month, she stopped by Huntington Bank's interactive video kiosk in the University of Toledo's student union. The freshman made her selection on the touch screen and talked to a banker who appeared on the video screen.

"I've always been intimidated by big banks," she says. "But this was easy to use."

A growing number of banks are betting consumers like Woodyard will prefer the convenience and speed of electronic devices that process loans and credit-card applications. And the banks see technology as a way to cut costs. Small banks, in particular, see video links, loan machines and World Wide Web sites on the Internet as an easy way to extend their reach beyond their branches and grab a bigger piece of the huge consumer-loan market. U.S. consumers have racked up $1 trillion in outstanding installment debt.

But consumer advocates argue that high-tech lending will make it so easy to get a loan that people will borrow money on impulse and buy things they can't really afford. And they complain that machines, which use computer programs to decide who qualifies for a loan, will arbitrarily exclude borrowers with less-than-perfect credit histories.

About 15 banks are trying out automated loan machines made by Affinity Technology Group of Columbia, S.C. These machines can complete a loan on the spot and issue a check — all in about 10 minutes. The machines make only unsecured personal loans now, but they could be used to make more complicated secured loans, such as auto and home-equity loans.

But not every effort will succeed. New York Life Insurance, for example, recently closed a subsidiary that produced interactive loan kiosks when efforts to sell the business failed.

Still, the banks testing Affinity's machines like them. Among the reasons they give:

▲ Many consumers, such as Woodyard, are more comfortable with a machine. They are not intimidating, says Beverly McKinney, president of Bank One West Virginia, which has installed nine machines that make loans of $1,000 to $10,000. One is located in a 24-hour Wal-Mart. Many experts say consumers prefer the anonymity of the machines because they don' t have to face a loan officer if their application is denied.

▲ The machines are inexpensive. Kenneth Rous, vice president at Reisterstown (Md.) Federal Savings Bank, says a machine can process a loan for less than half the cost of a traditional loan. Banks don' t own the machines. Rather, the banks pay Affinity a fee for each loan, ranging from about $40 to $65 a loan, depending on the number of loans.

Reisterstown's parent company, Susquehanna Bancshares, has set up six machines at its subsidiaries. Farmers & Merchants Bank and Trust in Hagerstown, Md., for example, is passing on some of its savings to machine users by offering a 9.99% introductory rate vs. rates that can go as high as 21%.

Lending electronically

Banks and other lenders are experimenting with what they hope will be cheaper and easier ways to make loans.

AUTOMATED LOAN MACHINES

▲ Customers use a touch-screen keyboard to fill out loan application.
▲ Computer checks credit report, says whether they qualify for a loan and spits out a check or deposits money directly to bank account.

INTERACTIVE VIDEO KIOSKS

▲ Customers can apply for loans, open accounts or check account balances.
▲ A bank representative on screen processes loan applications. Customers find out immediately if they're approved, but they have to get a check during banking hours.

INTERNET

▲ If bank has a secure system, customers can fill out a loan application from their personal computers.
▲ Borrowers don't get immediate decision. They are contacted later by electronic mail or phone.

(Cont.)

As long as the machines are issuing only small personal loans, however, cost savings will be marginal, says Robert McCormick, president of First Manhattan Consulting Group in New York City.

▲ The machines help banks attract customers. "Our goal is to (bring in) younger consumers," says Luke Yancy, executive vice president of Union Planters Bank in Memphis, which has 11 machines. Research shows younger customers are most likely to try new technologies.

But Huntington National, based in Columbus, Ohio, considers automated loan machines too confining. It has worked with NCR to develop interactive video kiosks, called Personal Touch machines.

"We wanted to replicate what you can do at a traditional branch," says George Jeffers, vice president in charge of electronic banking at Huntington. Although the technology is expensive to develop, it lets customers print out account statements, get product information and calculate loan payments using various interest rates and down payments. And it can call a banker who will appear on the video screen and help a customer apply for a personal line of credit, credit card or installment loan. Huntington's machines can't yet complete a loan and issue a check. But an advanced version that can do those things should be ready in 6 months to 12 months, Jeffers says.

Some experts believe machines will have a limited appeal. "There will be a role for machines," says William Keenan, senior vice president of NatWest Bank Delaware. But, given a choice, consumers will prefer to bank at home, using the Internet or interactive television, he predicts.

Now, however, only a few lenders, such as First Union Bank of Charlotte, N.C., are accepting loan applications on line from personal-computer users. Other lenders require those customers to print out an application from the lender's Internet page or call a toll-free number.

Banks are moving slowly because of concerns about Internet security. But those concerns have been overblown, says Sherri Neasham, president of Financenter, an Internet-based service that helps consumers get loans and other personal-finance information. Her company has been offering on-line home-loan and credit-card applications using Netscape Navigator since early this year.

Low overhead makes it possible to offer some Internet services at below-market prices. Neasham's company has arranged to sell mortgages issued by American Finance and Investment, a mortgage banker in Fairfax, Va. Financenter claims applicants can get the lowest rate in the USA on a standard loan, low fees and a credit decision in 48 hours. The lender also waives the credit report fee, so consumers can apply for credit without any upfront charge.

Elsewhere on the Internet, Credit Card Network is a clearinghouse that lets computer users shop for a card from among hundreds of listings. Mark Muchnick, director of the Seattle-based network, says about 80 credit-card issuers let consumers apply on line. He says they are increasingly embracing the Internet because the direct-mail market has been saturated.

Credit Card Network and Financenter are part of a growing number of Internet financial intermediaries. They can be a benefit to consumers by making it easy to shop and encouraging price and rate competition, says Bill Burnham, an associate in the financial-services group of consultants Booz Allen & Hamilton. But consumers need to remember intermediaries are not regulated.

"It's 'buyer beware,' not only in life in general, but on the Internet as well," Burnham says.

Although some consumer groups are concerned that high-tech lending encourages people to take on too much debt, lenders say consumers already are inundated with credit-card solicitations and have plenty of opportunity to get into debt.

Consumer advocates also fear high-tech lending, which relies on computer models to rate applicants, is too rigid. For years they pressured banks to develop more flexible standards, so poor people and minorities were not turned down because they have a nontraditional or less-than-perfect credit history.

"I think if banks go to a formula approach, they will be moving backward," says Janice Shields, banking researcher at the Center for Study of Responsive Law.

But some lenders, such as Union Planters Bank, automatically review applications turned down by a machine. "If we feel the machine did not give them due consideration, we call the borrower," Yancy says.

And there is one important benefit for consumers: Unlike loan officers, machines are colorblind. "They make an objective decision," says Burnham. "There is no room for prejudice to enter the lending process."

Copyright 1996, *USA Today*. Reprinted with permission.

Internet shopping for loans, credit

Internet addresses for companies in the story doing business there:

Financenter: Information on mortgages, credit cards, buying cars. http://www.financenter.com

First Union Bank: http://www.firstunion.com

Credit Card Network: clearinghouse for credit card shoppers. http://www. creditnet.com

Power Struggle: Deregulation Sparks Marketing Battle

By Ross Kerber and Benjamin A. Holden
Staff Reporters of The Wall Street Journal

Green Mountain Power Corp. is advertising with a hot-air balloon 10 stories high. **Working Assets Funding Service** Inc. of San Francisco, is giving away pints of Ben & Jerry's ice cream. And **Freedom Energy** Co. promises long-term price cuts of up to 25%.

With the kind of intensity normally used to hawk corn chips or compact cars, companies are starting to woo customers for one of New England's hottest commodities — electrical power.

Later this month, New Hampshire will allow 16,487 residences and businesses, or about 3% of the customer base, chosen by lottery, to pick an electricity supplier just as they now choose among AT&T, MCI, or others for long-distance phone service. A bill expected to pass the state's legislature would expand electrical choice to all consumers by Jan. 1, 1998.

The pilot is being closely watched within the industry and by other states as a case study of what consumers can expect as deregulation accelerates around the U.S. The state's dominant utility, Public Service Co. of New Hampshire, or PSNH, is facing about 29 competitors, both local and out-of-state.

It's too early to answer many of the larger questions about deregulation, like how much prices will fall; whether some small businesses and rural residences will be left out in the cold; and who will pay for costly investments, like nuclear plants, that utilities were previously guaranteed to pay off through rate increases. But this much is clear so far: Consumers can expect a marketing free-for-all and a confusing array of products.

So far in New Hampshire, pitches have included pledges never to rely on nuclear fuel, discounts for conservation, and free insulation. Unitil Corp., a utility based in Exeter, N.H., has even tried to make an issue of PSNH's out-of-state ownership. "Unitil," its ads proclaim, "a New Hampshire company working for New Hampshire."

Xenergy Inc., a unit of **New York State Electric & Gas** Corp., plans to provide energy-management services to as many as 2,500 customers as part of a partnership with Freedom Energy, says senior manager Bill Hatch. The services may include free insulation, remote controls to turn on kitchen appliances, and itemized, on-line billing services that would "show the customer exactly how much it costs to run the basement fridge."

Of course, the inducement that New Hampshirites want to hear most about is price. Consumers in the state pay about 11.3 cents per kilowatt-hour for electricity, the highest rate in the U.S. and 64% above the national average of 6.9 cents. The state's Public Utilities Commission has forecast that the pilot could produce immediate rate cuts of about 10%, and the companies like Houston's Enron Corp. have been hinting they may top that.

Deregulation's popularity among consumers rests on such promises. "Our rates are obscene," says Craig Benson, chairman of Cabletron Systems Inc., a big computer-networking equipment maker in Rochester, N.H., who helped push the deregulation legislation. "Low rates are a necessity for businesses to survive," says Barry Sanborn, vice president at Hodges Cos., a Concord, N.H., real-estate firm.

However, it may not be so easy for consumers to pick out the lower prices amid a deluge of complicated packages. Even Jacqueline Lake Killgore, an attorney who has worked in deregulation issues, finds the campaign confusing. Since joining the pilot program, she has received brochures from three different units of PSNH's parent, **Northeast Utilities,** based in Berlin, Conn. One promises energy-efficient lights and emergency flashlights; another offers some power for a penny a kilowatt-hour; a third guarantees its rates won't rise. "It would be hard just to make sense of these three alone," says Ms. Killgore.

The campaign for customers is a harbinger of larger struggles as deregulation spreads. Congress encouraged states to deregulate power markets in 1992, and California is developing a massive deregulation plan that will take effect in stages.

In Peoria, Ill., **Cilcorp** Inc.'s Cilco unit this month will allow eight industrial customers, three residential areas and a shopping center to choose their electricity supplier. The three Illinois communities, Heyworth, Manito and Williamsville, have

an aggregate population of about 5,000. Michigan, meanwhile, has angered some existing big customers by inviting new businesses — but not existing ones — to shop for power from the cheapest source.

Despite its popularity, the deregulation bandwagon leaves many issues unsettled. In New Hampshire, electricity is particularly expensive, partly because rates — based on the traditional regulatory formula that fixes prices at a premium over costs — include some expensive nuclear facilities owned by Northeast Utilities. That has provided an opening for resellers, which make their profit by buying and reselling excess power available on regional power grids, to attack PSNH.

At a recent get-to-know-you forum between electricity sellers and state businesses at Concord's Makris Lobster & Steak House, PSNH was hammered from all sides by would-be competitors. An emissary of Freedom Energy, a local reseller set up to take advantage of deregulation, argued that consumers shouldn't have to pay for Northeast's nuclear-investing mistakes. A decision expected from the state Supreme Court soon could accelerate Freedom's entry into the market.

Robert A. Bersak, a PSNH lawyer, noted that the higher prices also reflect regulations that require it to buy from alternative suppliers, such as small, wood-burning power plants. He hinted that PSNH may sue to block the pilot if it determines that the new competitive environment will be unfair.

PSNH has started to appeal to the public with ads meant to raise doubts about reform. "Solid factual answers . . . have to come before, not after, we commit to overhauling this industry," says Jack Atkinson, president of a Nashua company, in one ad appearing in New Hampshire newspapers recently.

But the arguments leave many customers cold. One participant in the pilot program, Manchester attorney Paul R. Kfoury, says he is looking to cut his home's $200 monthly power bill, and doesn't care about Public Service's explanations. "New Hampshire shouldn't be paying the highest rates in the country," he says. "We're entitled to lower rates, period."

Reprinted by permission of *The Wall Street Journal,* © 1996 Dow Jones & Company, Inc. All Rights Reserved Worldwide.

Microsoft and Justice End a Skirmish, Yet War Could Escalate

Company Agrees to Unbundle Internet Software; Will Regulators Widen Case?

Why Netscape Still Frets

By David Bank and John R. Wilke
Staff Reporters of The Wall Street Journal

Microsoft Corp. settled a legal skirmish with the U.S. Department of Justice, but its hardball tactics have set the stage for what may be a wider and costly war.

The software giant Thursday accepted terms to avoid a contempt-of-court citation sought by the Justice Department for allegedly violating a federal court order. It will do what the agency has sought, and a federal judge has wanted, for weeks: give the nation's personal-computer makers the right to ship the current version of its best-selling Windows 95 operating system on their machines without also being forced to display Microsoft's software for browsing the Internet.

But the company, by its effort to defer compliance and its aggressive — some say arrogant — posturing in the case, has committed what is widely seen as a colossal public-relations blunder, angering both presiding Judge Thomas Penfield Jackson and the antitrust regulators. Now, Justice Department investigators are building a new antitrust case against the software giant that could reach far beyond the narrow issue before the court Thursday, and could affect Microsoft's planned introduction of Windows 98 later this year, lawyers and officials familiar with these efforts say. The case — if it goes forward — would attack the heart of Microsoft's strategy of using Windows to muscle into new markets.

"Bill Gates finally understood he made a huge strategic and public-relations blunder in the way the company tried to respond to the judge's order," says Sam Miller, a San Francisco attorney who was part of the Justice Department team that pursued an initial antitrust case that led to a 1995 consent decree. "It finally sank in that their arrogance backfired."

Federal prosecutors wouldn't comment on the prospects of a new case and say they have made no final decision. "We have an active and continuing investigation into several Microsoft business practices," says Justice's antitrust chief, Joel Klein. Practices under investigation include Microsoft's investments in new video technology, its stake in former rival Apple Computer Inc. and, more broadly, its effort to extend its dominance of desktop software into new markets.

But the looming introduction of Windows 98 — and the threat that it would crush competition in the Internet-browser market — is what most worries antitrust enforcers.

This dust-up is but the latest in a series of skirmishes that go back to 1994. Justice sued originally on the grounds that Microsoft was using its licensing practices with PC makers to smother competition. Mr. Gates cagily settled that case with a consent decree in 1995, agreeing to make minor changes and preserving Microsoft's right to develop "integrated" products. It was considered a major victory for Microsoft, which continued its startling growth. The browser case is actually a reprise of the 1994 litigation; browsers, which connect PC users to the ever-expanding Internet, are already a huge business.

Microsoft may yet wriggle out of harm's way, in part by adopting a more conciliatory attitude. Thursday's settlement began to jell when Mr. Gates's top attorney called Mr. Klein last Thursday to propose the settlement, after he briefed Microsoft's CEO on the company's progress in court. In two days of hearings, Judge Jackson signaled increasing impatience at Microsoft's stance.

The settlement won't diminish Microsoft's immense marketing power much. The PC makers say they will continue to voluntarily bundle the company's browser because it is free and a powerful product. "We aren't making any changes," said a spokeswoman for Compaq Computer Corp., the world's biggest PC maker.

Microsoft could settle the Justice Department's suit, and perhaps any future suit, on the same terms without losing much clout. That's because its Windows operating systems have already become the standard for the computer industry, and it has so much scale and momentum that a huge army of software developers will still continue to build programs, including ones for Internet commerce and interactive television, for Microsoft and Microsoft alone.

On the other hand, Microsoft's hard-line attitude so far seems only to have emboldened, not discouraged, regulators. According to antitrust lawyers familiar with the government's investigation, one approach under consideration is that the Justice Department demand that Microsoft provide a version of Windows 98 without Internet access to computer makers who want it. That would give Netscape Communications Corp., Microsoft's chief browser rival, a fighting chance and ensure that Microsoft wouldn't be able to capture a lock on consumer access to the Internet, some of those close to the investigation believe.

These people say the government also is reviewing Microsoft's contracts with Internet-service providers, the companies that connect consumers to the Internet and distribute browsers. These contracts could be challenged in court if they give preferential treatment to Microsoft's Internet Explorer, they say. Justice Department lawyers are also asking questions across the computer industry and are poring over hundreds of contracts Microsoft struck in the past two years with major providers of information or entertainment on the Internet.

Justice Department officials remain wary of stopping Windows 98 outright, and Microsoft said Thursday that it expects no delays in the product's launch. But the government's success so far in court — which surprised even Justice Department officials — and negative public reaction to Microsoft's hard-nosed legal tactics have heartened the government.

Still, the decision of whether to file a broader antitrust case against Microsoft under Section 2 of the Sherman Antitrust Act, which outlaws monopolistic behavior, depends in part on whether the Justice Department prevails in a pending appeal sought by Microsoft that will be heard in Washington on April 21. Microsoft has said that Judge Jackson overstepped his bounds last month when he ordered Microsoft to stop forcing computer makers to preinstall its Internet software as a condition for getting access to Windows 95.

On the courthouse steps Thursday, Mr. Klein hailed Microsoft's sudden decision to settle. "Competitors and innovators should know that their products can compete on their own merits and not be snuffed out by Microsoft's use of monopoly power."

Microsoft's lead counsel, Richard Urowsky, said the agreement leaves other issues in the larger case unresolved, including Microsoft's claim that it has the right to integrate its Internet software with its Windows system. "Microsoft will continue to defend the software industry's right to update and enhance products without unnecessary government interference," said William Neukom, Microsoft senior vice-president and general counsel.

Mr. Neukom declined to speculate on whether the Justice Department would file a broader antitrust case. "We're a company that has allocated a responsible amount of resources to understanding the laws that bear on our business," he said. In antitrust law, "the fundamental notion is, 'What's good for the consumer?'" he said. "As long as the answer is, they're getting better goods and services and lower and lower prices, then there can't be a violation of antitrust law."

The settlement came as Microsoft took other steps to soften the harsh image it has projected in the case. Microsoft just hired Haley Barbour, former head of the Republican National Committee, the GOP's fund-

(Cont.)

raising arm. The company also has hired Mark Fabiani, the former White House lawyer who fielded questions about Whitewater and other Clinton administration scandals, to work on its Internet-product strategy.

Separately, Netscape said it would give away its Navigator browser free in an effort to add millions of new users. Microsoft already gives its browser away and has gained market share rapidly at Netscape's expense.

Certainly the settlement announced Thursday will do little to stanch the losses at Netscape. Once in command of more than 90% of the browser market, Netscape's share has steadily dwindled, and it is now spilling red ink and planning layoffs in the face of Microsoft's marketing blitz. "This is one small step in a very long march," says James Barksdale, Netscape's chief executive officer, who is hoping for additional action by the Justice Department.

Gary Reback, an attorney who has represented Microsoft's competitors, says the Justice department has to do more than launch "surgical" strikes against specific practices of the company, which Mr. Klein, the agency's antitrust chief, has previously indicated would be the department's strategy. "These are markets where if you step in early, you can do arthroscopic surgery," Mr. Reback said. "The free market will then take over and the better products will win. The longer you delay stepping in, the more drastic the remedy has to be to restore competition."

According to Thursday's agreement, Microsoft will let computer makers install Windows 95 but delete the Internet Explorer icons from the computer's desktop.

The agreement came after it began to look more likely that Microsoft was headed for a defeat before Judge Jackson. The company has challenged the judge at every turn in the case, which was filed in October and alleged that Microsoft violated the 1995 agreement with the Justice Department. That agreement, among other things, prohibited Microsoft from tying computer makers' use of other Microsoft products to the use of Windows. The government said the link between Explorer and Windows was a violation; Microsoft called it a permissible and natural integration of the products.

After the judge's initial ruling last month restricting the way Microsoft markets the products, Mr. Gates chose to comply by offering computer makers a commercially worthless version of Windows 95. Next, when the judge named a Harvard law professor to advise the court on technical matters, Microsoft accused the expert, Lawrence Lessig, of bias. Mr. Gates's lawyers even scolded the judge in court, declaring that his order was "senseless," and filed immediate appeals of each of his rulings.

Those tactics damaged Microsoft in the court of public opinion. Steve Ballmer, the company's executive vice president and Mr. Gates's top lieutenant, recently admitted that the number of people who are enthusiastic about the company and its products had clearly taken a dip. He also admitted that the company's morale had suffered.

People inside the company say Microsoft lost sight of how the perception of common sense and courtesy could profoundly shape its prospects. "You have some of the most serious negative attitudes and perceptions that the company has ever experienced, and it's beginning to seep into other sectors," says one former Microsoft executive who remains in contact with its inner circle.

While a Fortune magazine poll concluded this week that 73% of business executives consider Microsoft one of America's great businesses, a more recent Merrill Lynch survey indicated that the company's standing among technology opinion-leaders has suffered. In a survey of 50 corporate chief information officers, 59% said they believe that Microsoft abuses its power, though 62% believe Microsoft should be allowed to integrate its Internet browser and operating systems.

Major Microsoft customers say they currently have no plans to stop supporting the Microsoft standard. And PR strategists say Microsoft can still restore its public image, just as Intel Corp. did after suffering a PR disaster by insisting the company, rather than customers, would decide whether to replace a defective microprocessor, creating the famous "Pentium flap." But Microsoft will have to change tactics, fast, they say.

"I'm astonished at the way Microsoft is presenting its case to the public," says Gershon Kekst, a PR veteran of many merger wars between big companies. "If they don't frame the issue persuasively, then if they haven't already suffered irreparable damage, they will." Antitrust lawyers say Microsoft clearly underestimated Judge Jackson. Known to friends as "Pen Jackson," he has spent 16 years on the bench, winning a reputation as visceral and blunt, dealing harshly with defendants who dare to defy the court.

"He's not sympathetic to cute or clever arguments," says Steve Newborn, a former federal antitrust enforcer who successfully argued for the Federal Trade Commission in one of the judge's few prior antitrust cases. "If you try to put one over on him, you're going to be in deep trouble."

Federal auto-safety regulators felt the judge's wrath when he found that they had rigged brake tests as evidence in a 1980s case alleging that a line of General Motors Corp. cars was unsafe. In a sharp rebuke, he threw out the charges. In another celebrated case, the judge gave the maximum prison term allowed under sentencing guidelines to Washington Mayor Marion Barry, who had been videotaped smoking crack cocaine.

Lawyers who have practiced before Judge Jackson say the former litigator is more impressed with a tough cross-examination than a scholarly legal brief. In four days of contentious hearings on the government's charge that Microsoft hadn't complied with his order, he grew visibly frustrated with Microsoft's highly technical arguments.

Microsoft's defense rested on its belief that it knew more about the black art of software development than the government — and the judge — and it repeatedly stressed that point. It couldn't comply with the order as written, the company said, because removing Internet software from Windows would disable the operating system. But the government's attorney responded to the judge's questions with simple answers, and used Microsoft's own "add/remove" tool that comes with Windows to do what the judge had asked Microsoft to do.

Microsoft's tactic raised this question, though: If it knew so much about programming, why couldn't it just do what Judge Jackson asked? Harvey Goldschmid, a Columbia University antitrust expert, said the company's strategy seemed more focused on tripping up Judge Jackson than on complying with his order. "They tried to make the judge look foolish" in the hope that an appeals court might later reverse him, Mr. Goldschmid said. Judge Jackson's frustration with Microsoft finally exploded when he responded last week to the company's efforts to remove technical expert Mr. Lessig, calling the efforts "trivial ... defamatory ... and not made in good faith."

The court strategy, authorized by Mr. Gates personally, speaks reams about the company's self-image and psychology, which is synonymous with the personality of Mr. Gates. Its managers have learned to aggressively attack detractors and competitors inside, and outside, its high-tech world.

"Bill Gates is Microsoft," says Alan Brew, a partner in the San Francisco corporate branding consultancy Addison Seefeld and Brew. "The character of the whole company is cloned in the form of this combative, young, arrogant leader."

DON CLARK AND MICHAEL SCHROEDER CONTRIBUTED TO THIS ARTICLE.

Reprinted by permission of *The Wall Street Journal,* © 1998 Dow Jones & Company, Inc. All Rights Reserved Worldwide.

22

Pick Up on This: Just Don't Answer, Let Freedom Ring

Odds Are, That Telephone Call Isn't Worth the Bother; Of Slaves and Ms. Masters

By Christina Duff

Staff Reporter of The Wall Street Journal

WASHINGTON — The home phone rings. Shelly Masters, a lawyer, reclines on her love seat, flipping channels. It rings again. She cranks up the TV volume and stays put.

And why shouldn't she? Ms. Masters, age 33, is quite comfortable letting a ringing phone ring.

The answering machine clicks on. "Shel? SHEL-LY! Will you pick up the phone? I know you're there . . ." Ms. Masters stares at CNN. A life blissfully uninterrupted.

The caller, a friend, doesn't see it that way at all. Reached later — and on the first ring — Reagan McBride is fuming. "She's like, lying to me," Ms. McBride says. The 32-year-old graphic artist makes a point of answering her phone, and she expects others to do likewise.

A Freudian Possibility

This is a country of callers sadly divided. On one side are those who remain phone slaves. These souls continue to treat each ring like a fire alarm, disrupting dinner, interrupting lovemaking, muting the TV and shushing the kids. Often, experts say, these are anal-retentive types who overly respect authority. They probably don't jaywalk. And no doubt they eagerly rip open junk mail.

On the other side are those who have conquered the 122-year-old device. Growing numbers of people are learning to get an answering machine or voice mail, toss in a Caller ID unit — and get a life. To screen calls is simply to have e-mail that talks. Pick up if your boss is calling, otherwise return messages at your leisure and erase the verbal spam. Let's face it: Increasingly, it appears that these people are on the right side of history; they are winning the battle.

Answering machines were considered "insulting" by many in the 1970s, but by 1987, people were evenly split on their worthiness, says James Katz, social-science director of Bellcore, a telecommunications-consulting firm in Morristown, N.J. Today, two-thirds of U.S. households have them, and of those, fully half use them to screen calls, according to the marketing-research firm Roper Starch Worldwide. Grandparents will always answer their phones. But their kids and beeper-reared grandchildren practice guilt-free screening. The plugged-in crowd wants to know who's calling before picking up, which, after all, is a form of commitment.

"Appalling," says Peter Crabb, associate psychology professor at Pennsylvania State University at Ogontz. He did a two-year study of electronic chitchat. "A ringing telephone," he writes, "serves as a summons to interact." Yet, by screening, "callees appear to ignore the established answering norm and to engage in behavior that violates it." The result: "Social isolation," Mr. Crabb says.

Jingle of Social Change

In truth, phone behavior had to change. The wife used to be home manning the phone. Now, the last thing she wants to do after a day's gainful employment is chew the fat. Telecommuters turn off the ringer after hours to help divide work and home life. And with New Age "team" structures at work, many others are talked out by the time they leave the office.

It's "sheer survival," says Christena Nippert-Eng, assistant sociology professor at Illinois Institute of Technology, in Chicago. "We're trying to counteract a life under siege." Trained like dogs to jump at a ringing noise, "we must de-brainwash ourselves," Ms. Nippert-Eng says. She herself picks up only when expecting a call, or when "feeling adventurous."

Like potty training, learning phone avoidance can be painful, but the end results are less messy and save time and sanity. Guilt and shame quickly turn to secret delight. Empowerment. Freedom.

Realistically, what are the chances a call is going to be more interesting and rewarding than what you're already doing? "Million to one," figures Roxy Roxborough, head of Las Vegas Sports Consultants, the world's largest independent oddsmaker.

Match that against the odds that the caller is a telemarketer, an in-law, or some other undesirable. "Three to one," Mr. Roxborough wagers.

In Kansas City, Mo., Ben Goodall was having a lovely time sipping a cold beer on his back porch on a balmy spring evening when, brrrring! the phone rang. Mr. Goodall, a 44-year-old roofing contractor and father of three, leapt from his recliner and spun too quickly, sending his Heineken into the geranium and severely spraining his left ankle.

All for a soccer mom wanting cupcakes for the last home game. "The shame," Mr. Goodall laments. Obedient no longer, he now relishes the chance to sit and screen. "It feels so good," he says.

It's also totally fair. Take it from etiquette umpire Judith Martin, a k a Miss Manners. "The wildly condemned practice" of screening "is not rude," though it is hard "to make the irate understand that," she writes in her book "Communication." Actually, Ms. Martin says, "it is no more possible or wise always to accept all calls as they are made than it is to leave one's front door wide open." The caller is rude not to realize that.

Technology has made it far too easy to reach out and smother someone. Look at beepers, multiple phone lines, call-waiting. Consequently, victims of telephone assaults have no recourse but to arm themselves with technology of their own and fight back. If a caller refuses to leave messages, a Caller ID box can still reveal his name and number. It was intended as a safety device. Now, "people use it for the control," says Joan Rasmussen of Bell Atlantic Corp., which took eight years to sell its first million Caller IDs and just one year, 1996, to sell the second million.

Voice mail is a cool option. No more bulky machines. But it has one drawback: Callers can't be overheard leaving messages. To this, too, there is a solution: SoloPoint Inc., in Los Gatos, Calif., makes miniature speakers for the phone so voice mail messages can be heard as they come in. Virginia Yorgin, a 63-year-old retired case worker in San Diego, signed up for a pair. Now, she never answers her phone.

Telemarketers and others desperate to get through can electronically mask their number, and not even Caller ID can decipher it. So for the hard-core screener, there's software. YoYo Call Tracker can actually disable the ring for some, all or just unidentified callers and bump them to a machine.

Technophobes improvise. Advice columnist Ann Landers doesn't even own an answering machine, but she takes the phone off the hook during her sleeping hours: 1 a.m. to 10 a.m. "No one's going to call me until I'm ready," she says.

It's time to recognize that screening transcends society, maybe even time and space. When the phone rings, "the bell creates in us a kind of vibration, maybe some anxiety," says Vietnamese Zen master Thich Nhat Hanh. Who is it? What do they want? Do I owe them money?

Mr. Hanh suggests meditation. When the phone rings, don't move: It's a temple bell. Begin to breathe. "Breathing in, I calm my body. Breathing out, I smile," he says. "This is very beautiful." In the French monastery where he lives, near Bordeaux, Mr. Hanh sucks in air and allows a nun to answer the phone.

Of course, there is an ugly side to this. Jason Fries, a 33-year-old sales manager in Chicago, hates the idle-chat-on-the-phone phase of dating. He tried to sneak a message onto a young woman's answering machine one afternoon when he expected her to be at work, but she was there — home sick — and she answered the phone. Startled, Mr. Fries blurted out the truth: "I just wanted your machine." Screeners often prefer to call at odd hours to avoid conversation.

And after the screening habit is learned, it

(Cont.)

can go too far. Bert Garrett, a family practitioner in Austin, Texas, is often paged in the middle of the night. He rushes to call the patient — and gets an answering machine. That's overscreening. To retaliate, Dr. Garrett quickly spits out, "Doctor called," and slams down the phone. "I mean, hell-oo-o. Who else do they think is calling at 3 o'clock in the morning?" he says. "Why not just pick up and say, 'Hi'?"

Struggling to stay relevant, phone fanatics use a universal scold: "I know you're there." To which screeners respond: I know you know I'm here. I'm still not answering. What phone slaves haven't gotten hip to yet is that screening has rendered the once-powerful telephone practically impotent.

Better it than you. One summer evening in the Freeman family's Fort Wayne, Ind., home, the lights were dim, the wine bottle drained, the James Taylor on. In the middle of a particularly amorous moment with his wife, 30-year-old Kevin Freeman heard the high-pitched ringing of a nearby phone and lunged for it.

Now, Amy Freeman turns off the ringer most nights when she and her husband are home. "I'd be a fool to complain," Mr. Freeman says.

Reprinted by permission of *The Wall Street Journal,* © 1998 Dow Jones & Company, Inc. All Rights Reserved Worldwide.

Buyer Behavior

Empty Nests, Full Pockets

Most empty nesters are sitting on annual disposable-income 'bonuses' of $5,000 or $10,000 as financial obligations to their kids diminish. Many youth-obsessed marketers don't seem to have figured that out yet. *By Terry Lefton*

Ask Sterling Group president Simon Williams about empty nesters and he'll recount a recent focus group where the differences between the baby boomers at 50 and any previous generation became readily apparent.

"I've got two groups of friends," Williams recalls hearing from one man whose last child had recently left home. "Half of them are worried about what their stomachs look like on the outside and the other half are worried about what they put in their stomachs."

The first of the 77 million-strong baby boomer generation turns 50 this year. Understanding generational nuances like a passion for fitness with the usual increased health concerns of 50-somethings is becoming an imperative for a marketing community that has largely ignored the over-50 set.

"As the boomers move into this phase of life, you'd have to think marketers will follow them," said Myra Stark, who tracks trends as svp/director of knowledge management at Saatchi & Saatchi, New York. "But advertising and marketing to this group have a long way to go."

Ignore this group at your own risk. With the biggest population boom in U.S. history fueling their growth, empty nesters are a group that will be on the rise until the year 2015. According to a study done by Roper Starch, N.Y., for the American Association of Retired Persons, in the next 25 years, the number of Americans over 50 will increase by 47.2 million—larger than the entire Generation X culture that marketers are increasingly desperate to reach.

Having spent years accumulating goods, they are now seeking experiences. And with no children to support, many will finally have the disposable income to pay for them.

A recent study by Age Wave Communications of 1,007 new empty nester couples with household incomes of $50,000 or more found more than one-third reporting an annual "empty nest bonus" of $10,000 or greater; two thirds of those surveyed reported bonuses of $5,000 or more.

"As the boomers have moved through different ages they have been the most marketed-to generation of all time," said Denise Fedewa, vp and associate research director at Leo Burnett. "So you'd have to believe the numbers themselves will change that. Some clients are starting to ask us to study that market. But overall they are the minority."

The demographic handwriting on the wall has been glaringly apparent for some time. So why aren't marketers targeting empty nesters with the same zeal they attack Gen X or even women? After all, this is a group that will be the mainstream market before long. Some point to the fact that many advertising execs and brand managers are 30 or younger. And changing American marketers' preoccupation with the culture of youth will be as easy as it is for a 50-year-old to pull on the jeans he or she wore 20 years earlier.

"It's not fashionable or glamorous in any marketing-driven business to appeal to anyone old," said Williams, who has done work for Johnson & Johnson in the 50-plus field. "Take a walk in your local mall. What's aimed at older people? Nothing. So there's a huge opportunity for marketers to segment against them as they grow into a predominant group."

There also seems to be a "one-size-fits-all" mentality among some marketers who assume that a broad campaign can reach empty nesters. "Any marketing messages aimed at this group need to be just as tailored as they are for Generation X," said Mike Rybarski, svp and director of target marketing at Age Wave Communications, who directed the recent empty nester survey as part of a campaign for Kemper Funds. "One-size-fits-all is not true now and it will be less true as this group grows exponentially."

Another misconception about empty nesters is that they have already made all their brand decisions. Marketers familiar with the demographic say that empty nesting is such a formative time that it is as important to be in front of this group as it is to pound away at young adults forming their first brand loyalties.

"A lot of companies segment by age, because it's easier, but a better indicator of consumers ready for new and different goods and services is people going through a life change, which new empty nesters obviously are doing," said Kathy Schofield at Doner Direct, Baltimore, which handles advertising for AARP. "They will be dealing with things like divorce, remarriage, starting second families, death, inheritance and grandchildren."

A Roper Starch study for the AARP concluded that those aged 50-60 experience more "life-changing events" than in any other decade of their lives.

Adds Saatchi's Stark: "We no longer think of this time of life as a downward slope. It's a next step, and anytime that happens, people have new needs as consumers."

And age, in and of itself, is less of a marketing imperative than ever. "Age as a driver of market segmentation is not as relevant," said Laurel Cutler, vice chairman of FCB/Leber Katz, N.Y. "The age of one's children is a far stronger driver."

One national marketer already targeting this group is Choice Hotels, which has converted about 10% of the 7,000 rooms in its Rodeway and Econo Lodge brands to senior-friendly suites, with brighter lighting, larger-button telephone and TV remotes, and grab bars in showers. Based on reservation line advance bookings, the rooms are generating $5 million in annual incremental revenue.

> **"Companies segment by age because it's easier, but a better indicator of consumers ready for new and different goods is people going through a life change."—Kathy Schofield, Doner Direct**

"It's a group that travels more and stays longer, especially at times of year when other travel is off, so it was incumbent upon us to target them," said Tim Shuy, Econo Lodge vice president and brand manager. Choice markets to seniors via its venerable TV campaigns in which celebrities pop out of suitcases, with one recent execution featuring comedian Jonathan Winters extolling the virtues of the senior suites.

The way boomers spend their empty-nest "bonus" reveals a lot about their psychographic profiles. For example, while the Age Wave/Kemper study found that 60.4% of those surveyed admitted to not having put away enough for retirement, only 40.7% were earmarking all or most of their newfound disposable income for retirement savings. More often, the bonus is used to pay for new experiences, which is why the travel market has already been targeting in a number of unorthodox ways.

"They are looking for new and different experiences, even more so than 20-year-olds," said Dennis Marzella, svp of strategic marketing at YP&B, an Orlando, Fla., travel-marketing firm. "People think that most of the exotic trips to Nepal and what-have-you are done by only the young and vigorous. The fact of the matter is that, attitudinally, empty nesters are more adventurous than younger travelers. And, of course, they have the money to afford adventure trips."

Still, one can't assume that empty nesters automatically have higher disposable incomes. With more children living at home than at any time since the Depression, it shouldn't be surprising that the Age Wave survey found fully one-third of those surveyed have "boomerang" children. Even those with kids that have flown the nest still have financial responsibilities for them: 69.5% of those surveyed said they were using some of their empty nest bonus to help children with expenses, ahead of retirement savings, at 55.7%. And of course, there will be the added financial burden of aging parents.

"These are people devoid of the responsibility of raising zero to 22-year-olds," observed Brookings Institution economist Gary Burtless. "But marketers should be mindful of the squeeze a lot of them will be in nonetheless."

So what's a marketer to do, especially the plethora of financial services companies zeroing in on a group for whom retirement no longer seems so far away? In the case of Kemper, Age Wave concluded the right approach was to confront the problem directly and assure empty nesters that they were not alone in their worries about not being able to save enough for retirement.

"We found that what's really on their minds is that they think it's just too late," said Rybarski. The solution was a direct approach, in which a Kemper employee tells a prospective empty-nest customer that most people at their life stage share similar concerns about retirement income. Having had those fears somewhat allayed, customers are then sold funds designed for those starting late on retirement savings.

"Most of them don't think they can make up for lost time, so before you can sell this group anything you've got to be cognizant of that," said Rybarski. "That could apply to someone selling financial services or fitness equipment or health and beauty products."

"The boomer mindset has always been one of immortality and that won't change just because they've turned into 50-ish empty nesters," said Williams. "My speculation would be that anyone who can market products that tap into that feeling and say 'here's how' will do well."

It's a group with a newfound sense of freedom, whose greatest needs are now self-fulfillment and self expression. That would indicate opportunities for the arts and for marketing of time-consuming hobbies, like painting or woodworking. Just ask Rich Gore of EMG Worldwide, N.Y., whose company did an about-face from marketing popular music to arranging tours of the most popular TV chefs after he discovered empty nesters couldn't get enough of them.

"Cooking becomes entertainment for these people, who are looking for new ways to pass the time more than new things," he said.

Dining was also cited as an industry that could be

targeting this group. "It's possible some of the larger restaurant chains feel they'd risk the younger audience, but that is a real opportunity right now," said Joel Steckel, a marketing professor at New York University's Stern School of Business.

> **"Most empty nesters don't think they can make up for lost time, so be cognizant of that before trying to sell them financial services or health and beauty products."—Mike Rybarski, Age Wave**

It's a generation that will bring its addiction to physical fitness with it, so athletic equipment marketers might do well to follow the lead of Nike, which produced a TV spot of 50-plus runners with talk of "wrinkled, but not old." Those kinds of efforts are supported by a survey conducted by American Sports Data for the Sporting Goods Manufacturers Association. It showed recreational participation in record numbers for this demo, with fitness walking, stationary bike riding and treadmill exercise all more popular than golf, the sport usually associated with this group.

"We've identified this group tactically as someone we've got to address, especially with our legacy in aerobic and walking shoes," said Stephen Stocks, Reebok's director of U.S. marketing. "But really, I haven't seen anyone spending real money against it yet."

"My mother's generation felt that at age 40, you could give up having a good figure and relax into middle age, which is something this group will never do," said FCB's Cutler. "They expect to always be young and beautiful, and will fight to maintain it."

Much of the marketing efforts aimed directly at empty nesters have centered on real estate. But for all the lavishly appointed "empty nests" built in this country in recent years, few plan to leave their current residence. According to the Age Wave/Kemper study, 68.6% of those polled said they don't plan to move. Of those who did move, 38.1% said they did so because they no longer needed the space their former home offered. And some are investing in vacation homes they will eventually use as a retirement home.

"The real estate angle possibly has been overblown," said Williams. "But I do believe that since this group tends to believe they are starting over, there is an opportunity for home furnishing and home remodeling products."

Not that empty nesters are entirely self-indulgent.

The Age Wave study showed a healthy opportunity for toy makers to target empty nesters, with 45.1% spending $1,000 or more per year on toys, clothes or entertainment for grandchildren.

One can debate just how brand-loyal this group is. What is certain, though, is that this is the most marketed-to group of all time.

And as the heaviest group of media consumers, it is easy to reach. But just like an old fish that's seen and turned away from every lure, it isn't an easy sell. Perhaps that's why Kemper found the best approach to be a straightforward one. The consensus seems to be that this is the most brand-loyal group, but one that is nonetheless exploitable, since it is making so many new purchase decisions.

"The brands that have traditionally hit this demo hard, like vitamin supplements or luxury cars, will clearly have to change their pitches, and I'm also convinced there's a lot of opportunity for new brands that can target empty nesters in creative ways," said Burnett's Fedewa.

"This is a group that is skeptical to begin with," said Cutler. "They will stay loyal to brands that stay loyal to them. For everything else, they will buy private label or on price."

"They are demanding and they look or value over price," said Econo Lodge's Shuy. "But as a group, I'd say they are more brand-loyal, because the older you get, the more you don't like surprises."

So how should marketers approach this group? Other than taking a direct approach, one key is playing to the boomers' preoccupation with immortality by never mentioning age directly. If it is mentioned, show that it doesn't matter, as Nike does. Jeans manufacturers have already caught on: remember, the jeans aren't for old, fat people, they just have "a *scoche* more room."

"If my dad gained weight, he'd buy a larger size of pants," said Rybarski. A baby boomer has to be sold something that's a "relaxed fit" instead.

And remember that the self-image these people have is always a lie. "When you market to this audience, you are always going to depict someone 10 to 15 years younger, because their mental picture is that much younger, even up into their 70s," said W.B. Doner's Schofield.

"You *never* mention age," said FCB's Cutler. "If it's skin care, you talk about drying out. You bring up concerns of aging, but avoid mentioning age itself like the plague."

© 1996 ASM Communications, Inc. Used with permission from *Brandweek* magazine.

24

U.S. advertisers slowly learn to speak Spanish

By Melanie Wells
USA TODAY

A handsome, dark-haired man discovers he's fresh out of his favorite instant coffee. Strolling on to his apartment balcony, he spies a woman next door enjoying a steaming cup of java. His favorite brand. They smile, flirt and then savor the coffee.

This isn't the Taster's Choice couple. The duo drink Folgers. And they're Hispanic.

Until recently, they were also advertising afterthoughts. To many Hispanics, they still are. Although Hispanic marketing is becoming a hot button on Madison Avenue, the top 50 mainstream U.S. marketers spent less than $300 million targeting Hispanics last year. That's barely a sliver of the $160 billion U.S. ad-spending pie.

Procter & Gamble, the nation's biggest advertiser and largest advertiser to Hispanics, spent $40 million selling Folgers and other goods to Hispanic audiences last year. But that's the same amount P&G spent on advertising just for Crisco oil.

There's more to it than translating and dubbing

Critics say Madison Avenue is ignoring a powerful, fast-growing market. The U.S. Hispanic population hit 27.4 million last year. By the turn of the century, it will be the USA's largest ethnic minority group. Average annual Hispanic household income is $31,582,vs. $43,133 for all U.S. households, the Census Bureau says.(Average household income for the nation's 33.4 million African-Americans is $29,259).

"For Hispanics being 10% of the population, they only make up 1% to 2% of everyone's ad budget; that's not enough," says Hector Cantu, managing editor of Hispanic Business, whose advertisers include American Express and Chase Manhattan.

Hispanics spent about $228 billion in 1995, up 25% from 1991, according to Miami-based Strategy Research, a market research firm. They spend a disproportionately large amount on nonessential consumer products, such as TVs, stereos, apparel and beauty aides, experts say. And Hispanic consumers are often more receptive to commercial messages than the advertising-saturated mainstream market.

"It's a rapidly growing market and one that's less saturated with advertising messages than the mass market," notes Dr. Jeffrey Humphreys, director of economic forecasting at the University of Georgia. "Dollars spent by advertisers in the Hispanic market may be more profitable than dollars spent in the general market." Marketers are slowly realizing there's a huge, relatively untapped market for financial services, and they're moving aggressively to tap it:

▲ Allstate is airing its first-ever Hispanic ads, a $3-million campaign to get more consumers to buy insurance. One spot intones: "There's someone who knows that your little girl is afraid of the bogeyman. And that you would do anything to protect your whole family."

▲ NationsBank is airing commercials — one features a Spanish-speaking bank operator — to make Hispanics feel comfortable and welcome at bank branches.

▲ Discount brokerage Charles Schwab is advertising its bilingual services, which include a toll-free number for Spanish-speaking customers. Howard Dade, senior international manager, estimates 4% of Schwab customers are Hispanic.

▲ Citibank is sponsoring conferences held by the National Society of Hispanic MBA's to beef up visibility among Hispanic consumers and job applicants, says Denise Montana, Citibank's director of diversity management.

"Banks and financial service companies see a huge market out there, because statistics show that Hispanics are making money and ones who are newer to this country are making first-time decisions about which to use," says Cantu.

Al Aguilar of San Antonio-based ad agency Sosa, Bromley, Aguilar, Noble compares today's Hispanic consumers to mainstream consumers of the 1950s: "There is an open-arm attitude that says 'Tell me more; give me more information.'" The agency's newest client, Clairol, wants ads to boost sales to Hispanic customers.

Among other marketers hoping to make big tracks in the Hispanic market through ads, promotions and event sponsorships:

▲ Nike is sponsoring Major League Soccer on Univision, one of two Spanish-language cable networks in the USA. Jorge Campos, a Mexican goalie, will appear in ads next month.

(Cont.)

▲ Coca-Cola is sponsoring a Tejano music award ceremony in San Antonio this week. The company also hopes to attract Hispanic teens to Summer Olympics promotions.

▲ Miller Brewing has begun airing two Hispanic commercials for its new Miller Beer brand. "We have significantly increased our marketing spending for (Hispanics) in 1996," says Noel Hankin, Miller's ethnic marketing director. "Hispanics are becoming a bigger part of the beer category."

▲ Sprint is going for collect calls with an ad campaign from Sosa Bromley Aguilar for 1-800-TU-CASA. Sprint raised its Hispanic ad budget 9% last year to $7 million.

▲ Mazda hopes a $3 million ad effort in Miami — the nation's third-largest Hispanic market after Los Angeles and New York — will increase sales of its luxury Millenia model by 11% this year.

Mazda is redubbing English TV spots into Spanish — a once-popular practice that's considered a no-no by Hispanic marketing experts these days.

Some marketers think the consumer isn't savvy enough to realize when a commercial is dubbed over, says Luz de Armas of Conill Advertising, the Hispanic arm of agency Saatchi & Saatchi.

Creating good, effective commercials that are as sophisticated and as sensitive as the best in the mainstream market can be a challenge. Increasingly, marketers are asking Hispanic ad agencies to help, says agency search consultant Arthur Anderson of Morgan Anderson, which has offices in New York and Mexico City.

"It's a very young market and the advertising is starting to reflect that more and more," de Armas adds. "It used to be you couldn't have a Hispanic commercial unless you had a cute little Hispanic grandmother in it."

Emotional, family appeals are still recurring themes in some Hispanic ads. That often means a marketer has to jettison its mass-market campaign theme — especially when humor is difficult to translate. For example, the humorous California Milk Processor Board's "got milk?" campaign was popular with mainstream consumers. But it soured Hispanics.

The board hired Anita Santiago Advertising, a specialist in Hispanic ads. It's "Generations" spots asks mothers if they've given their families enough milk.

Santiago didn't try and replicate the sloppy-burger humor of general market ads for Carl's Jr. when it

Top Hispanic market advertisers

Advertising targeting the Hispanic market topped $292 million last year, up 8% from '94.

	Change from '94	'95 spending (millions)
Procter & Gamble	5.1%	$39.5
AT&T	4.2%	$20.0
McDonald's	7.1%	$12.0
Anheuser-Busch	-4.8%	$9.9
Sears Roebuck	2.2%	$9.5
Phillip Morris	3.3%	$9.5
Colgate-Palmolive	-10.4%	$8.6
J.C. Penney	10.3%	$8.6
Ford Motor	3.8%	$8.1
Quaker Oats	2.7%	$7.6

Source: Hispanic Business
By Julie Stacey, USA TODAY

was given the California-based restaurant chain's Hispanic ad account. Instead, the agency created festive ads featuring dancing kids, couples and families. "Hispanics are offended by people being sloppy or playing with food. We did something with more family values," she says. "When marketers air commercials that aren't relevant to the Hispanic market, they're telling consumers 'We want your money but we're not going the extra mile to reach you the appropriate way.'"

Similarly, Sears adopted a theme for the Hispanic market even though its "Softer Side of Sears" mainstream campaign translate easily into Spanish. The Hispanic theme: "Everything for you" from agency Mendoza Dillon.

Changing the theme line was a "very calculated decision," Sears marketing chief John Costello says. "Hispanic customers are more aspirational than general market customers," he says. "They shop with the whole family and shop a greater breadth of merchandise."

Costello predicts consumer product companies increasingly will add Hispanic advertising to their mix. "Marketers need to view this not as targeted marketing but as the evolution of marketing to a multicultural society," he says.

Contributing: Laura Petrecca

Copyright 1996, *USA Today*. Reprinted with permission.

25

THE NEW WORKING CLASS

by Rebecca Piirto Heath

As recently as two years ago, leading newspapers were announcing the death of the working class. That obituary now seems premature. Although the structure of the working class is shifting, its spirit is thriving. What's changing is the working-class stereotype of a hard-hatted, blue-collared, middle-aged, white man. As the industrial age becomes more of a dim memory, the image of the group of people who drive the economy is changing, too. Indicators suggest that the working core of Americans is becoming younger, more ethnically diverse, more female, somewhat more educated, and more alienated from its employers.

> *In a supposedly classless society, nearly half of Americans consistently identify themselves as working class. This group is more diverse than it was a generation ago, and now it includes people from all walks of life. Perhaps the greatest common bond of working-class Americans is their belief in the combined strength of working people — through unions.*

Trying to pinpoint the precise nature of this shift, however, is a prickly proposition. The difficulty comes from our uniquely American view of class. The common belief on these shores is that America, unlike Europe, is a classless society. We admit to racial, ethnic, gender, and cultural divisions. But to class? Most Americans think of class the same way they think of the British monarchy — something foreign.

Economic indicators show a steady polarization between incomes of the top-earning households and the lowest-income households. Only the richest Americans have seen any real income growth in the last decade. Incomes of the top 5 percent of Americans grew 37 percent between 1984 and 1994, compared with a meager 1 percent increase on the bottom.

Despite this evidence, many Americans find it most comfortable to believe that class divisions, if they exist at all, are minor obstacles. Even supposedly jaded baby-boomer parents still teach their children they can be anything they want to be. Despite growing rumbles of doubt,

most of us still believe the old adage that an individual with enough gumption can pull himself up by his bootstraps, especially with a little hard work and a good education.

"No one wants to be working class in America," says Peter Rachleff, professor of history at Macalester College in St. Paul, Minnesota. For those who take issue with that statement, Rachleff asks another question: "When was the last time you saw a U.S. film about the working class?" British films, on the other hand, are full of working-class heroes. "We are bombarded by so much popular culture that tells us continually that this is a middle-class society," says Rachleff.

Michael Moore, author of Downsize This and a popular director and producer, has made a name for himself by poking fun at America's "classlessness." Roger & Me was a surprise hit documentary about Moore's attempts to track down General Motors CEO Roger Smith to ask him why the company's auto plant in Flint, Michigan, was closing and laying off thousands of loyal long-time workers. Moore says that getting a distributor for his films has always been an uphill battle. "There's something about working-class satire and irony that seems to be missing from our national language," he says.

This lack is ironic in itself, considering the relative novelty of a large middle class in this country. "The middle class didn't even exist until this century," says Moore. So what's behind all this American denial of its working-class roots? "It all started to change after World War II, when working-class people were able to own a home, buy a car or two, take extended summer vacations, and send their kids to college. Once they got some of the trappings of wealth, they got the illusion that they were like the man who lived in the house on the hill," says Moore.

CLASS IN A CLASSLESS SOCIETY

One reason why many surveys don't reveal the state of the working class is that they don't ask about it. Many definitions of the middle class are based on income. By one definition, the middle class includes households with incomes of $15,000 to $75,000. Such socioeconomic categories rarely include an explicit working-class group.

One survey that does is the General Social Survey (GSS), conducted by the National Opinion Research Center. Since 1972, it has asked Americans to classify themselves as lower, working, middle, or upper class. In

1994, 46 percent of American adults said they were working class, virtually equal to the 47 percent who claimed middle-class status. These proportions have varied little over the past 22 years.

In an effort to get at the characteristics underlying class affiliation, Mary Jackman, a professor of sociology at the University of California-Davis, and her husband, political scientist Robert Jackman, published Class Awareness in the United States in 1986. It was based on a landmark survey conducted by the University of Michigan's Survey Research Center in 1975. The study has been called "the most important study of class identification since Richard Center's 1949 Psychology of Social Classes." The Jackmans intentionally crafted the question to include five class divisions — poor, working, middle, upper-middle and upper. "This way middle was truly in the middle, which is more how people think of it," says Jackman. With this grouping, 8 percent identified with the poor, 37 percent with the working class, 43 percent with the middle class, 8 percent with upper-middle, and 1 percent with the upper class.

The Jackmans went on to analyze why people classified themselves the way they did. They asked them to rate the relative importance of attributes such as income, education, and occupation, as well as lifestyle and attitudes. Topping the list for most people was occupation, followed by education and people's beliefs and feelings. Up to 49 percent rated the kind of family a person came from as not important at all. "It seems that, for most people, social class is a combination of fairly hard-core economic attributes that you can identify pretty quickly and other cultural and expressive attributes that you can't identify quite so quickly — their lifestyles, values and attitudes," says Jackman.

Income turned out to be less valuable a predictor than occupation or education. "Education ends up being so important because it's a piece of social capital that reflects Americans' long-term focus," Jackman says. Occupations also played a role, although a less clear one. "The occupations that caused the most confusion about working- or middle-class status were the upper-level blue-collar jobs or skilled tradesmen," says Jackman. Lower-level clerical jobs also created confusion. But there was no debate over assembly-line workers and seven other solidly blue-collar occupations.

The occupational line is blurring even more today. With more companies downsizing, outsourcing, and turning to temporary workers, some highly qualified workers have been marginalized and are underemployed or working for lower pay and fewer benefits. At the same time, formerly semi-skilled blue-collar jobs demand higher-level skills. Even auto mechanics, a solidly working-class occupation in the 1970s, now require sophisticated knowledge of electronics. "For most functions, you just can't use a mechanic anymore. You really need technicians who can solve problems at a much higher level than in the past," says Myron Nadolski, dean of automotive and technical training at American River College in Sacramento, California.

TODAY'S WORKING CLASS

The work force isn't the same as it was 40 years ago. Neither is the working class. Since the Jackmans' study hasn't been updated and the General Social Survey doesn't ask respondents why they label themselves the way they do, differences between working- and middle-class Americans must be inferred by their answers to other questions.

The average age of working- and lower-class Americans is declining, while the age of the middle and upper classes is increasing in line with national trends. On the other hand, the working class has become more average in its gender mix. The proportion of working-class Americans who are female increased from 48 percent in 1974 to 54 percent in 1994. The other classes have been predominantly female all along.

One of the most significant changes in the working class that is also in line with national trends is its increasing racial diversity. Back in the mid-1970s, Jackman found a clear delineation between the races in class attitudes. "You really have to deal separately with blacks and whites because the distribution is so different," Jackman says. This is because, historically, blacks were left out of the economy altogether and have only recently begun to rise into the working and middle classes.

Racial diversity among the lower, working, and, to a lesser extent, middle class is increasing, while the upper class is becoming less racially diverse. Between 1974 and 1994, the proportion of whites who claimed working-class status decreased 9 percent, while the proportion of blacks grew 3 percent and those of other races rose 5 percent. The shift was even more pronounced for the lower class, and somewhat less so for the middle class. Meanwhile, the proportion of whites claiming upper-class status increased, while the proportion of blacks decreased.

The GSS supports the notion that income level plays an unclear role in class identification. In 1994, 74 percent of the working class and 63 percent of the middle class reported household incomes between $15,000 and $74,999. But 10 percent of the upper class also reported making less than $15,000, and 4 percent of the lower class reported making over $50,000 a year.

Educational level is a more reliable indicator that rises steadily with social class, although educational level for all groups has increased. The upper and middle classes still have the preponderance of bachelor's and graduate degrees, but higher degrees are becoming more common among the working class. The proportion of bachelor's degrees held by working-class adults more than doubled between 1974 and 1994, from 4 percent to 10 percent. The proportion of two-year degrees held by working-class respondents increased by 5 percentage points, to 6.5 percent. Two percent of the working class had graduate degrees in 1994.

Similarly, the occupations that make up the working class are less clear-cut. Between 1988 and 1996, the proportion of managers and professionals in the working class increased by 4 percent, to reach 17 percent in 1996. The proportion of technical, sales and administrative workers also rose slightly. Conversely, the proportions of service employees, farm workers, and craft and skilled workers have declined. (It is not possible to compare occupations before 1988 because the classification scheme changed.) In addition, the number of part-time workers has increased across the board, but part-timers remain most prevalent in the lower and working classes.

What does all this mean? Changes in the working class reflect changes in the work environment itself, says David Knoke, professor of sociology at the University of Minnesota, who is currently conducting a panel study of 1,000 work environments around the country to measure shifts in outsourcing, part-time and temporary employment, and cutbacks. "The number of people involved in non-full-time work has quadrupled in the past decade," says Knoke. Up to 30 percent of all U.S. workers are now "contingent" workers — temporaries, part timers, subcontractors or independent consultants, according to Knoke.

Knoke and colleagues theorize that increased global competition has forced the elimination of companies' internal job markets. "It used to be that if you got a job with IBM out of college, you were set for life," Knoke says. "A series of job ladders was built into the organization that allowed people to count on a slow but steadily rising standard of living."

The likely effect of these shifts on workers is already being seen. "People involved in part-time work have a looser stake in the organization. There's more of a sense of having to fend for themselves," Knoke says. "People see themselves as more working class and having less of a stake in the middle class." Jackman agrees. "I believe there has been a hardening of awareness of class boundaries in the last 10 or 15 years because the situation for American workers has gotten grim, and it's happened so quietly."

The UPS strike last year crystallized these issues for American workers, which is one reason why the 180,000 striking teamsters had such overwhelming support from the public. "Workers across the country could identify with the striking UPS workers because they're all feeling the same pinch," says Deborah Dion, AFL-CIO spokesperson.

UNION RESURGENCE?

Not surprisingly, interest in organized labor is one of the attributes most common among the working class. "You can be working class without being a union member, but it's difficult to think of a union member who is not aware of working-class issues," says Rachleff of Macalester College. This relationship is borne out in GSS data. Union membership is one of the clearest delineators between the working and other classes. Although union membership among U.S. workers has fallen across the board, for the last 25 years it has remained highest among those who claim working-class status.

Unions understand the changing structure of the new working class and are targeting somewhat younger, more ethnic, better-educated workers, and different occupations than they did 25 years ago. Coincidentally, just around the time UPS capitulated to strikers' demands for more full-time jobs and a better pension arrangement, the AFL-CIO launched a five-city pilot ad campaign to help boost sagging union membership. More than one-third of all American workers belonged to unions in 1950. By 1997, less than 15 percent of workers (only 10 percent of nongovernment workers) were union members.

A recent AFL-CIO poll found that 44 percent of the general public employed in a non-supervisory job said they would vote to form a union at their workplace. Another 20 percent were less certain but still positive, saying it was better to join together at a work site to solve problems. "That 20 percent is made up of the same people we're trying to reach with our campaign — minority groups, young people, and women," says Dion.

The ads are four personal stories from real union members. Mike, a construction worker, represents the traditional white, male, blue-collar core of the membership, but with a twist — he's young. A young black nurse named Arthereane talks about her love of helping children and her conviction that hospitals run best when they're run by doctors and nurses, not the profit motive. Erin, a working mother, balances family and her job as a chef with the help of her union. Michael, a worker at a Harley-Davidson plant, sings the union's praises for keeping the company from closing the plant, and making jobs more secure and the company more profitable. The tag line is: "You have a voice, make it heard; today's unions."

"These issues are the key because they are issues that workers everywhere are concerned about. Everything's going up except workers' fair share — the stock market's going up and executive salaries are skyrocketing," Dion says. She believes this is a pivotal time for unions to get this message out to people who may not realize the historic power of unions to raise wages and secure better benefits for workers.

Filmmaker Michael Moore also sees this as a pivotal period. "I think we're going to see a resurgence in interest in unions," he says. "In the last five years, it's dawned on a lot of people that unions have been asleep at the wheel. They really don't have that much in common with the man on the hill."

> **It used to be that if you got a job with a company like IBM out of college, you were set for life.**

Moore features some of the newest members of the United Food and Commercial Worker Union in his latest film, *The Big One*. The 45 booksellers who start at $6 an hour at the Borders Books store in Des Moines, Iowa, voted in the union in December 1996. They are mostly young, with bachelor's or even graduate degrees. Many came to Borders from other professions — teaching, the arts, or independent bookstores driven out of business by the big chains. They say it's not about money so much as it is about respect.

"The way they pay us and treat us is a paradox," says employee organizer Christian Gholson. "On one hand, they say the employees are the reason for Borders' success, then they say this is a transitional job and you aren't worth more than $6.50 an hour." So far only four of Borders' 200-plus stores have organized, but Gholson sees it as a worthwhile struggle. "In my perfect world, I'd like to make $8.00 an hour. That's not so much when you see the volume of business that goes through this store," he says.

The trend toward unionization is growing among health-care professionals as well as among upscale service businesses that depend on younger workers. Stores in the Starbucks Corporation and Einstein/Noah Bagel Corporation chains have also voted for union representation in the past year. As for Gholson, their issues are better wages, full-time hours, health benefits — and respect.

Social scientists see historic similarities between today's labor issues and those of the 1930s. "After the Depression, everybody's job became a lot more insecure," says labor historian Rachleff. "There were a lot of efforts by white-collar workers to unionize. The intervention of anti-communism stopped that and threw the labor movement back onto a much narrower social foundation." Knoke says that the contract between employers and workers has once more ended in the 1990s. "For a lot of people, it's turned into something like it was before World War II," he says. "There is great uncertainty. People are being forced out of jobs that are disappearing."

If globalization is creating a working class with a wider social base, what does a person like Gholson, who considers himself a writer and a poet, have in common with an auto-plant assembly-line worker? It seems like a clash of cultures. "It's very funny watching these enthusiastic young kids trying to get the old fogies of the union to take action and get involved," says Mike Moore.

The Jackmans' study found that beliefs and feelings were an important determinant of class in the 1970s. For today's working class, the commonality just might be age-old issues such as job security, autonomy on the job, occupational prestige, and the belief that hard work should be rewarded. The working class has always been the group most likely to rate job security as the most important reason for taking a job, according to GSS data. "There are differences between us and the old union people," admits Gholson. "But there's a middle ground where we all agree."

The mere fact that working-class identification has stayed so stable over the last 20 years, despite myriad macro economic and social changes, is significant in itself. "If we find people continuing to identify themselves as workers, there must really be something going on socially," says Rachleff, "because there's so much stacked against their doing that."

BEHIND THE NUMBERS

The General Social Survey (GSS) has interviewed a nationally representative sample of American adults aged 18 and older on an almost annual basis since 1972. Questions on social-class affiliation have been asked on a consistent basis throughout the survey's history, as have many other questions about demographic, social, and economic characteristics and attitudes. For more information about the GSS, contact the National Opinion Research Center, 1155 East 60th Street, Chicago, IL 60637; telephone (312) 753-7877. The cumulative database is in the public domain and is available from the Roper Center at the University of Connecticut in Storrs; telephone (203) 486-4882.

Reprinted from *American Demographics* magazine with permission. © 1998, Cowles Business Media, Ithaca, New York.

Low-Key LUXURY

Younger consumers have redefined the luxury goods market, elevating backpacks, bikes and microbrews, but so far keeping a skeptical distance from Rolex and BMW. *By Elaine Underwood*

Caught by an ad agency camera crew for a man-on-the-street interview, a young New Yorker was trying to explain his compelling attraction to smoking expensive cigars.

"I see myself smoking a cigar, sitting in an old, wood-paneled room in a wingback chair with a glass of brandy," he said, thoughtfully. Dressed casually, in a burgundy polo shirt and khakis, he looked to be about 30 but sounded like a charter member of the Yale alumni club.

Dubbed counter-culture slackers a few years ago, Generation X might have seemed an unlikely target for cigar marketers. But the age group has proved to be a market worth chasing, and not just for cigars. The Census Bureau numbers them at 66 million, while Roper Starch Worldwide puts their spending power at $125 billion annually. And their purchasing and lifestyle choices appear to be influencing some of their elders, too, among the youth-obsessed Baby Boomers.

But if the old-money image of luxury conjured up by the young cigar smoker might have come straight from the pages of *Playboy* magazine, circa 1965, GenXers are selecting some of their status icons from categories that back then might have seemed uncongenial, even antithetical, to the luxury market: daily fixes of Rhumba Frappuccinos at Starbucks ($4.50 for the extra large, or Venti, portion), Prada knapsacks ($500), Y Bikes from Trek ($3,000). Technology items like Iomega's removable Zip drives and the impossible-to-find $300 Pilot hand-held computer, which transfers data from the desktop to a model small enough to fit in a shirt pocket, have augmented high-end stereos and other consumer electronics items as status symbols.

Meanwhile, icons such as the Rolex watch and BMW car are so strongly associated with the *Dynasty* 1980s that they haven't truly clicked with young adults. Other traditional luxury goods purveyors such as Gucci, Chanel and Louis Vuitton are making a play for this emerging group of luxury shoppers by revamping both their product lines and their advertising. Established names like TAG Heuer watches and Davidoff cigars that were lucky enough to be anointed by Xers now actively market to them, too.

Matriculating into a dispiriting job environment, the generation is supposed to be the most self-reliant, entrepreneurial one yet. Although a fortunate slice of them are making big money in activities like software and Internet development, research shows that many are pessimistic about attaining a standard of living that their parents took for granted.

After years of Boomer-driven consumerism, young adults now are the key drivers of new products, designs and advertising that find their way to other demographics. Gucci's new designer Tom Ford put the luxury label at the forefront of the current "rich hippie" look, pairing psychedelic shirts with acid-bright hip huggers and patent-leather thong sandals to attract young trendies and somewhat older women. Gucci, which went public last year at an opening price of $22 a share, is now trading at $70.

Calvin Klein's CK One fragrance was created specifically for GenXers. But this year, it also ranked among the top Mother's Day gifts.

Nothing goes against the stereotype more than the burgeoning yen for cigars and the fogey-style pursuits that go along with them. Other young men—and women—interviewed by O'Leary Clarke & Partners, N.Y., which creates advertising for Davidoff cigars, said they liked to smoke their $20 stogies on the golf course and while socializing in the specially ventilated rooms at restaurants, taverns and cigar bars springing up in major cities around the country.

"A lot of people are smoking cigars because the social doctors of our society say 'no' to everything," said Alice O'Leary, the agency's president/ceo. "Smoking three to four cigars a week is better than cigarettes. What's more, you can network and have fun."

Geneva-based Davidoff's 1995 worldwide sales rose 60% to $1.5 billion, mainly in cigars but also in ties, brandy, men's fragrances (notably Davidoff Cool Water) and cigar accessories such as $300 guillotine-style cigar snippers.

O'Leary's print campaign features George Sand, Chopin and Al Capone, all famous cigar smokers, and pitches the smokes as being, "For those who are obsessed with quality." Davidoff's U.S. president, Christof Kull, crisscrosses the country staging $200 to $300 dinners where the bill of fare includes a gourmet meal, single malt scotch and Davidoff cigars.

If anything, people in their twenties are even more conscious of brand names than Boomers. "Look at Tommy Hilfiger, Calvin Klein and Polo Sport," said

David Lauren, son of Polo Sport designer Ralph Lauren and editor/publisher of the GenX magazine *Swing.* "Those brands are still strong and doing better than ever with this generation." To Lauren, who is 24, and his co-horts, status brands include Oakley sunglasses, Rollerblade in-line skates, Trek mountain bikes and Jeeps. "It isn't surprising to find someone on scholarship having a beautiful bike," Lauren said.

Citing research compiled by Roper Starch World-wide in 1993, *Mademoiselle* magazine puts the dispos-able income of women in their twenties at $2,820, slight-ly less than baby boomer women who may earn much more but have added family responsibilities.

A recent set of focus groups by *Mademoiselle* had GenX women group brand names into the categories "for us" and "for them," "them" being boomers and even older Americans. "Us" brands included Gucci, Chanel and Ver-sace, global status names that have managed to stay cur-rent. The young women also identified with Absolut vodka, DKNY sportswear, designer Ralph Lauren's trendy Polo Sport collection and Estee Lauder's Origins line.

Relegated to the dust heap of "them" brands were Estee Lauder, Ralph Lauren's primary collection, Coach Leathergoods and BMW. The women identified with every major piece of plastic, deciding American Express, Visa and MasterCard all sufficed for them.

"When you're in your early twenties, luxury brands tend to mean more on the whole," said *Mademoiselle* publisher Catherine Viscardi Johnston. "If they can't af-ford a Chanel suit, they'll buy a Chanel lipstick or nailpolish and move up later."

To recapture the pull it had with 20-somethings in the '60s, Volkswagen is trying to exploit the cachet of one hot bike. In TV and print ads, VW is offering a limited-edition Jetta Trek model whose $14,500 base price in-cludes bike rack and Trek mountain bike. A TV spot by Arnold Fortuna Lawner & Cabot, Boston, spends more time romancing the fun consumers will have on the bike than pitching the attributes of the car. "If there's anything more fun than driving a Volkswagen, it's driving a Volk-swagen with a bike on top," a print ad states.

"We've been very happy with the promotion," said Dick Moran, marketing manager at Trek USA. "Cus-tomers have to pick up the bike at one of our stores, so our dealers like it, too." At the stores, shoppers will find Trek shorts, tops, helmets and other accessories. Volkswagen also is co-sponsoring a four-man professional mountain bike team with Trek.

Trek sells bikes in a spectrum of price ranges, but last year it introduced the Y series of mountain racers that retail for $3,000 and up. Moran says he pitches the line to people who actually face steep inclines, but the bold bikes, with yellow frames and rapid-adjustable damping, or RAD, mechanisms sell well with wannabes, too. Wa-terloo, Wis.-based Trek USA's sales skyrocketed to $350 million last year from $200 million in 1993.

Some luxury goods makers have established credi-bility by tying themselves convincingly to GenXers' pre-ferred activities. Trek spends much of its $4 million mar-keting budget outfitting local bike shop racing teams and offering a van service that allows bike shops to easily plan mountain biking excursions for their customers. "For the younger audience, the real impact comes from employees at the shops, most of whom are college students working part-time and graduating college students," said Moran. "They're the influencers and the most important compo-nent in our sales."

Those active lifestyles spawned a new category in the handbag trade, designer backpacks, when GenXers, liking the outdoorsy cues they suggested, kept carrying practical backpacks after college. Now, they're catered to with high-fashion Prada, Donna Karan and Gucci back-packs costing hundreds of dollars.

To become a more integral part of Xers' lifestyles, some marketers are emphasizing event marketing. Swiss watchmaker TAG Heuer holds sponsorships for the annu-al World Mountain Biking Championship in Vail, Colo., Formula One racing, and Boston's Charles Regatta, which attracts Ivy League students and alumni. On the Charles River, regatta crew wear TAG T-shirts and anoraks, and buoys are printed with the TAG slogan, "Success. It's a mind game."

"We always strive to be the official timekeeper of these events," said Fred Reffsin, president of TAG Heuer USA. "We avoid like the plague multi-layer sponsorships, where we'd be one of 20 sponsors."

If in markets like Japan heritage is very important, "what's important here is authenticity and credibility," Reffsin said. The company spends 40% of its $75 million worldwide marketing budget on sporting events and guards its image so carefully it won't allow retailers to in-clude the brand on their Web sites. (TAG currently is de-veloping its own site.)

In the past five years the average price of a TAG Heuer has risen as its customer base has gotten more comfortable about splurging on a timepiece. Five years ago, Americans were buying $300 watches; now they're trading up into a range of $600 and up. Later this year, it debuts a $40,000 platinum model.

According to Mediamark Research, N.Y., men age 18 to 34 spent $607 million on watches in 1994, outpac-ing the supposedly affluent boomers in the 35-49 demo

(Cont.)

by $133 million. Other categories show a similar trend.

Details magazine is more than happy to share with potential advertisers research data showing that only 20% of GenXers conform to the slacker stereotype (it calls them "postponers"). "Overall, the generation is comprised of spenders, not savers," said associate publisher Susan Cappa.

In an effort to attract younger men to its stores, retailer Saks Fifth Avenue carries wide selections of trendy Gene Meyer, Moschino and Gucci menswear. This September, Details and Saks will co-host a benefit for Gen Arts, a group that raises money for young people in film, the arts and fashion, at the retailer's Los Angeles store. "Saks knows its median age is in the fifties and it is using *Details* to get to the younger people," Cappa said.

Trendy shoppers are hitting the boutiques of contemporary designers Anna Sui, Todd Oldham and Prada. Another retailer to the carriage trade, Neiman Marcus, Dallas, views catalogs as a way to reach young consumers who might not venture into its stores.

"On the one hand, we have less competition; it's just Neiman's and Saks, because I. Magnin has disappeared," said Bernie Feiwus, president of Neiman Marcus Direct. "On the other hand, the number of designer boutiques has proliferated. Fifteen years ago, Dallas had two; now there are dozens."

Feiwus pitches to younger shoppers a catalog of basics named Essentials that, for Neiman's at least, are moderately priced. He also sees them responding to catalogs of gourmet foods. The specialty store's Christmas book is also carrying more items for $25 or less to ease perceived price barriers at the chain.

"The important thing about our brand is we've been able to balance prestige and luxury with accessibility," said TAG Heuer's Reffsin. TAG also takes an egalitarian approach, equipping its cheapest and most expensive watch models with the same functions. "There's none of that, 'Wow, you have the Baby Benz' stuff with us," he said. "No matter where they come in on our price range, we're able to tag them."

© 1996 ASM Communications, Inc. Used with permission from *Brandweek* magazine.

27

New Bug goes upscale but draws on nostalgia

By James R. Healey
USA TODAY

DETROIT — Riding a wave of optimism and nostalgia that would shame a Ronald Reagan speech writer, Volkswagen rolled its long-awaited New Beetle into public view here Monday.

The product is no surprise. Versions have been seen at shows and in the press since 1994. But the price — $15,700, more than $1,000 below forecasts — created a stir.

It's a price that will appeal to younger buyers in a car designed to attract the baby boomers who made the first Beetle a huge success.

VW hasn't sold a Beetle in the USA since 1979. The enduring design has continued production in Mexico, but those cars don't meet U.S. safety and pollution regulations. Once VW's life-and-death model, the old Beetle has become an afterthought, a nostalgic muse.

The New Beetle — a far different car, except for its half-round shape — goes on sale in March. It, too, is built in Mexico, and mechanically is similar to the VW Golf compact sedan, also manufactured there.

The differences are major: The old Beetle never had more than 60 horsepower; the new one won't have less than 90. The old car had its engine in back, where it powered the rear wheels and was cooled by air — a radical setup, then and still. The new car has its engine up front, where it drives the front wheels and is cooled by water — a conventional arrangement

VW expects to sell about 50,000 New Beetles a year in the USA. The best-selling VW in the USA is the Jetta at about twice that number a year.

Ever since VW, almost on a lark, exhibited a Beetle-esque show car here in '94, the company has been inundated with inquiries. "We got such a favorable reaction from the public, our dealers and the press. To say the least, we were overwhelmed. We were almost forced by the customer's voice to make it a real car," VW Chairman Ferdinand Piech recalled.

Added VW director Jens Neumann: "We got thousands of letters and phone calls from around the world asking: 'Are you really bringing the Beetle back?'"

"The answer is, 'Nope.' We're not bringing the Beetle back. We're bringing out the New Beetle."

Neumann, the German board member in charge of North American operations, who introduces himself as "director of Beetle affairs," calls it a car for the 21st century.

NO HUMBLE BUG

Fans of the simple Beetle of yore won't find that simplicity in the New Beetle. A Golf underneath, New Beetle is as computerized and complicated as any modern auto. But inside, there is at least a hint of the original's unupholstered unpretentiousness, and a cute bud vase is built into the dashboard to accent the retro-style round gauges.

Top VW executives, in from Germany for the unveiling, bubbled.

The New Beetle is "optimism on wheels," and "a dream come true . . . for people who see the world's glass as half full," Neumann said.

Even the normally icy Piech was thawed by the surfeit of feel-good fuzzies. He professed affection for America, which first hung the label "Beetle" on the original half-moon-shaped VW sedan decades ago.

> "The Beetle came just when Americans were revolting against the wretched excess of America's turgid, jelly-bodied blobs of the time."
> —Ken Gross, director, Petersen Automotive Museum

And he modestly called the car's launch merely "one of the highlights" of the North American International Auto Show here, which opens to the public Saturday.

The original Beetle was popular for several reasons. "The car itself was pretty good. And it was classless: Wealthy people owned them; kids owned them. And the BBDO (agency) ads were fabulous. They called it a lemon; they said to think small," noted Ken Gross, director of the Petersen Automotive Museum in Los Angeles. And the timing was right. "The Beetle came just when Americans were revolting against the wretched excess of America's turgid, jelly-bodied blobs of the time."

Judged against that list, the New Beetle has some strengths.

For one thing, VW ads seem to blend the simplicity of the earlier ones with enough attitude to pique the been-there, done-that '90s buyer. Print ads will omit technical details, just showing the car and using a simple headline, as the old ads did. Some examples of what they'll say:

(Cont.)

▲ "The engine's in front, but its heart is in the same place."

▲ "Less flower. More power." reference to the '60s hippies, who adopted the Beetle and the VW van as icons of a simpler life.

▲ "0-60? Yes." Making fun of other automakers' emphasis on muscular mobiles that accelerate quickly to 60 miles an hour.

▲ "If you sold your soul in the '80s, here's your chance to buy it back."

▲ "See what happens when we all wish for the same thing."

And, as before, the New Beetle seems classless. VW studies of prospective buyers show the car appeals to all ages, all nationalities, all incomes, both genders. "The reaction of everybody is the same. They smile," Neumann said.

Timing once again could be fortunate. Though big sport-utility vehicles and pickups are America's darlings, they are under fire from environmentalists for pollution and profligate fuel use. If social conscience intrudes or the pendulum of taste swings, the New Beetle might be in the right place at the right time.

BEETLE FANS ALL OVER

Industry analysts and other professional skeptics verbally hugged the new Bug.

"It's cute," smiled Joe Phillippi of Wall Street's Lehman Bros.

"I just sat in it. I like the way it feels," grinned Bob Knoll, senior auto consultant for *Consumer Reports* magazine.

"They got the price right for this market," said Susan Jacobs, head of Jacobs and Associates auto-industry consulting firm. "It's doable for young people, and it'll make the New Beetle a hot car, one that sells out."

President Michael Basserman and Executive Vice President Michael Jackson of Mercedes-Benz North America watched the New Beetle unveiling. "I'm coming back later," Jackson told Basserman as they walked away.

Even General Motors Vice Chairman Harry Pearce, who led GM's legal attack on VW over industrial espionage allegations involving former GM purchasing boss J. Ignacio Lopez de Arriortua, offered praise: "VW has a long and rich history. They are

---

THE BEETLES: YESTERDAY AND TODAY

Volkswagen first manufactured the Beetle in 1938, but it wasn't until 1949 — well after World War II — that the first two Beetles made their way to the USA, where they went for about $800 each. VW now is preparing for a spring launch of its New Beetle, hoping to capitalize on baby boomers' nostalgia. It will be the first Beetle to the U.S. market since 1979, but the New Beetle, a VW Golf chassis with a rounded body, is nothing like the old one.

1949 Beetle		1998 Beetle
$800 (approx.)	**Price**	$15,700[1]
30	**Horsepower**	115
Air-cooled, rear-mounted, 1.1-liter, four-cylinder	**Engine**	Water-cooled, front-mounted, 2-liter, four-cylinder
Rear-wheel	**Drive**	Front-wheel
About 65 mph	**Top speed**	About 120 mph
34 mpg highway	**Fuel economy**	29 mpg highway[2]
1,600 pounds	**Weight**	2,700 pounds
160 inches long 61 inches tall 60.5 inches wide 94.5-inch wheelbase	**Size**	161.1 inches long 59.5 inches tall 67.9 inches wide 98.9-inch wheelbase
Cheap, basic transportation	**Intent**	Upmarket, nostalgic money-maker and image enhancer

1 - includes destination charge; 2 - optional 90-hp diesel engine is rated 48 mpg highway
Source: Volkswagen and *Standard Catalog of Imported Cars* 1946-1990

---

strong competitors."

But there were reservations, too. Mainly this: Can VW's dealers, drained of enthusiasm by being starved of exciting models for years, take advantage of the excitement the New Beetle is sure to generate?

"Their dealers died years ago," said Jerry Forbes, auto analyst.

Another concern is whether New Beetle has the staying power of its predecessor. About 22 million old Beetles have been built, making it one of the world's most popular cars. If the New Beetle is hot today, gone tomorrow, VW's plan to reassert itself in the USA will take a dramatic hit. The car will be sold worldwide, however, so VW probably won't be hurt financially unless interest wanes in many markets at once.

Despite the red flags, there is, the powerful push of nostalgia as aging baby boomers reach for any symbol to prove they're still young.

Says Gross: "There are just enough people who remember the old Beetle fondly to give the New Beetle a lot of homes."

Contributing: Micheline Maynard

Copyright 1998, *USA Today*. Reprinted with permission.

28

ARE TECH BUYERS DIFFERENT?

Marketers say new consumer categories are needed

To the bright young founders of WebTV, it looked like a home run: hook televisions up to the Net and tap into the vast market of couch potatoes curious about this new thing called the World Wide Web. But after burning through an estimated $50 million to advertise the new service during the 1996 holiday season, WebTV and partners Sony and Philips Electronics counted a disappointing 50,000 subscribers.

The problem, WebTV now acknowledges, was the wrong marketing message. Couch potatoes want to be better entertained, while computer users are content to explore using small PC screens. A revamped campaign now emphasizes entertainment over education.

WebTV's marketing myopia isn't unique. As the $280 million consumer market for technology soars, companies that sell stuff ranging from cellular phones and computers to software and Internet services have some surprising blind spots about who their customers are and what motivates them.

Enter market researchers, sniffing opportunity. Unlike soup or soda, technology products are often complex and evolve rapidly. And the failure of a few well publicized products, such as WebTV or Kodak's PhotoCD, to hit it big with a mass market has convinced a growing number of companies that when it comes to high tech, conventional marketing research doesn't go far enough. "The traditional approach pretty much always falls back on the ancient taxonomy of early adopters and followers," says Peter M. Winter, president of Cox Communications Inc.'s Interactive Media unit. "That's not precise enough."

MOTIVATION. The result has been a scramble among researchers to find out what makes technology customers tick—and whether consumers behave differently when they buy technology than when they purchase other consumer products. Of course, consumer-goods makers figured out long ago the value of understanding consumer habits, even for seemingly mundane stuff such as toothpaste. But to gain similar insights into technology consumers, some marketers argue, research must go beyond demographics and buying patterns—it must capture how people really use technology day to day, and how they feel about it.

Some market-research firms, such as San Francisco-based Odyssey Research and pollster Yankelovich Partners' Cyber Citizen, are focusing on the way consumers use the Internet. Others, such as SRI Consulting Inc., are using traditional market-research methods that combine demographics information with an analysis of consumer emotions to predict how tech buyers will behave.

But the most ambitious effort so far is a scheme from technology consultant Forrester Research Inc., which contracted with polling and research firm NPD Group to survey 131,000 consumers annually about their motivations, buying habits, and financial ability to purchase technology products. Dubbed Technographics, the first survey results won't be completed until later this month. But already, some big-name clients, including Tele-Communications, Sprint, Visa, Ford, and Bank of America, have signed up for a look. "Technology is not just changing the way consumers spend time," says Gil Fuchsberg, director of new media for ad agency Interpublic Group, a Technographics client. "It's also changing the way nearly every company is making, selling, and delivering products. We've got to understand that."

Of course, plenty of technology companies have prospered without such tools. But Jim Taylor, who ran Yankelovich before he became senior vice-president for marketing at computer maker Gateway 2000 Inc. in 1996, thinks technology-specific research will be increasingly critical as PC makers and others learn to segment their markets to keep up growth. The difference, he says, is that traditional consumer research will tell you who bought a computer. But it won't tell you that four different people in a household use it—or how their needs differ. Marketing to the wrong member of the household can sink a product, he says. "In this business, you don't have to screw up much to screw up a lot," he says.

To help companies zero in on their target customers, Forrester's scheme separates people into 10 categories. Some, such as career-minded "Fast Forwards" who own an average of 20 technology products per household, and their less affluent colleagues, known as "Techno-Strivers," are at ease with technology and use it at home, in the office, and at play. Others range from "New Age Nurturers" who spend big bucks on technology, though primarily for family use, to "Hand-Shakers." These older, wealthy consumers—often managers—let younger assistants handle computers and other technology

in the office (table).

CLEAR TARGETS. Some Forrester clients have already started identifying products and services they're likely to rework. At Cox Interactive, for example, Winter plans to use Technographics to identify more clearly the target viewers for his Web sites. Once he has a stronger handle on who they are, he'll reshape content to better draw them in.

To get a glimpse of how it will work, consider Cindy Williams, 46, an administrative secretary for a health-maintenance organization in Tulsa, Okla. She and her husband Gary, a 44-year-old maintenance supervisor, have one PC they bought three years ago and no Internet connection. They are mulling an upgrade since their sons, ages 11 and 12, want speedier games than their sluggish machine can play.

Thanks to their family status and income—two traditional signposts—a conventional consumer-research profile would highlight them as promising technology buyers. But Forrester claims those factors are misleading and that any tech company pitching sophisticated products to the Williams would likely be wasting its money. Technographics pegs the Williams as Traditionalists—family-oriented buyers who are relatively well off but remain unconvinced that upgrades or other new techno-gadgets are worth buying. Why? A key factor in the Williams profile is the age of their PC. Three years old is ancient by tech standards.

So an online grocery service starting up in Tulsa might use Forrester's information to bypass the Williams, despite their superficial demographic fit. Unlike other family-oriented consumer groups such as New Age Nurturers or Digital Hopefuls, Traditionalists "wait a long time before upgrading. That's not a very fertile part of the online market," says Forrester analyst Josh Bernoff.

But Technographics should also help a company find new buyers. Carol Linder, 46, is a customer-service manager for Ameritech Corp. in Milwaukee. She and her husband Robyn, a 53-year-old CPA, already have three school-age children, two pagers, and three PCs. By the end of the month, they plan to buy two more computers. Robyn spends time online for work. Although similar to the Williams family in income and family status, they are light-years away in how they use technology. The Linders are classic Fast Forwards, using computers and other gadgets for job, family, and individual pursuits. So a

(Cont.)

company selling ISDN phone lines that speed computer connections might use the Technographics profiles to target the Linders while avoiding the Williams.

Such distinctions should also come in handy as tech companies struggle with marketing to a broader audience as they shift away from early adopters. That's the challenge facing Tele-Communications Inc. The cable-TV giant wants to use Technographics to help develop and sell new products as its cable-modem business goes mass market. "How we market the product initially, and how we target and talk to our customers changes over time," says John Najarian, director of consumer research for TCI.

TCI knows that speed and performance have been important to early users of cable-modems. But that's not necessarily what will appeal to new types of buyers. So Najarian says it might use Technographics to help create kid-friendly Internet marketing targeted to family-oriented New Age Nurturers, for example. Or it might develop ways to download TV clips that appeal to entertainment-hungry Mouse Potatoes.

NEW BOTTLES? Similar plans are under way at Delta Air Lines. The Atlanta-based carrier hopes that by analyzing its own customer database using Technographics' categories, it can better target online ticket sales. Delta plans to create marketing campaigns aimed at time-strapped Fast Forwards and New Age Nurturers, for example. Just as important, it figures to save a bundle by using Technographics to eliminate customers who appear to be technology pessimists from its solicitations. High income or not, they're unlikely to use such a service. "Traditional marketing research gives you a picture of the universe but doesn't focus on the people more likely to book online," says Paul Lai, manager of marketing research for Delta.

Despite the interest Forrester has sparked,

more traditional researchers argue that it's doing little more than putting old medicine into new bottles. "Consumers are consumers," says Bill Guns, director of SRI Consulting's business-intelligence center. "Nothing in the data we've seen over 20 years suggest that somehow people are different beings when they are buying technology." SRI's research, called Values Lifestyles Survey, leans more on emotions, delving into whether or not customers like technology or are intimidated by it.

But retail consultant Wendy Liebmann, president of WSL Strategic Retail, says the slow start of Net shopping and the frustrated expectations of many consumers new to online services clearly show the need for more targeted technology marketing. Companies are providing services that consumers ignore. Meanwhile, consumers sign up for other services and are disappointed. With a mountain of data on tap, Forrester is hoping it can carve out a new category for itself: techno-matchmaker.

By Paul C. Judge in Boston

Reprinted from January 26, 1998 issue of *Business Week* by special permission, copyright © 1998 by McGraw-Hill, Inc.

TECH CUSTOMERS: THE OPTIMISTS . . .

MORE AFFLUENT　　LESS AFFLUENT

FAST FORWARDS	NEW AGE NURTURERS	MOUSE POTATOES
These customers are the biggest spenders, and they're early adopters of new technology for individual use.	Also big spenders, but focused on technology for home uses such as a family PC.	They like the online world for entertainment and are willing to spend for the latest in technotainment.
TECHNO-STRIVERS	DIGITAL HOPEFULS	GADGET-GRABBERS
Use technology from cell phones and pagers to online services primarily to gain career edge.	Families with a limited budget but still interested in new technology. Good candidates for the under-$1,000 PC.	They also favor online entertainment but have less cash to spend on it.

DATA: FORRESTER RESEARCH INC. ©BW

. . . AND THE PESSIMISTS

MORE AFFLUENT　　LESS AFFLUENT

HAND-SHAKERS	TRADITIONALISTS	MEDIA JUNKIES
Older consumers—typically managers—who don't touch their computers at work. They leave that to younger assistants.	Willing to use technology but slow to upgrade. Not convinced upgrades and other add-ons are worth paying for.	Seek entertainment and can't find much of it online. Prefer TV and older media.

SIDELINED CITIZENS　Not interested in technology.

DATA: FORRESTER RESEARCH INC. ©BW

PUSH FROM ABOVE

To lower costs, corporations are making new demands on small suppliers. And the suppliers have little choice but to comply.

BY LEE BERTON

Let the supplier beware: You have to be more accommodating to your big-company customers.

Pushing hard to lower their costs, large companies are changing their supply arrangements— asking suppliers to absorb more costs, ship more efficiently and take on more services than ever before. Not surprisingly, many small suppliers are taking hits. And, if they can't accommodate, they end up losing the contract.

Santee Cooper, a large utility based in Moncks Corner, S.C., recently got rid of the 90 photocopy machines it owned. Rather than buying new copiers, though, it only wanted to pay for copies that its employees made on machines owned by a distributor.

For Santee, it was a logical move. "We're saving ourselves about $20,000 a year," says Wade Ferguson, contract administrator of the state-owned utility.

But the original supplier, **Modern Office Machines** of Charleston, S.C., which made money by selling and servicing the utility's copiers, wasn't able to make the change, and so lost the contract to another distributor. "We just couldn't figure out a way to make money on the new contract," says Anthony Brush, regional sales manager for Modern Office.

Mr. Brush says that since losing that account and others as customers push for lower prices and more service, his company has learned to become more flexible and is developing new contracts that involve leasing the machine and setting charges per copy.

In the past, companies ordering supplies were "fat, dumb and happy and willing to pay the premium for control and flexibility in using the product," says Santee's Mr. Ferguson. Now, "all companies, including utilities, are under enormous competitive pressures, and have to think more carefully before they spend extra dollars."

While increased competition is a major reason for the change, improved technology at many companies is also playing its part. "Increased usage of sophisticated computer software data is making smart consumers of all buyers," says Robert Novack, an associate professor of business logistics at Pennsylvania State University's Smeal College of Business in State College, Pa.

Often, small vendors are being asked to do jobs, sometimes at no extra charge, that their customers used to do themselves, says David Rachman, a professor of marketing at Baruch College's school of business at City University of New York. Big supermarkets are asking suppliers to do more on-site inventory checking and ordering to keep shelves stocked with fast-moving merchandise — a role usually done by the supermarkets, Prof. Rachman says.

"And instead of shipping big orders to the retailer's warehouse," he says, "vendors are being asked to break down the orders and ship them separately to each store." This helps reduce the retailer's warehouse and trucking costs and pares time between ordering and store delivery, he notes.

At **Wal-Mart Stores** Inc., a buying strategist says the company is wringing "more inefficiencies and inconsistencies out of the supply chain" by requiring more than 3,000 vendors to "cooperate with our efforts" to pare costs and improve deliveries. And officials at **Federated Department Stores** Inc., which operates Bloomingdale's and Macy's, says that since 1992 it has pushed suppliers harder "to reduce costs and increase efficiencies."

Similarly, **Xerox** Corp. two years ago began asking more than 400 small companies to ship spare parts for copiers to five warehouses throughout the nation, says Frederick Stenross, a Xerox manager for inventory strategy. "We used to ship all the parts to one central warehouse, so by eliminating the second shipment, we reduce some parts costs by up to 5%," he adds.

Volume Savings

Companies are also squeezing bigger discounts from suppliers. **James River Paper** Co., Richmond, Va., has pared the number of its small vendors for office supplies, raw materials and other items to about 100 from nearly 500 three years ago, says Sid A. Brown, the company's purchasing manager. That allows the company to order more supplies from each remaining vendor. "With bigger orders, we can get larger discounts and save up to 10% for some items," he says.

All this is taking a toll on the suppliers, which don't have much choice but to give in to the customers' requests.

"In the past, when I shipped our line to department and discount stores, we simply put the merchandise in a big box and sent it off," says Herman Bernstein, chief financial officer for **Tracy Evans** Ltd., a New York sportwear maker that sells to retail outlets of Wal-Mart, **Kmart** Corp., **Caldor** Corp. and **Petrie Stores** Corp. "But over the last two to three years, the buyers have foisted on us the new jobs of labeling the product and even putting bar codes on the label for point-of-sale automation" with a price scanner.

These changes are trimming his profits, he says. "While I haven't figured out exactly how much [the labels] cost, I don't welcome such changes because increased competition prevents us from recouping their cost," he says.

Boxed In

Some suppliers are finding it difficult to keep up with the competition as customers seek lower costs. Three years ago, big department stores began to change their orders from **Climax Manufacturing** Co., a small, closely held packaging maker in Lowville, N.Y. Instead of buying high-quality gift boxes, the companies switched to less-expensive versions that were less profitable for Climax. "The new boxes cost [the department stores] 20% less," says Urban Hirschey, a co-owner of Climax.

At the same time, other suppliers began to lower their prices even more than Climax did for the cheaper boxes, and Climax couldn't keep up. "We've lost some big department-store chains as customers because we just couldn't afford" to meet the competition, says Mr. Hirschey. And a large consumer-products company that had asked Climax to produce boxes for retail sales scaled back its order, he says. "Two years ago, the customer found someone who could make the boxes at a lower price," he says, "so they just want the die-cut blanks or patterns" that the competitor needed to make the boxes.

Now, to make up for the lost business, Climax is trying to supply production patterns to other box manufacturers that are more able to meet buyers' demands. "We're talking to 150 other members of the National Paper Box Association to try to drum up such business," Mr. Hirschey says.

MR. BERTON IS A STAFF REPORTER IN THE WALL STREET JOURNAL'S NEW YORK BUREAU.

Reprinted by permission of *The Wall Street Journal,* © 1996 Dow Jones & Company, Inc. All Rights Reserved Worldwide.

THE PUSH TO STREAMLINE
SUPPLY CHAINS

Whether it's whittling inventories or pressing suppliers to do a bigger share of the work, companies are honing the way they buy materials. ■ *by Eryn Brown*

Just a decade ago, which seems like ancient history in the new computerized world of inventory control, Eastman Chemical of Kingsport, Tennessee, kept on hand a three-month supply of wood pulp, one of its principal feedstocks. The company now gets by on a nine-day supply, which is not allowed to creep back up. Not until 1,000 tons of wood pulp, say, have left the company after being transformed into one of dozens of products does Eastman order more. Following the iron dictate of demand-pull, the company tells suppliers to send just enough to replace what was used, not an ounce more.

Welcome to another triumph of lean, mean supply-chain management. Consultants, eagerly capitalizing on industry's ardor for the concept during the past five years or so, have reported some pretty astounding results. A study by Pittiglio Rabin Todd & McGrath (PRTM), a consulting group in Weston, Massachusetts, shows that, depending on the industry, companies in the top quintile for supply-chain performance achieve saving equal to 3% to 7% of revenues compared with their median-performing peers.

"Companies used to compete on product and cost," says Bill Helming, a PRTM director. "Now they compete on supply-chain management." Economywide, the results from inventory savings alone are awesome. According to Everett Ehrlich, undersecretary of the U.S. Department of Commerce, manufacturers have cut inventories by 9% since the Eighties, freeing up to $82 billion for other purposes.

It's becoming increasingly clear, though, that there's more to supply-chain management than hard-nosed procurement and Scrooge-like inventory controls. Think of the supply chain as a collection of pathways beginning upstream at the sources of a company's rawest of raw materials, proceeding through the company's internal logistics and production system, and extending down-

stream to customers. To manage the supply chain, a company tries to eliminate delays and cut the amount of resources tied up along the way.

Some companies concentrate on streamlining internal processes. Externally, supply-chain management most often means pushing inventory costs out of the company and putting off delivery—and payment—until the stuff is truly needed. Companies may also ask suppliers to shoulder more development costs or switch to providing complete subassemblies instead of mere parts. Such arrangements foster closer relationships with fewer suppliers, who play along because they can help assure a revenue stream for years to come. In today's climate a company has little choice but to demand more from suppliers, because downstream it's getting the same kind of pressure for improved service and just-in-time delivery from its own customers.

Within a company, enormous changes in attitude are needed to make supply-chain management work. The core concept—viewing and controlling procurement, manufacturing, and distribution processes as a unified flow—often requires people at every level of an organization to look beyond the narrow old rules that told them how to do their jobs. Nick Semaca, a vice president at A.T. Kearney consulting firm in Chicago, calls it "killing the sacred cows." Resistance is common. A procurement chief may be told that merely buying from the lowest bidder isn't always best, and he may not like it. An engineer may have to let a supplier's engineer come in and tweak his precious design. A production worker may need to respond to customer-service inquiries or scan bar codes for inventory tracking, whereas before he only bolted widgets.

A company has to function as a single organism, supply-chain gurus say, with a single pair of eyes recording what's going on and a single brain processing it all. Today's computer systems have helped make it all possible, and the investments in information tech-

nology can be huge. Fielding Rolston, Eastman Chemical's vice president for customer service and materials management, says his company's computer installation, called Globiis, cost "the equivalent of bringing up a plant." Good software is obviously essential, though Bruce Richardson, a vice president at Advance Manufacturing Research, a consulting firm in Boston, cautions: "Software is not the magic diet pill. All it can do is reinforce your best practices."

Hungry for information on those practices, many companies have sought out Chrysler Corp., whose Score program (for Supplier Cost Reduction Effort) is widely reputed to represent the best thinking in Motown. The automaker racked up over $1 billion in savings in 1996 alone, and it shares the savings with suppliers that come up with money-saving ideas and product innovations. Drawn by Score's good press, every organization from IBM to the Air Force's U.S. Transportation Command has inquired how it's done. Chrysler's executive vice president for procurement and supply, Thomas Stallkamp, is willing to talk but insists: "What we're doing is tailored for Chrysler. People come in here and expect us to show them our little formula. We're not saying this is necessarily going to work for them."

Maybe not, but the general principles applied at Chrysler and elsewhere can work in a wide range of businesses. FORTUNE recently visited five companies, whose products range from pills to locomotives, to learn how each, in a different way, has fine-tuned its supply chain.

Eastman Chemical, nestled among the eastern Tennessee hills, was founded as a division of Eastman Kodak in 1920. Longtime boss George Eastman wanted a facility to produce methanol, which is involved in the photographic process and comes from wood, a ready resource thereabouts. The division later branched into a wide variety of products, from commodity plastics to carefully tailored "fine chemicals." Today, Eastman, spun off from Kodak in 1994, boasts $4.8 billion in annual sales and profit margins that are higher than the industry average.

Eastman Chemical's processes call for 1,500 different raw materials that arrive from 850 suppliers. But an outsize one-fourth of revenues comes from products based on cellulose esters, which are created by mixing cellulose derived from wood pulp or cotton with acetic anhydride, which the company produces from coal. Cellulose esters ultimately go into everything from photographic film to acetate yarn to hair barrettes.

Once Eastman was turned loose as a company, CEO Earnest Deavenport accelerated a process, already under way, for optimizing the flow of materials. Exaggerating to explain why improvement was needed, Deavenport recalls: "In the past you'd have five departments, each wanting infinite inventory of raw materials so it would never run out and an infinite inventory of finished product so the customer would never be caught short."

To make sure that as little inventory as possible sat idle, Eastman had devised what it calls "stream inventory management." Rolston, the customer-service and materials-management VP, offers a view from the top of how the latest refinement of the system works: "We try to see this whole supply chain operating like a pipeline. When the order comes in from the customer, we take one pound of product out of the tail end. We've then got the raw material function working with the supplier to put another pound in on the other end. We want to achieve a continuous flow."

These days stream inventory management requires gigabytes of information, crunched by the company's Globiis computer, which stands for Global Business Integrated Information System. Using software from Germany's SAP as a platform, it's able to manage inventories worldwide on a real-time basis. The new approach also requires a novel organization under Rolston, called Customer Service and Materials Management, through which all incoming orders and outgoing purchase orders pass. Most companies, Deavenport says, would have established teams that bring together representatives from the usual functional turfs—sales, finance, or procurement. "We said, 'Let's define the process and put all of that in one organization.' The only thing we didn't put there is the actual manufacturing of the materials."

Rolston and his staff keep inventories small by looking at each raw-material stream as a single companywide number instead of tallying up separately the assorted amounts and reformulations of the material along the stages of the manufacturing process. The inventory number for cellulose embraces, among other things, rolls of wood pulp, pulp that has been turned into powder, and pulp that has been mixed with solvents to produce a cellulose ester. Whatever the form, Globiis converts it to standard units of cellulose. Gone are fragmented inventory measures that don't promote a big-picture view. "One person tracks inventory," Rolston says. "Me."

Here's an example that follows the path of one material in a manufacturing process. Suppose Eastman's materials planning people have decided to maintain 2,500 tons of cellulose in the supply chain for acetate tow, the material used in the manufacture of cigarette filters, in which Eastman has a major position. An Eastman customer service representative sits at a Globiis terminal in the brand-new Eastman Business Center in Kingsport, where key customer service and materials-management functions are handled. He receives an order through Globiis from a major cigarette manufacturer requesting its regular monthly shipment of four million pounds of acetate tow. The customer service person, familiar with the tobacco company, gets in touch with Eastman's logistics team, which, thanks to Globiis's forecasting tools, is positioned to ship four million pounds of baled acetate tow just as the product is produced.

But Globiis is looking upstream too. Acetate tow is one of Eastman's products made from pulp-derived cellulose esters. Accordingly, the customer service representative notes than 1,200 tons of cellulose have been removed from the acetate-tow-chain inventory. He then uses the computer system to request 1,200 tons of wood pulp from Rayonier or International Paper to replenish the supply. Within seven days the pulp arrives in Kingsport via train and enters the production process. The original 2,500-ton inventory figure has been maintained.

Stream inventory management has delivered a pretty payoff. Because Eastman can monitor inventory while it's still at the supplier, and because it can also generate more accurate production forecasts, it no longer needs a cushion of large stockpiles. Not content with telescoping inventories of wood pulp from a three-month to a nine-day supply, the company hopes to pare them further to four days' worth. The trend is under way in other raw materials as well. Twenty years ago Eastman kept 18 million pounds of paraxylene, a material that winds up in polyethylene terephthalate (PET) plastic soda bottles, to support 520 million pounds a year of PET production in the U.S. Today, Eastman keeps only 14 million pounds of paraxylene, even though its U.S. PET production has grown more than threefold. Companywide, Eastman's inventories have fallen from 11.5% of sales in 1989 to 8% last year.

In 1991 sagging profits gave pharmaceuticals giant Eli Lilly no choice but to tighten up its supply chain. HMOs had gained huge buying and negotiating power, key patents had expired, and even the runaway success of Lilly's Prozac antidepressant couldn't fully offset these trends. Taking its first quarterly loss in decades, the Indianapolis company worried about being swallowed whole in a takeover. "We wanted to stay on the left side of the hyphenated name of some new company," jokes William Smith III, Lilly's executive director of global manufacturing services.

So Lilly tore into a massive reorganization, staking out procurement as one area for improvement. With help from A.T. Kearney, Lilly has been implementing the consulting firm's "strategic sourcing" approach. The goal is to save $190 million on an annual basis by 1998, which the company is on track to achieving. Lilly's director of global supply management, Stephen McCracken, says that the first step was to "understand our own spending." Each of Lilly's 28 plants was handling purchasing independently—an arrangement that didn't allow for much strategic sourcing at all. In response the company created 12 global commodity managers, each of whom takes responsibility for a portion of Lilly's spending and handles all the relevant decisions and strategies.

Centralized purchasing has given Lilly greater buying clout. For example, one global commodity manager is responsible for the entire company's procurement of primary containers, right down to such items as the aluminum seals on vials of insulin for diabetics. He or she studies Lilly's worldwide purchasing patterns as well as aluminum-market trends, develops a buying strategy, and completes a purchase contract. Whereas previously a buyer at each site would handle negotiations for aluminum, now all that buyer has to do is tap into the global commodity manager's contract. The on-site buyer is responsible for monitoring a supplier's price, delivery, and quality performance, and for reporting back to the global commodity manager, who then uses the information to improve the aluminum contract to Lilly's benefit—or to replace the supplier.

The company doesn't just extract better terms from suppliers. It has also been working more closely with them. Lilly long printed its own bottle labels, boxes, and pamphlets with information on dosages and precautions. But in 1993 it went to 100% outsourcing. Keller Crescent, a printing and packaging company in Evansville, Indiana, won 99% of Lilly's U.S. business. Eager to accommodate, Keller set up a 68,000-square-foot printing facility in Indianapolis, a 20-minute drive from Lilly's manufacturing plants.

Keller Crescent today holds most of Lilly's

(Cont.)

inventory of labels, pamphlets, and boxes, though the quantity it sits on has fallen 45% since 1993 and is still headed down. In return for its big capital investment, the supplier gets a long-term contract and the opportunity to peek at Lilly's production schedules.

This doesn't mean that Keller Crescent can sit back and assume that its position as Lilly's sole supplier is for keeps. Just last year, according to McCracken, Lilly scrutinized Keller Crescent's performance as part of a routine strategic-sourcing study. "We met with Keller Crescent and explained to them that we were going to review spending and decide if we needed to allocate differently. The possibility of switching suppliers was real, but at the end of the day we ended up not taking that course."

That's no surprise, for the partnership has been fruitful. One recent coup: The two companies kept their lines of communication open as the FDA finished putting the OK on a new antischizophrenia drug, Zyprexa. When approval came, Keller Crescent was able to leap on printing pamphlets for the packages, and the drug arrived on some pharmacy shelves within three days.

The big General Electric locomotive plant in Erie, Pennsylvania, has also been building intimate relationships with suppliers. One is Dominion Castings, a Hamilton, Ontario, unit of Chicago's NACO. GE Transportation Systems, as the locomotive operation is called, is the largest of its kind in the world, capable of annually rolling out 700 behemoths weighing up to 200 tons. NACO provides trucks, the complicated wheel assemblies on which a locomotive rides.

In 1993, when the two companies negotiated a long-term contract, NACO was responsible only for delivering truck casings, the H-shaped steel skeletons that hold a locomotive's wheels, axles, and motors in place. Managers at GE were impressed with NACO's work, as well as its enthusiasm for GE quality initiatives, such as the corporationwide Six Sigma program that aims to cut defects to 3.4 per million. When the time came to develop a high-adhesion truck—a truck with especially great pulling capacity—GE decided to let NACO participate in the development. Time to completion? One year, practically minutes as such projects go.

Then, in 1995, GE came up with a new approach—a steerable truck whose design allows a locomotive to take a curve at higher speed—and decided to outsource its manufacture. "It was a natural to let NACO help in the design process," says GE Transportation executive Jim Alvino. "We had developed a pretty damn good partnership." The development phase was another success. NACO integrated its computer systems so that it could look at GE's design drawings and quality information online. The company also let GE

engineers work at its own engineering center. "It was like they had become an extension of our organization," Alvin says.

NACO is taking on more and more of the production process for steerable trucks. Whereas at first it delivered only castings, it now assembles complete trucks for GE, including wheels, axles, and motors. In mid-1996, GE got an order from the CSX railroad system for 138 locomotives, including 80 with steerable trucks. GE and NACO worked together to achieve what Alvino calls flawless execution. "The trucks came in one day, and in the very same day, a locomotive sat on top of it," he says. "We carried no inventory."

GE, which says its partnership with NACO has delivered high product quality, solid design support, and a "favorable cost position," plans to keep upping the ante. By the end of this year GE will entrust NACO with procurement for all the parts for steerable trucks. "The NACO folks," Alvino sighs, "if I could clone them across the supplier base, it would make the job so much easier."

The NACO tie-up fits into a larger GE strategy that targets just-in-time delivery from suppliers and significant inventory reductions. In 1996, the demand-pull approach saved GE Transportation $20 million in inventory costs. This doesn't mean that suppliers are always left holding a bigger hot potato of inventory. Joseph A. Seher, NACO's CEO, says that because his company gets prompter notice of GE's requirements than in the past, it has taken advantage of the planning jump to push inventory responsibility back on its own suppliers. NACO's stocks are not up, says Seher, but down—by 40% in 1995, for example, for high-adhesion truck castings.

S upply-chain management takes a somewhat different twist at the A.W. Chesterton Co., a family-owned seal, pump, and packings manufacturer in Stoneham, Massachusetts, with about $200 million a year in sales. One important role of the company's seals and packings is to curb pollution from factories. Revamping its supply strategy with help from the PRTM consulting firm, Chesterton has whittled the number of vendors dramatically, from 1,300 in 1993 to 125 today. Since 1993, when the company got serious about its supply chain and other matters, inventories have fallen 35% and profits have tripled.

Chesterton's managers say they give service and quality twice as much importance as price when selecting suppliers. The company expects suppliers to advise it on matters of product design, which can represent 80% of manufacturing cost in the mechanical seals business. Suppliers sit on 80% of Chesterton's inventory of certain materials and deliver just in time. Two years ago the average lead

time for mechanical seals parts delivery was 12 to 16 weeks; now it's down to two to four weeks, and sometimes as little as 72 hours.

Is Chesterton squeezing its suppliers excessively? Senior executive vice president Greg Plakias shrugs. "If the supplier can't compete among our top three suppliers in price, quality, and service, they won't be able to work with us. Call that a squeeze if you want." Survival in the new era may give Chesterton little choice but to demand more. PRTM's Bill Helming likens the company's tactics to an A+ essay in a lesson he calls Supply Chain 201—the notion that truly successful supply-chain companies must run lean because they're part of someone else's chain. "We have to be in the top three suppliers for each of our customers too," says Plakias. "If we aren't, we can't be a preferred supplier."

So, while putting the pressure on Chesterton's own suppliers, Plakias and his team have spruced up service to the company's customers. These days they expect delivery within days or even hours. Given that Chesterton's seals, pumps, and packings are usually built to order—in some 30,000 possible configurations—this has been quite a challenge.

Chesterton has reorganized, cutting out 218 positions in the first major layoff in its 113-year history. With the help of money saved from this move and lower inventory costs, the company has created a set of cross-functional customer service centers, à la Eastman Chemical. It has also installed computer systems that allow customers to transmit drawings and engineering specs directly to the plant floor, where new, updated tools speed manufacturing.

Supply Chain 201 doesn't just dictate that you look at your customers' supply chains. It also urges you to look in the other direction, to your suppliers' needs. Take Ford Motor Co. as an example. As part of a lean manufacturing initiative, the company in late 1994 instituted something called In-Line Vehicle Sequencing (ILVS) at its Wixom, Michigan, plant that assembles Lincolns. While aimed at cutting Ford's manufacturing costs, ILVS gives suppliers important information they need to streamline their own supply chains.

Here's how it works. Customers at a dealership in St. Louis have ordered a burgundy Lincoln Continental, a blue one, and a brown one. The company routes the orders to the Wixom plant. At Wixom, materials planners determine that the three cars will need such items as matching interior-door trim. Six days before the cars are scheduled for assembly, Ford sends a requisition to the supplier of this item, Prince Corp. of Holland, Michigan, which makes interior-door trim for Lincoln Continentals and Town Cars. On the day of assembly, Prince delivers the trim to the point of use at Wixom, arranged in the same bur-

(Cont.)

gundy-blue-brown order in which Continentals will be assembled. The trim parts are placed on movable racks with other pieces that go into each car at that point on the line.

The advantage for Ford? Zero lead time and practically zero inventory. Whereas Wixom once used to hold three days' inventory of selected parts, it now keeps only enough for half a day. The advantage for suppliers? More reliable information to manage their own production and inventory. Once Ford sends an ILVS order to a supplier, it claims, the order does not change—ever. Says Chuck MacIver, Ford's North American vehicle and option scheduling manager: "Originally the suppliers didn't think we could hold the schedules firm. Now they have confidence in us, and they really like it."

Prince Corp. has been part of Ford's ILVS setup since the beginning. Mark Cooney, Prince's logistics coordinator, says, "The biggest benefit for us has been education. We're taking what we learn and applying it to our own supply base." That means making Prince's suppliers bend to its own zero-lead-time, zero-inventory regimen. While it's still too early to quantify gains, Cooney says that the "total supply chain has improved."

The new era, of course, has a harsher side. Speaking privately, many suppliers grouse that serving today's impatient, exacting, prying industrial customers is a headache. Surprisingly, though, some suppliers like demand-pull manufacturing, even though it would seem to expose them to disruptive new ups and downs in production. Wasn't life easier in bygone days, visitors ask, when producing for big inventories permitted smoother production schedules? Not really, says Prince's Cooney. Using a new scheduling system that takes industry forecasts and internal data into account, his company has been able to level out its production rate. Cooney says that Prince has not had any idle periods, not even in the third quarter of 1996, when Wixom was shut down part of the time for various reasons, including sagging Lincoln sales.

Cooney swears that he prefers the demand-pull environment to the old "push" system. The old way, he says, "the car companies would produce until they had exorbitant stocks. Then they would shut down for a month or two. When they ramped up again, they would come back at a faster pace because dealership lots would be empty. Now, with demand-pull, the peaks and valleys are more gentle."

So what will they teach in Supply Chain 301? How about: Act locally, think globally. In some industries these days, says Hal Sirkin, a Boston Consulting Group vice president, competition is between entire supply chains rather than between mere companies. "The chains are lining up on a worldwide basis," he says. Now might not be a bad time to jump onboard.

© 1997 Time Inc. All rights reserved.

Getting Information for
Marketing Decisions

DATA IS POWER.
JUST ASK FINGERHUT
It's able to offer credit cards to a lower-income market

For Marilyn Gnat, the Fingerhut catalog is a godsend. It has allowed the retired dime-store salesclerk from Eagle River, Wis., to buy everything from pots and pans to a teddy bear cookie jar with matching salt and pepper shakers—all on the installment plan. "When I started out, Fingerhut was the only place that would give me credit," says Gnat, who raised nine children on her modest income.

Fingerhut sells everything from toy phones for $20 to big-screen TVs for $2,000. But its real business is extending credit, at rates of about 24% a year, to people who would otherwise have to pay cash. Its catalogs list monthly payments in bold type and actual prices in fine print. Even a pair of $40 sneakers can be amortized over 13 months with payments of just $4.79 a month.

To serve its market, the $2 billion retailer has built a cutting-edge database that stores more than 500 pieces of information on each of more than 50 million active and potential customers. That allows Fingerhut Cos. to sort through its records and zero in on the best credit risks among America's low- and moderate-income households, its chosen niche since the Minnetonka (Minn.) company got its start in 1948. Now, it's banking on a new way to leverage its expertise in consumer credit: Fingerhut has quietly become a major issuer of credit cards.

Fingerhut, the second-largest consumer catalog marketer in the country behind J.C. Penney Co., gathers a lot more than names and addresses in its database. It collects demographic details such as age, marital status, and number of children. It tracks hobbies and birthdays and uses that knowledge to hit customers with personalized catalogs when they're most likely to buy. "Fingerhut is one of those pioneering companies that is making intense knowledge of their customer a core competency," says Thomas Blischok, a retail consultant at Coopers & Lybrand.

Early last year, Fingerhut launched its own co-branded Visa and MasterCard. The 750,000 accounts opened by yearend generated more than $500 million in receivables, making Fingerhut the nation's 23rd-largest issuer—and one of the few catering to lower-income consumers, without demanding collateral. The lender's yearend 1996 goal: 1 million accounts and $1 billion in receivables. "They're new to the card business, but they're old-timers in the credit business," says James Daly, editor of *Credit Card Management* magazine.

FINANCING. Still, mining this end of the market is risky. Credit-card issuers' bad-debt levels rose to 4.4% at the end of 1995, up from 3.7% a year earlier. Fingerhut is reserving for losses of about 6%. To finance its rapid buildup of customer debt, Fingerhut will spin off all or part of its stake in its credit-card unit through an initial public offering later this year. "We have our hands on a very successful business," brags Chairman and CEO Theodore Deikel.

He had better hope so. Deikel, the son-in-law of company co-founder Manny Fingerhut, has headed the company since 1990, when Fingerhut was spun off by Primerica Corp. after four years of stalled growth. By 1993, Deikel had increased sales 50%, to $1.8 billion. But in 1994, startup costs associated with a cable-TV shopping venture and the credit-card business knocked third-quarter earnings down by 50%. The stock fell 22% in a day. Last year, it got hit again by double-digit increases in paper and postage costs.

Deikel, 60, laid off 200 middle managers, tightened credit criteria, and cut back the number of catalogs mailed. That helped push earnings up 11% last year, to $50.9 million on revenue of $2.1 billion, though that's 32% below 1993's earnings. So far this year, sales have picked up, and consumer delinquencies have stabilized. But Wall Street isn't convinced. Fingerhut stock is hovering around

14 a share, down from a 1994 high of more than 33. What does Deikel think about the stock price? "What's below ridiculous?" he sneers. Still, Fingerhut has big plans. "It all goes back to the database," says Deikel, who predicts the company may someday be a major player in car loans, insurance—and even home mortgages. Watch out, Citibank.
By Susan Chandler in Minnetonka, Minn.

Reprinted from June 3, 1996 issue of *Business Week* by special permission, copyright © 1996 by McGraw-Hill, Inc.

FAMILY FILE

The $2 billion retailer's database stores scores of facts on each customer

NAME, ADDRESS, SOCIAL SECURITY NUMBER

LAST PURCHASE

NUMBER OF KIDS

HOUSEHOLD INCOME

PAYMENT HISTORY

BIRTHDATES OF FAMILY MEMBERS

SPANISH OR ENGLISH CATALOG

ACCEPTS TELEMARKETING CALLS

New passenger services keep fliers in touch

By Donna Rosata
USA TODAY

41,000 FEET OVER FLORIDA— "New evidence in the Simpson case, new theories and a different view of the courtroom players," proclaims Greta Van Susteren, co-host of CNN's *Burden of Proof*, on three TV screens.

This is up-to-the-minute TV news, but the story here is who's watching it: 110 passengers on this Delta Air Lines Boeing 767, the only airliner in the world showing live TV.

Ready or not, fliers soon may grasp yet another umbilical cord to Mother Earth. Fading fast is an era when you could be out of touch with the boss, loved ones and the latest news because you were in a plane. Communication services already common on many domestic flights—such as seat phones, ground-to-air paging and fax services—are killing excuses for being out of the loop. Live TV will knock off another.

This jet—called the Spirit of Delta because employees bought it for the company in 1982—is a flying laboratory for cutting-edge passenger services. Delta is two months into a six-month test of DirecTV, which operates like the direct broadcast satellite TV seen in homes. Delta also is testing electrical outlets in first-class seats so fliers can plug laptops in and save their batteries. There's a phone in arm's reach of every seat. Passengers can be paged from the ground, too.

Delta isn't the only airline closing the communications loop. Continental Airlines will begin installing live TV this spring. Passengers will choose up to 24 channels. In January, American Airlines will put power ports in first class and business class on international flights. British Airways and Singapore Airlines both are testing an interactive entertainment system that will let fliers gamble, play trivia games with other passengers, shop and track the progress of a flight.

Catching the Spirit of Delta isn't easy because it doesn't fly the same route every day. And Delta doesn't know more than 24 hours in advance where the Spirit will be flying.

SEEING IT NOW

First-class passenger Fernando Fernandez is thrilled when he finds out Delta will be broadcasting live TV on this 3-hour, 10-minute flight from Atlanta to San Juan, Puerto Rico. Fernandez, a Norcross, Ga., businessman, has flown Delta on this route three times the past month. "I don't want to see *Mission: Impossible*

one more time. Frequent fliers need more options when they fly," Fernandez says. TV beats watching the same movie again. "I like to keep up with what's going on in the world."

Across the aisle, Joe McCloskey is thumbing through *George* magazine with a Marilyn Monroe-esque Drew Barrymore on the cover. He's bored. "I'd love to watch ESPN or CNN. I'd pay for it," says McCloskey, who is headed home to San Juan. McCloskey will have to wait to get his sports fix. Delta only has the rights to show CNN, Headline News, Discovery Channel and Nick at Nite.

After flight attendants deliver meals of short ribs and steamed vegetables, passengers throughout the plane are given complimentary headsets. TV programs are shown on three large screens spaced equally through the plane. A commercial for Cycle dog food flicks on the screen. A cooking show on the Discovery Channel appears before CNN comes on. Van Susteren is on, chatting with Joseph Bosco, author of *A Problem of Evidence*, a new book about the O.J. Simpson trial. The picture is sharp and clear.

In seats 2A and 2B, Ross and Lydia Buckley immediately put on their headsets. The couple are headed for vacation in Nevis, an island east of Puerto Rico. The Buckleys think live TV will really catch on in planes. "Bookstores are going to be disappointed," Ross says.

Everyone isn't glued to the screen. Back in coach, the man in 25B is snoozing. A father in 23A is trying to keep his daughter occupied with a coloring book. But many of the 94 coach passengers are watching CNN attentively.

Jodi Dunlap, Delta's technology expert, is aboard to monitor the live TV system. "A lot of people still think they're watching a taped show. We're trying to get the rights to show the World Series . . . later this month," says Dunlap, who notes that live broadcasts of the Republican and Democratic conventions were popular with passengers in August.

A commercial for American Airlines flashes on the screen. "See, we don't edit anything," says Maurice Maige from Hughes Avicom, which helped Delta design the TV system. Maige says he helped install a system for TWA to screen the first in-flight movie in 1961.

What Maige says isn't quite true. If there's an airline accident, CNN has agreed to notify Delta's operations center before CNN airs the news. The operations center then contacts pilots, who will shut the TV system down. Passengers will be told only that the satellite feed has been interrupted. "We don't want passengers to find out about an accident while they're on a plane," Dunlap says.

Delta says it plans to install video screens in the backs of seats on this plane this spring so passengers could watch any channel they want. But it costs nearly $3 million to install such a system for an entire plane. "We think we can recoup the cost of the system if we can get passengers to pay for it. But we can't buy the system if passengers aren't willing to pay," says Kathie Lonvick, project manager for Delta. Lonvick says Delta likely will charge passengers in coach $5 to $8. First- and business-class passengers will get live TV free.

"I'd pay for live TV, but I still won't watch the commercials," says coach passenger Minerva Ramirez, a West Virginia doctor.

On Headlines News, a gruesome video of fighting on the West Bank is being shown. Then the screen goes blank. But it isn't a problem with the system. "Passengers still want their movie," says flight attendant Martina Goscha as *Mission: Impossible* appears on the screen. Plus, DirecTV can't broadcast outside the USA, so Delta can't show TV programs once this plane is over water.

POWER IN THE SEAT

Flying the Spirit from San Juan back to Atlanta, Jim Darby is thrilled as he watches the battery on his laptop charge up. Darby, sitting in first class, is using an adapter Delta gave him to plug his laptop into a power port on the seat. A green light shows the power is on. But the outlet, placed about calf-level on the front of his seat, is an awkward reach.

Darby is having a problem sending the electronic mail he composed on his way to the airport. He plugged his phone line into a jack on the GTE Airfone in the armrest, but couldn't get a connection to send the e-mail.

But his colleague, Angela Brav, likes the power ports: "I fly to the West Coast a lot, and I refuse to carry heavy batteries for my laptop."

Goscha, a Delta flight attendant for 17 years, is glad Delta is testing a power source for laptops. Fliers often ask for a place to plug in theirs. "Passengers are always trying to go into the bathroom and plug their computer into the outlet for shavers. It just blows their computer up," she says.

Delta is considering installing power ports in first-class and business-class seats on international flights. It will be a while before coach fliers get power ports, and when they do, they'll have to pay to use them. "These systems are so expensive to install. We have to make sure it will generate enough revenue for us to recoup our costs," Lonvick says.

PHONING HOME

The Spirit of Delta's phone system has some bugs. Several passengers using the phone to call colleagues get cut off in mid-conversation. Passengers can receive calls forwarded from a home or office phone, too. It's like being paged. You register from the seat you're in so calls can be routed to you. The phone rings and the caller's number appears on the handset. You decide whether to call back. The cost is a flat $15 if you call back; no charge if you don't. But several attempts by one passenger to receive a call from the ground didn't work. Brav says she often has problems with phone connections on planes. GTE, which provides the phone service, says the problems happened because the flight's course between San Juan and Atlanta took the jet over water and out of range of GTE's ground stations.

That's no problem for travelers who like being out of touch. "You can't work 24 hours a day. When I'm on the plane, I want to relax," says A.P. Singh, of Huntsville, Ala.

But fliers like Singh are going to find it harder to hide. Delta says it plans to give fliers access to the Internet from an in-seat video system. Now, a passenger with the right software in their laptop can tap the Internet by connecting a laptop into a jack on the seat phone. But it's an awkward system. "We want people to pull up the Delta web site, plan trips and book tickets in the air, just like they can do from their home PC," Lonvick says.

Coming to your airplane seat: DirectPC.

Copyright 1996, *USA Today.* Reprinted with permission.

33

Retailers in search of customers for life

by Bruce Horovitz
USA TODAY

Kids want everything. The right clothes. The right Christmas and Hanukkah gifts. The right car to be driven to school in.

Because so many kids seem to want so much so often, it is kids who have become wanted. They are wanted by virtually every major company in America. As customers. For life.

Right now, between Thanksgiving and Christmas, is when the drumbeat of marketing to kids sounds loudest. "The influence of kids goes up when the jingle bells ring," says James McNeal, author of *Kids as Customers*.

But even after the holidays are over, kids will be followed, observed, scrutinized and lured by familiar brand names — such as Levi's, Sega, Mattel and even General Motors — in ways unimaginable just a few years ago.

There's no kid-glove protection from this effort. Just a grinding need for new customers that forever has changed the way many of the nation's biggest marketers treat kids as young as pre-schoolers.

Once upon a time, kid marketing was limited to toys and breakfast cereals. Now, marketers realize kids as young as two can influence everything from where the family will vacation to the next car in the garage.

By age 2, kids are nagging their folks for the latest gizmo they saw hyped on TV, says Dan Acuff, author of *What Kids Buy and Why*. And this is just the beginning of kids' struggle for control over what once were solely parental decisions. It should be no surprise that many of the nation's biggest marketers are siding with the kids.

In many families, this power struggle reaches a crescendo when the Christmas tree goes up and the Hanukkah candles are lighted. That's why toys ads are hogging the airwaves. The typical Saturday morning television viewer is seeing a TV spot for a $110-plus toy, K'NEX Hyperspace Training Tower, four times a week right now, estimates Paul Kurnit, president of the ad agency Griffin Bacal, which created the ad.

"Kids like frequency," says Kurnit, an expert in ads that target kids. "This is the time of year to be in sight and in mind."

But critics say there's no proper time of year to chase kids. "It's hard to believe that so many marketers are sitting around thinking of ways to invade young peoples' space at a time youngsters are just trying to figure out who they are," says Marianne Manilov of the Center for Commercial Free Public Education, a consumer group.

Driving this youth frenzy is one thing: economics. And the amount of money kids spend or influence is far, far greater than most marketers have previously believed.

Until now, it was widely believed that kids were spending or influencing spending of about $150 billion annually. But new research by McNeal, who many regard as the nation's top authority on kid spending, dwarfs earlier estimates. In 1997, the nation's estimated 34 million children age 12 and under will have spent or influenced spending of a record $500 billion, says the marketing professor at Texas A&M University.

That $500 billion is about what Americans will spend on all forms of legalized gambling this year.

But marketing to kids is no gamble. It's regarded as a must. Overall spending for kids is growing at a torrid 20% annual clip, says McNeal. At that rate, it could surpass $1 trillion in less than five years.

KIDS VIEWING 20,000 ADS PER YEAR

It's no accident, then, that the typical American child sees 20,000 ads a year, says the American Academy of Pediatrics. And marketers are aware that TV spots targeting kids lead to peer pressure as early as age 3, says Victor Strasburger, professor of pediatrics at University of New Mexico.

Marketers also know that kids form brand loyalties early — sometimes as early as 2, says Debbie Solomon, senior researcher at the giant ad firm J. Walter Thompson. The majority of American adults, she says, still use the same toothpaste, peanut butter and canned soup that their folks bought.

"There is not a company on the globe that does not have some vested interest in marketing to kids," says Devorah Goldman, senior editor of the *Selling to Kids* newsletter.

Perhaps that helps to explain why, like never before, major marketers are stepping over the invisible line that once separated them from the private lives of America's youngest consumers. Consider:

▲ They're in the bedroom. Mattel commissioned a global study in a dozen countries — from the United States to China — where it looked at everything that youngsters had hanging on their bedroom walls. One purpose of the study was to see what brands kids were using, says Gene Del Vecchio, who creates Mattel ads for Barbie at Ogilvy Mather.

▲ They're taking pictures. Levi's supplies kids with throw-away cameras and video cameras and asks them to record diaries about how they and their friends spend their time. "Kids serve as reporters for us by showing us what's going on in their own world," says Andre Richards, marketing research manager for Levi Strauss Co.

▲ They're spending the night. While consulting for Esprit, teen marketing expert Marian Salzman had three girls — all about 14 — stay with her in a guest bedroom of her New York apartment for six weeks. The girls also worked as interns at her teen research firm. "This gave me an incredible insider's perspective," says Salzman, now at Young Rubicam.

▲ They're watching on weekends. Several years ago, Pepsi's ad agency, BBDO, arranged for about 30 high school kids to spend an entire weekend at a posh hotel in New Jersey, along with adult chaperones. The agency talked to them about new Pepsi ads. Many of the sessions were videotaped.

▲ They're using the schools. Grade schools in Connecticut have, for a $5,000 fee and some real-world courses in media, given marketers wide access to interview 10- to 12-year-old students after school inside classrooms. The money funds after school activities.

▲ They're following on-line. Every Wednesday afternoon, Nickelodeon has on-line chats with 150 kids between 7- and 11-years-old. The most recent was about their favorite movies. The network even has asked kids to send photos of their pets. "Knowing what kids want is critical to our success," explains Cyma Zarghami, general manager of Nickelodeon.

▲ They're amassing huge databases. Sega of America has dialogues on-line with kids, capturing thousands of names every day for future prospects. Since the program began this year, Sega has been capturing 2,000 names per week of kids aged 12-17, says Anne Moellering, director of marketing.

▲ They're getting kids to do the work. Many marketers, including Eveready's Energizer battery, have retained the research firm Kid2Kid, which hires kids as young as 14 to moderate focus groups of peers. Four years ago, Kid2Kid was one of the first to test this controversial format. Now, says Kid2Kid president Jim Holbrook, "it's become just another tool."

▲ They're paying for information. Some marketers, including Levi's, have handed kids $50 to $100 cash, then asked the kids to record how they spent every nickel of it.

KIDS ON THE COMPANY PAYROLL

All of this is happening with parental approval.

Levi Strauss has tapped 700 kids nationwide — ages 11 to 19 — to report to the jeans' giant on their habits, hangups and day-to-day lives. Kids are recommended to the company by other kids Levi's already talked to. They're paid $20 to $100 to complete a research project.

Renee Cruz, a 15-year-old 10th grader from Miami, Fl., was paid $75 to photograph her outfits every day and glue the pictures in a scrapbook. To make sure the task was done right, Levi's even sent her the gluestick.

When the project was done, two Levi's representatives came to her house and spent about an hour talking to her in her bedroom. They mostly wanted to see the clothes in her closet. And they videotaped the session.

"I think of it as an even exchange," says Cruz. "I got $75," she says, "and they got a lesson on what's cool."

Never mind that Cruz doesn't own a single pair of Levi's.

Across the country, in Santa Monica, Calif., Levi's also has 14-year-old Valerie Adeff, a 9th grader, on its trends panel.

She's convinced that Levi's listened closely to her advice. Less than a year after she showed Levi's a pair of funky, baby-blue corduroy bellbottoms that she bought at a thrift store, she spotted a remarkably similar Levi's version of the same pants at the mall near her house.

But this kind of research is not foolproof.

That's why many companies, without letting parents know, are collecting personal information from kids who browse Internet web sites. In a Federal Trade Commission survey of 126 Web sites, 86% were collecting names, e-mail and postal addresses and phone numbers, the agency reported this week. But only 4% asked for parental permission.

That's one key reason why the FTC plans to review Internet information-collection practices for a report to Congress in March. The agency will investigate the extent to which Internet sites, including children's sites, are posting privacy policies.

This new arsenal of sophisticated marketing weaponry is not kid's stuff. But many marketers convincingly claim that children are empowered — not exploited — by being brought into the decision-making process at every level. When kids help decide the look of the next style of blue jeans or the tone of some video game ad, that's giving them a vote, they say.

"You can't force a trend to kids," says Rena Karl, executive editor of the *Marketing to Kids Report,* a monthly newsletter out of Encinitas, Cal. "Kids are the tail that wags the dog."

Kids grouped by their advertising ages

All youth marketers want to know how to raise kids' eyebrows.

There is no single answer. But Dan Acuff, co-author of *What Kids Buy and Why,* offers these tips on how marketers target kids through the years.

▲ Birth to age 2: Appeal to Mom and Dad. Parental agendas for gifts for their kids rank in this order: safety, love, stimulation.

▲ Ages 3 to 7: The "nag" factor begins. Kids nag parents for things they see advertised on TV. The influence of kids on parental buying decisions increases. This is an age of fantasy, and a time when kids seek more power and control. Cabbage Patch Kids and Power Rangers were hits because they appealed to those needs.

▲ Ages 8 and 9: Kids get attracted to "causes," and seek toys and games that fulfill these goals. It's why Johnson & Johnson is developing Endangered Species shampoo for kids.

▲ Ages 10 to 12: There's a new interest in games of challenge, and sports are important. Figures like Michael Jordan are featured in ads.

▲ Ages 13 to 15: Kids have a growing need to "fit in" with friends. At the same time, there is a push for self-identity. Brand-consciousness takes over. Apparel and music become enormously important.

▲ Ages 16 to 19: Childhood's over. No more toys and games — unless they're CD players or pagers. There's a longing for controversy — sensed by marketers like Calvin Klein.

EVEN SANTA GETS INTO THE ACT

Critics charge it's all turning the nation's kids into the sum total of their spending power.

"It's not about love or caring," says Alex Molnar, author of *Giving Kids the Business.* "It's about selling."

At some of America's biggest malls, Santa isn't doling out candy canes. Instead, at several malls in Northern Virginia, he's handing out samples of Post Cereal's new Honey Nut Shredded Wheat cereal. In a gift bag, of course.

"We could have put 20 more ads in the bags," brags Clarke Green, merchandising director at the White Flint mall near Bethesda, Md., "but we didn't."

As Wall Street pressures companies for bigger profits, many firms are reaching out to a segment of the population they previously ignored.

Also driving this youth marketing mania: parental guilt. A new world of dual-income families has left parents anxious to make up for so much time away.

Laments Donald F. Roberts, professor of communications at Stanford. "The dominant message kids in this country hear is, `Buy, buy, buy.' "

Especially on Saturday mornings.

The cost of 30-second commercial slots on network Saturday morning kids shows can increase 50% during the hectic fourth quarter. Ad industry executives refer to these last eight weeks of the year the "Hard Eight" because toy makers and others fight so hard for the key Saturday morning time slots.

Some ads, such as Mattel's spot for the Workin' Out Barbie Doll, can take four months to create. The ad, which opens with a life-size, life-like Barbie exercising on the beach, is made with the aid of computerized graphics imagery.

"Some may cry exploitation or materialism," says adman Del Vecchio, "but for a little kid — on a cold, dark night — who gets to hug her Barbie doll, this is just a fantasy fulfilled."

No detail is too small when it comes to kids marketing. Ask McDonald's. The giveaways in its current Happy Meal promotion for the re-release of Disney's *Little Mermaid* were the result of intensive research. That included interviewing hundreds of kids as young as 4.

Interviews convinced McDonald's executives to sprinkle some Happy Meals with special gold-painted versions of the *Little Mermaid* characters. Most of the Happy Meals get the characters painted the same color they are in the film.

Some parents have had it with all this marketing to kids madness.

Take Sloane Smith Morgan, of Oakland, Calif. Her 2 1/2-year-old son, Paris, recently received a birthday gift from Aunt Fern. The gift: a book on counting.

But it's not about counting numbers. It's about counting M&Ms. The book, *The M&M's Counting Board Book,* looks exactly like a package of M&Ms. Each page is dotted with photos of M&Ms.

Morgan threw out the book. She didn't want her son to learn to count M&Ms. "My son can learn to count using grains of sand, beans or his fingers," she says, "but he's not going to learn with M&Ms."

Copyright 1997, *USA Today.* Reprinted with permission.

Novel P&G Product Brings Dry Cleaning Home

BY YUMIKO ONO

Staff Reporter of THE WALL STREET JOURNAL

Procter & Gamble Co., the laundry detergent powerhouse, wants to take a spin with all those clothes that normally get sent to the dry cleaner.

In February, the consumer-products giant plans to begin test-sales of a product it hopes will open up a huge new market: home cleaning kits to be used in household dryers. Dubbed the Dryel Fabric Care System, the kit contains pieces of moist cloth which are tossed into an accompanying nylon bag along with dirty clothes.

As the dryer tumbles, P&G says, heat-activated vapors emerge from the cloth, penetrate the clothes and "volatilize," or remove, odor molecules. Instructions urge consumers to remove spotty stains first with stain remover, provided in a separate bottle.

The stakes are high for P&G, which has been searching for the next blockbuster to add to its annual $35.8 billion sales, but has recently been criticized for reacting slowly to emerging trends. Research for Dryel (pronounced "Dry-ELLE" stretches back five years, P&G says — including testing the product with 10,000 consumers and 36,000 loads of clothing.

One challenge will be marketing Dryel without setting off alarms in consumers' minds about toxic fumes and other potential health hazards sometimes linked to conventional dry cleaning. P&G officials say Dryel doesn't use perchlorethylene, or "perc," the toxic solvent used in most of the nation's 37,000 professional dry-cleaning plants. They won't say exactly what Dryel does contain, other than "biodegradable wetting agents" commonly used in other household products.

P&G officials stress that Dryel isn't meant to replace the corner dry cleaner, especially for really tough stains. "We view this as a great complement, to let consumers care for their [dry clean-only] products at home," says Jamie Egasti, a marketing director for P&G's laundry and cleaning products division.

But the $8 billion professional dry-cleaning industry is already sweating. Dryel "will have an impact — how big or small depends on how good their marketing is," says William Seitz, executive director of the Neighborhood Cleaners Association International, a New York trade group. "Procter, when it comes to marketing, knows its way around the terrain," Mr. Seitz adds.

Mr. Seitz, a 53-year veteran of the industry, says that while Dryel may not clean clothes as thoroughly, it could steal away the business of clothes that are merely stained by cigarette smoke or need to be freshened up.

Mr. Seitz says P&G officials approached him yesterday about working together to expand the entire business for dry-clean-only clothes, and perhaps even sell Dryel through professional dry cleaners. He doubts his members would want to sell a competing product in their outlets, but says he plans to discuss the issue.

The maker of Tide and Cheer says its research revealed that only 40% of Americans regularly go to the dry cleaners — another 40% never go. And as many as 70% of consumers, P&G's statistics show, avoid buying dry-clean-only clothes because they are such a hassle to care for.

Interviews found that some people go to interesting lengths to avoid the expense and trouble of lugging garments to the dry cleaner. Some consumers simply wash and iron clothes meant to be dry cleaned. Some people wear the same sweater or suit time after time before dropping them onto the dry cleaners counter.

To persuade consumers to break with tradition by throwing silk shirts into the dryer, P&G plans to bombard consumers in its test market, Columbus, Ohio, with samples and product demonstrations in shopping malls. Ads, created by Chicago's Leo Burnett, are expected to carry the tagline, "A fresh new choice for dry clean only fabric care."

A starter kit will cost $10 to $11 and can be used for 16 garments. By contrast, dry cleaners can charge $5 or more per garment.

Other companies have been trying to develop similar dry-cleaning alternative products for years, with spotty results. During the 1970s, some manufacturers created do-it-yourself dry-cleaning machines that looked like washing machines, and installed them in laundromats. But the effort fizzled after people discovered their clothes came out smelling of solvent — and not much cleaner.

For the last three years, a company called Creative Products Resource Inc. in Fairfield, N.J., has been selling its own dry-cleaning kit, first through the QVC shopping network and now through supermarkets and drug stores in East coast cities from Maine to Baltimore. Custom Cleaner, as it is called, also uses the dryer, and includes a plastic bag and moist cloth containing ingredients found in a window cleaner and a seaweed extract called carageenan. Custom Cleaner sales are expected to reach $4 million this year, the company says.

Reprinted by permission of *The Wall Street Journal,* © 1997 Dow Jones & Company, Inc. All Rights Reserved Worldwide.

Test Market USA

By Betsy Spethmann

Kathy Jo Brihn is laughing in her car, but when she walks into the supermarket in her hometown of Eau Claire, Wis., her face goes blank. As she strolls through the aisles to pick up a box of macaroni & cheese and a tube of toothpaste, she never drops her poker face. Kathy Jo is one of the few people in town, or in the whole country, who knows which products have been brought to Eau Claire for top-secret test marketing, but she never gives it away. She's an unassuming woman who looks more like the head of the PTA than the head of one of the country's most extensive product-testing operations, but her code of confidentiality would impress the CIA.

"It may seem like we're paranoid, but it's ingrained into us. What we see and hear at work stays at work," she said. "When I interview new employees, I always apologize that I can't tell them more about what the job really involves."

Ask to see the 30,000-square-foot warehouse and the staff breaks out in a sweat. Little wonder: It houses manufacturers' whole inventories, with as many as 100 SKUs in test at a time, all ordered, stocked and policed by IRI. Manufacturers get so skittish about keeping new products hush-hush, one even ran a test here without telling the local sales rep.

New products is one of few growth avenues left to packaged good companies pressured by Wall Street to increase profits. Downsizing and ECR have cut costs, and private label precludes price hikes. "They can't expect category growth, economic growth, price increases or cutting costs to carry the day anymore," said Jim Findley, IRI president of testing services. "New product development is key, but the industry's lousy at introducing new products."

Of all the products introduced in 1992 by the top 10 ad-

> **The fate of the nation's new packaged goods is determined by results in Anywhere, America. Like Eau Claire, Wis., population 57,000.**

vertisers, 72% failed, and 55% of line extensions failed, IRI reports. Less than 1% of new brands earn $200 million or more in the first two years. At about $15 million a crack to introduce a new product (not even including the cost of product itself), that's not great odds on the ROI.

"One reason failure rates are so high is because marketers want to rollout products very quickly; they're in a huge hurry because of the pressure they feel to perform financially," Findley said. But a heap of failures doesn't do

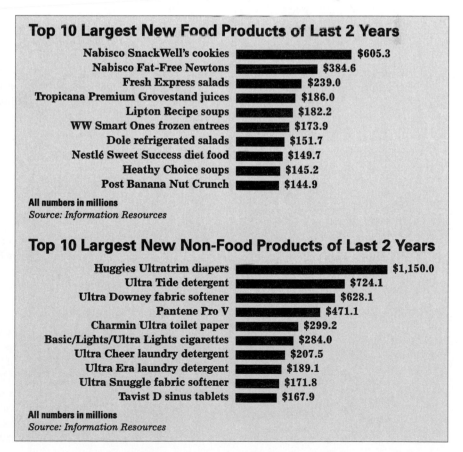

Top 10 Largest New Food Products of Last 2 Years

Product	Sales
Nabisco SnackWell's cookies	$605.3
Nabisco Fat-Free Newtons	$384.6
Fresh Express salads	$239.0
Tropicana Premium Grovestand juices	$186.0
Lipton Recipe soups	$182.2
WW Smart Ones frozen entrees	$173.9
Dole refrigerated salads	$151.7
Nestlé Sweet Success diet food	$149.7
Heathy Choice soups	$145.2
Post Banana Nut Crunch	$144.9

All numbers in millions
Source: Information Resources

Top 10 Largest New Non-Food Products of Last 2 Years

Product	Sales
Huggies Ultratrim diapers	$1,150.0
Ultra Tide detergent	$724.1
Ultra Downey fabric softener	$628.1
Pantene Pro V	$471.1
Charmin Ultra toilet paper	$299.2
Basic/Lights/Ultra Lights cigarettes	$284.0
Ultra Cheer laundry detergent	$207.5
Ultra Era laundry detergent	$189.1
Ultra Snuggle fabric softener	$171.8
Tavist D sinus tablets	$167.9

All numbers in millions
Source: Information Resources

(Cont.)

Information Resources Inc. was founded on product testing in the early '80s, when scanners were new and scarce. BehaviorScan, the flagship of the testing division, accounts for 82% of all tests. But business has gone down in recent years after scanners sprouted up everywhere and manufacturers eager to cut costs took a lot of testing in-house.

"They think they can just put the product in a market and watch scanner data, but there are a lot of elements you can't count on," said Jim Findley, president of testing services for Chicago-based IRI. That gives marketers a false read on performance about half the time. IRI's eight BehaviorScan markets get an accurate read about 94% of the time, Findley said, because so many elements of the mix—advertising, number and size of stores, shopper demographics—are tracked or controlled.

Eau Claire, Wis.: Cedar Rapids, Iowa; Grand Junction, Colo.; Visalia, Calif.: Rome, Ga.; Marion, Ind.; Pittsfield, Mass.; Midland, Texas. Why did IRI settle on these relatively obscure towns?

"We chose markets that are representative of their region, in demographics and in the number and type of stores. The right mix of chains and independents," Findley said. "They're relatively isolated towns, with their own newspapers and cable TV so we can control ad support. Any they're small enough that manufacturers don't have to invest too much in media support, and need to make only a small batch of product."

Rome and Visalia can't test TV, and advertisers have to buy Atlanta newspapers to reach Rome residents, but the rest of the towns are isolated enough to blanket just through local media.

IRI always tests a product in at least two markets. To pick which ones are appropriate, it researches category data to find markets that best represent that category's national sales. "Brand managers usually want to go into the highest-indexing markets because the brand will do best there," Findley said. "Hey, they're the champions of the brand, they really want it to succeed. But we have to make sure to get the most accurate data we can, not necessarily the best product performance."

Most often these days, marketers are testing advertising rather than new products. One manufacturer is going into its third year of previewing the next year's advertising and promotional campaign before rolling out the ads.

much for the bottom line, so thorough testing is coming back into favor.

"We've been through three cycles with a few manufacturers who go out and test on their own, and then come back," Findley said. "They're very lean these days, so they don't have the internal testing expertise they did 10 years ago."

That's just fine for the guinea pigs in Eau Claire, the 4,000 families in this quiet town of 57,000 about 90 miles east of Minneapolis that get first crack at the latest from R&D. These hand-picked panel members show their "Shoppers' Hotline" card at checkout; every purchase is tagged with the shopper's six-digit number, every coupon bagged for data entry back at IRI's inconspicuous office, tucked away in a residential neighborhood. IRI has retailer contracts to do about 100 tests a year in the seven groceries and five drugstores, and is negotiating with the Wal-Mart, Target and two Shopkos in town.

Brihn and her 85-member crew have three goals as they put test products on shelves: Be normal, be normal, be normal. Anything that makes a product stand out, or changes the way consumer panelists shop, throws off the data. The staff, overwhelmingly female, nurtures new products like babies. "We baby the products, do everything we can to make them fly," Brihn said. They negotiate hard with store managers to get the end-aisle display or number of facings a manufacturer wants, and then when they're shopping, "the store managers tease us; they'll say, 'Aha! I don't see that in your cart,'" said Sue Norgaard, assistant market manager.

Three retail test coordinators each oversee a grocery, drugstore and mass merchandiser, acting as the retailers' main contact and maintaining each product on shelves. Each week they scan every product that's on display, using a handheld computer to record UPCs and display location. They also collect data for customized reports, whatever variables a marketer wants to track: number of facings, size and type of display, shelf location for itself or competitors. "We don't give any more competitive data than anyone could get just walking in the store and looking at the shelf," Brihn said. But this is no casual stroll through the store.

The 50-person data entry department keys in every packaged good ad in newspapers for 17 markets in the Great Lakes and North Central regions, noting the ad's size, any coupon offers and the most excruciating details on the product: flavors, sizes, type of discount. Data on product movement, displays and ad features for every product in the market is transmitted daily to IRI's Chicago headquarters. Somewhere in that discreet little building there's 14 years worth of data on every product that's moved through every store in town, and two years worth of every ad that ever ran in the 17 markets the Eau Claire office tracks.

IRI maintains its own TV studio in each market, splicing in TV spots to target Shoppers' Hotline households. The system uses two cable TV channels to override regularly scheduled network, local and cable TV spots with test TV spots. The system is so precise it can run a TV spot in one household and skip the next-door neighbor's.

Brihn said manufacturers have done a lot of sampling in the last year, but like the rest of the business,

(Cont.)

that's cyclical. The best part of the job is hosting brand managers who come to see their pet projects come alive on the store shelves. Sometimes they'll pump IRI staffers for info on competitors' products, but Brihn swears they get nothing. BehaviorScan clients get category exclusivity for a certain time period, so no one else is testing in their category at the same time. All competitive data is given in aggregate, so manufacturers never see their competitors' sales figures, Findley said.

There are a few improvements IRI wants to make in the system. It needs to be faster and cheaper, Findley said, to suit today's hurried-up, slimmed down corporate environment. Tests now run for $200,000 to $500,000 and average three to six months for new products, a year for ad testing. And the system needs to track mass merchandiser sales better. The stores will stock product, but haven't agreed to process Shoppers' Hotline cards.

"Wal-Mart is growing so fast they don't want to reprogram their system to include us, and don't need the money we offer as an incentive," Findley said. "We're talking with them and Kmart, offering to do tests in exchange for data." Kmart, which spends nearly $40 million on Sunday circulars, is most interested, he said.

At checkout in Eau Claire, Brihn shows her Shoppers' Hotline card, pays for her toothpaste and pasta, and watches the cashier put her coupons and receipt in a bag. As she walks out of the store, Brihn starts to smile. She gets into the car, pops a piece of bubble gum in her mouth, and then she's laughing again.

© 1995 ASM Communications, Inc. Used with permission from *Brandweek* magazine.

36

Preparing for 2000, Census Bureau Tests Carrots vs. Sticks

By John Pierson
Staff Reporter of The Wall Street Journal

Picture two envelopes:

One is imprinted with a bright yellow circle (like a smiley-face button) enclosing white letters that say: "Count me in!" The other bears a black-bordered rectangle surrounding bold, black letters that warn: "YOUR RESPONSE IS REQUIRED BY LAW."

Which one are you more likely to open?

The Census Bureau is field testing these and other envelopes (with test questionnaires inside) to determine what package it will drop through the mail slots of 120 million U.S. households on a day in the spring of 2000. During the past census, in 1990, only 65% of Americans mailed back the census form, a significant drop from 78% in 1970. Enumerators are hired to go door-to-door in search of the missing, but every silent household they find costs the government $200, compared with the $2 it spends on counting a household by mail.

A lot rides on the census, including state and community shares of federal funds for schools, housing, hospitals and services to children and old people — as well as the number of representatives each state sends to Congress.

So, since 1991, the bureau has redesigned and tested a variety of alternatives to the 1990 package, in search of the right balance of carrot and stick, simplicity and comprehensiveness that will increase the rate of response to the mailing. By the middle of the decade, Congress wasn't favorably impressed with the results.

Waving one of the test forms at a hearing last year, Republican Rep. Hal Rogers of Kentucky, who heads the House subcommittee that handles money for the census, told census officials that it looked as though it had been designed by someone with "a doctoral degree in how to confuse people."

Since then, the bureau has increased its efforts toward a more successful tally in 2000. It sought advice from private pollsters but found their input unpromising. Private companies usually poll by telephone instead of mail, limit their calls to a sample of perhaps 2,000 people and are happy with a 2% response, says Martha Farnsworth Riche, director of the census and a former national editor of American Demographics magazine. "We have to count 100%," she says.

So the bureau turned to consultant Don Dillman, a former census employee and director of the social and economic sciences research center at Washington State University, Pullman. Mr. Dillman believes in providing a census form with a "very clear navigational flow" — unlike the 1990 multicolumn short form, which folded out to 28 inches.

A Dillman form being tested has a different page for each person in the household and uses white spaces in a light green background as "targets" wherever answers — check marks or letters — are required. Ms. Riche praises the design as providing "the bones" for the 2000 census form.

Over the past year, the bureau has also sought design help from a team comprising graphic designer Sylvia Harris Woodard and Two Twelve Associates, both of New York. The team has provided "meat" on the Dillman bones, says Ms. Riche. One of the team's packages now being tested includes the use of bright yellow, pale yellow and royal blue, along with black and white. With icons and words, the form's cover tells people how they benefit from the census.

Even as the test is under way, however, some of the design team's meat has begun to stick in Washington's craw. The "Count me in!" button on the envelope has drawn fire; it will have to be replaced by something "more official," a census official says. "We've softened that form too much; we've got to beef it

up," Ms. Riche says. To save money, she adds, the team's suggested color scheme could lose its royal blue.

Rep. Rogers has suggested that the bureau use a postcard as the main census form, but census officials have decided against that. Mr. Dillman says a postcard that asked only two questions, the names and ages of all household residents, didn't improve response.

Tests are likely to continue through 1997, when the size of the census forms must be settled. Ms. Riche says her bureau can continue to "tweak" the design until printing time in 1998 or 1999.

If funds permit, the form will be preceded by a letter telling households to expect the census questionnaire. Then the form itself would be sent, followed by a letter that would thank those who responded or appeal to those who didn't; if a response isn't elicited by that letter, a duplicate form would be sent to the same person. Meanwhile, the bureau hopes to have the funds to urge response through a major advertising effort.

But money worries continue to plague the bureau. Rep. Rogers said he wanted a less expensive census. Thus, notwithstanding Ms. Riche's dismissal of pollsters, the bureau plans to borrow from their methods and use sampling once it has counted 90% of the population. Ms. Riche now predicts that the 2000 model will cost $3.9 billion, up from 1990's $2.6 billion — but below the $4.8 billion estimated cost without the sampling.

The bureau hopes to send the census packages by first-class mail, which would permit the forms to be delivered on a single day. As in 1990, the Direct Marketing Association says it will remind its 3,000 U.S. members that they have a "vested interest" in a successful census and urge them to give the census "a window of time" to arrive alone in mailboxes.

Reprinted by permission of *The Wall Street Journal,* © 1996 Dow Jones & Company, Inc. All Rights Reserved Worldwide.

Product

37

Munchy maker hungers for taste of low-cal success

By Bruce Horovitz
USA TODAY

EAST HANOVER, N.J., INSIDE SNACK-WELL'S TEST LAB — Here, amid the stainless steel rows of baking bowls and kitchen widgets, one crucial ingredient bedevils goody makers. It threatens to halt the relentless SnackWelling of America.

Calories.

Nabisco, maker of Snackwell's, does a dandy job whacking the fat out of cookies, crackers and other munchies. But darned if it can figure out how to kill more of the calories. But it had better. And soon.

The problem: Low fat, alone, doesn't cut it anymore.

For wildly successful Snackwell's, it boils down to the marketing world's most familiar but frustrating mantra: What have you done for me lately? There is nothing even remotely sweet about the battle for America's $40 billion sweet tooth. Rather, cutting-edge technology is at play. Just as whiz-bang technology determines who's the big wheel on the Information Highway, only complex kitchen technology can find a way to feed consumer hunger for low-cal cookies.

Snackwell's isn't alone anymore. Everyone from Keebler to Pepperidge Farms to Famous Amos has figured out how to remove fat from cookies. That's one reason Snackwell's cookie sales are crumbling. They've thinned a painful 27% through Oct. 7, while Snackwell's cracker sales have shrunk 16%, Information Resources reports.

Fat-free isn't passé. A record 2,000 products that claim to be low-fat or fat-free will be introduced before the year ends, says *New Product News*, a trade publication. That's more than three times the number when Snackwell's were introduced in 1992. But fat-free isn't new. And in the marketing world, newness is coolness. So, besides junking the fat, cookie and snack makers are scrambling for new ways to appear healthy. Above all, they're trying to cut calories without killing taste. That's no cakewalk.

"They may have to find people without taste buds," warns Carol Kroskey, senior bakery editor at *Bakery Production and Marketing,* a trade magazine.

Instead, a team of 20 technicians at Nabisco are now undertaking an urgent mission. They are doing everything scientifically possible to cut more calories from Snackwell's cookies — even its popular Devil's Food Cookies. "We are determined, dedicated and fix-

TOP-SELLING GROCERY STORE ITEMS		
1. Coke Classic	$1,784	
2. Pepsi	$1,695	
3. Campbells soup	$1,185	
4. Kraft cheese	$936	
5. Folgers coffee	$927	
6. Diet coke	$846	Est.'96
7. **Snackwell's**	$810	sales in
8. Marlboro Lights	$759	millions
9. Budweiser beer	$750	
10. Tropicana Pure Premium orange juice	$681	

Source: Information Resources Incorporated

ated on cutting the calories," says James Postl, the rarely interviewed president of Nabisco Biscuit Co., who took the post one year ago. His goal: to reduce the calories in Snackwell's cookies and crackers 33% to 55% within a year.

Good luck. It is one thing to remove fat. But that doesn't remove all the calories. When fat is taken out, it must be replaced with another ingredient. In Snackwell's cookies, skim milk replaces whole milk. And egg whites replace whole eggs. A super-secret baking process allows Snackwell's to bake cookies with less fat, yet still retain moisture. But certain high-calorie necessities like sugar are in its cookies. So Snackwell's continues its search for a way to make low-cal cookies taste not only decent, but decadent.

"We've made a good deal of progress," Postl says, "but nothing we are totally satisfied with."

SNACKWELL STEALTH

No name has been concocted yet for Snackwell's super-secret project. Six years ago, Nabisco's original project for creating Snackwell's was code-named Project Zero — which stood for zero fat. But zero calories aren't really an option with cookies — especially if they have taste.

"We'll have to come up with a good name for the project," says Postl. "Any suggestions?"

Well, how about Mission Impossible. Certainly,

(Cont.)

the early going has been rough. To reduce calories, Snackwell's scientists have tested nearly 50 sugar substitutes — none of which has passed the consumer taste test, says Richard McFeaters, head of new product development for the brand. "We'll look at anything," McFeaters concedes.

Until Snackwell's masters the recipe for a truly tasty, low-cal cookie, it has found another way to grow: multiplication. It is extending its low-fat and no-fat brand into every aisle of the grocery store.

Snackwell's has been rolling out products this year faster than you can slap its chocolate fudge frosting on a cake made from its devil's food cake mix. Both are new. In 1996, Snackwell's introduced an astounding 47 low-fat and fat-free items — from blueberry muffins to raspberry cereal bars to chocolate ice cream.

It's hard to overstate Snackwell's success.

In five years, it has become the seventh best-selling brand name at the supermarket, ranking just below Diet Coke in annual sales. Nearly 61% of the households in America at least tried Snackwell's the past year. "Snackwell's is a success by any standard," says Lynn Dornblaser, publisher of *New Product News*.

LOW-CAL FOR FAT SALES

Snackwell's now sells 74 different items. And more are on the way. Snackwell's candy, with 70% less fat than leading chocolate brands, is on tap for next month. Early buzz on the candy line is that it could quickly garner almost as much hoopla as Snackwell's cookies. To get the word out on all of its new products, Nabisco will nearly double Snackwell's ad budget next year to $60 million, Postl says.

With so much new stuff, Snackwell's overall sales surely will continue to climb. Sales should surpass $810 million this year. And by decade's end, Postl expects sales to exceed $1 billion. But the company knows only one thing will get Snackwell's to that magical billion dollar mark: a lower-calorie cookie.

It won't come cheaply. Industry experts estimate Nabisco spent up to $50 million to develop Snackwell's cookies. It could cost that much — and more — to develop a low-calorie cookie that passes America's taste test.

All kinds of inventors and scientists keep badgering Snackwell's with suggestions how to do it. "Suppliers are knocking down our doors with ideas," says William DeLauder, senior vice president of product development.

To no avail. Earlier this year, test-marketing of a low-cal Snackwell's cookie at a New Jersey shopping mall bombed.

Sadly, this desperate search for a low calorie cookie is breaking Snackwell's costly cookie-making ma-chinery. When fats and calories are removed from cookies, the dough can get very sticky. As a result, some of the older motors on the giant mixers simply conked out.

SEE-FOOD DIETS

The costly quest for low-calorie's Holy Grail is threatened by one intangible: consumer fickleness. "Consumers talk a good talk about wanting to eat healthy," says Tom Vierhile, general manager of Marketing Intelligence Service, "but put a couple Arch Deluxes in front of them, and, poof, so much for good health."

Wall Street experts say Nabisco desperately needs to take its Snackwell's cookies and crackers to the next level. "They defined the category," says Steven Galbraith, analyst at Sanford C. Bernstein & Co., "but their cookies and crackers have been hemorrhaging for the past two quarters."

These days, it seems everyone's picking on Snackwell's. "Since most people think Snackwell's are good for them, they eat many more than they should," says Jean Freeland-Graves, nutrition professor at University of Texas at Austin.

And some health food stores have junked Snackwell's altogether. "They did not meet our quality standards," explains Peter Roy, president of Whole Foods Market.

Five years ago, a shortage of Snackwell's Devil's Food cookies caused a run at the supermarket. The company picked up on the theme and created a character for its TV spots, "Cookie Man," who is hounded by shoppers trying to get their hands on his cookies.

But if Snackwell's doesn't find a new cookie formula, Cookie Man could eventually find himself as lonely as the Maytag Repairman.

To boost sales, early next year Snackwell's will offer discount coupons on all of its products at the same time, Postl says. Coupons mean lower profit margins. And the brand has never had to do that before.

"This isn't as much fun as when you're growing 100% a year and you can't make enough to keep up with demand," says Postl.

But he's intent on Snackwell's low-cal mission.

Back in the test kitchen, seven rows of a super-secret, possible new line of devil's food cookies sit on a drying rack. For the scientists, it's sometimes more like a torture rack. "The issue isn't just what a cookie tastes like, but what it looks like," says McFeaters. On a rack of otherwise fine-looking cookies, he points to one sadly-shaped reject, which looks more akin to a fossil than a cookie.

"Would you eat that cookie?" he asks.

At Snackwell's, the answer to that question means everything.

Copyright 1996, *USA Today*. Reprinted with permission.

38

Investigators Follow A Trail of Shampoo To Some Dry Ends

Phony Head & Shoulders Had Quite a Journey, Starting In P&G'S Own Factory

Missing: the Don of Dandruff

By Raju Narisetti

Staff Reporter of The Wall Street Journal

Investigators are scratching their heads over thousands of bottles of fake Head & Shoulders dandruff shampoo.

For a year, they have tracked the fakes across two countries, beginning in a rundown Toronto building where the shampoo was bottled by a Pakistani biochemist and her three daughters. The bottles then traveled to Miami and later to New York, and from there onto store shelves and into homes across the Midwest and Northeast. The bottles changed hands numerous times and somewhere along the way mysteriously got Head & Shoulders labels before 25,000 of them were seized by U.S. marshals and padlocked in a rented warehouse on New York's Long Island.

But the private investigators employed by Procter & Gamble Co., the maker of the real Head & Shoulders, are still stumped. They wonder who and where is one Frank Pandullo, the apparent mastermind of the shampoo caper.

A Flurry of Lawsuits

Not only P&G is trying to pin him down; Quality King Distributors Inc. is, too. P&G sued the national consumer-products distributor last August in federal court in Uniondale, N.Y.; it accused Quality King of selling counterfeit shampoo and violating trademarks and sought monetary damages of at least $10 million. Quality King countersued, contending that P&G itself made the shampoo and that Quality King ended up with counterfeit bottles only because P&G managers didn't dispose of it properly. It is seeking $50 million because, it says, its reputation was damaged and as a result of P&G's actions three large clients have reduced or terminated their business ties with Quality King.

Quality King is "not disputing we bought and sold this merchandise," says Alfred Paliani, a lawyer for the distributor. "We would not have been in the position we are in

today had P&G been more careful in the way it disposed of shampoo in Canada." P&G's lawyers dismiss that argument as legal maneuvering akin to a car thief saying the owner was careless in leaving the car door open.

Over the years, P&G has steadfastly fought to protect its brand names, filing dozens of lawsuits alleging trademark and copyright infringement. But this case is especially vexing to the Cincinnati-based consumer-products giant because it allegedly involves a murky mess of counterfeiting with multiple intermediaries that frequently pay cash and don't seem to bother with receipts or bookkeeping, leaving nary a piece of a paper trail. In all, the shampoo at issue was sold at least nine times from the time it left a P&G factory as gratis scrap and appeared on store shelves, and its price escalated to $3.99 a bottle from about 49 cents. In addition, dozens of other names and businesses have cropped up in hundreds of pages of depositions, each opening up a new line of investigation that P&G is now chasing.

Costly for Companies

Counterfeiting costs U.S. companies nearly $200 billion in annual sales of genuine brands, says the International Anticounterfeiting Coalition, a Washington industry group. For P&G, which says it has spent at least $100 million in advertising Head & Shoulders between 1990 and 1995, the actual value of the fake bottles is marginal. But the company is spending thousands of dollars investigating the caper. So far, it has nailed down just about everything but Mr. Pandullo.

The fraud was discovered last summer when a P&G salesman spotted the fakes at a Kroger Co. supermarket in Cincinnati. Although the bottles and labels looked similar to real ones, the impostor bottles were long-necked — P&G had replaced that design months earlier with a rectangular-shaped bottle — and also lacked a recycling symbol at the bottom. So, they weren't left over from an old P&G consignment.

Alerted by P&G, Kroger put out a "Class One Recall," usually reserved for life-threatening problems, and then helped P&G quickly trace the shampoo to Quality King. Armed with a court-issued seizure order, P&G attorneys, accompanied by three people wearing windbreakers identifying them as U.S. marshals, searched Quality King's warehouses on Aug. 7, 1995. By the end of the day, they had loaded a tractor-trailer with plain cardboard boxes containing nearly 25,000 Head & Shoulders shampoo bottles and had taken them to the Long Island warehouse rented by P&G. Quality King had already sold about 35,000 bottles to retailers.

Then, P&G launched a media blitz, warning retailers, doctors and consumers in a news release and half-page advertisements in 27 newspapers that the shampoo was fake — and possibly contaminated with bacteria. P&G also set up a toll-free hot line for free replacements and said it had sued Quality King, which is based in Ronkonkoma, N.Y.

"People trust our brands, and we're not going to let anyone violate that trust," proclaimed John Pepper, P&G's chief executive officer in a widely distributed statement.

What P&G didn't say publicly — and Quality King noted in its countersuit — is that some, if not most, of the shampoo in the counterfeit bottles originated at a P&G factory in Hamilton, Ontario, where managers had found a cheap way to dispose of waste shampoo that had been spilled onto floors or scraped from barrel bottoms. Instead of dumping it in expensive landfills, P&G was regularly giving it away in 45-gallon drums to a local company, Ianco Envirotech Inc. It even delivered the shampoo free of charge in P&G trucks.

Philip Kalifon, Ianco's owner, said in a deposition that before receiving the shampoo, he had signed an agreement with P&G that forbade him to sell it as human or animal shampoo. But he admitted it usually ended up as human shampoo, sometimes labeled Elegance, and had been sold as far away as Jamaica and Hungary. He added that the shampoo also was turned into floor cleaners, tub and tile cleaners, or shampoo for dogs, cats and horses, by adding water, dye and table salt to thicken it.

Ianco, whose stationery says "You create, we recreate," even tried to peddle the shampoo to local service stations as carwash, though that idea flopped because the shampoo left a film on cars. "We couldn't find a way, a chemical to add to remove the film," Mr. Kalifon testified.

Some Bad Batches

Throughout his deposition, Mr. Kalifon contended that managers at the P&G plant knew what he was doing and that once the waste became "a bastard product," it was understood that he was welcome to do anything he wanted with it. P&G says it never authorized any deviation from the agreement. Mr. Kalifon said P&G stopped sending "goodies" in 1994 and when he started getting shampoo that was bad — some even contained sand — he often poured it down the drain, although he admits he was "not supposed to do that."

So when Ayesha Alam, a former Ianco employee whose job had been to mix chemicals and dyes, asked him for some of the shampoo, he says he sold her drums of it from P&G, plus bottles and caps.

Enter Mr. Pandullo. In June 1994, a man variously described as tall, slick, solidly built and in his early to mid-40s, with dark curly hair and a mustache, strode into the one-room office of A. Gruda Products Co., an Ontario buyer and seller of closed-out merchandise as diverse as croutons, soft drinks and liquid cleaners.

Introducing himself as Frank Pandullo, owner of Oxford Surplus Traders, he asked whether A. Gruda could supply as many as 120,000 bottles of blue shampoo. In subsequent visits, he even brought along a plain bottle, which resembled a long-necked Head

(Cont.)

& Shoulders bottle, and a label for a brand called Morello, which he said would be affixed to the bottles.

Paul Doubilet, an A. Gruda co-owner, agreed to find a supplier for the nattily dressed stranger who was soon referred to in Gruda ledgers as "The Don." Mr. Doubilet telephoned Ms. Alam, a biochemist who then was running her own company, OMA International, and she told him she could fill the order with the barrels of Head & Shoulders then in her possession.

Mixing It Up

Questioned by P&G attorneys, Ms. Alam, who said she never got around to incorporating OMA International because she didn't have money to do so, testified that she used eight drums of P&G's Head & Shoulders. She said she added to the shampoo four drums of water and salt, several drums of white shampoo and drums of shampoo blends. Over several weeks, she filled white bottles with the blue shampoo and sent them to a Toronto warehouse as instructed by Mr. Doubilet, who promptly paid her cash. Ms. Alam testified that the bottles she sent to the warehouse in Toronto had no labels and that she never met nor heard of anybody named Frank Pandullo until P&G investigators contacted her.

Between June and August of 1994, Mr. Pandullo would appear unannounced at A. Gruda's office, driving a dark Mercedes and paying cash for consignments sent to the warehouse. In August, he vanished, allegedly skipping out on the last payment, for about 2,000 bottles. He never returned telephone messages left by Mr. Doubilet, who says he never really cared about Mr. Pandullo's credentials as long as the cash was coming in. Oxford Surplus couldn't be found at the address on Mr. Pandullo's business card, P&G investigators say.

While buying the shampoo, Mr. Pandullo was trying to sell it to Beverly Zoeller, who ran Zoeller International Trading, which deals in health and beauty-care merchandise out of a condominium in Toronto. Mr. Pandullo approached her, she testified, and offered to sell her Head & Shoulders shampoo in bottles that he claimed were coming from P&G because the company was shifting to a new bottle.

Ms. Zoeller, who said in her deposition that "my business is diversion" (mostly buying in Canada and selling in the U.S. products meant for the Canadian market), didn't verify Mr. Pandullo's credentials, either. She testified that in her work she was used to a lot of "fax jockeys," people who promise all sorts of products but never deliver. Mr. Pandullo seemed serious; he had sold her a small quantity of Hershey chocolate in the past year, and this time he showed her samples of the shampoo.

A Major Qualm

Her big reservation was that he brought them in a stapled Kellogg's cereal box, which she said raised questions about whether the bottles were obtained legitimately. (Some Tylenol and Rollerblades offered to her by others in the past, her daughter, Erika Weber, testified, turned out to be stolen goods.) Mr. Pandullo said P&G would provide plain cardboard boxes, but he told her that the company insisted she not sell them in Canada. Ms. Zoeller agreed, sealing the deal in a local deli, where she handed him 33,000 Canadian dollars without asking for a receipt.

Ms. Zoeller then contacted Sal Arzillo, a Miami-based freight forwarder and an old business acquaintance, who had helped her sell Marlboro cigarettes that the manufacturer had earmarked for sale only in Indian reservations. He agreed to take the shampoo and paid her by check. Mr. Arzillo's Rapid Air & Ocean Inc. sold it to Omnisource International Inc., an Aventura, Fla., distributor. Omnisource resold the shampoo to an old customer, Quality King, for $2.50 a bottle — five times as much as what Ms. Alam had first received. P&G eventually added Rapid Air and Omnisource as defendants in its lawsuit.

It isn't clear where or how the bottles got the Head & Shoulders label, which has a different type font but otherwise looks nearly identical to the real version. So far, everyone P&G and Quality King have talked to is claiming ignorance. Ms. Zoeller says the bottles in the Toronto warehouse used by Mr. Pandullo were already labeled. Ms. Alam, who sent the bottles to the warehouse, says there were no labels on her shipments. The warehouse manager never saw the bottles themselves because they were sealed in boxes, but she says no one could have come in and glued on labels without her knowledge.

A full explanation seems to lie with the missing Mr. Pandullo. Investigators from P&G and Quality King have found little, despite months of tracking down names, aliases, addresses and phone numbers.

Stood Up

But shortly after P&G's investigators began retracing the shampoo's trail, Mr. Pandullo called Ms. Zoeller, she testified, and told her that he was in Mexico putting together a coffee deal. She told him to call P&G and get its investigators off her back. Mr. Pandullo assured her, she said, that the shampoo wasn't counterfeit and promised to explain matters.

They agreed to meet on a street in Niagara Falls, N.Y., but he never showed up. He called once more, saying he was at the rendezvous but left because he saw someone else in the car and assumed it was a P&G representative. It was Ms. Zoeller's daughter, there to jot down Mr. Pandullo's license plate number.

"For a while I believed that Frank Pandullo didn't exist," says Mr. Paliani, Quality King's lawyer. "But too many people have seen this guy. I am sure he is tall, dark and handsome Mediterranean-looking guy. He just can't be found." Donald Tassone, a P&G spokesman, says the company's extensive efforts show how far it will go to protect its brands. "It is very important to continue to track down the real culprits here," he says.

P&G still has time. The shampoo mess isn't likely to go to trial until next year.

Reprinted by permission of *The Wall Street Journal,* © 1996 DowJones & Company, Inc. All Rights Reserved Worldwide.

39

Lettuce enjoys salad days as a time-saver

By Bruce Horovitz
USA TODAY

The head of lettuce is on the chopping block.

If you're wondering who put it there, it may have been you. This should not be surprising if you are among the one in four Americans who regularly buys pre-packaged, pre-washed, pre-chopped lettuce.

Prepared salad's startling success seems almost preordained. It's a time-saver, a waste-saver, a cut-on-the-pinkie-saver and some would argue — with less leftover lettuce gurgling down the disposal — a money saver. Ten years ago, the retail lettuce-in-a-bag industry didn't even exist. But this year, retail revenue from bagged lettuce — often mixed with shredded carrots and red cabbage for color — is expected to top $1 billion.

| **Convenience spurs change in ways to sell fresh produce** |

Talk about money in the bag. Some lettuce prognosticators say bagged lettuce may eventually outsell head lettuce. Eight in 10 Americans bought at least one bag last year. Some predict lettuce-in-the-bag could become as common as mashed potatoes in the box. Or fresh pasta in a plastic container. Or pre-roasted chicken. "A whole generation could grow up without seeing a head of lettuce in the house," says a wishful Edith Garrett, president of the International Fresh-Cut Produce Association, an industry trade group.

Grocers say the bagged lettuce category, also known as packaged salads, ranks as the single fastest-growing grocery segment over the past five years. A record 62 types of pre-packed salads were introduced during the first nine months of 1996, says Marketing Intelligence, a new product research firm.

A handful of companies that once mostly made their livelihoods growing and selling heads of lettuce are now bagging it, too. The top five bagged lettuce producers all reported double-digit growth in 1995 — for the fifth consecutive year. But with a wild scramble under way to rank No. 1 nationally, the packaged salad industry's salad days may be ending.

Fresh Express, the industry leader, will sell $300 million worth of bagged lettuce this year, compared with less than $9 million in 1992. Over the next week, alone, Fresh Express will sell 2.5 million bags of its lettuce. "We call it the home meal solution," CEO Steve Taylor says.

But it is Dole, perhaps better-known for its canned goods than fresh produce, that has just raised the stakes. Dole recently began to broadcast the country's first national TV ads for bagged salads. The $2 million ad campaign boasts about Dole's bagged Caesar salads. "We have to educate people that produce is now a packaged good," says Kelley Maier, marketing head at Dole Fresh Vegetables.

To juice sales, the major competitors are trying everything. They're selling fancy mixes of romaine, radicchio and bib. They're adding doodads like croutons, bacon bits, even chicken strips. Single-serving salad kits were recently introduced. Even kids are being targeted. And to add some allure to the category, plucky Ready Pac plans to soon announce it will link with chef extraordinaire Wolfgang Puck of Spago in Los Angeles. "We're talking about selling the same salads he serves in his restaurants," says Ready Pac's executive V.P., Chris Nelson.

Spurring the demand for bagged lettuce is one thing above all: convenience.

Ask avid lettuce-eater Carla Stanley of East Liberty, Ohio. The mother of three hasn't purchased a head of lettuce in three years. "I'm lazy," she explains. For that matter, her 10-year-old daughter Nicole Egnot can't even recall the last time she saw a head of lettuce in the house. "It's been a long, long time," says the fifth-grader. "Longer than I can remember."

Even corporate produce honchos increasingly are buying lettuce by the bag.

Among them is Dick Spezzano, who oversees produce purchasing for Vons, one of the largest grocery chains on the West Coast. Over the past five years, Vons has spent about $3 million to add special coolers for the bagged lettuce in its 325 stores in California and Nevada. "We've now got customers eating lettuce and carrots who never ate them before," Spezzano says.

Spezzano has one especially crucial customer who has made the switch to bagged-only: his wife. "I haven't bought a head of lettuce in four years," says Carole Spezzano, a professional food broker. "For working people, packaged salads are the best thing since sliced bread."

She insists it saves her money because unlike head lettuce, none of it goes to waste. Most bagged salads

(Cont.)

can last 10 days to two weeks in the refrigerator.

This newfangled way to sell lettuce is turning produce sections on their ears. And possibly changing the way produce makers will compete in the future. Almost overnight, produce sections have become packaged goods sections. No longer is the produce corner a bastion of nameless heads of lettuce and brandless tomatoes that fail to register with shoppers. These packaged salads all carry name brands — and product codes that can be carefully tracked at the cash register. And consumers increasingly are asking for the brands by name, says Thomas Vierhile, general manager of Marketing Intelligence.

"The battle to be No. 1 is titanic," says Ken Hodge, who three years ago decided to devote an entire magazine to the topic, Fresh Cut, whose circulation is now over 10,000 — and growing.

Of course, bagged lettuce comes at a premium — it typically costs anywhere from 25 cents to $1.00 more than a conventional head of lettuce. And some of the fancier brands, stuffed with extra ingredients, can cost up to $3.99 for a single bag. But producers argue that by wasting less lettuce and saving time, consumers ultimately save money.

The success of bagged lettuce has ushered in a slew of other fresh-cut items like bagged baby carrots and broccoli florets. As a result, the number of items in the typical grocery store produce section has doubled in about five years from 150 to 300, says the produce group's Garrett. Fresh fruit producers, too, are starting to study the technology, she says.

A breakthrough in packaging technology in the late 1980s made it possible for bagged lettuce to keep crisp for up to two weeks. The new packages are able to take in needed oxygen and let out unwanted carbon dioxide. That keeps the lettuce from turning brown or wilting.

Lettuce turns over a new leaf

	Revenue
1989	$ 82 million
1990	$ 91 million
1991	$106 million
1992	$168 million
1993	$312 million
1994	$577 million
1995	$889 million
1996	$ 1.1 billion

Sources: International Fresh-Cut Produce Association, Information Resources

By Elys A. McLean, USA TODAY

> "A whole generation could grow up without seeing a head of lettuce in the house."
> — Edith Garrett
> International Fresh-Cut
> Produce Association

Technology aside, it may be psychology that is playing the biggest role of all, says Jerald Jellison, professor of psychology at the University of Southern California. Most packaged salads require consumers to select and pour on the dressing. "There's still a sense that you created it yourself," he says.

There may be a status factor, too. Purchase just the right blend of pre-packaged lettuce for a dinner party and it can make anyone appear kitchen savvy, says consumer psychologist and ad executive Renee White Fraser.

Nutritionally speaking, there's little difference between a head of lettuce and a bag of it, says Chris Melby, professor of nutrition at Colorado State University. "Anything that improves our ability to eat greens is a good thing," he says.

But not everything's peachy on the produce aisle. No thanks to bagged lettuce, sales of head lettuce have declined by 15% in some parts of the country. And as consumers increasingly view pre-packaged salads as complete offerings, sales of items like tomatoes are declining, too.

Also, there's the problem of keeping bagged lettuce cold until consumed. Odd things can happen to bagged lettuce that is kept below 38 degrees for several hours. One company that tried hauling it in trucks across the Rocky Mountains discovered thousands of lettuce bags exploded like tiny time bombs.

Then, there's plain-and-simple resistance. Women buy most of the bagged salads. Men mostly resist. Even Rick Antle, president of the giant lettuce grower and cutting-edge fresh-cut packer Tanimura & Antle, says his preference still is to step out into one of his many lettuce fields and pluck a fresh head to bring home. "Me?" says Antle, whose company just began selling processed salads in individual bowls that include forks and napkins. "Well, I like to make a salad from scratch."

Contributing: Barbara Hansen

Copyright 1996, USA Today. Reprinted with permission.

Seeing Red Abroad, Pepsi Rolls Out a New Blue Can

BY ROBERT FRANK

Staff Reporter of THE WALL STREET JOURNAL

Foreign markets are becoming ever more crucial to U.S. soft-drink makers, but Pepsi's message has been losing something in the translation.

Overseas, some Pepsi billboards are more than 20 years old — and its image is all over the map: A grocery store in Hamburg uses red stripes, a bodega in Guatemala uses '70s-era lettering and a Shanghai restaurant displays a mainly white Pepsi sign. A hodge-podge of commercials feature a variety of spokespeople, ranging from cartoons and babies to doddering butlers. Worse yet, consumers say the cola tastes different in different countries.

So **PepsiCo** Inc. is unveiling a radical, if risky, comeback plan this morning in London. Code-named "Project Blue," it's expected to cost $500 million over the next year and a half. It calls for revamping manufacturing and distribution to get a consistent-tasting drink throughout the globe, as well as an overhaul of marketing and advertising.

Pepsi is even scrapping its signature red-white-and-blue colors in favor of electric blue. Starting this year in more than 20 countries, the new blue will be plastered on all its trucks, coolers, cans and bottles. The switch is expected to reach the U.S. by the year 2000.

"It's a gutsy move," says Gary Stibel, of New England Consulting Group, a global marketing firm. "Pepsi drinkers overseas are a small and loyal group. They might not take kindly to any changes."

All agree, however, that Pepsi has to do something. As the U.S. soft-drink market matures, the entire beverage industry is staking its future overseas. Last year, the U.S. market grew 3.6%, compared with about 6.5% in 1985, according to Beverage Marketing Inc. **Coca-Cola** Co. remains the U.S. market leader, with a roughly 43% share, to Pepsi's 31%, according to Beverage Marketing.

While overseas sales of both Coca-Cola and Pepsi are growing between 7% and 10% a year, Coca-Cola outsells Pepsi abroad nearly 3 to 1. And Coca-Cola already earns more than 80% of its profits abroad, compared with Pepsi's 30%.

"It's ridiculous that we're not growing faster," says Christopher Sinclair, PepsiCo's global beverage chief. With Project Blue, he aims to boost Pepsi's overseas growth rate to the "double digits" and close the gap with Coke to under 2-to-1 by the year 2000.

Project Blue began two years ago, when Mr. Sinclair and others began delving into why, despite an outlay of $3 billion to bolster its foreign manufacturing and distribution, sales were falling below company expectations.

During visits to stores in Europe, one thing became apparent: Coca-Cola's red logo dominated the shelves, all but obliterating Pepsi. "You had to squint to find us," Mr. Sinclair says.

Nor did customers always like what they got. In some countries, cans and bottles had been sitting on shelves for years. A focus group in the United Kingdom called the brand "an embarrassment to drink."

So, working with the San Francisco-based corporate-image consultants Landor Associates, Pepsi devised the new blue look after studying the success of Pepsi Max, its popular overseas diet drink that comes in a blue can.

What began as a merchandising project quickly ballooned into a total product re-launch. At an executive retreat in Montana in late 1994, Pepsi's overseas marketing chief, John Swanhaus, presented the redesign to Roger Enrico, who soon thereafter became PepsiCo's chairman and chief executive.

"Why stop with the design change?" Mr. Enrico asked. "Why not change what's inside the can?"

Thus, Project Blue also includes new freshness standards and quality controls. The company is even training a team of tasters to sample drinks from around the world.

Yet Project Blue carries big risks — especially in light of Coca-Cola's ill-fated attempt a few years ago to reformulate classic Coke. Pepsi hasn't made such a drastic logo change in more than 40 years. And with the project's high costs come high expectations: Pepsi is counting on nothing less than a long-term sales turnaround. "If it becomes a quick sales hit and doesn't motivate the whole business, we've failed." says Mr. Sinclair.

Pepsi's bottlers are also nervous. Many of the independent companies that make and sell Pepsi overseas will have to scrap or redo all of their red-white-and-blue signs and vending machines, plus over 30,000 trucks and more than 10 billion cans and bottles. Though Pepsi will pick up some of the costs, its U.K. bottler, for instance, has had to boost marketing spending by 30% to 40% to support Project Blue.

"We're all concerned about the cost," says Stephen Davies, managing director of Britvic Soft Drinks Ltd., Pepsi's U.K. bottler. "But we think it will pay off."

Another concern is whether repackaging will exacerbate Pepsi's overseas identity crisis. Coca-Cola's red has become the world standard for soft drinks, and many marketing experts say Pepsi will have a tough time bucking that tradition with blue.

"The danger is that they're stepping outside the conventional graphic cues for the category," says John Lister, chief executive of Lister Butler Inc., a New York image-consulting firm. Still, he calls the package change "the easy part. They have to send a clear signal to consumers that something is different, and tell them how it's different."

Pepsi's only test of Project Blue took place last November, when it commandeered a small shopping district on the Persian Gulf island of Bahrain, a market that Pepsi dominates. It painted shop signs and sidewalks blue, and erected a giant blue neon sign.

Surveys show that Pepsi improved its public image, and consumers drove from as far away as Saudi Arabia to buy the blue cans. Still, its market share slipped slightly during the first month of the launch, while volume rose only in the single digits. Though only the packaging had changed, about a third of Bahraini consumers surveyed thought the drink's taste had changed — 17% for the worse.

Pepsi insists the test portends a winner, and is doing its best to make sure the world thinks so, too. It's kicking off a new ad campaign, featuring supermodels Claudia Schiffer and Cindy Crawford as well as tennis star Andre Agassi. Over the next 18 months, it plans a host of stunts: enveloping the Danube in blue fog, wrapping a Cairo skyscraper in blue, painting blue logos on thousands of tuk-tuk passenger cycles in Thailand and painting a Concorde plane blue. It's even sending a Pepsi Blue banner into space, to be unfurled in the Russian space station Mir.

Reprinted by permission of *The Wall Street Journal*, © 1996 Dow Jones & Company, Inc. All Rights Reserved Worldwide.

P&G Uses Packaging Savvy on Rx Drug

BY RAJU NARISETTI

Staff Reporter of THE WALL STREET JOURNAL

Researchers have pinpointed the bacteria that cause peptic ulcers, and drug makers have found ways to eradicate the germ. But developing user-friendly packaging for the complex combination of pills seemed daunting.

Enter **Procter & Gamble** Co., the nation's pre-eminent packaged-goods company, making its first major foray into the U.S. prescription-drug market. Using the main ingredient in its Pepto-Bismol antacid, it developed Helidac, an intense ulcer-treatment course. The drug, which began shipping 10 weeks ago, has a cure rate in tests that matches those of its competitors.

But it is P&G's packaging of Helidac that is turning heads in the pharmaceutical industry. The company —whose clout with consumers has made such brands as Crest toothpaste, Tide detergent and Bounty paper towels No. 1 in their markets—focused on helping people use Helidac properly, and it priced the drug as much as 50% below rivals' prices.

"Most drug companies target physicians, who are their customers, but we put the focus on the consumer," says Christopher Warner, the Helidac project leader.

P&G's efforts to develop distinctive packaging began in 1994, when the company formed an eight-person in-house team and brought in four behavior-modification consultants to provide insights into what makes people stick to such health regimens as diets and nicotine patches. P&G coined an acronym for what it learned: PERM, or packaging, education, reminders and motivation.

The task was a tough one: Patients taking Helidac have to gobble 224 tablets, representing three types of drugs, over two weeks. P&G's rivals—**Glaxo Wellcome** PLC, whose Tritec was introduced last August, and **Astra-Merck** Inc., whose Prilosec came out last April—offer less complex treatment with fewer pills over a four-week period.

It isn't just quantity that poses a problem. Helidac users have to follow their regimen every six hours: First chew two pink tablets, then swallow a white tablet, then take an orange capsule with at least one glass of water. Missing even a few pills can sharply reduce the drug cocktail's success rate, and in some cases, the ulcer-causing bacteria can reemerge, sometimes in a more drug-resistant form.

In focus groups, ulcer patients told P&G they wanted their medicine to be portable and compact, but the simplest solution—a separate bottle for each type of pill—was a no-no. "I don't want to be walking around so you can hear me jangling down the hall" was a common refrain, says Mr. Warner. Meanwhile, the pharmacists P&G talked to didn't want extra bottles cluttering up their shelves.

The result: Each day's pills are held on a separate blister card so that consumers can slip a day's dosage into a coat pocket or purse.

The blister card helped make the medicine child-proof. But it also caused problems for old people. In tests, many older consumers tried to push the tablets out the wrong side—through the transparent but strong plastic covers—rather than peeling the thin aluminum foil off the backs of the sheets and popping the pills out.

This discovery helped P&G zero in on yet another problem: People rarely bother to read fine print on packaging. And so the company asked the older people in its focus group to write their own instructions. The result was a simple, 14-word text, accompanied by three drawings, that was printed on the side of the box. Another consumer suggestion adopted by P&G: dividing each blister card into four perforated squares, one for each six-hour tablet supply, with labels reading "breakfast," "lunch," "dinner" and "bedtime."

The P&G team then rewrote the mandatory information leaflet that lists side-effects. Out went any word that couldn't be understood by an eighth grader. Bacteria became germs, for instance. Complex instructions became symbols that could be understood at a glance, such as a picture of a liquor bottle and wine glass in a red circle with a line through them. Rather than printing all that on a piece of paper folded many times over, as most drug companies do, P&G designed a glossy 20-page booklet that fit squarely into the box.

But there remained the daunting problem of reminding patients to take their pills regularly. P&G pondered using its massive consumer-products hotline to phone each patient three times a week. Some consumers liked the idea, but many others felt it would turn P&G into Big Brother. The team considered issuing each patient a tiny battery-operated beeper or a vibrating buzzer, set to go off every six hours, but that was deemed too costly, as well as potentially embarrassing. Physicians also worried that their offices would be inundated by patients who couldn't program the devices or stopped taking the tablets if a buzzer malfunctioned.

P&G's solution was stickers. Inside the package, patients get a sheet of four stickers—decorated with balloons—that they can affix to a visible spot wherever they tend to be when it's time to pop the pills.

But P&G felt patients needed something extra to keep them motivated. Rewarding them with a $5 P&G gift certificate was considered, but it wasn't clear who should get the money if a patient was on Medicaid. And so the team fell back on a motivational tool used by self-help groups: daily affirmation cards. The cards carry pithy slogans and can be peeled off to mark the passing of each day. Day 1 says "look at how the stack of blister packs is going away."

Helidac has impressed some doctors. "It's packaged in a way to help patients take it correctly," says Alan Cutler, director of gastroenterology research at Sinai Hospital in Detroit.

Bill Chapman, a spokesman for rival Glaxo, doesn't think patient compliance is "a major issue with our prescription." He says the drug's efficacy, not packaging, is the key.

But P&G may be onto something. Interest is growing in attempts to prevent unintentional prescription-drug misuse. Nearly two million Americans land in the hospital each year because of it, and another three million have to visit their doctors. Two weeks ago the federal government launched a voluntary plan to ensure that more patients receive comprehensive—and comprehensible—information in writing about adverse drug interactions and other risks.

Reprinted by permission of *The Wall Street Journal,* © 1997 Dow Jones & Company, Inc. All Rights Reserved Worldwide.

Colgate Places a Huge Bet on a Germ-Fighter

BY TARA PARKER-POPE

Staff Reporter of THE WALL STREET JOURNAL

New germ-fighting ingredients have won raves from Americans in everything from soap to cat litter. But will consumers pay more to have them in their toothpaste?

Colgate-Palmolive is betting $100 million they will, starting with televised "teaser" ads today for the biggest new-product launch in the company's history. Hoping to kick rival **Procter & Gamble's** Crest in the teeth, Colgate is going all-out to whet the American appetite for Total, a toothpaste popular abroad whose main claim to fame is that it contains triclosan, the same germ-fighter found in many soaps, deodorants and hand lotions.

Colgate is heading into the new year with an unprecedented U.S. marketing and distribution push, bypassing warehouses to ship directly to retailers and sending out 30 million samples to get the products onto store shelves and into consumers' mouths in record time. The company even has changed the famous Colgate clock overlooking New York's Hudson River, putting a giant replica of a box of Total toothpaste next to it.

"We believe this toothpaste is the biggest innovation since fluoride," says Ian Cook, president of Colgate U.S. "We are prepared to invest mightily to gain market share with it."

The arrival of Total in the U.S. market sets up a pitched battle with rival Procter & Gamble, which in July launched its own new product, Crest MultiCare, backed by nearly $60 million in marketing and advertising. Both products promise to clean better than regular toothpaste, but only Colgate's Total has won U.S. Food Drug Administration approval to be marketed as helping to prevent gum disease. The toothpaste will cost about 25% more than other Colgate toothpastes, or about $3 for a six-ounce tube.

For Colgate, the U.S. launch of Total, which already is sold in more than 100 countries, is the biggest test yet of the turnaround in its U.S. business under Chairman and Chief Executive Reuben Mark. Although Total has been a big hit abroad, and helped Colgate steamroll rival P&G in the Canadian market, the U.S. consumer may prove to be a tougher sell.

For one thing, American mouths are among the healthiest in the world. Fluoridated water, improved brushing habits and elementary-school dental-hygiene campaigns, many of them sponsored by Crest toothpaste, mean cavities aren't the problem they used to be. And although Colgate has closed the gap with rival Crest, brand loyalty among Crest users remains high, fueled by a new "Crest kids" advertising campaign that shows adult Crest users waxing nostalgic about the toothpaste they grew up with.

P&G's chief executive, John Pepper, conceded this summer that the Cincinnati company had stumbled in its oral-care business by failing to introduce new toothpaste products quickly enough. In the past few years, dozens of rival products boasting of whitening ingredients, baking soda and tartar-control properties have hit the market, eroding Crest's dominance.

Just who is leading the U.S. toothpaste market currently is in dispute, partly because different data providers track different outlets. According to Information Resources, a Chicago market-research firm, Crest remains the clear favorite with about a quarter of the U.S. market, compared with roughly one-fifth for Colgate. But according to AC-Nielsen data, New York-based Colgate edged ahead in the past few months, with 26.2% of the market, compared with 25.3% for P&G. That marks the first time since 1962 that Colgate has overtaken P&G in the toothpaste business, the data show.

P&G says its current array of products, including MultiCare and a new whitening toothpaste, now gives consumers the range of choices they want. "The combination of the product lineup and the advertising we now have on the air is going to enable us to continue to build our share," said P&G Vice President Bill Dobson.

Colgate executives counter that they will rely on the same advertising and marketing efforts that have made Total a hit abroad to make Colgate the "undisputed" market leader in the U.S. Of the $100 million launch budget, $60 million will be spent on traditional print, billboard and broadcast advertising. By comparison, P&G spent about $70 million in the U.S. advertising all of its Crest products in the 12 months through July, according to Competitive Media Reporting.

The new 15-second Total teaser ads simply show a box of Total, as an announcer boasts that the product is "the only toothpaste in history" to win the seal of acceptance from the American Dental Association for fighting a series of maladies, including gum disease and bad breath. In another version, the announcer says "Only one toothpaste works all day" to fight bad breath, cavities and other mouth worries.

In mid-January the main Total advertising campaign will begin, featuring people brushing their teeth with Total. As they go to work, exercise, sleep, smile or do just about anything, the brushing sound continues. "Now, there's a toothpaste so advanced, it even works when you're not brushing," the ads say. All the ads were created by Young Rubicam, New York, which handles Colgate advertising worldwide.

The advertising is nearly identical to Total ads in other markets, including Canada, where the Total launch helped Colgate overtake P&G. Before Total's introduction in the fourth quarter of 1993, P & G led the Canadi-

an market with a 35% share, ahead of Colgate with 21.5%, according to ACNielsen data provided by Colgate . Following the launch, Colgate gained three to five percentage points a year, and now boasts 36.3% share of the market, compared with 27.3% for P&G.

The difference between Total and other toothpastes is triclosan, an antimicrobial agent that destroys the cell walls of bacteria and prevents them from multiplying. In the past few years, hundreds of new bacteria-fighting products, from toys to pillowcases to scouring pads, have hit the market, playing into consumer worries about germs and disease. Many of those products contain triclosan.

In the U.S., no other toothpaste uses triclosan, although P&G does sell triclosan-based Crest Ultra in Canada. It took the U.S. FDA five years to approve Total, but it seems likely the process would be shorter for another triclosan contender if one surfaced in the U.S. For the time being, it appears P&G is putting its marketing muscle behind its MultiCare product.

Although Total toothpaste has been clinically proven to help prevent gingivitis, plaque, cavities and tartar, Colgate says the daily benefit consumers experience is that their teeth feel cleaner and their breath tastes fresher for longer after brushing. "Consumers love the idea of being protected between brushings," says Jack Haber, vice president, oral care, for Colgate U.S.

Leaving nothing to chance, Colgate has taken some unusual steps to ensure that U.S. consumers who see the new advertising can try Total. In October, Colgate sent 100,000 samples of the toothpaste to dental offices across the country in an effort to create a buzz in the professional community. Retailers, including Pathmark Stores, based in Woodbridge, N.J., and Cincinnati-based Kroger supermarkets have posted "coming soon" signs to spur early interest among consumers.

And although most product launches require about six to eight weeks to get products from plants to store shelves, Colgate claims it has cut the time to six to eight days. The company says that in many cases, it is bypassing retailers' warehouses and shipping tubes of Total directly to individual stores from its plant in Indiana. In addition, some retailers are sending trucks directly to Colgate warehouses rather than wait for the product to be shipped. Colgate also sent 104,000 in-store product displays to retailers; that compares with just 16,000 such displays shipped for the recent launch of its whitening toothpaste.

Even Colgate employees have gotten into the act, checking their local drug and grocery stores for the product during the past few days and alerting Colgate executives if they can't find Total on the shelves.

Reprinted by permission of *The Wall Street Journal,* © 1997 Dow Jones & Company, Inc. All Rights Reserved Worldwide.

Updating a Classic: 'The Man in the Gray Spandex Suit'

BY SUSAN WARREN

Staff Reporter of THE WALL STREET JOURNAL

Better business suits are made with . . . *spandex?*

That's what **DuPont** Co. is telling designers, makers and customers of men's clothing. The chemical giant claims that adding a smidgen of its Lycra brand of spandex to suiting results in the perfect material for tailored men's clothing.

It's a tough sell.

Spandex is noted for its elasticity — just what a lot of men aren't looking for in a business suit, which DuPont acknowledges. "When you say stretch to a guy, he's thinking men-in-tights. He's thinking Batman and Robin. He's thinking, 'This is not for me,'" concedes Brian Gallagher. He's the DuPont marketing manager charged with overcoming the stigma of a fabric long associated with women's undergarments and body-hugging exercise apparel.

Introduced by DuPont in the early 1960s, the elastic thread originally replaced rubber in women's girdles, then quickly spread into hosiery. Now as Mr. Gallagher tries to hasten its spread into menswear, he has immersed himself in the fashion business and operates out of offices in New York's garment district, far from the labs at DuPont's Wilmington, Del., headquarters.

A typical day finds him supervising the shooting of fashion ads for the menswear trade magazine Daily News Record. Browsing through Geoffrey Beene dress shirts and Haggar sports coats, he chooses a navy Claiborne suit to show off his stuff.

Flexing his shoulders in that same Claiborne suit, model Grant Luther admits he never really thought of spandex as something to wear to the office. "It evokes bikers and hookers as opposed to businessmen," he says.

Mr. Gallagher, who describes Lycra's benefits as "elastification," is just one cog in a much larger fashion machine built by the chemicals industry to boost sales of fibers such as nylon, polyester and spandex. Global powerhouses like Germany's **Bayer** AG and **Hoechst** AG routinely sponsor fashion shows, curry favor with major designers and commission cutting-edge designs to showcase new fabrics. Wellman Inc., a polyester-resin maker in Shrewsbury, N.J., sponsors an annual collaboration between top designers and fashion students, who create styles from its fabric made from recycled plastic bottles.

At DuPont's garment-district offices, two fashion directors search for trends to offer retailers and designers in regular color and style forecasts. Part of the mission is to promote new twists on old fibers. A few years ago DuPont rolled out Micromattique, a silky polyester. Next year it will introduce Supreva, a nylon that mimics wool.

But it also must find new markets for old products like Lycra. Analysts estimate that Lycra generated sales of $1.5 billion last year and that it accounts for about 60% of the world's spandex market. Seeking to stretch that market, a DuPont team at headquarters is working on adding Lycra to women's leather shoes in an effort dubbed the "Cinderella strategy." Another team is experimenting with Lycra in luggage.

Out in the field pushing Lycra in menswear, Mr. Gallagher is doing his best to overcome men's skepticism about clothes that stretch. At his first meeting with a major garment maker, company officials shooed him away after advising him, "You've got an uphill battle." Even when he got in the door at Baltimore-based retailer **Jos. A. Bank Clothiers** Inc., he says he faced a room of salespeople sitting with arms crossed and eyes down, already convinced that "never in their wildest dreams would they wear a stretch suit."

As Mr. Gallagher recalls, one protested: "I typically sell to businessmen who make $100,000 or more a year, and they're just not going to buy it." Another asked: "Does the suit come with a cape?"

A turning point, he says, came last spring when DuPont joined with the Fashion Association to hold a fashion show featuring 60 ways to dress a man in spandex. Models wore tailored suits, golf slacks and sports jackets. After the show, Mr. Gallagher says, some in the audience asked to try the garments on.

In fact, Mr. Gallagher often encourages clients to try on his own size 40-regular suit coat and do what he calls "the chicken dance"— the elbows-up-and-down motion many men make when trying on a jacket.

His days visiting retailers and clothing manufacturers are paying off. About 2.5 million men's suits, or about 15% of those sold in the U.S., contained spandex last year, up from almost none in 1996. Major menswear designers including Calvin Klein, Hugo Boss and Armani have used a touch of spandex in their men's suits. **J.C. Penney** Co. offers its own line, called "Traveler Plus."

Federated Department Stores Inc. introduced a 98% wool/2% Lycra blend into its midpriced Alfani suits last year and the line has sold solidly, says John Fowler, men's fashion director for the Federated Merchandising Group unit. The suits have fewer wrinkles and wear longer, he says.

Percy Carter, a menswear salesman at Macy's in Dallas, says that when suits with Lycra began appearing on the racks last year, "a lot of men were afraid of it." He adds: "They saw the word spandex on the tag and they freaked out."

Macy's customer William Ard, 24 years old, believes the last time spandex touched his body was in his high-school football uniform. "I don't really have the figure for spandex," he jokes. But Mr. Carter goes to work, snatching a stretchy black Hugo Boss suit priced at $950, grabbing the corner of the jacket and wadding it into a tight ball. "Look at that," he says after letting go. "No wrinkles." He then urges Mr. Ard to slip on the coat. "This feels all right," says a surprised Mr. Ard. (He doesn't buy it, though; the suit is out of his price range.)

Even as Lycra makes inroads in menswear, a challenger is emerging. Fabric makers are rolling out a new "mechanical" stretch, achieved with a special weave and twist to the fiber that creates a flexible fabric without requiring man-made elastic. Dallas-based Haggar Corp., for one, has introduced a wool-with-Lycra blend but is opting for the mechanical stretch in its all-cotton products.

Chicago's **Hartmarx** Corp., maker of Perry Ellis tailored clothing, has already tried spandex and abandoned it. "Mechanical stretch is the new thing," says Mark Alden Lukas, Perry Ellis creative director.

Marks & Spencer PLC's Brooks Brothers tries to have it both ways. In its lower-cost outlet stores, it sells a wool with Lycra suit for under $300. But its other stores are all-wool only (about $600). Gordon Schwartz, vice president of men's tailored clothing, prefers the mechanical stretch to Lycra, which he says "has a little bit of a rubber-band feeling to it."

Reprinted by permission of *The Wall Street Journal,* © 1998 Dow Jones & Company, Inc. All Rights Reserved Worldwide.

Camera System Is Developed but Not Delivered

BY WENDY BOUNDS
Staff Reporter of THE WALL STREET JOURNAL

For more than three months, yellow Kodak fliers at a Rite-Aid drugstore have promoted the Advanced Photo System with the line: "The Dawn of a New Era in Photography Is Here!"

The question is: Where? This Wilkinsburg, Pa., store hasn't gotten any of the cameras or film, and nationwide, other retailers are also waiting for the cameras, which were supposed to arrive in stores in late April.

Five of the world's largest photo manufacturers, including **Eastman Kodak** Co., developed the new photography system to spur ailing sales and counter new competitors in the computer industry. The system, which is incompatible with 35mm technology and is priced about 15% higher, is supposed to solve some of picture-taking's most vexing problems. For instance, the cameras are small and light, making them more convenient to carry, and they come in a variety of designs. Photographers can take three sizes of pictures on the same film roll: classic (4 inches by 6 inches), group (4 by 7) and panoramic (4 by 10). Errors in the use of the flash can be corrected at the photofinishing stage.

But more than six months after the cameras were unveiled, production problems and demand miscalculations have kept the new systems off most retailers' shelves. Poor packaging has spurred some consumers to buy the new film cartridges thinking they will fit old cameras. Advertising has drizzled off, and in-store marketing is haphazard.

Meanwhile, the togetherness that created the Advanced Photo System is over. For nearly a decade, the five rival developers pooled their technological skills to create the system. Along with Kodak, the companies included **Fuji Photo Film** Co., **Minolta Camera** Co., **Canon** Inc. and **Nikon** Inc. But when the time came to market the film and cameras, collaboration was unthinkable, they insist. "That's collusion," says William Janawitz, Kodak's general manager, Advanced Photo System.

Collusion is indeed the issue in pricing, but the players couldn't even agree on a single name. Instead, there are Kodak's Advantix, Minolta's Vectis, Nikon's Nuvis among others.

"This has to be the worst product launch in the history of the photographic industry," says Paul Gordon, director of U.S. marketing for Japan's **Konica** Corp. (Konica isn't one of the five original developers, but it manufactures cameras and film for the system as a licensee.)

"I call it the nonlaunch," says Michael Adler, chairman of **Moto Photo** Inc., a photofinishing franchiser. Desperate for cameras so that customers would use the new film and get it developed, Mr. Adler last month instructed his 375 U.S. franchisees to buy any cameras they could find from mass merchants.

But **Wal-Mart Stores** Inc., the nation's largest photofinishing retail outlet, still doesn't have cameras in all its 2,252 stores. **Phar-Mor** Inc. is still waiting for the system, and a spokesman says he doesn't think "we'll have a lot of it real soon." Says Don Franz, an industry consultant: "Retailers are missing out on the big summer vacation picture-taking opportunities. They are bound to feel deceived and let down."

Internally, companies discussed postponing the April 22 shipment date, but each feared its rivals would forge ahead. "I truly believe the system should have been introduced and not rolled out until June," says Fuji's Mr. Almeida. But Kodak's Mr. Janawitz says, "When I look back at what we did, I don't think the cards could have been played a whole lot differently."

System developers, including Fuji and Kodak, blame unexpectedly high demand and startup kinks for the shortages. Some say cautious reviews by the trade press tempered their production projections.

Japanese developers, for example, trimmed planned camera shipments to the U.S. because negative trade-press reports consistently questioned whether consumers wanted a new system. But developers now concede that they were partly to blame because information about the system's benefits was kept top-secret. Concedes Fuji's Manny Almeida, vice president of U.S. marketing: The trade press "only knew what we were spoonfeeding them. They didn't know all the details."

At the Photo Marketing Association's late February trade show in Las Vegas, manufacturers realized the depth of their problems.

Dealer and retailer orders poured in at unexpected levels, spurred by a spate of advertising, including the start of a $100 million campaign by Kodak. By the show's third day, Mr. Almeida says, Fuji salesmen were warned against promising on-time deliveries. Kodak's Mr. Janawitz, too, says, "we knew we couldn't supply them all."

Big retailers at least were forewarned about low supply. Drugstore chain **Eckerd** Corp., the nation's third largest photofinisher, mounted its own media campaign in core markets like Dallas, Miami and Atlanta, warning local press that "there could be shortages," says Eckerd spokesman Gerry Hoeppner. "We needed to let people know we couldn't guarantee every day that cameras would be there."

Meanwhile, Kodak gave the QVC home shopping channel a big chunk of Kodak cameras in April. Smaller photo dealers cringed. "I'm not whining, but I've been selling the concept of APS to my customers for a year," says Guy Danella of Danella Photographic in Utica, N.Y. Mr. Danella ordered his cameras in March but in May received only film and Kodak APS stickers for his store window.

In Europe and Japan, similar problems arose. A group of French retailers printed a catalog advertising the system but dumped 10,000 copies in the trash when they got no cameras.

Developers now promise manufacturing kinks are solved and output is rising. Kodak has mailed apologies to its U.S. dealers and says it's "discussing" additional APS-related manufacturing expenditures. Mr. Almeida says Fuji is currently shipping 300% more cameras to the U.S. than originally forecast.

Kodak advertising heated up again during the Olympic Games in Atlanta. Fuji has waited until this month for major promotions, when more cameras will be available. Photofinishers like Mitch Goldstone of 30 Minute Photo Etc. in Irvine, Calif., postponed advertising too.

Nearly one-third of U.S. buyers surveyed earlier this year said they intended to purchase the Advanced Photo System — if they could only find it. Says Konica's Mr. Gordon: "If we don't recover quickly, the Advanced Photo System could be the Edsel of the photographic industry."

Reprinted by permission of *The Wall Street Journal*, © 1995 Dow Jones & Company, Inc. All Rights Reserved Worldwide.

Place

45

Convenience is what firms are selling

By Lisa Green
USA TODAY

DETROIT — The time is midnight, but the lights are burning inside the Kinko's copy center at the corner of Mack Avenues and Moross Road. Copy machines are cranking. IBM computer screens invite customers to sign on.

Freelance artist Joseph Ferraro is one of the half dozen people in the shop. He's getting an image from a floppy disk transferred to a color proof. He needs it for an 8:30 a.m. meeting. "You talk to any artist, and this is almost like a godsend," says Ferraro.

Kinko's and its round-the-clock hours is one of the higher profile examples of a growing trend: businesses open all hours to cater to a demanding consumer.

They range from standbys such as grocery stores, to couriers and pharmacies.

They serve customers who can't find time during what once were considered normal business hours — 9 to 5 — to pick up prescriptions from the drug store or get a suit to the cleaners. They cater to those who work late shifts.

They serve business people who are wheeling and dealing with clients in different time zones. Some must respond to news from Tokyo, for example, where the stock market opens during evening hours in the USA.

And though many businesses that now operate 24 hours reach their slowest period after 10 or 11 p.m., they're willing to be accessible at all hours for the extra revenue.

After all, one of the best ways to make money in the '90s is to "sell convenience," says Anil Menon, an assistant marketing professor at Emory University in Atlanta.

Even for businesses where the revenue gains are small, employees are usually busy in the night hours — working on other projects for customers, making sure store shelves have plenty of inventory, or handling paperwork.

The past three years, Walgreen has more than doubled its 24-hour drugstores from 149 to 315.

"We try to have enough 24-hour stores to give us a good geographic coverage so you never have to drive too far," says Michael Polzin, spokesman for the retail and pharmacy chain.

Wal-Mart Stores opened its first 24-hour store seven years ago and now has 386.

On the East Coast, you can even golf 24 hours a day. Real estate developers Adam and David Wolkoff, along with their father Jerry, opened the nine-hole Heartland Gold Park in Islip, N.Y., in May.

The cost: $15 during the day, $20 at night. About 70% of customers are there between 6 p.m. and 3 a.m.

"Not everybody has the schedule and not everybody has the money to join the country club," David Wolkoff says.

> **For some 'it's as if the day never ends and a new one never begins'**

Whether you have the munchies at midnight or want to read a book until dawn, businesses are waiting.

▲ **Al Phillips, the Cleaner,** in Las Vegas. Eight of the company's 16 dry cleaning stores are open 24 hours. "How many times have you rushed to the cleaners for something you had to wear the next day and it's closed?" asks Mel Shapiro, company treasurer. The first 24-hour shop opened 25 years ago.

▲ **Preventive Dental Associates** in New York City. The practice is flexible. Early evening appointments are available. And an answering service will beep a dentist for emergencies. It's rare someone has to return to the office in the middle of the night. "Most dental emergencies can wait until the morning," says Dr. Mitchell Charnas.

▲ **Auto Zone,** in Glendale, Ariz. "It's as if the day never ends and a new one never begins," says store manager Brian Pierson. Auto Zone caters to the do-it-yourselfer, many of whom prefer to work after the often-sweltering sun has set. Employees can run simple tests to help car owners figure out their problem, and then provide technical assistance and tools.

▲ **Emery Worldwide,** based in Palo Alto, Calif. About 10% of the average 11,000 daily calls to the delivery service come after 10 p.m. and before 6 a.m.

And Emery announced last week the start of a new company to help focus on the demand for round-the-clock service. Emery Expedite gives additional options for door-to-door freight shipments for manufacturers, suppliers and other customers with tight deadlines and emergencies.

"It's a 911 type of service," says Expedite's David Quin.

▲ **Fidelity Investments,** based in Boston. The nation's top mutual fund company answers investors' calls round the clock, though most inquiries occur

(Cont.)

when markets are open.

▲ **Lands' End** in Dodgeville, Wis. It's the nature of the catalog business to be available day and night. Lands' End spokeswoman Anna Schryver says calls peak around 10 a.m. Central Time and drop to their lowest between 2:30 a.m. and 5 a.m. Between midnight and 5 a.m., Lands' End calls can usually be handled by five to 10 sales representatives. Unless, of course, it's the holiday season. Typically, an average day shift at Lands' End can be managed with 200 to 300 sales reps.

Those on the late shift or early morning shifts often talk to people like Joan Oishi of Ann Arbor, Mich. She usually looks at catalogs before going to bed. Once, she called at 3 a.m. Her children's winter coats had grown too small, and when Oishi saw coats she liked in the catalog, she ordered right away. "I told the lady when I called, 'If I don't buy tonight, there'll be a snowstorm.'"

▲ **Terry Neese Personnel Services** in Oklahoma City. Office hours are 8 a.m. to 5 p.m., but an employee is always available by pager. Panicked employers have called at 5 a.m. because they need temps for a project.

"We had employers who would call us and one of the first questions they would ask us is if we had a 24-hour service," says Terry Neese.

Neese estimates accounts have increased 10% because scheduling snafus can be handled anytime.

Back at the Detroit Kinko's, it's about **1:50 a.m.** Carrak Norton comes in because he needs 25 copies of a four-page exam for students he teaches at a high school.

"I have to be at the school at 7, so I'll have about four hours of sleep," Norton says.

2:20 a.m. Peter Zeiler, assistant manager, and Mark Van Eckoute, a supervisor, make a quick run to an adjacent 24-hour Amoco station for sodas and chips.

Mary Moran, a field manager for Oracle, a database software company, arrives. She uses an IBM computer to prepare a presentation for a client and also needs some faxes sent.

3:55 a.m. Cheryl Semmler couldn't sleep, so she comes in for color copies of material her fourth-grade daughter needs for a school project due in two days.

"I've been in at 6 (a.m.) here and it's much busier than this," says Semmler, who lives in nearby Grosse Point.

Between 2 a.m. and 5:30 a.m., 30- to 40 minute gaps between customers aren't unusual, says Zeiler, the assistant manager.

But employees can't let up. "There have been occasions," Zeller says, "when we've had a $7,000 or $8,000 job come in at 2 or 3 a.m."

Copyright 1995, *USA Today.* Reprinted with permission.

46

Middlemen Find Ways to Survive Cyberspace Shopping

What's a Distributor to Do If the Internet Connects Buyers and Sellers?

By David Bank

Staff Reporter of The Wall Street Journal

Middlemen are back in style.

Not long ago, the betting was that the Internet, with its power to directly connect sellers and buyers, would wipe out the link in the chain of commerce occupied by brokers and distributors of everything from fish to flowers to fighter planes.

These days, some of the busiest dealmakers in tech are network matchmakers that promise to bring buyers and sellers together in the electronic marketplace. The new niche has the potential to generate what has been in short supply in electronic commerce to date: real sales.

Using an Internet service to gather information on the availability of a particular pearl-beige Nissan Altima GLE with sunroof helped Bruce and Diane Fleischer of Herndon, Va., for instance, land the one hard-to-find car that had caught their eye. After a few weeks of broken promises from their original dealer, they were resigned to special-ordering the car from the manufacturer at an added cost of $1,000.

Then a colleague suggested that Mrs. Fleischer try **Auto-By-Tel** Corp., which runs a Web site that lets users click through a set of forms to select the make and model of their dreams. The Fleischers' order was instantly forwarded to a Nissan dealer in nearby Maryland, who called with a quote nearly $3,000 below the car's sticker price. Auto-By-Tel gets a monthly fee from participating dealers, but charges no commission on each sale.

"It was like ordering Chinese food to go," says Mr. Fleischer, a photography teacher. "We just signed the papers and drove away."

Insurance Buyers, Sellers

Intermediary sites are also popping up to serve other electronic commerce sectors such as computers, books, wine, insurance, travel and even homes. The Web site of **InsWeb** Corp., for example, serves as a buffer between life, auto and health insurance buyers and sellers by letting users compare quotes from several insurance companies, but doesn't sell policies itself. InsWeb sends customer information along to brokers or insurance companies only when the customer is ready to buy.

"We're about to reach a critical mass, where a wave of commerce-enabled merchants meet a lot of Web surfers who are ready to buy," said Julio Gomez, an analyst at Forrester Research Corp. "What the sellers need are intermediaries to help them scoop the buyers up."

There are several factors behind the trend. Many ordinary consumers find the Web a bewildering place and are happy to have a guide. Beyond that, rapidly improving computer technology makes it cheaper and easier to add links in the transaction chain between producers and consumers; indeed, many analysts believe that electronic commerce will support more, not fewer, intermediaries.

The key to success for the matchmakers, analysts say, is credibility and independence from any particular vendor. Instead, trusted, independent information on a wide selection of products and technology that can guide buyers through complex decision-making brings customers together. Once assembled, customers can be delivered to merchants, on-line or off, in return for a subscription or transaction fee, or a commission.

Collecting a fee of even a few percentage points on each transaction could turn into a nifty business. Total revenue from on-line shopping is projected to rise from $518 million this year to $6.6 billion in 2000, according to Forrester.

The computer industry is using itself to test the case for digital middlemen. Computer hardware and software already makes up the largest category in electronic commerce, accounting for an estimated $140 million in on-line sales this year and rising to $2.1 billion in 2000, according to Forrester. **PcOrder.com** Inc., an Austin, Texas, information clearinghouse for computer hardware sales, wants to do for selling computers what the Sabre reservation system has done for selling airline tickets, by integrating manufacturers, distributors and retailers into one information system.

PcOrder's database and software powers Web sites for wholesale distributors and retail resellers, who in turn offer services to their customers. A half-dozen wholesale distributors supply up-to-date information on 150,000 products from more than 800 manufacturers. Resellers and large corporate buyers can then use the system to compare prices, locate hard-to-find parts, configure computer systems from multiple sources and place orders over the Internet. PcOrder gets a percentage commission on each transaction.

Software retailers and distributors would seem to be a prime candidate for being edged out of the transaction chain, as more software is distributed electronically, rather than in shrink-wrapped boxes. But **Microsoft** Corp., the world's biggest software maker, is pushing for a system for electronic distribution of software that preserves the financing and customer service roles of existing intermediaries in the sales channel, from distributors like **Ingram Micro** Inc. to resellers such as **Egghead** Inc.

To cover the costs of establishing the new distribution system, Microsoft is passing along to its sales-channel partners its savings on the boxes, manuals and diskettes, items that aren't needed for software distributed on-line. Such costs total about $10 for a software program priced at $100 at retail.

Tracking Licensing Pacts

Microsoft's model, which is being adopted by much of the industry, even adds a new intermediary: electronic clearinghouses that keep track of software licensing agreements and the distribution of the digital keys needed to unlock the software before it can be used.

Other new intermediaries handle tasks such as credit authorization, billing, payment processing and providing shipping information. **TanData** Corp., Tulsa, Okla., for example, provides merchants with a database sys-

---

An Evolutionary Tale:

On-Line Commerce Business Trends

Once, there were middlemen, or intermediaries, in the physical world that helped customers and sellers find each other in the chaos of the marketplace. These intermediaries included advertisers, brokers, distributors, shippers and lenders.

Then came the Internet and, with it, predictions that direct connections between producers and consumers would cause **disintermediation,** or the elimination of middlemen of all sorts.

"Not so fast," said the middlemen, many of whom scrambled to find new niches for themselves in the electronic marketplace, gathering customers and information, extending on-line credit and providing services to complete transactions. And that process was called **reintermediation.**

But in the end, some of the old intermediaries went away and new ones emerged. And so it was that Paul Saffo, director of the Institute for the Future in Menlo Park, Calif., coined the phrase **disinter-remediation.** As Mr. Saffo says: "The ones that don't adapt disappear. Others change and survive. New ones appear. It's a tumultuous and evolutionary process."

(Cont.)

tem for comparing price and service information from freight carriers like **Federal Express** and **United Parcel Service**. For Internet commerce, that means customers get the best shipping charge instantly.

The proliferation of new intermediaries raises a host of issues about who will win or lose as electronic commerce spreads. One issue: Some sellers are worried that the inter-mediary who brings them a customer won't ever let go.

"Some intermediaries are arguing, 'I should get a piece for everything the customer does because I brought them to you,'" says Forrester's Mr. Gomez. "Sellers are saying, 'You're a referral source, just like advertising. You get a one-time flat fee.'"

In the end, Mr. Gomez says, the customer will decide. "The pressure is on the intermediaries to make them come back through," Mr. Gomez says. "They need to continually prove their value."

Reprinted by permission of *The Wall Street Journal,* © 1996 Dow Jones & Company, Inc. All Rights Reserved Worldwide.

47

Russia's Retail Revolution

By Christopher Bailey

A couple of Russian entrepreneurs were in my office recently, complaining about the sales of their food products. Just two years ago, their company could fly in a planeload of goods and they would sell out almost as quickly as Russian stores could be stocked. Those were the days of barren shelves and very little choice. Now, shelves are full, competition has heated up and they realize they need to spend more time establishing their brand. Their experience is a good indication of how quickly things are changing on the retail scene in capitalist Russia.

Surprises lurk around every corner in this unstructured, evolving market. Upon first look, one would find only a handful of what Americans consider supermarkets, as retail goods are sold mostly in the tens of thousands of small city kiosks and open markets. But then you stumble across the GUM, an organized retail outlet near Red Square that is now dominated by upscale retailers, including Nike, Reebok and other Western brands. These extremes illustrate both the contrasts in the Russian marketplace and the speed at which it is evolving, making the tasks of identifying consumer needs and building brand awareness far different—and more difficult—than in the United States.

In this newly thriving marketplace, brands can suffer an identity crisis. Partly to blame, and indicative of the accelerated pace of growth, is an underdeveloped distribution infrastructure for domestic companies. This has led to problems in establishing brand recognition because of inconsistencies in manufacturing, distribution, store presence and even the actual product itself.

U.S. consumer product companies are accustomed to keeping brands true to their promises—whether Americans buy their Kool-Aid in Boston or Texas, it is a given that it will taste virtually the same in each locale. This is not the case throughout Russia, where it is far more difficult to retain a sense of consistency. Mix water with Brand X in one part of the country and compare to another region and you'll see what I mean: different water, a different product.

The in-store environment is chaotic, especially for American brand marketers used to maintaining a uniform shelf presence across stores. While Russian retailers seem to have great respect for brands (when a Coke cooler goes in a store, it is stocked only with Coca-Cola products), maintaining a semblance of consistent shelf placement is a challenge for any brand or category. Baked goods can be found next to cosmetics in one store and bubble gum in another. Weak distribution systems are partly to blame. When a brand sells out, it may be weeks or months before that store can get it again, so shelves are rearranged around merchandise that's in stock.

Point-of-purchase advertising is not terribly sophisticated either; it often consists of taping labels to the windows of a Moscow kiosk. And to compound these issues, Russian product cycles are shorter. Categories are just being built, and they become obsolete more quickly than in the United States.

Those interested in tracking a brand's sales will find the methods archaic. There may be bar codes on some packages, but Russian retail does not use scanning equipment yet.

The future of Russian retail is hazy, with continuing change the only certainty. Right now, it is easiest to iden-

DOMESTIC HELP

Similar to Tang in the 1960s, Russian company C-PRO distributes powdered soft drinks positioned on convenience and nutritional value. Offerings under its brand, Invite, have now expanded to other powdered foods, such as oatmeal and soup.

To compete more effectively for the attentions of Russian consumers, C-PRO and others have turned to American companies to learn how to create brand awareness and package products. There is also a strong movement toward setting up manufacturing infrastructures, starting with building factories and creating domestically produced items.

Traditionally, C-PRO's products have been co-packed outside the country, but its entrepreneurs see tremendous opportunity in production at home. The company is currently in the process of building a factory to begin domestic manufacturing, yet it will also try to retain images of quality that Russians associate with prestigious imported products. —C.B.

(Cont.)

tify consumer needs and trends by looking at the cosmopolitan inhabitants of Moscow and St. Petersburg, but the urban population is beginning to move outside the city into suburbs growing on the outskirts, and brand awareness is even slowly creeping into rural areas. This will cause a natural evolution—or revolution—in the way people make purchases, and the retail scene will need to adjust. Expect to see consolidation as kiosks and open markets merge into larger stores.

As these changes take place, sooner rather than later, brand identity will become more important. But what will the Russian consumer consider the highest priority? Will it be value? Prestige? Imports? Domestic brands? It will be difficult to predict, but worth finding out.

© 1998 ASM Communications, Inc. Used with permission from *Brandweek* magazine.

Casket Stores Offer Bargains to Die For

BY GORDON FAIRCLOUGH

Staff Reporter of THE WALL STREET JOURNAL

Joseph H. Schoepe has always watched his pennies. That's why, although he's still going strong at 85 years old, he's already bought himself a discount casket.

Mr. Schoepe, of Avalon, Calif., got one for his 71-year-old wife, too. He feared their survivors would be pressured into buying expensive coffins. "I've worked hard for everything I have," says Mr. Schoepe, who spent 40 years putting roofs on homes in Los Angeles County. "And I don't want to waste money."

He found his casket discounter, Direct Casket, in an industrial complex in nearby Costa Mesa. The company and a handful of other cut-rate casket chains have sprung up since 1994, when the Federal Trade Commission ruled that funeral homes couldn't charge handling fees on coffins purchased elsewhere.

The discounters aim to yank the lid off the tightly controlled casket business, dragging it from the somber confines of the mortuary to the fluorescent light of the shopping center. Their goal: to make the emotion-laden purchase of a casket more like buying a piece of furniture.

You can shop in a showroom, call an 800 number or order on the Internet. Many companies offer 24-hour delivery. For those who buy their own caskets, some discounters hold the sum invested in trust until the customer's death. Under FTC rules, funeral homes can be fined $10,000 for refusing to accept caskets purchased elsewhere.

"We take a very straightforward approach. We're offering a consumer product," says John Iwaniec, Direct Casket's executive vice president and part owner. "Eventually, this has got to change the course of the industry." Why, he asks, "pour money into what is literally a hole in the ground?"

But shaking up the $10 billion funeral trade—known to insiders as the "death-care business"—won't be easy. Americans are used to one-stop shopping in their local funeral homes. And the industry doesn't take kindly to discounters.

Many of the 1.9 million caskets sold annually in the U.S. are produced by just two companies: Batesville Casket Co., a subsidiary of Hillenbrand Industries Inc. in Batesville, Ind., and York Group Inc. of Houston. Analysts estimate that Batesville's share of the market is 45%; York has 15%.

These giants ship only to licensed funeral directors; neither will sell to the upstarts. "We feel our products are best handled by death-care professionals," says Mark E. Craft, a Hillenbrand spokesman.

Typically, funeral homes mark up casket prices by 300% to 500%. They are often the most expensive part of funerals, which cost an average of $4,624 in 1995, up nearly 24% from $3,742 in 1991, according to the National Funeral Directors Association in Milwaukee. Of that, the association estimates $2,146 goes for the casket, although prices vary widely depending on the materials.

In the old days, the town undertaker was usually the local carpenter, who knocked together a pine box for the body and then "undertook" to bury it. When embalming came into wider use during the Civil War, being a mortician became full-time work. Costs rose as funeral directors offered more services. In recent years, many small mortuaries have been bought up by giant funeral-service companies, and this consolidation has pushed up prices in some markets.

Accordingly, more consumers are shopping for lower-cost alternatives, such as cremation or no-frills burials. Even when they deal with traditional funeral homes, they are choosing lower-priced caskets more frequently, says Bill W. Wilcock, president and chief executive officer of York Group. "It's gradual, but it's there," he says. "Consumers are smarter and very conscious of the price of everything, funerals included."

The discount casket showrooms expect to capitalize on this new frugality. "For $900, I can put you in a very nice casket," boasts Raymond S. Silvas, the 31-year-old president of Direct Casket's West Coast operations. The company recently opened its fifth store, located in the New York borough of Queens. It plans to have 30 outlets open within the next 18 months.

Direct Casket offers 40 models, among them the luxurious "Lincoln" in baby-blue burnished metal with a velvet lining for $1,595. At rock bottom is the $275 "Congressional," a corrugated-cardboard box covered with gray flannel and lined with twill. Direct Casket's biggest customers are baby boomers arranging funerals for their parents and planning ahead for their own. The company declines to disclose sales.

Other discount chains are also growing. Casket Royale of Hampton Falls, N.H., has more than 50 dealers and distributors across the country. The company had sales of about $2.1 million last year and expects to do more than $5 million this year. "It's just taking off, it's incredible," says owner Robert Ginsberg.

ConsumerCasket USA, a chain based in Erie, Pa., puts out a glossy, full-color catalog of caskets, urns and headstones. Within a year, it plans to add 10 stores to the four now in operation. Its president and chief executive, James M. St. George, is the former owner of a funeral home who lost his license after a brush with the law. Mr. St. George pleaded guilty in 1993 to mail fraud in connection with federal charges that he had misappropriated money customers had placed in trust to pay for funerals. He served 10 months in prison and is still on probation.

Now 31, he says those days are behind him. He vows to fight what he calls "widespread abuses" in the industry. Casket discounters decry the sale, for example, of expensive "protective" caskets. These are metal and come with a rubber gasket to keep out air and water, but some funeral directors fail to mention that the body will decompose anyway.

Traditional funeral directors are equally scornful of the discounters. "These are aggressive people who aren't interested in the well-being of families," says Richard Heath, the 43-year-old owner of Inglewood Mortuary in Los Angeles. Mr. Health says that as discounters have moved into his area, he has had to adjust his pricing. He has lowered the average cost of a casket by $400, while raising the average fee for services by the same amount. With others in the industry following suit, he predicts that even with lower casket prices, the total cost of a funeral will remain the same.

It's hard to say how much business the discounters eventually will be able to pull away from traditional funeral homes and their casket suppliers. After all, plenty of bereaved families still flinch at the notion of skimping. "You're dealing with a cultural issue here," says Joseph Chiarelli, an analyst at J.P. Morgan Securities who follows the industry. He doubts that most people are "ready for a discount funeral."

Reprinted by permission of *The Wall Street Journal,* © 1997 Dow Jones & Company, Inc. All Rights Reserved Worldwide.

THE VIRTUAL MALL GETS REAL

Online buying is expected to hit $4.8 billion in '98, and the Net may now be the place retailers have to be

For the past two months, Office Depot Inc. has been using the image of Dilbert, the cartoon character, in its advertising to help sell everything from staples to personal computers. But now, the wisecracking Dilbert is going interactive. On Jan. 16, when Office Depot launches its online store, the cartoon character will double as a sales clerk who helps cybershoppers find what they're looking for and walks them through their first online purchase. Office Depot figures Dilbert may make the experience easier as a new crop of shoppers flocks to the Net this year. "People have voted with their mouse clicks that if you make it more convenient, they will come," says Paul Gaffney, Office Depot's vice-president for systems development. "There is a huge opportunity here."

Indeed, online sales have never been better. In the quarter just ended, cybernauts snapped up everything from airline tickets to tennis rackets, to the tune of nearly $1 billion—twice the volume for the same period a year ago and higher than any previous quarter, according to Forrester Research Inc. Experts now say that 1998 is the year when electronic commerce could finally begin to fulfill its promise as a vast new marketplace. Online sales are projected to reach $4.8 billion this year, double that of 1997. "We're moving people from being window-shoppers to buyers," says Robert W. Pittman, president of America Online Networks, the division that runs the No.1 online service.

So whose virtual cash registers are ringing in the New Year? The early winners are those hawking computers and other high-tech gear—$863 million worth in 1997, a total that's expected to grow 85% this year, to some $1.6 billion. Dell Computer Corp. is the PC king on the Net, selling an average of $3 million a day. But even lesser-knowns are making hay. Computer reseller NECX, based in Peabody, Mass., sold $60 million on the Web in 1997, a fivefold jump over the previous year.

The computer crowd won't hold sway forever. Sales of everything from music CDs to shoes are on the upswing. But the biggest corner of cyberspace activity could be in travel. Web merchants selling airline tickets and booking hotel and car reservations accounted for $654 million in sales last year. Travelocity, Preview Travel, and Microsoft's Expedia, for example, are booking more than $2 million a week, on average. And Travelocity says it has topped $3 million several times in recent months. It could get better yet. By 1999, travel is expected to be the No. 1 electronic commerce category, with some $2.8 billion in total sales, according to Forrester.

OPEN WINDOW. Why are online sales taking off? For one, the number of U.S. households dialing into the Web is on an upward path: from 20 million in 1997 to an expected 26 million by the end of 1998, says market researcher Yankee Group Inc. That has prompted a slew of brand-name companies to open shop, including Bloomingdale's, the Gap, Sears, and Clinique—which, in turn, draws more shoppers. "This is a great way to get to a large number of people," says Angela Kapp, vice-president for special markets and new media for Estee Lauder Inc., which owns Clinique. "There is a window of opportunity here now."

Just so. Merchants hopping on the Net say that some of the impetus is seeing the success of early pioneers, such as Amazon.com. The Seattle-based startup was the first to open a mega-bookstore online, offering 2.5 million titles—more than any bricks-and-mortar counterpart. Amazon's huge selection, easy-to-use site, and hacker-free track record helped propel 1997 sales to an expected $131.7 million, up from $15.8 million a year ago, estimates Hambrecht & Quist Inc. Now, Barnes & Noble Inc. is fighting back, investing in its own Internet site, and bookseller Borders Inc. has plans for the Web, too.

The lesson: Getting on the Net early can be a huge advantage, especially for tiny startups. Even big-name retailers can't afford to wait. "I'm constantly pounding the tables, telling the companies whose boards I sit on, 'Don't get Amazoned,'" says James F. McCann, president of 1-800-FLOWERS, which has been selling online for three years. Clearly, cybershoppers have signaled they won't wait for the brand names if Net startups can offer a good selection, discounts, convenience, and security. Danielle Battle, a housewife in Bedford, Mass., is a point in case. She has spent about $1,500 over the past couple of years at fledgling online stores, including Amazon. "With the modem and the PC, you have the world before you," she says. "It is a bit of fun and a big convenience."

WISH LIST. It's also getting more customer-friendly by the day. In recent months, many Web-site operators have gotten smarter about how to appeal to buyers. Walt Disney Co.'s site, for example, has made it easy to find

Key Categories:	1997*	2000*
	(millions of dollars)	
PC HARDWARE AND SALES	$863	$2,901
TRAVEL	654	4,741
ENTERTAINMENT	298	1,921
BOOKS AND MUSIC	156	761
GIFTS, FLOWERS, AND GREETINGS	149	591
APPAREL AND FOOTWEAR	92	361
FOOD AND BEVERAGES	90	354
JEWELRY	38	107
SPORTING GOODS	20	63
CONSUMER ELECTRONICS	19	93
OTHER (TOYS, HOME, ETC.)	65	197

DATA: FORRESTER RESEARCH INC.   * Estimates

(Cont.)

shopping online by putting links to its virtual store on the opening page of its site—no more plowing through Web page after Web page. And this week, iQVC, the online division of QVC Inc., launched a separate section on its site called Gemsandjewels.com that offers general information about gold and stone cuttings. QVC also features a new

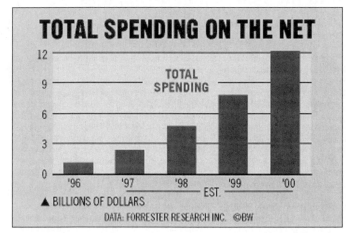

TOTAL SPENDING ON THE NET

TOTAL SPENDING

12
9
6
3
0

'96   '97   '98   '99   '00
EST.

▲ BILLIONS OF DOLLARS

DATA: FORRESTER RESEARCH INC. ©BW

service that lets visitors set up a wish list of items friends or family can look through when searching for a gift.

At the same time, merchants are streamlining the online shopping experience with better technology. They have improved so-called cybershopping carts that let consumers put the products they want in a virtual basket. That way, shoppers can continue browsing the site rather than having to pay for each product before selecting the next one on that site. And merchants, such as

Amazon and L.L. Bean, are using passwords to preserve billing and credit-card information so that once shoppers register at a site, they don't have to fill in that data again.

E-merchants also are making headway in figuring out how to grab Web surfers' attention. Many online merchants have begun using the heavily trafficked Net search engine sites as a springboard to their sites. Consumers using No. 1 search engine Yahoo!, for example, can click on an icon that links directly to Hallmark Cards Inc.'s Web site, where the greeting-card company offers 17,000 graphics and messages—some for free and others for a fee. And Yahoo!, AOL, Lycos, Infoseek, and Excite! have all introduced or redesigned shopping areas to highlight specific online shops, such as Eddie Bauer, Barnes & Noble, or J.C. Penney. Merchants can pay millions of dollars for top billing on these popular sites. "From a retailer's perspective, you can build a great store, but if the traffic isn't there, it's like a phone number in the white pages," says AOL's Pittman. "You've got to be where the people are."

SECURITY FEARS. Even with the improvements, shopping online isn't always a breeze. Consumers still have to type in order forms at each separate site. And the Web has a ways to go before it delivers on the promise of easy-to-find goods for every taste and price range. In November, Yahoo! and Excite introduced shopping tools that are designed to search according to price or product. Still, they include only a few hundred merchants. Technology that can scour the entire Web and the thousands of shops out there isn't available yet. And it's still hard to judge colors and sizes on Web pages. "I'm waiting for the online avatar that can make suggestions and show me how things look on me," says Harold Wolhandler, director of research at ActivMedia Inc., a technology consultant based in Peterborough, N.H.

Concerns also linger about security, especially among those consumers who are new to the Web. Technology developed by Visa USA Inc. and MasterCard International Inc. that outlines how credit-card transactions are handled by merchants and banks is still in the testing phase. That means that the marketing machines of two of the most trusted credit-card companies haven't begun pushing consumers to buy online—yet.

Still, some experts say the grassroots growth of cybershoppers is almost making the endorsement by credit-card companies a non-issue, especially when giants such as AT&T and IBM are pushing electronic commerce in TV and print ads. That could help put the Internet on any savvy shopper's list of places to shop till they drop.

Reprinted from January 26, 1998 issue of *Business Week* by special permission, copyright © 1998 by McGraw-Hill, Inc.

50

Selling Jewelry, Dolls and TVs Next to Corn Flakes

By Calmetta Y. Coleman

Staff Reporter of The Wall Street Journal

OMAHA, Neb. — At one HyVee Food and Drug store here, Barbie and Elmo dolls perch atop frozen-food cases and a model train races across a salad bar topped with faux snow. Decorated trees in nearly every aisle showcase the store's holiday decorating service.

What's happening to this supermarket? Grocery chains have always done a big business in food at this time of year, but now some are undertaking a much more ambitious goal: They want to become places where people do all their holiday gift shopping.

HyVee, a supermarket chain based in West Des Moines, Iowa, recently began holding open houses to highlight gift items like a $210 decorative clock, a $250 miniature tea set and a $270 humidor with cigars. **Wegman's Food Markets** Inc., Rochester, N.Y., offers to ship customized gift baskets filled with fruits, wines, coffees or bath accessories anywhere in the continental U.S.

Schnuck Markets Inc. of St. Louis this year mailed a catalog of plants, fruit baskets and other workplace gifts to 93,000 businesses. Last Christmas, Schnuck's regular grocery circulars featured jewelry boxes, cherry-finished coffee tables, ab-toning machines and bed linens. Big sellers included televisions and VCRs.

"Our gift business has increased every year as we've done a better job of marketing it," says Craig Schnuck, chairman and chief executive of the 87-store chain.

All this is the latest punch in supermarkets' ongoing battle to protect market share from a growing number of retailers selling food. Three big mass merchandisers, **Wal-Mart Stores** Inc., **Kmart** Inc. and **Dayton Hudson** Corp.'s Target, all have supercenters with full-service grocery sections. And at Christmas, even chic department stores get into the act, selling fancy food baskets and wines.

"Supermarkets are beginning to see ways to regain market share by treading in some nontraditional areas," says Jon Hauptman, a supermarket-industry consultant with Barrington, Ill.-based Willard Bishop Consulting Ltd. The result: a blurring of categories, as supermarkets and department stores all converge into one cornucopia selling everything.

Total sales of nonfood items increased 2.6% at supermarkets last year, a Progressive Grocer magazine study shows. Sales of toys — always a hot Christmas category — rose 4.5%.

Some supermarkets branched out beyond food years ago. **Kroger** Co. has boasted perfume counters for years, and jewelry and apparel have long shared space with food at Fred Meyer stores. But at many stores, today's hurried lifestyles have shrunk the cooking-ingredients section, clearing the way for even more general merchandise. Many supermarkets are devoting the extra space to seasonal products.

HyVee, for instance, has two fewer grocery aisles now than it did a year ago. Much of the space has gone to prepared meals, but still more of it makes up a large corner of the store that changes with the seasons. For Valentine's Day, for example, that could mean a selection of heart-shaped charms and knick-knacks.

"We're striving to be merchants rather than just grocery stores," explains John Allen, director of the Omaha store.

Some consumers are buying this pitch. Sandy Miller ducked into the HyVee Food and Drug store at the end of a recent workday to buy a $25 Cabbage Patch Kid, a Christmas present for her new granddaughter.

Groceries were just an afterthought. "As long as I'm here, I may as well get a few things," said the 55-year-old cafeteria cook.

Distributors are pushing the trend too. Fleming Cos., based in Oklahoma City, assists its supermarket clients with product marketing, including tips like displaying some Christmas merchandise as early as the beginning of October. This year the distributor expects to do big business in Elmo dolls and virtual pets. Bob Dickson, vice president of marketing and procurement, says the company is trying to change its image as merely a grocery supplier in order to expand its sales.

That fits in with supermarkets' efforts to be more like department stores. The 240-store HyVee chain first began holding Christmas presentations for its employees five years ago. Gift-wrapping experts give advice on colors and styles, and trendwatchers talk about which toys and clothes are expected to sell each year.

This year, HyVee chairman Ron Pearson directed some store managers to try to create "the ambiance of an upscale department store" for Christmas. To that end, Mr. Allen spent two days with a decorator from a Neiman Marcus store in Scottsdale, Ariz. "I learned a way of marketing that isn't just stacking pops on pallets," says the 30-year HyVee veteran.

The result was a three-day holiday show for which Mr. Allen invited 400 Omaha businesses to see the store all decked out for Christmas. Some highlights: A tuxedoed soloist sang Christmas tunes near the checkout counter, and VCRs around the store played holiday videos that were already gift-wrapped for sale. And in the parking lot, a Cadillac Catera and an El Dorado were displayed for sale.

The centerpiece of the show was a red-carpeted Holiday Gift Center decorated with a sofa and chairs from a local furniture store. Decorative candles, framed artwork and pricey porcelain figurines were all for sale. "I really wanted to make it look like someone's home to set the right mood to shop," Mr. Allen says.

The Cadillacs didn't sell and were returned to the dealer after the weekend show, but the unlikely supermarket display prompted one surprising impulse purchase: Julie Grauer bought two chairs from the display at $300 each.

Mrs. Grauer says she had long been dissatisfied with chairs she already owned but hadn't been moved to go furniture shopping. Notes the 65-year-old homemaker, "You have to go to the grocery store."

Reprinted by permission of *The Wall Street Journal,* © 1997 Dow Jones & Company, Inc. All Rights Reserved Worldwide.

52

BAXTER'S BIG MAKEOVER IN LOGISTICS

Even before the managed-care squeeze, supplying hospitals was a thin-margin business. So Baxter went back to the drawing boards. ■ *by Mary Connors*

At 7 A.M. a patient, let's call him Joe, rolls into an operating room for coronary bypass surgery at the big 1,100-bed Duke University Medical Center in Durham, North Carolina. Nearby, a scrub nurse busily unloads trays from what looks like an oversize room-service cart, fresh off the operating-suite dumbwaiter. Over the next half-hour, out come some 200 items, packed in the precise order that the surgeons and nurses will use them during the four-hour procedure. Here is skin marker to trace a seven-inch incision, bone wax to stanch the bleeding after a sternal saw does its work, suction tips to clear blood from the patient's chest cavity, plus scalpels, sutures, and, oh yes, gloves and gowns.

Don't tell Joe, but the small arsenal of products lined up for his operation, worth several hundred dollars, came not from the hospital stockroom but straight from the supplier's warehouse, 12 miles away in Morrisville, North Carolina. In fact, Joe checked into the hospital long before his supplies did, under a just-in-time contract tightly negotiated between Duke and Baxter International of Deerfield, Illinois, a major supplier.

Welcome to the every-thin-dime-counts business of supplying hospitals and other health care providers, which Baxter has been drastically revamping in its bid to remain No. 1 in the field. This $4.5-billion-a-year piece of the company delivers 200,000 different products, not counting all the sizes and shapes. They range from cheap-as-air cotton balls to vials of magnetic particles used to isolate a patient's stem cells in cancer treatment, delivered in dry ice and costing up to $450 each.

The prompt delivery of Joe's surgical kit epitomizes two of Baxter's strategies for remaining on top: just-in-time methods that relieve the hospital of carrying inventory, and a bold new risk-sharing arrangement in which Baxter and Duke set targets for reducing the cost of surgical supplies and share the gains

or losses. Risk sharing is already paying off, says Dr. Bruce Capehart, assistant administrator of the Duke medical center: "We're not simply slowing the rate of increase in the cost of health care. We've achieved a real decrease."

The logistics revolution at Baxter, which has transformed its dealings with all medical providers, big and small, couldn't be more timely. This fall the company will spin off its distribution arm and a surgical products manufacturing operation to form a new company called Allegiance Corp. The new entity's goal is to deliver not just products to hospitals, physicians, and nurses but also cost-saving methods that extend right to the operating table, worked out with the help of the company's own consultants. The rest of Baxter, focused on high-growth medical-technology and international businesses, will continue under the existing name.

The distribution unit—including the old American Hospital Supply, which Baxter bought a decade ago—is engaged in something far more subtle and sensible than mere downsizing by edict. Hundreds of working-level employees have been enlisted to help figure out ways to streamline the operation. And while a leaner operation is the overriding objective, the company has resisted some economy moves that might jeopardize a valued customer's quality of service. In some cases, moreover, Baxter is not just shaving costs but is also tacking on fees—atop generally flat prices—for extra service that previously carried no surcharge. Results to date: The distribution arm has cut operating expenses by $48 million a year and reversed a decline in cash flow. Some of the changes, recently worked out, have yet to bear fruit. "It's not done yet," says Lester Knight, a Baxter executive vice president who will head the spinoff company.

Rethinking its entire logistics system has

entailed a wrenching cultural change for Baxter. For years, the company's easygoing approach could be summed up by the words "Just say yes." Furnish what customers want, when they want it, in as many as 47 different bedpan styles, if that's what it takes. But in its dealings with hospitals, which account for the lion's share of revenues, cutthroat competition had eroded the distribution arm's markups to just 5% to 6% by the early Nineties. And the outlook was becoming even grimmer in today's revenue-constrained health care environment, in which managed-care companies wring discounts from hospitals and Medicare imposes a flat spending limit for each diagnosis. "We realized that if we didn't change the way we do business, at some point we would lose money," says Robert Zollars, Baxter's distribution chief and principal architect of the turnaround. In fact, one of Baxter's distribution rivals, $3-billion-a-year Owens & Minor of Richmond, did experience red ink for the first time last year, losing $11 million.

Baxter's new era in logistics began in 1989, when the company launched a just-in-time delivery system called ValueLink. Going beyond similar programs in other industries, ValueLink eliminates most stock keeping by customers, which each save $450,000 a year, on average, by not having to maintain big inventories. With a sophisticated computer system, Baxter is able to meet demand for supplies far more accurately than hospitals can on their own. The service took off, growing fivefold in three years. But Baxter, it turned out, was giving away the store. The deals it cut with its earliest just-in-time customers barely covered costs, and in some cases were not profitable.

"It was our Achilles' heel," says Zollars. "We didn't charge enough for all the extra services. We didn't articulate to our customers all the cost savings we were bringing them." A little articulation—along with new fees for fancier levels of service and stricter payment terms—put Baxter back on track. Contracts signed in the past 18 months have provided higher rates of return. Last year ValueLink sales increased 30%, to more than $650 million, while service fees from the 133 customers rose 60%, to nearly $20 million. This took place while Baxter was holding the line on basic prices, not counting those fees, in the face of continuing medical inflation.

The Duke medical center, for one, believes the savings from ValueLink more than offset the fees. The center no longer bears the cost of keeping on hand 30 days of supplies, and has turned 18,000 square feet in the basement formerly used for this purpose over to such revenue-generating operations as a pediatric endoscopy lab and a "telemedicine" department where physicians confer with doctors and patients worldwide.

In a much more daring change, piloted in an agreement with Duke in 1994, Baxter pushed beyond the just-in-time concept. By entering risk-sharing agreements with customers, it puts itself financially on the line to bring down their costs. Duke wanted to reduce the $20 million it was spending annually on operating-room supplies, and do so without hurting the quality of patient care. Over five years, the goal is to save $4 million in surgical-supply costs. Each year, Duke and Baxter split the savings fifty-fifty—or jointly cough up for overruns.

So far, the partners have pocketed savings. Baxter has helped the hospital staff to standardize and reduce the number of items used per procedure wherever possible. In the case of arthroscopic knee surgery, Baxter got eight physicians to eliminate excessive variety and use more of the same items. That move reduced the cost of supplies by 25% per operation, or a total of $32,000 a year in savings to Duke. Overall, the medical center's surgical-supply costs per procedure fell 5% in the second half of 1995. That's a drastic change. Previously, Duke's bill for all kinds of medical supplies had shot up 31% between 1991 and 1994.

Duke's Bruce Capehart, who says the risk-sharing agreement with Baxter may later be broadened beyond surgical supplies, believes the partners are breaking important new ground. "We're beginning to see some standardization of clinical care," he says, which would not have occurred on such an extensive scale had Baxter not pushed for the use of standardized materials. "What we're doing here has the potential to change the way health care is delivered in the United States."

Last year, Baxter's sales under risk-sharing agreements rose 30%, to $180 million. The company now has such deals with 34 major medical centers and hospitals, including three that signed up just in May; it hopes to win 200 more customers in the next four years. But risk sharing may not be for everybody.

Baxter figures that by 1999 only a fifth of its customers will embrace the concept.

That's one reason why the company has launched its most far-reaching effort, reinventing the way it delivers to all its customers. This got under way in 1993 with the help of Tennessee Associates International, a management consulting firm in Alcoa, Tennessee. The firm had previously advised a Baxter division on continuous-improvement strategies. But for companies battling cost pressures in a glutted market, says Gerald Sentell, Tennessee Associates' chief executive, "just continuously improving what you always have done may not be enough. In fact, it may be deadly."

Many of the steps Baxter has taken make familiar reading in the Nineties. Six operating divisions were melded into one, and the organizational pyramid was flattened. Before, five layers of managers separated Zollars from the frontline sales rep. Today, only two do. In a process that Zollars describes as "traumatic and difficult," many costs were lopped off. The number of warehouses from which Baxter supplies customers was trimmed from 99 to 69, and the company saved $35 million a year in freight costs by negotiating better deals with trucking firms that deliver supplies to it and by reducing the number of firms it uses. (For outbound shipments to hospitals and other medical producers, Baxter has its own fleet.)

More radical was a drive to rationalize the whole supply chain by dramatically narrowing the range of products held in warehouses close to customers. After slicing and dicing the data, Baxter discovered to its shock that 57% of its products accounted for just 2% of sales. The majority sat around, expensively, waiting to be ordered. Last year Baxter instituted a three-tier system, based on how quickly items go out the door.

Only the products that hospitals order frequently—popular styles of gloves, caps, needles, and sutures—are stocked in the 68 regional distribution centers close to customers. Items that hospitals order somewhat less frequently—odd sizes of gloves, say, or a special type of suture—are now shipped nationwide from a center in Waukegan, Illinois. And Baxter has sloughed off carrying the slowest sellers: These items go out directly from manufacturers, which now keep the inventory. That move, of course, shifts costs to the manufacturers.

Baxter's gold standard for warehousing fast-moving items is its $65 million Midwest distribution center, also in Waukegan. Opened in 1993 and boasting floor space equivalent to 13 football fields, it serves a five-state area, replacing eight facilities that Baxter closed. Products arrive and leave in a

mind-boggling array of configurations: a pallet of assorted supplies for a suburban Chicago hospital, a case of catheters for a Michigan clinic, and a recyclable plastic tub of products to be supplied just in time to a hospital in Milwaukee (contents: three dispensers of liquid hand soap, a 12-pack of single-fold towels, and 18 rolls of toilet paper).

In its brief life, the center has already become more efficient. The value of inventory held there has shrunk from $55 million to about $49 million, while the volume of products moved, and the speed with which they arrive and leave, has climbed impressively. In the past 12 months, Baxter has managed to cut by 25% the number of days' inventory it must have on hand. Credit for this improvement goes both to Baxter's revamped logistics system and to information technology. Some 214 people work at Waukegan in three shifts around the clock, but computers rule in nearly every process that takes place.

Computers aboard trucks bound for Waukegan, for example, give electronic notification of what supplies are en route and when they will arrive. That's just the beginning. Back in low-tech days prior to 1988, a shipment arriving in a Baxter warehouse might have been deposited in a preassigned spot or simply put down in the closest available nook. Today, Waukegan's computer talks to the company's order-management computer. Based on daily updates of product demand trends, the warehouse computer constantly adjusts the floor locations for optimum use of space. Best-sellers go to the front, slow sellers to the back.

Computers also tell drivers of forklift trucks where to stow newly arrived stuff. When the drivers pick up an incoming load at the dock, they use an optical scanner to read the bar code on the arriving pallet or case. A digital display panel at eye level near the driver's seat spits back the floor and shelf assignment. The truck, a "narrow turret" type that can maneuver down the center's tight aisles—whose narrowness allows for greater storage density—follows a guide rail to the reserve storage area, where pallets are berthed in racks up to 25 feet high. The driver scans a bar code on the shelf to confirm that the goods have reached the proper place. If they haven't, the forklift truck's digital display beeps and flashes "Wrong location!"

Despite the belt-tightening throughout its distribution business, Baxter has managed to achieve a higher level of customer satisfaction. Service ratings, defined as the number of lines on a hospital's order sheet that Baxter is able to fill immediately, have climbed from the high 70s to more than 95%, including a 3.5-point improvement in the first quarter of this year. This success may owe something to the careful way Baxter made the changes happen.

In summer 1993, Zollars, Tennessee Associates' Sentell, and others began a series of "flyarounds," visiting more than 500 managers and 10% of the work force, and proclaiming the need to streamline. In each major region, they met with large groups of employees for question-and-answer sessions, and held one-on-one meetings with customer-service reps, sales reps, even truck drivers. Those meetings often lasted until 2 A.M. "The key is to be open in communication," says Sentell. "Baxter's leaders told their people up front, 'There won't be as many of you here as when we started.' When major events took place, there were no surprises."

One reason is that troops in the trenches, not just bosses at headquarters, helped to design and implement the changes. When Baxter decided to chop $26 million in distribution costs in 1994, each region got a target to hit, and workers assisted in wielding the budget ax. "You can't come in like Simon Legree," says Sentell. "The point is to build a new way of doing things. You don't do it to employees, you do it with them."

Tamara Sager, 31, the quality inventory control supervisor at the big Midwest center, was among 100 employees who received three weeks of training from Tennessee Associates as HPO—for high-performance organization—facilitators. Her first assignment: "Tell us, Tamara, should we shut down our Indianapolis distribution center?"

Sager gulped, pulled together ten distribution, transportation, and sales colleagues from the Chicago area and Indiana, and flew to Indianapolis for an initial meeting. "I was very nervous," she says. "People were defensive. They could lose their jobs." Brian Kay, operations manager for the Indianapolis region, admits there was some Hoosier apprehension—"even my own"—in the early minutes of the first meeting. "But when asked to assess, you assess."

Things got easier as the group loosened up. "We were being asked, we weren't being told," says Sager. "Instead of giving us an order to close down the facility, they told us to look into it."

About two months later Sager brought a recommendation back to her superiors. Don't close Indianapolis. To do so would threaten a large just-in-time contract then up for renewal at Indiana University's big medical complex. A competing distributor had just entered the market. "Our determination was that it would save money, but we'd lose customers," says Sager. As an alternative way to economize, the team proposed supplying customers in South Bend from Waukegan instead of Indianapolis, a labor-saving move that would save $150,000 a year. Back at headquarters, executives questioned Sager closely but implemented the change in April 1995.

Similar procedures were used elsewhere. Each time, Baxter employees representing a range of functions came up with joint findings. At the Hayward, California, distribution center, truck drivers took part is sessions that led to the elimination of a delivery route and the design of more efficient runs. Marjorie Wilson, a truck driver for six years, was tapped to help work out the changes. "I can't say the reaction of the drivers was truly positive," Wilson says. "Their overtime was cut. But they knew we needed to cut costs. And the changes helped them operate more efficiently."

While rank-and-file participation helped prevent reckless economizing, the overall results were disappointing. Design teams in Baxter's eight regions nationwide came up with about 60 cost-saving changes. Sample: reducing driver overtime 50% in the Carolinas and three neighboring states. But in all, the groups fell short of the $26 million goal, saving only $16 million a year in distribution expenses. Baxter management, not the workers, took the blame for the shortfall. "We stubbed our toes," admits Mark Ehlert, VP for quality and regulatory affairs. The company will go on using grass-roots facilitators but has laid down additional standards to guide them.

To reinforce these changes, Baxter makes each employee accountable for his or her performance according to a one-page set of objective measures tailored to each job. "It's a technique straight out of General H. Norman Schwarzkopf's book about the Gulf war," says Sentell. "I will hold you accountable for everything on this page. If it's not on this page, you're not accountable." Thus, a truck driver is rated by such yardsticks as the number of on-time deliveries and the number of miles driven without an accident. The hard part: There's no place to hide if you don't hit the targets.

Accountability has already changed Baxter's culture for the better, Zollars says. "Two years ago, I could have visited one of our facilities and asked, 'How's receiving going?' And there might have been no answer, or a group answer. Today I'll visit Los Angeles, say, and the person who owns the receiving process answers."

Baxter hopes to emerge from the makeover a much stronger player. Though detailed performance data won't be available until the company discloses financial information on the new Allegiance Corp. early this summer, the distribution arm's head count has been reduced by 10% in the past three years. Zollars says a majority of those who lost jobs have found new positions elsewhere in Baxter.

Security analysts generally take a favorable view of the distribution company's solo prospects. "Large hospitals need help in controlling health care costs, and Baxter can differentiate itself here," says Kenneth Abramowitz of Sanford C. Bernstein in New York City. He expects the new company's revenues to grow annually by 5% to 7%, outpacing the 3% to 4% growth in the medical-supply distribution business. "The spinoff will be able to focus on distribution without being encumbered by the high-tech end of Baxter," Abramowitz says. Safeguarding market share and stepping up risk sharing are key to Allegiance's future, adds Jay Silverman of New York City's Schroder Wertheim & Co.: "Once they're able to lock in a lot of these programs with managed-care outfits and hospital groups, by the end of 1997 they will be getting the kind of results they want."

Still, given the complexity and the low margins, it's not an easy business to be in. Distribution chief Knight, Allegiance's boss-to-be, says the toughest moments for him so far have been in "soul searching" meetings with hospitals about to take the plunge into just-in-time deals. "They look us in the eye and say, 'If you don't deliver, we'll have somebody die on the operating table.'"

Back at Duke, heart patient Joe is doing well, thank you. And Knight is counting on the same for his bottom line.

REPORTER ASSOCIATE *Ani Hadjian*

© 1996 Time Inc. All rights reserved.

53

A PC Maker's Low-Tech Formula: Start With the Box

BY EVAN RAMSTAD

Staff Reporter of THE WALL STREET JOURNAL

It's come to this: A guy can start a personal-computer company by figuring out what size box Federal Express considers optimal.

That was one of the first pieces of research for Doug Johns, a **Compaq Computer Corp.** refugee who wanted to run his own business. FedEx told him the ideal dimensions for a package between 15 and 25 pounds were 19 inches by 19 inches by 9.5 inches. Mr. Johns and his wife Jane dug shoeboxes out of her closet and taped them together to form a box that size.

The result was **Monorail** Inc., a little company that's thriving thanks to the upheavals that are wrenching other PC makers. Mr. Johns saw that PCs are becoming lookalike commodities with plunging prices. The way to compete, he concluded, wasn't with superior technology, but rather superior logistics.

To keep costs low, he contracted out manufacturing, customer support and even some accounting. Rather than promote technology, he marketed his computers' design and quick delivery. To fit FedEx's specs, he designed a hybrid machine that's easier to ship than a desktop PC but more powerful than a notebook computer.

Today Monorail is grabbing lucrative shelf space and becoming a notable niche player in the market for personal computers costing less than $1,000. Debuting just about a year ago with a $999 machine, Monorail has been blessed with good timing. Sales of computers costing less than $1,000 now account for about one-third of the computers sold at retail in the U.S., compared with less than 5% a year ago.

On the other hand, that trend is bringing the PC world's heavyweights onto Monorail's turf. Compaq and International Business Machines Corp. are adding low-priced computers to their lines, robbing Monorail of its advantage as one of the few choices in that price range. In addition, imitators are emerging: The founder of Power Computing Co., which recently was sold to Apple Computer Inc. is drawing up plans for a PC company with product designers but no factory.

Mr. Johns, 49 years old, didn't intend to jump back into the computer business. Tired of long hours, he left his job as president of Compaq's personal computer division in 1993 and moved to Atlanta. He spent the next two years taking long vacations and volunteering at his kids' elementary school.

Watching the industry from a distance, he concluded that the competition had changed. Rather than producing the best technology, the winners in computer sales were leaders in the mundane areas of packaging and logistics. In fall 1995, he typed up a business plan for a company that would chiefly hire designers and managers and contract out everything else.

Early on, he enlisted FedEx as Monorail's distributor, giving it the ability to send PCs from factory to stores overnight and, sometimes, directly to customers. Since the box FedEx recommended wasn't big enough to hold a separate monitor and PC, Mr. Johns and his first employees designed a computer with the flat-panel display of a notebook computer on top of a dictionary-sized metal box filled with desktop computer innards. They came up with a machine that's 80% smaller than an ordinary desktop PC, but twice as heavy as a laptop.

Using a direct distribution system helped avoid a problem Mr. Johns says he saw often at Compaq in the early 1990s in matching factory output and customer demand. "It seemed like we always had monitors in Singapore when we needed them in Europe or too many computers in Germany when we needed them in Italy," he says. However, Monorail still isn't quite as efficient as giants Dell Computer Corp. and Gateway 2000 Inc., who custom-build PCs and ship right to a customer.

Mr. Johns hired a company that thinks up corporate names and told it to stay away from "Cyber" and "Tek" and come up with something friendly. He used $2 million of his money from Compaq stock to build a prototype and hired several friends, including former Compaq designers. A hire from Sun-Trust Banks Inc. forged a deal in which the Atlanta bank acts as Monorail's accounts receivable department. Since spring 1996, other investors have put another $28 million behind Mr. Johns's idea. Mr. Johns won't disclose revenue or profitability.

The company's biggest break came when CompUSA Inc., the nation's biggest computer superstore chain, agreed in fall 1996 to sell Monorail's system. Monorail promised that it could help the retailer keep inventories low. Larry Mondry, CompUSA's merchandising chief, says he ultimately took the product because of its unique look and low price.

Indeed, many buyers were drawn to its size, offering a little more than a notebook but not quite as much as a desktop PC. "Instead of devoting half a room to a computer by the time you get the wires and monitor hooked up, this only takes an edge of the desk and a slide-out place for your keyboard," says Deryl Danztler of Macon, Ga., who a year ago bought one for his office and a second for his mother. Florida Blood Services in Tampa equipped each of its 20 bloodmobiles with two Monorail units for registering and checking blood donors' histories.

Southwestern Vermont Medical Center bought 14 Monorail PCs this summer, rigging some to mobile stands typically used for intravenous solutions so nurses can wheel them from bed to bed. "Our experience has been that laptops last 18 to 24 months with constant use," says Dennis Amadon, technology administrator at the 124-bed facility in Bennington, Vt. "This way, we have a system that costs less and is nearly laptop size, but if the keyboard goes bad, we can replace it without having to replace the entire computer."

The trade-off is that the Monorail has a sealed case, so it must be sent back to the company for modifications, such as adding memory chips. In addition, its "passive matrix" screen isn't very bright. The better "active matrix" displays, used in the best laptop PCs, are too expensive for a low-price computer.

Monorail's obsession with low overhead exacted a cost last year when the die used to stamp out the computer's steel case broke. Mr. Johns had lined up contingencies for many potential problems, but he didn't have an alternative metal stamper. "That's when I started yearning for my money back," he says.

Production stopped and in just a few days, store shelves were empty. Luckily, a subcontractor created a new die in five days. Mr. Johns has since developed another contingency plan.

Last month, shipping stopped temporarily again when Monorail switched to a larger contract manufacturer, Synnex Information Technologies Inc. of Sunnyvale, Calif., which also produces PCs for Compaq and Hewlett-Packard Co. Though planned, the change left some CompUSA stores without products for a few days.

To keep growing, Monorail executives say the company next spring will begin rolling out other computer products, though they won't elaborate. Still, Monorail won't try to break new ground with technology. It will stick with products that use proven components that are widely available to keep inventory and costs low.

"It doesn't have to be a unique, ultraslim desktop PC," says Andrew Watson, Monorail's marketing chief. "Our sustainable advantage is we can sell anything through this model."

Reprinted by permission of *The Wall Street Journal*, © 1997 Dow Jones & Company, Inc. All Rights Reserved Worldwide.

Promotion

54

The Tricky Business of Rolling Out a New Toilet Paper

BY TARA PARKER-POPE

Staff Reporter of THE WALL STREET JOURNAL

Marketers of bathroom tissue have used everything from puffy clouds to cuddly babies to advertise their products. Now **Kimberly-Clark** wants to talk about the real reason people use toilet paper.

Testing the limits of how much consumers want to hear about what goes on in the bathroom, the maker of Kleenex Cottonelle is spending $100 million to promote the brand as the toilet paper that wipes better than regular tissue, thanks to a new "rippled texture." New ads begin today and ten million free samples will be hung on doorknobs in the eastern U.S., where the product will first appear.

The new texture is "designed to leave you feeling clean and fresh," promise the ads from **WPP Group's** Ogilvy Mather in Chicago. Another ad claims that "discriminating toilet paper users" prefer the tissue because it "left them feeling cleaner than the leading brand." The name, Kleenex Cottonelle, will remain the same, as will the price. The tagline: "Your fresh approach to toilet paper."

Talking about the way a toilet paper performs is a major departure for a category that for years has focused on squeezable softness, quilted softness and cottony softness. Are consumers who remember seeing Mr. Whipple squeeze the Charmin ready to hear even a hint of what he did with the product?

Kimberly-Clark is convinced that they are. And the ads call it by the name most consumers use: toilet paper. This is, after all, familiar territory for the maker of Kotex, the first feminine-care product ever advertised. The company also pushed the boundaries of personal-care advertising when in 1981 its Depends brand launched the first national-television advertising for an adult-incontinence product. More recently, the company has tacitly acknowledged the unpleasant task of cleaning baby bottoms as it boasts that its Huggies baby wipes "clean like a washcloth."

"If we have news that's important for a consumer, then we can find a way to tastefully communicate it," says Tom Falk, group president of Kimberly-Clark's North American tissue, pulp and paper business. "It's graphic, but [the textured tissue] really feels very different."

This is Kimberly-Clark's biggest push ever in the $3.5 billion-a-year U.S. toilet paper business, where it is a relative newcomer. Its original Kleenex toilet-tissue brand struggled after its introduction in 1990. The company merged with Scott Paper, maker of the Scott and Cottonelle brands, in 1995 and created Kleenex Cottonelle, which helped Kimberly-Clark gain a 23% share of the market. But it trails rival **Procter & Gamble's** Charmin, which has 30%. Among premium tissues, Kleenex Cottonelle still ranks a distant fourth behind Charmin, Fort James's Northern and Georgia-Pacific's Angel Soft.

Overall, bath-tissue sales are flat and premium brands are losing share to economy-priced tissue. Many toilet-paper consumers treat the brands as interchangeable and simply shop for the best deal. Even the industry's most recent innovation — the triple-sized roll from Charmin — is about value, rather than improved performance.

Kimberly-Clark hosted focus groups to talk to consumers about toilet paper, and asked them to compare leading brands with the new Kleenex Cottonelle textured tissue. They discovered that even though tissue advertising doesn't talk about how well a toilet paper wipes, that is what customers are thinking about.

Nonetheless, Kimberly-Clark marketing executives quickly discovered there were limits to what they could say. In advertising focus groups, it became clear that words such as "hygiene" and "cleansing" conjured up unpleasant images about the "process" of using toilet paper, rather than the final benefit.

"You can quickly cross a line where consumers say, 'Yeah, that's what the category is all about, but please don't go there,'" says Kent Willetts, marketing director for Kleenex rolled products. "Our big challenge was how do you talk to people about it."

The advertising solution is an anthropomorphic roll of toilet paper with a heavy British accent (the voice of London actress Louise Mercer from the old NBC sitcom "Dear John"). "I'm new Kleenex-Cottonelle toilet paper, and I understand you have a cleaning position available," the tissue says. "I have a unique, rippled texture designed to leave you feeling clean and fresh. I'd love to show you what I can do."

In another ad, the tissue brags that consumers prefer it to the leading brand. "Looks like all my bottom-line thinking is paying off," the tissue says. For now, the ads will claim only that consumers say the new tissue leaves them feeling cleaner than other brands, but Kimberly-Clark is "working on a way to objectively measure cleaning better," says Mr. Willetts. "There's no method right now."

The rippled texture is the result of a patented technology that dries the tissue during manufacturing without crushing it flat and later embossing it, the older approach. This method also allows the tissue to hold its rippled shape when wet, allowing it to clean better, the company says.

Thanks to a $170 million investment in a Beach Island, S.C., manufacturing site, the process uses less fiber while improving the bulk and strength of the tissue. As a result, the company's manufacturing costs per roll are 20% less than those for other premium tissues.

Bathroom Brawl

Kimberly-Clark hopes a new rippled texture will boost its Kleenex Cottonelle brand. Here are sales of toilet-tissue industry leaders, in billions of dollars for 52 weeks ending Nov. 23.

COMPANY	TOTAL SALES	CHANGE FROM 1996
Charmin	$1.052	− 2.4%
Northern	0.481	+ 0.6
Scott	0.434	− 2.6
Private Label	0.387	+ 4.2
Angel Soft	0.373	+ 8.6
Kleenex Cottonelle	0.360	(n/a)[1]
TOTAL CATEGORY	3.487	+ 0.3

[1] New brand following merger of Kimberly-Clark and Scott Paper

Source: Information Resources, Inc.

(Cont.)

With the price to consumers remaining the same, the extra margin will help Kleenex Cottonelle better withstand the price wars plaguing the tissue category and let the company spend more on marketing and advertising to grab market share.

"It's a very delicate thing, but it has the potential, if it's done right, of taking a major share of the toilet paper market," says George Rosenbaum, chief executive of Chicago market researcher Leo J. Shapiro Associates. "When you revisit cleaning, you're opening up a number of issues that years of product promotion have been silent about."

The $100 million launch budget is more than double what Kimberly-Clark spent on the brand last year. About $20 million to $30 million will go toward national television advertising, including 18 weeks of prime-time TV. In addition to the door-to-door sampling, another million single rolls will be available in stores for 50 cents each in the Eastern U.S.

As is typical in the paper-products industry, it probably will be at least 18 months before the product is available elsewhere, because Kimberly-Clark will have to build a new tissue-making plant to supply the remaining two-thirds of the country.

In the meantime, the company will launch a new, softer version of Kleenex Cottonelle in the rest of the U.S. Those more-traditional ads show a bubble drifting onto folds of toilet tissue. But the product package includes the "clean, fresh feeling" promise, in an effort to prime consumers for the eventual appearance of the textured tissue nationwide.

Reprinted by permission of *The Wall Street Journal*, © 1998 Dow Jones & Company, Inc. All Rights Reserved Worldwide.

Pore Strips Clean Up With Grimy Pitches

BY YUMIKO ONO

Staff Reporter of THE WALL STREET JOURNAL

It wasn't the easiest of ad assignments: The product's name was hard to pronounce. Consumers didn't know how to use it. And sales depended on convincing people that their noses are unbearably dirty.

Biore Pore Perfect is a white bandage strip. Basically, it yanks grime from pores on the nose, the way Scotch tape lifts lint from clothing. What **Deutsch,** a midsize advertising agency in New York, came up with for the Biore (pronounced bee-OR-ay) strip is a print ad that bluntly promised to extract "more dirt, oil and blackheads than you ever knew you had."

Developed by **Kao,** a Japanese consumer-products giant, Biore Pore Perfect has racked up an estimated $55 million in U.S. sales since its launch last summer. Despite the price, $5.99 for a box of six strips, some drugstores have reported shortages of the product.

In September, giant **Unilever** launched a similar product called Pond's Clear Pore Strips. Unilever says sales are going "phenomenally well," but declines to give specific figures. One of its print ads — part of a campaign created by **WPP Group's** Ogilvy & Mather — shows a magnified photograph of a sample extraction, which looks like a forest of tiny dark hairs.

This in-your-face approach, complete with grimy images, is a novelty in the skin-care industry, accustomed to ads with airbrushed faces and promises of radiant or rejuvenated skin. Many benefits of skin-care products are hard to illustrate, but the nose strips seem to have gained popularity expressly by showing results that are dramatically visible. And ugly.

The intended first reaction is, "That's so gross!" says Jeff McCurrach, director of new business at Andrew Jergens, the Kao unit that is distributing Biore Pore Perfect in the U.S. Then, he adds, comes relief that the skin is clean.

Although the Jergens brand has long been known for skin lotions and soap, Mr. McCurrach says the company chose to market the product under its Japanese brand name, Biore. It was thought to be hipper than Jergens, and thus more suitable for its target audience of women in their teens and 20s.

The hype draws caution signals from some dermatologists, who warn that the benefits of cleansing pores are cosmetic and temporary. Besides dirt, pores contain natural oils and proteins that are oxidized on the skin surface, turning them dark. And after a few weeks, clean pores clog up again.

"It doesn't mean you're dirty," says David Becker, an assistant professor of dermatology at the New York Hospital-Cornell Medical Center. "It just means that you're a normal human being."

Normal or not, women use a host of crude remedies, from steaming to scrubbing, to get rid of dirty pores. Albert M. Kligman, a dermatology professor at the University of Pennsylvania School of Medicine who invented Retin-A, an antiwrinkle lotion, has even used Krazy Glue on patients' noses.

Sophia Nissen, a 21-year-old college student in New Paltz, N.Y., first tested a sample Biore strip in Cosmopolitan magazine, and then ran out to buy more. "They're addictive, regardless of whether they're good for you," she says. One satisfying ritual, for her: holding up a grimy strip to the light.

Both strips require water. The Pond's strip is moistened, applied to the nose, then peeled off 10 to 15 minutes later. The process is the same for the Biore strip, except a user moistens her nose before applying the dry strip.

But the two companies employ different technology. Jergens says the Biore strip uses a patented molecule called polyquaternium-37, or C-bond, part of a family of molecules used as softening agents in hair conditioners. Because C-bonds are positively charged, they attract dirt and blackheads, which are more negatively charged than the skin, says Richard Maksimoski, Jergens's director of research and development.

Michael Indursky, a category director at Unilever's U.S. home and personal-care division, says the Pond's product uses a different adhering ingredient called PVM/MA Copolymer. He adds that Unilever's internal tests showed that the Pond's and Biore strips were "comparable" in effectiveness.

Kao, Japan's largest consumer-product company, launched Biore Pore Perfect there in 1996, to capitalize on a pore-cleaning craze that sparked more than a dozen new creams, masks and look-alike bandages.

The decision to introduce the product in the U.S. was risky, given Kao's checkered history here. Its fizzy bath solvent called ActiBath fizzled, and its shower gel, Jergens Refreshing Body Shampoo, was quickly washed away by heavily marketed products from Unilever and **Procter & Gamble.**

To create a buzz, Jergens first gave away samples on college campuses, in magazines like Glamour and Self, and at last year's Lilith Fair, an all-women's rock tour. It stacked postcards affixed with samples in trendy restaurants. And it persuaded Howard Stern and his staffers to try the Biore strip during his irreverent radio show. (His nose was fairly clean, more so than some staffers'.)

With a modest ad budget of $20 million, says Jergens's Mr. McCurrach, "You've got to market differently than P&G or Unilever."

To develop the Biore ad, Jergens and Deutsch conducted focus groups with hundreds of women. The research showed the need to demonstrate the effectiveness of the strips vs. facial cleansers. The problem: Showing a magnified used strip on the air would repel many viewers.

In the end, Jergens decided to show a cartoon diagram of a cross section of skin, with the strip prying debris from the pores. The commercial also shows a self-confident woman who peels off her strip, takes a peek and grimaces. She says the results are evident on the strip, "if you like looking at that sort of thing."

Despite the heavy targeting of women, word has also spread to some adventurous men. Seeing the results of using nose strips he got from his sister, Daniel Brescoll, a 29-year-old New Yorker, said his reaction was, "Wow, that's really intense." Both Pond's and Biore recommend once-a-week application, but Mr. Brescoll found he didn't need them that often.

If the cleanliness fascination begins to fade, Jergens is already prepared with its next grime fighter. This month, the company began shipping Biore Pore Perfect Face Strips, for the chin and forehead.

Reprinted by permission of *The Wall Street Journal,* © 1998 Dow Jones & Company, Inc. All Rights Reserved Worldwide.

The Biore Pore Perfect strip. It's a leg wax for your pores. Minus the yeoooow.

Biore: how it works:

Biore and Pond's go nose-to-nose in print ads for pore strips

Will Good Housekeeping Translate Into Japanese?

BY YUMIKO ONO

Staff Reporter of THE WALL STREET JOURNAL

When Good Housekeeping magazine popped up on newsstands in Japan last month, many Japanese thought it was a journal for diligent housemaids.

It has been a real chore for publishing giant **Hearst,** trying to adapt Middle America's vintage household-service magazine to the land of *bento* boxes and cramped apartments. Cover-to-cover challenges range from the magazine's very name to its vaunted Good Housekeeping Seal of Approval.

Hearst and licensing partner Nihon Keizai Shimbun — a newspaper company known as Nikkei — debated using a Japanese translation of the title. But *kaji,* the closest Japanese equivalent of "housekeeping," literally means "domestic duties" and can connote servants' tasks.

So they stuck with English, to preserve the monthly's American cachet, but printed the word "good" on the cover triple the size of the word "housekeeping." Ads took the same tack. "Good room! Good food! Good fashion!" chirps the English-speaking Japanese narrator in a recent commercial. She adds almost parenthetically, "Good Housekeeping!"

Asian markets may be roiling, but Hearst, which already has Japanese editions of Cosmopolitan and Esquire, thinks the time is ripe for Good Housekeeping in Japan. Amid the long-running economic slump, many Japanese are questioning their workaholic ways. Anxious to devote more time to home and family, they are looking West for guidance — watching British gardening shows via satellite, for example, or buying waffle makers from **Williams-Sonoma** outlets.

Hearst boasts that Good Housekeeping's Japanese debut issue had about 100 ad pages, nearly twice what it expected, for products ranging from Royal Doulton chinaware to a low-calorie sake called Nana. It distributed an ambitious 300,000 copies of the first issue. But with disappointing sales outside the big cities, circulation was subsequently cut to 230,000. Nikkei officials say they are reaching their target audience and expect distribution to grow gradually as more consumers become aware of the magazine.

Nikkei, best known for its business newspaper, Nihon Keizai Shimbun, first approached Hearst early this year. In its pitch, Nikkei noted the growing number of foreign magazines published in Japan, including GQ, National Geographic, Figaro and Elle Japon. Nikkei suggested that Good Housekeeping's strong U.S. circulation of about five million copies and 112-year heritage would distinguish it from domestic competitors.

But wooing the Japanese woman is no easy task. Good Housekeeping was all but unknown in Japan before its launch, and it competes in a crowded field. No fewer than 25 magazines — with names like Orange Page, Lee and Domani — already target Japanese women over 30. All are scrambling to keep skittish advertisers in a weak economy. Last year alone, more than 200 new magazines squeezed onto Japanese newsstands. Typically, about 30% of them fail within a year, according to Dentsu, Japan's biggest advertising agency.

Hiroko Kumita, the 39-year-old editor of the Japanese edition, quickly decided most of Good Housekeeping's U.S. articles wouldn't fly in Japan. Harrowing tales of an ordinary woman's triumph over tragedy, like Wanda Ickes's survival after a tornado leveled her Texas home, would put off Japanese women accustomed to cheery stories, she says. And in a largely Buddhist nation, so would articles like "Best-Loved Bible Quotes."

Instead, the Japanese Good Housekeeping features "aspirational" articles about an idealized America, including a 16-page feature on sparkling New York kitchens as big as entire apartments in Japan. The Seal of Approval, which befuddled Japanese consumers, was scrapped. Instead, Japanese researchers, called "GH Checkers," do their own testing and rating of products such as breadmakers and washing machines.

"We have no interest in trying to export our product exactly as it is," says Ellen Levine, Good Housekeeping's editor in chief, who also oversees the magazine's editions in the United Kingdom, Latin America and Russia. "That would be cultural suicide."

For a start, the Japanese edition targets women younger than its 40ish average reader in the U.S. It also uses more expensive paper for an upscale image and costs 480 yen ($3.68) per issue, compared with $2.95 in the U.S.

Some women in Japan say they don't see much unique about Good Housekeeping . "It has everything that other women's magazines have — interior decoration, cooking, flower arrangement and travel," says Kanae Terakawa, 36, a wedding coordinator in a Tokyo suburb. "There are some articles about Western lifestyles, but they're very short."

She would like to see more practical articles, like one that published sample product-complaint letters, in English, to companies abroad.

Some articles from the U.S., in fact, translate perfectly well. An example is the advice column by Peggy Post, Good Housekeeping's etiquette doctor. A recent column suggested that thank-you notes should never be e-mailed.

Another direct lift from the U.S.: recipes for party snacks, such as goat-cheese crostini and roast-beef-and-potato bites. Despite the editors' initial concern that American recipes would be too rich and too generously portioned for Japanese tastes, the party snacks

U.S. and Japanese editions of Good Housekeeping

went over big. They were "quite tasty," Ms. Kumita says. Of course, unfamiliar ingredients require earnest explanation. "Horseradish is a Western *wasabi* in a jar to accompany roast beef," reads one article, comparing it to the spicy, green sushi condiment.

Most of the articles are by Japanese writers, including the one about glitzy American kitchens. A group of editors flew to New York and its suburbs to look the places over. The subsequent kitchen feature lavished praise on the pastry boards and french-fry makers, and showed the layout of every pantry, cabinet and shelf in tiny diagrams.

Although such kitchens are a distant dream for most Japanese, close-up photos of nooks and crannies, such as pull-out drawers and custom-made spice racks, are useful in even the tiniest of kitchens, Ms. Kumita says.

Reprinted by permission of *The Wall Street Journal,* © 1998 Dow Jones & Company, Inc. All Rights Reserved Worldwide.

Tractor Dealers Get Down in the Dirt Promoting Machines

As Farmers Harvest Profits, Equipment Maker Decides To Stage 'Showdowns'

By Carl Quintanilla

Staff Reporter of The Wall Street Journal

WOODLAND, Calif. — It is the tractor maker's version of the Pepsi Challenge. Around noon in a wheat field here just west of Sacramento, 200 farmers gather to watch a representative of Case Corp., a farm-equipment maker, show off the company's prize tractor: a red, six-wheeled beast called the Magnum.

"Who's ready for some action?" yells Terry Wilkinson, the local Case dealer, greeting his guests in jeans and cowboy boots. The farmers line up for a free lunch of Mexican carnitas and beans, when a surprise comes along: Case has hauled in a competing John Deere tractor and is daring farmers to test-drive both machines.

"What's that?" jokes David Hills, an agriculture professor at the University of California at Davis, spotting the green Deere tractor.

"Oh, don't worry," Mr. Wilkinson says smiling. "That's going to break down shortly."

Sales Gimmicks

Dirt is flying in the tractor business. Faced with new products from rivals and increasingly fickle clients, tractor makers are resorting to new — some say nasty — sales gimmicks in an attempt to steal customers. Caterpillar Inc. of Peoria, Ill., trying to peddle its Challenger tractors, has discovered a particularly dirty trick: some Case and Deere & Co. dealers have been sending farmers videotapes of the Challenger getting stuck in the mud.

"It's like the cola wars," says Jon Carlson, Case's vice president of North American sales and marketing. "Only here, there are $100,000 machines and no blindfold."

Why the aggressive salesmanship? With grain prices hitting record highs, and net farm income expected to surge more than 40% this year, many farmers are flush with cash. Their equipment, much of it bought in the boom years of the 1970s, is aging. That makes them ripe for a sales pitch from farm-equipment companies.

Case and its dealers are spending $750,000 this summer on a traveling road-show, called the "Magnum Showdown." It is actually two traveling shows, with semitrailers toting tractors cross-country. Each show pits a 215-horsepower Magnum 7250 against

a 225-horsepower Deere 8400, both of which retail at $125,000.

Spinning Its Wheels

During the event, which announces itself with a portable tent and purple-striped flags, Case reps take farmers for a ride through the field on the competing machines. They warn that the Deere tractor might spin its wheels in the soil. In Woodland, Case's tractor clearly outperforms Deere's, making local farmer Ray Yeung a little suspicious.

"Hey Terry, your tractor looks like it's running better," he says, pausing midmeal at his folding chair under the tent.

"Of course it is," Mr. Wilkinson says, laughing. "I've got it set up that way."

Woodland's John Deere dealer isn't amused. "It's a dirty sales trick," Mick Stoulil says from his office less than a mile from the showdown. Mr. Stoulil wasn't invited or even told of the promotion until customers brought it to his attention. Now, he expects clients to come back and "razz" him about Mr. Wilkinson. "We're not friends," he says of his rival.

Case, which is No. 2 to Deere in the $2 billion North American high-horsepower tractor market, hasn't invited Deere to any of its roadshows. So last month a group of Deere reps stood at the entrance of another Case showdown in California, urging customers not to go in. (Case is now screening guests at the door to ensure privacy.)

Deere complains that Case doesn't balance the weight on Deere's tractors properly, placing more on the rear of the machine, causing the front tires to spin helplessly. Case says it is abiding by Deere's operating manual.

'Farmers Aren't Dummies'

"Those are the kinds of games that are being played," says Robert Porter, Deere's senior vice president for North American agriculture marketing. "But farmers aren't dummies. They're not going to fall for these tricks." For one thing, he says, they might take a closer look at the machine itself. "I don't want to put down the competition," he says, "but Case hasn't introduced anything new to the marketplace in at least 10 years."

Mr. Carlson of Case retorts that there have been "hundreds of improvements" on the Magnum since its launch in 1987, "from the front all the way to the rear axles. It's an evolutionary product."

Deere came out with a new farm-tractor model in late 1994, and in its own quiet answer to the Magnum Showdown, flies prospective customers to a demonstration site near its Moline, Ill., base. Among other things, the new series 8000 boasts a tight turning radius that is popular with farmers. "No one can come near the 8000," Mr. Porter boasts.

Farm-equipment makers have always battled for business. But today, they knight their machines with names like "Commander" or "Genesis," adorn them with air-cushioned seats, digital dashboards, compact-disk players and even tiny refrigerators to stash cold drinks. Kent Lynch, a Caterpillar marketing man, says these days, "You're judged by how

many cup holders you have."

Many farmers love the bells and whistles. Everett Wessel, a 63-year-old corn farmer from Blue Earth, Minn., grew up on a tractor with an engine so loud it caused partial hearing loss. Today, he spends his 16-hour days in an air-conditioned Caterpillar Challenger cab, listening to country music. "We're all a lot more comfortable than we were starting out," he says.

Case has spared little expense in staging the Magnum Showdown. The trucks hauling the tractors are custom-painted. Bruce Klein, 47, a Case truck driver, wears a red Magnum Showdown jumpsuit and sleeps in the cab while on the road. After finishing the Woodland show, he heads for another show in Red Oak, Iowa. He has driven 7,000 miles since starting in Edna, Texas, in April, and will add thousands more before completing the tour in Circleville, Ohio, on Nov. 7.

Case, a Racine, Wis., spin-off from Tenneco Inc., bought up the farm-equipment business of the old International Harvester in 1985. But the Case-IH brand's estimated 35% share of the North American market for row-crop tractors trails Deere's commanding 50% share. (Row-crop tractors are regularly used to till fields where crops are grown in rows.)

Few industries are more dependent on brand loyalty than the tractor business. Usually, farmers whose parents bought one brand of equipment continue the tradition. Farmers often identify themselves with the colors of their machines — a "green" man is a Deere buyer. Mr. Wessel, the corn farmer, teases one of his employees that he "has a green appendix." Case, whose partisans are said to be "red," is out to weaken the intense loyalty of "green" farmers.

But Mr. Stoulil, the Woodland Deere dealer, doesn't think the Case showdown has done anything to erode Deere's name. "I doubt Terry got one new sale out of that event today," he says. "Most of those farmers probably went for the free food."

Wheel and Deal

Indeed, by the end of the day in the wheat field, barely a handful of farmers actually get behind the wheel of the tractors. Most sit around trading tales of broken fan belts or axles.

Jennifer Davis, a local AT&T Corp. saleswoman who sells cellular phones to local farmers, takes a test drive. So does 12-year-old Russell Hatanaka, a son of a tomato farmer, who has been driving tractors since he was five.

"Which tractor did you like better?" a farmer asks him.

"Mmmm, the red one," Russell says, pointing to the Case.

Mr. Wilkinson smiles at his prospective client. "Get that kid a cap," he says.

Reprinted by permission of *The Wall Street Journal,* © 1996 Dow Jones & Company, Inc. All Rights Reserved Worldwide.

Nestlé builds database in Asia with direct mail

Malaysia pilot shows success of defining market full of 'peculiarities'

By Suzanne Bidlake

[Petaling Jaya, Malaysia]

Malaysians unaccustomed to having big companies reach out to them by mail are inundating the local headquarters of Nestlé with phone calls. But they're not calling to complain about unwanted special offers, dietary tips or recipes; they want to create a dialogue with the Swiss food giant.

"As soon as we send out a mailing, people phone because they're so excited and want to call to say hello and thank you. It's an incredible way of finding out how people really feel," said Caroline Lim, a consultant with Ogilvy One, Ogilvy Mather Worldwide's direct marketing arm, who is working solely on Nestlé business across Southeast Asia.

TRADITION OF DIVERSITY

Such enthusiasm for direct contact plays neatly into Nestlé's global strategy, making Malaysia a suitable pilot for an Asian rollout of the serious database-building and one-to-one communication programs the Vevey, Switzerland-based company has embarked on elsewhere in the world.

Over the past year, detailed questionnaires on consumption patterns, lifestyle, race, religion and feelings about specific brands have been answered by 100,000 Malaysians, who were lured by the chance to win a new car.

The idea is to learn about the buying population in a country of 19.5 million people who speak one or more of three languages (Bahasa Melayu, Chinese and English), vary in their religion (60% are Muslim) and traditionally eat out only on special occasions.

'GOOD CORPORATE CITIZEN'

Nestlé's five-year plan forecasts a doubling in database numbers each year, building a sample which it will manipulate to suit its various brands.

The database seeks to serve a country Nestlé has been present in since the early 1960s and where Nestlé has all of its product categories represented. By building up its knowledge, the company hopes not only to target its marketing but also to adapt its products accordingly. For example, some Malaysian products are gelatin-free to respect Muslim sensitivities.

"There are lots of peculiarities in this market. [The information] helps us understand to emphasize certain things that will reinforce Nestlé as a good corporate citizen," Ms. Lim said.

COMPETITION SPURS ACTION

Every kitchen in Malaysia contains around three Nestlé brands, according to Ms. Lim, but the company now faces more competition from other multinationals as well as local rivals. As a result, the company hopes to give the Nestlé name greater prominence, especially by linking its many brands under an umbrella of consumer good feeling.

Ogilvy One developed the Asian-looking and multilingual "Nestlé boy" to usher this corporate message into Malaysian homes. The cartoon figure is seen in mailings saying lines such as "I wish I was bigger. Then I could eat even more Nestlé Corn Flakes cookies."

TARGETING BUSY CONSUMERS

Some of Nestlé's first targets in Malaysia are busy people who want combined products. Nestum 3-in-1, for example, is a cereal with milk, sugar and oats provided in a packet, while a Nescafe variant provides coffee, milk powder and sugar.

Other targets are those who want to cook traditional meals but don't have the skills nor the time. Mailings include recipes for a Malay breakfast, typically *nasi lemak* (coconut rice with a hard-boiled egg and chili sauce) with meat or fish, that makes use of Nestlé's Maggi sauces and mixes.

Ms. Lim noted that marketers of cigarettes, wine and spirits, credit cards and insurance already build databases in Asia, "but for [package goods] companies, doing this with a strategic goal is really something new."

Reprinted with permission from the January 1998 issue of *Advertising Age International*. Copyright Crain Communications, Inc. 1998. All Rights Reserved

MORE BANG FOR THE SUPER BOWL AD BUCKS

At $1.3 million, a 30-second spot needs to score extra points

Super Bowl advertising has been a big-time winner for Intel Corp. The chip-maker bought time last year, using the game to debut its now-famous bunny-suit people. These dancing pitchmen, clad in colorful "clean room" suits, have since played a starring role in transforming Intel's once-aloof techno image into something more hip and fun.

Still, Ann Lewnes, Intel's director for worldwide advertising, swallowed hard when she heard the price tag for this year's Super Bowl spots: $1.3 million per 30-second slot. "It freaked me out," she says. Nevertheless, Intel decided not only to return but to boost its presence to two ads. "Everybody is watching this game," she says. "As an advertiser, you have to grin and bear it."

"BEHIND THE CURVE." Intel has a stadium full of company. While the sky-high rates have caused some previous advertisers, such as Nissan Motor Co. and Porsche, to stay on the bench, most figure they've got no choice. Exorbitantly priced or not, with 120 million viewers, the Super Bowl remains the only real mass-market buy in town. And that has left companies scrambling to get more bang for their Super Bowl marketing buck.

Indeed, many companies are coming to the game with a slew of extras tacked onto their commercials in hopes of grabbing more sustained consumer attention. From promotions and contests to international marketing ploys, advertisers are looking for every pos-sible way to extend viewers' eyeball time beyond that 30 seconds. "If all you're doing is a commercial on game day, you're behind the curve," says Scott Becher, president of Sports Sponsorships, a Coral Gables (Fla.) sports-marketing firm.

That's a big shift from the traditional focus of Super Bowl ads. For years, most advertisers have viewed the game as a one-time event, and simply tried to outshine others by offering up the most creative spot. Although the game-day ads come and go in a flash—some are never used again—many companies spend as much creating their ads as they do to buy the airtime.

This year, companies are far less willing to put all their eggs into one high-profile basket. Consider the way Intel plans to use its two ads. The first, narrated by actor Steve Martin, depicts a theft from Intel's labs. As suspects are suggested, viewers are instructed to visit Intel's Web site to vote on who-dunnit. Intel has filmed three endings, and the voting will determine which one will air late in the game. Intel's goal: to use its two minutes of TV time to build Web traffic.

For some, the promotional gains started long before kickoff. By the time ads for Mail Boxes Etc. air in the third quarter, the San Diego-based chain of box-and-ship shops will have tallied most of its Super Bowl publicity. It stretched its spending by inviting small businesses to compete for the chance to appear in its ad. The contest, begun in the fall, generated thousands of entries—and months of free publicity. "It helped us go beyond 30 seconds," says Nancy Mammorella, vice-president for marketing.

IRRESISTIBLE. Similar efforts are under way throughout the Super Bowl advertiser roster. Instead of the stand-alone ad it ran last year, M&M/Mars is kicking off a millennium-themed campaign and contest that will extend into spring. Coca-Cola Co., in addition to buying ad time, is sponsoring the National Football League's effort to educate international viewers on the complexities of football with "virtual signs." Only viewers abroad will see the computer-generated signs, which will explain what a touchdown or a field goal is, alongside a Coke logo. And long-distance giant Sprint Corp. started its ad campaign—starring Tom Arnold and Rob Schneider as obsessed football fans—during postseason NFL games.

Still, the extra mileage is unlikely to quell critics who say the price of Super Bowl ads exceed their usefulness. "I tell my clients there are more effective ways to spend $1.3 million," says Jay Schulberg, CEO of ad agency Bozell Worldwide Inc. But for many, the chance to grab all those eyeballs is too powerful to pass up. This year, marketers hope to make the moment last.

Reprinted from February 2, 1998 issue of *Business Week* by special permission, copyright © 1998 by McGraw-Hill, Inc.

Intel Advertising Proposal Is Angering Web Publishers

By Thomas E. Weber
Staff Reporter of The Wall Street Journal

Intel Corp., maker of ultrafast computer chips, is promoting an unusual plan that could slow down the Web.

Intel has persuaded major Web sites, including those of CNN and computer publisher Ziff-Davis, to add features that slow down all but the newest and most expensive machines with the latest Intel chips. The sites are being asked to run a notice explaining, "Content on this page benefits from the performance of the Intel Pentium II processor."

In other words, if that Web page seems too slow, it's time to buy a new Intel-based personal computer. Intel is backing up the unusual request with a promise to pay bigger subsidies to advertisers who place "Intel Inside" ads on these sites.

The program, dubbed "Optimized Content," is roiling some big Web publishers, who are outraged at the notion of making their sites less friendly to the vast majority of their readers.

"This is unusual and untenable," says Kelly Conlin, president of **International Data Group** Inc., which publishes PC World and other computer magazines along with some 200 associated Web sites. "There is a line that we cannot and will not cross in regard to respecting the interests of our readers."

And because Intel's program requires these power-hungry features to be part of a site's editorial content — not its ads — some publishers complain it is an encroachment on their editorial independence. "Optimized content must be clearly owned by the proprietors of the Web site" and be "prominently" promoted on a site's main screens, according to an internal document Intel has been using to brief site operators on the plan.

Philip Lemmons, editorial director of PC World, wants no part of it. "It's like requiring TV producers to have programming that only looks good on a 35-inch set," he says.

Intel responds that it is simply trying to encourage the adoption of features and technologies that users will find exciting — such as three-dimensional "virtual reality" scenes. "I would think that sites would want it that way," says Jami Dover, Intel vice president and director of the company's cooperative marketing program.

Intel also disputes the notion that its program impinges on the editorial freedom of Web publishers. "We're not asking them to adjust [editorial content] at all," Ms. Dover says. "If there are sites that are interested in working with us and expanding the types of compelling information they can deliver, that certainly fits with our marketing interests." Ms. Dover adds that sites that decline to participate continue to benefit from the basic 50% subsidy.

The Intel Inside advertising program is a critical tool for the company to promote its most profitable chips at a time when consumers increasingly are buying low-cost PCs with less powerful processor chips. By extending the Intel Inside program to the Web, Intel has taken square aim at the most rabid consumers of technology.

Intel's decision last summer to begin subsidizing Web advertising just as it does print and broadcast ads was hailed as a potential windfall for struggling Web publishers.

Under the $800 million Intel Inside program — up to 10% of which has been earmarked for Web ads — computer makers who feature Intel's chips in their pitches receive reimbursement for half the ads' cost. Under the Optimized Content program, ads that run on qualifying sites receive an additional 25% subsidy from Intel.

Intel isn't offering any money to the Web sites directly. Individual computer makers purchase the ads, then receive reimbursement for a portion from Intel. But the extra subsidy could prove a powerful incentive for advertisers to select the "optimized" sites.

Intel is betting that high-tech consumers will be enamored of the glitzy digital add-ons encouraged by its program. As an example, it cites a feature called "3-D Globe" promoted on the front page of CNN's Web site. "The globe will work best with a Pentium II processor," CNN notes. This notice is bordered top and bottom by **Digital Equipment** Corp. ads touting its Intel-based computers. CNN executives in charge of the Web site couldn't be reached for comment late Thursday.

Told of the program, an executive at a major ad agency says adding features that slow down Web sites could be a risky move. "For many customers, the World Wide Web is already the world-wide wait," says Michael Baldwin, a senior partner at Ogilvy & Mather, which handles advertising for International Business Machines Corp., among others. "Anything that adds fuel to that sentiment is a disservice."

Fred Abatemarco, editor-in-chief of Popular Science, helped develop the American Society of Magazine Editors' guidelines for keeping editorial matter independent from advertising. He says Intel's program appears to "violate the spirit" of those guidelines, though the group didn't specifically anticipate an advertiser who seeks to influence the performance of a Web site instead of the words it contains.

"What you're seeing now is where the whole thing gets very muddy, and very complex," Mr. Abatemarco says.

Yet some Web publishers welcome the increased subsidies as a tool for attracting more advertising dollars. Ziff-Davis says the program allows it to attract more computer ads. "We would never compromise our editorial integrity," says a spokeswoman.

Dan Pelson, chief executive of **Concrete Media** Inc., a New York Web publisher participating in the program, says Intel's support could give a lift to the entire Web industry. Adds Mr. Pelson: "I don't see what they're doing as unethical or encroaching on our editorial [control] in any way."

Reprinted by permission of *The Wall Street Journal,* © 1998 Dow Jones & Company, Inc. All Rights Reserved Worldwide.

DON'T SURF TO US, WE'LL SURF TO YOU

The next wave: Sit back and let "webcasters" find and deliver the "programming" you want

Remember the good old days when surfing the Net was an adventure and you happily whiled away the hours searching out Web sites and waiting for pages to download? Well, if you're like most Web surfers, that initial infatuation gave way to a more weary reality: Surfing the Net can be a lot of work. And if you're one of the zillions of people trying to do business in cyberspace, you know that surfing is not a reliable way for customers to find their way to your cyber door.

> For advertisers, it's the Holy Grail: Pitches can be sent only to those who are most likely to buy

Now, there's a new approach to the Net that just might be the thing to let it fulfill its potential as a mass medium—and make it a far more predictable environment in which to run a business. Borrowing from the models of radio and television, dozens of companies are experimenting with what they're calling "webcasting"—a way to push information out across the Net rather than waiting for consumers to find it. It involves dispatching collections of ordinary Web pages, news updates, and, increasingly, live sound and video geared to a particular audience—even a particular person.

"Viewers" whose job involves corporate finance, for example, might log on to their computers and find a selection of new stories on the economy, along with a ticker on selected stocks and video of a recent Alan Greenspan speech. "The metaphor for the Web is going to shift from pages to channels," says Marc L. Andreessen, vice-president for technology at Netscape Communications Corp.

JUST LIKE TV. Already, webcasting is starting to click. Take PointCast Inc. Since May, some 1 million customers have downloaded the Cupertino (Calif.) startup's software, a screen saver that automatically dials up PointCast's server to receive and display news, sports, and scrolling weather reports and stock prices as specified by each PC owner. Just as on a TV channel, the service is paid for by the advertisers whose messages also flash on the screens. Even though it boasts no audio or video yet, PointCast is billing itself as the first commercial channel on the Net. Says PointCast CEO Christopher Hassett: "The Internet as a medium isn't an experiment anymore."

The buzz generated by PointCast quickly made webcasting the next battleground in cyberspace. Netscape and Microsoft Corp. are both adapting their browser programs to receive webcast content and to organize it into channels. Microsoft is striking deals with Web sites such as *The Wall Street Journal*, which will offer its online edition for free to users of Microsoft's new Internet Explorer 3.0 browser. With Internet Explorer 4.0, scheduled for release by yearend, the browser will be able to automatically download the content.

Netscape says its Navigator 3.0, announced on Aug. 19, already has webcasting capabilities. Using it, PC owners can get multimedia-enhanced Web pages from the *The New York Times* and at least two dozen other publishers in their electronic mailboxes.

Will webcasting turn a nation of couch potatoes into a nation of Net-channel surfers? Not anytime soon. There's a long list of technology kinks that need to be worked out, not the least of which is the Internet's limited ability to handle high-quality audio and video.

But the new approach to the Web may finally produce the kind of interactive TV that media giants have been spending hundreds of millions to develop. The key is the two-way nature of webcasting, which lets Internet users specify exactly what type of information they want to receive. It's as if you could not only choose which TV channels you want to watch but also specify what shows you want your channels to broadcast. You might sign up for a news service but request only stories on computers, the Yankees, and local weather, for example. Viewers can also respond to programs and ads—joining discussions with other viewers or clicking on an ad for more details, perhaps even placing an order.

These traits make webcasting appealing to advertisers and online retailers. On a webcasting site, advertisers can track how many people visit, discern what they're viewing, and often glean some detail about them. That way, marketers can begin to aim their appeals directly at the people who are most likely to

Webcasters

Some of the companies aiming to turn the Web into a broadcast medium:

TECHNOLOGY SUPPLIERS

PROGRESSIVE NETWORKS RealAudio software lets Net surfers listen to radio and other audio online

XING TECHNOLOGIES, VDONET Software "streams" live and recorded video over standard modems with no download delays

INTEL Intercast product sends TV-channel programming on the PC screen along with related Web pages

NETSCAPE New browser allows publishers to send entire Web pages automatically to Net surfers' E-mailboxes for faster viewing

MICROSOFT Its next browser software will download news to the PC screen

CONTENT CREATORS

INTERNET BROADCASTING Start-up webcasts both live and prerecorded music and news from its Web site

NBC MSNBC, a joint venture with Microsoft, marries broadcast TV, cable, and the Web

CBS Network provides live coverage of political conventions on the Web

NETRADIO Web-only radio station lets listeners program their own music and news

IF NETWORK Tim Conway Jr. runs nightly Net talk show

(Cont.)

CNET Cable network offers computer-related news on the Web

DISTRIBUTORS

POINTCAST Network sends news semiautomatically to PC screens

INDIVIDUAL NewsPage and FreeLoader services automatically E-mail news and Web pages to subscribers

INTERNET BROADCAST SYSTEM Startup sets up Web sites for TV stations so they can provide additional local news customized to each PC user's interest

AUDIONET Web site gives PCs access to broadcasts from 80 radio stations

APPLE COMPUTER QuickTime Live! Web site uses Apple and other technologies for live coverage of the Grammies and other events

---

buy—the Holy Grail for advertisers. "There's no other medium where you know your customer as well as you do on the Web," says Montgomery Securities analyst Betty J. Lyter.

The potential is not lost on media companies. CNN is making its content available through PointCast. NBC plans to webcast financial news to corporate desktops and is working with chipmaker Intel Corp. on a new scheme called Intercast. The system allows a PC equipped with a special circuit card to receive TV programming and also, employing a bit of unused TV bandwidth, to send Web pages associated with particular programs—say, historical statistics of the sports teams that are playing.

QUALITY LAG. For all the big names jumping in, the webcasting field is still wide open. Startup CNET, a cable-TV channel and Web site covering computer topics, is looking into webcasting. And there are a number of Web radio startups. NetRadio lets some 75,000 Web surfers in 90 countries choose what music and news they want to hear online—and surf to other Web sites while listening. AudioNet, a network of online radio stations, promises advertisers a unique audience. "We have a way to reach the in-office market that even TV and radio can't reach," says AudioNet President Mark Cuban.

Still, to build audiences to the numbers they'll need to draw advertisers, webcasters know they have to quickly come up with high-quality sound and video. The most promising solution so far is "streaming," a method of compressing multimedia information so it can be sent over the Net in a continual stream. With streaming, PC owners can start seeing and hearing clips within a few seconds instead of waiting for an entire file to download.

Progressive Networks' RealAudio soft-

ware, available for free on the Net, makes it possible to stream dozens of radio stations into a PC. The latest version of the program lets listeners preset "stations' ' and scan them, much the way a car radio does. Web sites are getting into the radio game, too. Sportsline USA plans to offer 70 hours a week of live webcasts starting Sept. 1.

Tackling video is proving more difficult. But a few startups, such as Xing Technology Corp. and VDOnet Corp., are offering software that compresses video so that it, too, can be streamed across the Net. It's nowhere near TV quality, but the Web provides an extra dimension that TV can't: During a VDOnet baseball webcast from Japan on Aug. 30, viewers could select from among several camera angles.

Another way to squeeze video across the Net may be through multicasting, a technology that promises to let an unlimited number of people view the same data stream. To handle large volumes of simultaneous broadcasts, though, every routing computer on the Internet ultimately will have to be updated or replaced. Notes Michael Wheeler, president of NBC Desktop Video: "Full-motion video on the Internet is years away.' '

If television-like programming on a PC becomes practical, will it be desirable? "No one's going to watch a half-hour show with a mouse in their hand," figures Halsey Minor, CEO of CNET. Maybe not, but with CNET and others hard at work on programming to keep twitchy Web surfers tuned to their channels, the Web won't look the same for long. Don't touch that dial—er, mouse.

By Robert D. Hof in San Mateo, Calif., with Elizabeth Lesly in New York

Reprinted from September 9, 1996 issue of *Business Week* by special permission, copyright © 1996 by McGraw-Hill, Inc.

62

Young and tech-savvy bypass Madison Avenue

By Dottie Enrico
USA TODAY

NEW YORK — Top graduates of the USA's best design schools and university advertising programs once flocked to Madison Avenue.

But these days, many of the best and brightest appear to see more promising futures at companies satisfying Corporate America's obsession with All Things Interactive — the Internet, CD-ROMs and interactive TV.

Techno-frenzy is fueling explosive job growth in New Media jobs. In the New York metro area, New Media jobs are expected to double to 142,000 by 1998. Many will be created at traditional advertising and marketing firms because more consumer product companies are looking to ad agencies to help develop Web sites and are exploring other interactive marketing efforts to sell products. But demand for tech-literate designers, copywriters and other specialists has created a seller's market for hot graduates from top design and advertising programs.

Traditional entry-level jobs on Madison Avenue — which often pay too little and offer slow career advancement and unchallenging work — are no longer a first preference for the young and tech-savvy. Some are opting for start-up firms, some are launching their own businesses and others are picking and choosing their work by free-lancing. Industry experts say this could eventually lead to a creative "brain drain" at mainstream Madison Avenue agencies, which could have trouble hiring — and keeping — workers capable of providing the hot New Media services clients increasingly demand.

"The traditional ad companies are going to have to change the way they present themselves," says Lisa Pines, director of career services at New York City's Parsons School of Design, one of a handful of prestigious schools known for developing top ad designers and art directors. "A talented person has many more options to choose from, and the idea of making less money and having less input on projects isn't what these kids are looking for."

Critics say many mainstream ad agency executives are technophobic and downplay New Media's role in advertising's future. That can be a turnoff to young job seekers.

"Today's grads speak a different language and are much more savvy about their career options," says Flinn Dallis, vice president of creative recruiting and development for ad agency Leo Burnett.

Some recent grads who've rejected traditional Madison Avenue jobs have found higher wages and a more congenial work environment, since most New Media companies are chock-full with employees in their 20s and early 30s. They also can have more input — and at a quicker pace — on projects than they could in traditional agencies.

Entry-level jobs at most ad agencies typically pay $18,000-$25,000 a year. An entry-level job as a Web designer or writer for a New Media firm might start at

> "Today's grads speak a different language and are much more savvy about their career options."
> — Flinn Dallis of ad agency Leo Burnett

$35,000, then can quickly jump to $50,000 to $75,000. Free-lance jobs can pay $50 to $100 an hour.

The Portfolio Center, an Atlanta school specializing in training students for advertising careers, says some ad agencies have significantly boosted entry-level salaries to match the pay being offered by more tech-oriented rivals. Some recent highly sought-after graduates were offered positions starting at $40,000 to $50,000 — nearly twice what graduates were getting in 1994.

Steve Fritz, 25, a 1995 graduate of New York City's prestigious School of Visual Arts, was offered several jobs working in broadcasting and other traditional media fields. Instead, he took a job as an art director at poppe.com, an on-line development unit of Poppe Tyson, an ad agency that specializes in integrated marketing services.

"While I was in school, I never thought I'd be as interested in the whole interactive thing," he says. "I expected to get a job in publishing or advertising. But when I began to interview, I realized what tremendous opportunities there were working in a field that was changing and growing so rapidly."

Fritz says peers working as entry-level art directors or copywriters in traditional TV and print advertising spend their first year in training and taking castoff assignments from senior employees.

(Cont.)

But Fritz can relate to even senior employees at poppe.com. His boss, Peter Adams, is 22.

Adams says finding experienced job candidates is virtually impossible. None of the New Media existed in their present forms that long ago. "I laugh when I see those classified ads looking for five years or more of experience," Adams says. "In this end of the business, one year is like a lifetime."

Many top ad agency recruiters and headhunters contend there is no creative brain drain on Madison Avenue, because the number of job applicants clamoring for jobs has remained steady the past few years.

But outside experts — professors and career counselors who help recent graduates make job decisions — say this attitude is one of the reasons why many of the most visionary creative talents are steering clear of the big traditional agencies.

"There will never be a shortage of people who want to create TV and print advertising. But that's assuming that these will always be the only ad mediums worth caring about," says John Murphy, professor of advertising at the University of Texas.

Many students say recruiters at most large ad agencies don't even ask to see examples of interactive Web sites or CD-ROM projects when they're reviewing creative portfolios.

"It's not that I have no interest in TV or print ads, I'm just hooked on interactive advertising for other mediums," says Cheyney Robinson, who graduated from Parsons in May.

Robinson, 23, begins a job in August designing graphics and interactive Web sites for Microsoft's on-line network and its interactive TV project. She received several offers — including a few from traditional agencies. But Robinson feared that she wouldn't get the pay, creative projects and youthful work environment that she'll find at Microsoft.

Other students and graduates are exploring job options while freelancing. Murphy says free-lance requests from major national companies looking for University of Texas students to create corporate Web sites have more than doubled the past two years. Many free-lance gigs pay undergrads up to $30 an hour, Murphy says.

A few recent grads lucky to strike early in the New Media craze have been able to write their own tickets with some major ad agencies.

Two years ago, brothers Adam, 26, and Eric Heneghan, 28, were barely old enough to buy their own beer when they left Iowa City for Chicago. There, they pitched ad agencies for free-lance work for Giant Step, the fledgling interactive multimedia business they started out of Eric's apartment while they were still in college.

Their interactive wrestling videos created on Macintosh computers and promotional pieces for clients like farm-equipment maker John Deere demonstrated both their creativity as visual artists and their high-level computer skills.

Within days of blowing into the Windy City, they were getting offers of hundreds of thousands of dollars from major national ad agencies for Giant Step. They were wined and dined by corporate recruiters who wanted to offer them jobs in art and media departments.

In an unprecedented move, Leo Burnett, which creates ads for McDonald's and Hallmark, offered them a chance to form an exclusive alliance.

These days, they work for the agency's clients as well as pursue their own business. After an 18-month "chemistry check" to see if they felt comfortable with Burnett's operating style (and vice versa), the agency recently bought a majority interest in Giant Step.

"We knew there was a demand for what we were doing, but we had no idea how much," says Eric Heneghan. "One day we were wondering if some advertising executive would take our call. The next day he was offering to buy our company or to hire us for some unbelievable salary. "

Copyright 1996, *USA Today.* Reprinted with permission.

63

New breed of sponsors race to NASCAR

By Bruce Horovitz
USA TODAY

BRISTOL, Tenn. — Before rushing to stock car races, sponsors have traditionally coaxed fans to grab a beer, a pack of cigarettes — and maybe an oil change.

But NASCAR is coming out from under its hood.

These days, new sponsors linked to the National Association for Stock Car Auto Racing, the sport's sanctioning body, also are trying to convince race fans that they also need designer furniture for their dens; a cable shopping network broadcast on their TV sets; and an on-line service provider flashing on their computer screens.

Look over in the passing lane, Miller, Camel and STP. The likes of Prodigy, QVC and Helig-Meyers furniture are bucking for camera time on the track and in the pits. And top NASCAR officials say they may be just months away from landing a giant computer maker as a sponsor.

NASCAR is trying to wipe the oil from its hands and present a sparkling new image to the marketing world. At stake: millions — if not billions — of dollars in additional sponsorships and merchandise sales. Last year, NASCAR revenue topped $2.2 billion — from racetrack admissions to fees from T-shirt sales. By one estimate, that figure could nearly double to $4 billion by the end of the decade.

"We're not just about car racing any more," says Brian France, NASCAR' s marketing director. "We're an entertainment company."

NASCAR's explosive growth is being propelled by a new marketing philosophy that has become its unstated credo: start acting more like Bloomingdale's and less like Kmart. Executives at family-owned NASCAR are convinced that the path to future sponsorship success is not lined with beer cans and cigarette butts, but more likely with computer disks and perhaps even espresso cups. And to continue expanding their fan base, they may want to mimic Walt Disney — and not the World Wrestling Federation.

Annual attendance at NASCAR's Winston Cup Series races has nearly quadrupled since 1980 — topping 5.3 million last year. That's one reason why McDonald's, backer of Bill Elliott's racing team, spent nearly $5 million for its 1995 sponsorship. For that, McDonald's received $15 million of TV exposure, says marketing expert Joyce Julius. "Those aren't just cars — they're moving billboards."

Numbers aside:

▲ The first NASCAR Thunder retail store is scheduled to open May 11 in Atlanta's chi-chi Gwinnett Place Mall. You'll be able to pick up $400 leather jackets with the NASCAR logo.

▲ In September, the first NASCAR Cafe will open in Myrtle Beach, S.C. The Hard Rock Cafe clone will have a NASCAR stock car suspended above the bar.

▲ This fall, a NASCAR-sanctioned, mini-amusement park opens in Irvine, Calif.

▲ A new NASCAR affinity MasterCard has become a hit with race fans. More than 200,000 have been distributed in less than a year.

▲ NASCAR has gone on line. Its World Wide Web site, just two months old, is generating over 3 million hits weekly.

What you're hearing is the purr of NASCAR's finely turned marketing engine. This isn't your grandfather's NASCAR. For that matter, it's not your father's, either.

Sports marketers generally credit Brian France for pushing NASCAR in its new, unconventional directions. France, 33, is the grandson of NASCAR's founder, William France and the son of NASCAR Chief Executive William France Jr. There are currently 110 NASCAR licensees who make everything from official T-shirts to baby bottles. But France does draw the line somewhere. He insists, "there is no official high-heeled shoe of NASCAR."

So far.

"Not even the Olympics have grown as fast as NASCAR," says Lesa Ukman, editor of IEG *Sponsorship Report,* an industry newsletter. "They've done the best marketing job of any sport in America."

"NASCAR wants to be considered in the same breath with the NFL and the NBA," says Ernie Saxton, publisher of *Motorsports Sponsorship,* a newsletter for race promoters. The fastest way to get there may be on the coattails of fans like 12-year-old April James.

Although James didn't attend last Sunday's rainshortened NASCAR race here in Bristol, her father, Mike James, did. Prior to the race, he waited in a lengthy line outside a merchandise trailer to purchase a $20 T-shirt for his daughter. The T-shirt didn't feature racing' s more traditional Coors Light or Skoal logos. Instead, it featured the kid-friendly mugs of Fred Flintstone and Dino the Dinosaur. They represent a new NASCAR sponsor that James found perfect for his daughter: cable TV's Cartoon Network.

"You can bet this will get her interested in racing," James smirked, before also buying a $30 Cartoon Network cap.

A sponsor for only six months, the Cartoon Network racing team already ranks among the top five NASCAR racing teams in 1996 merchandise revenue. Parent company Hanna-Barbera is even considering a NASCAR cartoon, says Tom Barreca, vice president at Hanna-Barbera Enterprises.

While pro sports like baseball and basketball have seen merchandise revenue slide, NASCAR's tie-in merchandise revenue has jumped nearly 1,000% the past five years — to more than $650 million. It's projected to top $1 billion by the end of the decade.

No wonder. Fans in search of merchandise waited in lines — sometimes up to five deep — before the Bristol race. Marlin Ballamy, a truck driver from Kingsport, Tenn., plopped down $125 for a QVC jacket that supported his favorite driver, Geoff Bodine.

The new breed of NASCAR sponsors are introducing a new breed of merchandise. Elliott's race team even sells $55 computer mouses and pads with the McDonald's racing logo.

At a NASCAR race last year in Daytona Beach, Fla., one fan stepped up to the McDonald's race team trailer and spent $1,896 on merchandise, ordering "one of everything," recalls Stacey Jones, a sales assistant.

NASCAR fans are almost rabidly loyal to sponsors. Over 70% of NASCAR fans say they favor products of NASCAR sponsors, says Performance Research, a research firm.

Just ask William DeRusha, CEO of Heilig-Meyers, a 723-store furniture retailer and NASCAR sponsor since 1992. The company is so convinced of fan loyalty that it now sells NASCAR-theme furniture. The line includes a $700 recliner with NASCAR-theme tapestry and a $1,200 oak grandfather clock, with race cars and checkered flags on its dial.

To further spread its influence from its Southern roots, NASCAR will stage a race at a new superspeedway in California in 1997. And, for the first time ever, a NASCAR exhibition race is planned this fall in Japan. But NASCAR is still struggling to rid itself of its reputation as a southeastern, redneck sport.

Maybe so. But when nearly 100,000 race fans poured into last weekend's race in Bristol, many self-admitted rednecks were out in force. "We're all rednecks," says Billy Olins, an 18-year-old entrepreneur from nearby Johnson City, who was doing a brisk business roadside before the race, hawking noise-muffling earplugs for $7 a pair. He admits he buys the earplugs for less than $2 a pair.

"These people will buy anything that says NASCAR on it," Olins says, then reconsiders. "Except maybe bottled water."

Copyright 1996, *USA Today.* Reprinted with permission.

64

Color Coordination

Program:
Gymboree/All-Color Cheer
Sampling

Marketers:
Gymboree, Burlingame, Calif.;
Procter & Gamble, Cincinnati

Key players:
Gymboree: Keith Harband,
vp-marketing; Theresa Backes,
vp-store operations; Mark
Syrstad, svp-store op.;
Cheer: Barry Shepard, brand
mgr; Brenda Gale, Frank
Lyman, asst brand mgrs

At first glance, Gymboree wouldn't seem to have a whole lot in common with packaged goods marketing giant Procter & Gamble. The growing children's apparel company, which operates about 375 mall-based retail stores that sell clothing under its own label, only recently introduced the term marketing into its vocabulary. Throughout its 20-year history, Gymboree's efforts had been conducted on a grass roots level, or, in other words, by word of mouth. The company didn't even have a PR firm until a few months ago.

But Keith Harband, who joined the company as vp-marketing last summer, saw a P&G brand as the ideal cross-marketing partner for Gymboree's first venture into traditional marketing. The result was a sampling program with P&G's newly relaunched All-Color Cheer that led to the distribution of 600,000 boxes of the detergent at Gymboree's children's apparel stores. It was conceived to leverage each brand's individual strengths and one common thread: color.

The manufacturing and selling of colorful clothes had always been Gymboree's strong suit and positioning, reinforced by its multi-hued logo and "Quality clothes, colorful kids" tagline.

"I made a list of brands that I thought were appropriate for us to work with, and detergent companies were at the head of that list," said Harband, a former marketer at Disney and Scholastic. "We needed somebody whose major equity was color."

In Harband's few, when all the detergent boxes were lined up, one stood apart as the clear choice for promotional synergy. He remembered Cheer and its color message from when he was a kid, back when it went by the moniker All-Temperature Cheer. It was known as Cheer with Triple ColorGuard when Harband called to inquire about interest in partnering with Gymboree. Little did he know that P & G was getting ready to relaunch the brand as All-Color Cheer.

When Cheer brand manager Barry Shepard an-swered Harband's call, childhood played a role as well. His daughter had received Gymboree apparel when she was born, "So he knew firsthand the color story of Gymboree," Harband said.

The promo also opened a new distribution channel in retail for the soon-to-be-relaunched Cheer. "We're always looking for new ways to get our messages to consumers," said P&G representative Damon Jones. "We know that Gymboree moms care about the way their children look [and] we know that consumers use Cheer because they care about colors. It was a natural fit."

Hoping the alignment would becomes more than just a one-off, Harband believed it was important for Cheer's executives to witness Gymboree in action, from operations at headquarters to field trips to visit merchants and play classes. He immersed Cheer's marketing team in the Gymboree culture, down to the official corporate observation of "snack time" at 3 p.m. every Wednesday, a convening of employees for cookies and milk. Harband wanted Shepard and his team to see that at Gymboree, "We celebrate childhood," he said.

"The Cheer people were very motivated to grow their business in a strategic way," he said. "After spending the day talking about my business and theirs, and how we could work together, it was off to the races."

> **"Aim high to work with the best brands; with that you get tremendous resources."—Keith Harband, Gymboree**

And the word "race" should be emphasized. As these talks were taking place in late summer with the Cheer re-launch set for October, very little time was left for implementation. Cheer had to design sample packs, fill them with detergent and send them out to the stores by late September. On the Gymboree side, the store operations department—led by svp Mark Syrstad and vp Theresa Backes—had to prepare its internal team. "We have a consumer who's very involved with her kids and their clothing," Harband said. "They needed to educate employees as to why it was a good fit and about Cheer's equity."

Additionally, distribution for the 600,000 samples among Gymboree's stores had to be determined so that shops of varying sizes and sales traffic weren't left over- or understocked.

Together, the companies produced a brochure of clothing care tips for distribution with the samples, one that contained a reworking of Gymboree's motto: "Gymboree All-Color Cheer keeps[sic] kids colorful." The cover of the booklet also doubled as an advertisement that P&G ran in the November issue of *Parents* magazine. Artwork was submitted too late to meet the deadline for the October issue, but because magazines generally hit newsstands far in advance of the actual cover date, the November book came out just in time to correlate with the October promo. As it turned out, timing was so tight they barely squeezed by in time for that issue's press run. Typical of the entire effort, "We got in by the skin of our teeth," Harband said. "Some people may say P&G isn't able to move quickly, but in our case, we found they worked at lightning speed."

Additionally, the alliance allowed the retailer to advertise, with the halo effect of combining its message with that of a trusted household name.

"You should aim high to work with the best companies and brands; with that you get tremendous resources," Harband said. "I don't have the budget to advertise in magazines, but with Cheer, I was able to do that."

Although he can't quantify just how much the sampling program affected store traffic or sales, Harband said Gymboree had a record quarter in terms of revenues, pushing him to establish mechanisms to better measure effectiveness in what for Gymboree is a new world of marketing. "I won't say [the promo] was the sole reason [for the sales increase], but I would say it had an incremental effect, absolutely," he said.

© 1998 ASM Communications, Inc. Used with permission from *Brandweek* magazine.

65

The DEATH *and* REBIRTH *of the* SALESMAN

Today's customers want solutions, and companies are remaking their sales forces to satisfy them. But total quality goals and sales quotas still clash. ■ *by Jaclyn Fierman*

I sold systems that people didn't want, didn't need, and couldn't afford.
—Bill Gardner, 23-year IBM veteran, now retired.

Not so long ago, many salespeople might have regarded Gardner's admission as the mark of a colleague at the top of his game, one so skilled he could persuade people to act against their own interests. Today, his dubious achievement is more likely to be seen as embarrassing, unenlightened, counterproductive, and even, under some new compensation systems, a shortcut to a smaller bonus. Merely pushing metal, as IBM insiders say, or slamming boxes, as Xerox salesmen daintily describe the act of closing a copier deal, won't carry a sales force in the Nineties. Companies now measure success not just by units sold but also by the far more rigorous yardstick of customer satisfaction. As vendors ranging from Hallmark Cards to Marshall Industries—and even IBM—have discovered, if you anticipate what your customers need and then deliver it beyond their expectations, order flow takes care of itself.

As more managers awake to the challenge, old stereotypes are fading faster than Willy Loman's smile and shoeshine. Forget the mythic lone-wolf sales ace; today's trendsetting salespeople tend to work in teams. The traditional sample case? It's more likely to hold spreadsheets than widgets, and the person hauling it around probably regards herself as a problem solver, not a vendor. These days you don't "sell to" people, you "partner

THE NEW SALESMAN

■ **Today's best salespeople see themselves as problem solvers, not vendors.**

■ **They gauge success not just by sales volume but also by customer satisfaction.**

■ **To reinforce that view, companies are increasingly making customer satisfaction an element in salespeople's pay.**

■ **Despite the new attitudes, selling requires the same mix of grit and persistence that it always has.**

with" them. At the rhetorical frontier of the new sales force, even the word "salesman" is frowned upon; the preferred title is "relationship manager."

Let's admit that the rebirth of the salesman in corporate America remains a work in progress. Not all companies or all salespeople will adapt equally well to the extra training

and teamwork that today's more cerebral sales approach requires. Moreover, as long as salespeople work on commission—as they do in virtually every major company today—the rhetoric of total customer satisfaction will inevitably clash with the reality of sales targets. "Come quota time, you still reach for the low-hanging fruit," says Robert Rodin, CEO of electronics distributor Marshall Industries in El Monte, California, one of the few companies to have eliminated commissions.

That said, companies that dismiss the new, more collaborative sales methods as a fad are likely to slip behind. Today's demanding buyers are running out of patience with more product pushers, whether at the new-car showroom, on the floor of a department store, or in the corporate conference room. Jon Gorney, head of information services and operations at Cleveland's National City Corp., captures the mood in speaking of one of this chief vendors: "I don't want IBM coming in here anymore and telling me they have some whiz-bang technology unless they can tell me exactly how it will help my business."

As it happens, IBM knows better than most the dollars-and-cents argument for a more customer-conscious sales approach. Robert LaBant, senior vice president in charge of Big Blue's North American sales and marketing, says every percentage-point variation in customer satisfaction scores translates into a gain or loss of $500 million in sales over five years. What's more, he says, developing new business costs Big Blue three to five times as much as maintaining the old. Says LaBant: "We used to be focused on moving products and were paid on the basis of which ones we sold—$500 for this, $1,000 for that. It was critical that we turn that around."

If ever there was a business that cried out for a new way of selling it's that of moving cars from the showroom floor to the driveways of America. The familiar but widely despised old approach is known among automotive historians as the Hull-Dobbs method, after Memphis dealers Horace Hull and James Dobbs, who reputedly created it following World War II. In the old Hull-Dobbs drill, customers exist to be manipulated—first by the salesman, who negotiates the ostensibly final price, then by the sales manager and finance manager, who each in succession try to bump you to a higher price.

Car buyers are fed up. A survey by J.D. Power & Associates found that only 35% felt well treated by their dealers last year, down from 40% a decade ago. Just 26% of buyers rated the integrity of their dealers excellent or very good in 1983; by last year, that figure had dropped to 21%. "People feel beaten up by the process," says Jack Pohanka, owner of 13 import and domestic franchises in the suburbs of Washington, D.C. "You think you got a good deal until you walk out the door. The salesmen are inside doing high fives, and the customer is lying out on the street."

Enter Saturn and its original, no-dicker sticker system. As everyone knows by now, the price you pay for a Saturn is the one on the sticker (between $9,995 and $18,675, depending on model and features). But that's only part of the package. Buy a Saturn and you buy the company's commitment to your satisfaction. A ritual reinforces the promise. When you pick up your new car, an entire team gathers around you, including a representatives from service, sales, parts, and reception. They let out a cheer, snap your picture, and hand you the keys. Corny? Maybe, but last year Saturn scored third in a J.D. Power customer satisfaction study, just behind Lexus and Infiniti, which cost up to five times as much.

A fervent convert to the Saturn gospel is Jack Pohanka. One of 180 Saturn dealers in the U.S., Pohanka has seen firsthand the method's effect on customer loyalty and salesmen's morale, and he has extended Saturn-like practices to all his other franchises. "You have to let people walk out the door and not harass them," he says. "That way they may come back or refer a friend to you." Take your car in for body work to any Pohanka dealership and you will get it back vacuumed, washed, and even polished. "Our goal," says Pohanka, "is to exceed customer expectations."

Transforming combative salesmen to customer servants required what Pohanka calls "Saturnization." Every one of this 465 employees, including mechanics and receptionists, went off-site for three days of classroom exercises and physical challenges, similar to the training that Saturn requires of all its dealers. The high point of the cultural remake was the familiar "trust fall"—a backward leap off a 12-foot stepladder into the arms of fellow workers.

Pohanka contends that postfall salesmen no longer compete with each other and so don't hesitate to refer customers to one another if a different Pohanka franchise would better meet a buyer's needs. He points to a 25% jump in sales at the company in the first five months of the year, twice the national rate for cars and small trucks. For his sales staff, the new system translates not only to higher commissions but also to a better frame of mind. Says his Saturn general sales manager Brian Jamison: "I was planning to get out of this business. I couldn't stand all the games we played with customers. This way feels a lot better."

Saturn and Saturn disciples like Pohanka reformed their sales methods to exploit a screamingly obvious market opportunity; for IBM a sales force remake was simply a matter of survival. The company has cut its cost of selling by close to $1.5 billion in the past two years. Its worldwide sales and marketing team, now 70,000 strong, is close to half the size it was in 1990.

Those who survived are part of a new operation that is a cross between a consulting business and a conventional sales operation. Big Blue now encourages buyers to shop for salesmen before they shop for products. Gorney of National City Corp., a superregional bank (assets: $30 billion), handpicked Dan Parker as his sales representative after interviewing a half dozen IBM candidates. Says Gorney: "I wanted this person to be a member of my team." An engineer by training, Parker maintains an office at National City, and Gorney has sought his help to drive down the bank's costs of delivering services within the bank and to retail customers in the branches.

Consultants obviously need a more sophisticated set of skills than metal pushers, and IBM has not stinted on their training. For the 300 people like Parker who head client teams, the company has developed a voluntary year-long certification program. The classroom component consists of a three-week stint at Harvard: one week devoted to general business knowledge, one to consulting, and one to the industry they specialize in serving. For the rest of the year, enrollees work on case studies and then write a thesis on their particular customer. Harvard professors grade the papers. So far, 28 IBM employees have received the certification, along with a raise. (Parker is in the midst of writing his thesis on National City.) Those who fail can keep trying.

In their new role as purveyors of solutions rather than products, IBM's sales teams don't always recommend Big Blue's merchandise. About a third of the equipment IBM installs is made by DEC and other competitors. Says senior vice president LaBant: "In the Eighties we never would have recommended another company's product because all we were paid to do was install Blue boxes."

Like IBM, Fletcher Music Centers in Clearwater, Florida, understands that the key to winning and keeping customers is to figure out what they need, sometimes before they figure it out themselves. A few years ago Fletcher was struggling along with other dealers in the moribund business of selling organs. "There is no natural market for organs," says Fletcher president John Riley, 42. "No one goes to a mall to shop for one." But after conducting focus groups with its main clientele, senior citizens who retire to Florida, Fletcher realized that what these people wanted wasn't so much a musical instrument as companionship.

Today Fletcher drums up business by positioning a "meet 'em and greet 'em" salesman at the keyboard within earshot of elderly mall patrons. "What's your favorite song?" he'll ask. And to the peels of *Chattanooga Choo Choo,* he'll begin his line of patter: "Where ya from? You just moved here? Do you play the organ at all? Ever seen one like this? It's specially designed for someone just like you with no musical background. Come on inside and try it out."

Once inside, the prospect is treated to a pitch heavy with subtext: Buy from us because we can help enliven your retirement years. Whether the customer springs for the $500 used model or the $47,000 top of the line, free weekly group lessons—good for a lifetime—come with the package. Says Riley: "We've seen a fair share of romances develop at these lessons."

Then there are the small details that show elderly customers how much Fletcher cares about their needs: large type on the keys and outsize knobs that arthritic fingers can easily manipulate. Says Sherman Wantz, 75, who just bought his fourth Fletcher organ: "They know how to treat elderly people without making them feel like children. They appeal to a desire in older people to continue accomplishing things in their lives." Such satisfaction is music to Fletcher's ears. Pretax profits reached $3.5 million last year on sales of $24 million.

Building durable customer relationships is one thing when you're hawking mainframes, cars, or organs; it's a rather different story when you're pushing a product as short-lived as a greeting card. That's why the sales force at Hallmark Cards, the world's largest greeting card company, concentrates on pleasing retailers. Says Al Summy, a vice president of sales and service for cards sold through large merchandisers like Target, Kmart, and A&P: "We're not selling *to* the retailer, we're selling *through* the retailer. We look at the retailer as a pipeline to the hands of consumers." Anything his salespeople can do to make Hallmark products more profitable for retailers, he figures, will ultimately benefit Hallmark.

As a result, Hallmark is reorganizing its entire sales and marketing operation into specialized teams designed to work effectively with product managers at major retailers. In the old days—less than 24 months ago—Hallmark sold pretty much the same mix of cards to every store. Now, using data derived from bar codes at the checkout counter and laptops that supply merchandising information from Hallmark headquarters, salespeople can tailor displays and promotions to a retailer's demographics.

James River Corp., which sells toilet tissue, napkins, Dixie cups, and the like, also understands that when it puts its head together with its retailers', both sides benefit. Specifically, James River shares proprietary marketing information with its customers that enables them to sell more paper products. For instance, it told its West Coast client, Lucky Stores, how often shoppers generally buy paper goods and which items they tend to buy together. Lucky has since reshelved all its paper products and managed to win market share in the category from competing stores.

James River has reorganized the way it calls on customers. Previously, three or more salespeople would approach a company like Lucky Stores: one with plates, one with cups, and one with toilet paper. If all three secured orders, Lucky was obliged to buy three full truckloads, one for each product, to get the lowest price from James River. Today, a unified team from James River will sell Lucky Stores one truckload with a mix of paper products at the lowest price.

At James River, as at Hallmark and IBM, building a sales force for the Nineties has meant a thorough rethinking of a salesperson's job. But an important aspect of managing a sales team hasn't changed much: how you motivate flesh-and-blood salespeople. It remains the same idiosyncratic blend of financial incentive, inspiration, and cajolery it always was. After all, sales is a tough job. Says Larry Chonko, marketing professor at Baylor University in Waco, Texas: "You still need fire in your belly, you still get rejected four out of five times, and you still need energy to get up in the morning and say, 'I can

do it,' even if you sold nothing yesterday."

One of the more visible motivators in the game today is Frank Pacetta, 40, who is something of a folk hero at Xerox for having turned around the company's flagging Cleveland and Columbus, Ohio, sales teams. Pacetta has also become a minor media presence of late, thanks to a profile in the *Wall Street Journal:* a major role in *The Force,* a new book about Xerox salesmen by David Dorsey: and the publication of his own manual for sales managers, *Don't Fire Them, Fire Them Up* (reviewed in Books & Ideas).

Pacetta uses a hyperbolic mix of praise and shame to inspire his team of 70 reps in Columbus. For his winners, Pacetta holds testimonial dinners, dispenses effusive hugs, and has them ring a ship captain's bell at the completion of a deal. Weak performers can expect a month-long visit on their desk from an ugly troll doll Pacetta swiped from his son. Salespeople who aren't sufficiently fired up after three consecutive visits from the troll are fired—the title of Pacetta's book notwithstanding.

Sales, Pacetta style, boils down to three simple steps: Identify the customer, make sure your product fits the customer's requirement, and ask for the sale. To minimize resistance on step three, Pacetta recommends the "presell," which he likens to a conversation he might have had when convincing his wife, Julie, to marry him:

"Julie: 'I don't like the way you dress, I don't think you make enough money, and you drive like a maniac.'

Frank: 'If I let you pick out my suits, if I doubled my income, and if I promise never to exceed the posted speed limits—will you marry me then?'"

In marked contrast to Pacetta's freneticism stands another master of sales motivation, 140-year-old Southwestern Co., America's oldest extant door-to-door sales company. It peddles Bibles and Bible study guides to millions of families, and its Nashville boot camp turns its young sales trainees, mostly college kids on summer vacation, into some of the most dogged salespeople in the country. How's this for a drill? After a week of classroom training, the graduates fan out to assigned territories across the country and settle down to work—up to six days a week, 13 hours a day. Southwestern salesmen ring as many as 65 doorbells a day to make 30 demonstrations, each lasting 20 minutes. Sticking to that schedule, they can expect to close one to three sales a day, enough to earn over $5,500 their first summer. The company, which is privately held, rings up over $100 million a year in revenues.

Don't discount Southwestern as an anachronism. The company's working alum-

ni, well over 100,000 of them, have carried their skills to places like IBM, Xerox, Procter & Gamble, and Wall Street and in many cases are leading the sales revolution going on today. Says alum Marty Fridson, 41, who runs high-yield securities research at Merrill Lynch: "There's nothing magical about sales. You want to be truthful and present a credible story so people will want to do business with you in the future. To sell effectively, you need to present the facts, list your supporting arguments, and learn all the nonverbal cues your customer gives while you're making your presentation."

With one element of sales motivation—how they pay their salespeople—many companies believe they can improve on tradition. IBM, for example, is following a budding trend to base compensation partly on customer satisfaction. Salesman Don Parker says that 45% of the variable component of his paycheck depends on how Jon Gorney at National City Corp. rates him. If Gorney is pleased with the way Parker has helped him meet the bank's business objectives, Parker says that he stands to make "a lot more this year then ever before."

At Hallmark, too, customers get a say in how well some salesmen are paid. In a pilot project, about 100 employees have taken a 15% cut in base pay and made that portion of their income variable, based on retail sales of Hallmark products. If results are good, those salesmen stand to make more than 15%. The point, of course, is to encourage these workers to focus on helping retailers do their job better.

Electronics distributor Marshall Industries has taken this thinking to the next logical step and eliminated commissions altogether. Marshall's 600 salespeople earn a straight salary, with a bonus opportunity of up to 20% more based on pretax corporate profits. In the latest fiscal year, with sales over $800 million, the bonus was 10%.

Marshall CEO Robert Rodin overhauled the compensation system when he realized the distortions that quotas and commission were creating in the system. "How can you say you're pursuing excellence if you give away TV sets to your top salespeople? Customers got their parts ahead of time so the salesmen could get their prizes. But guess what? Those customers wanted on-time delivery, not early delivery."

Rodin says his people hoarded inventory in their cars in case they needed it. And in the mad rush to meet monthly quotas, salesmen shipped "anything that wasn't nailed down, to any customer on our list, regardless of their credit standing." The mania strained the shipping department's ability to complete orders accurately: "You can imagine what bleary-eyed warehouse people do at two in the morning."

Rega Plaster, 32, a top Marshall saleswoman, worried at first when Rodin took away commissions: "I wondered where my motivation would come from." She says she was pleasantly surprised at her response: "Within a month, it was like being able to breathe again. This takes the sliminess out of selling. Now I can spend time with smaller accounts and nurture them, and I can do it with a clear mind and conscience." Sales at her Milwaukee branch have risen from a monthly average of $850,000 last year to over $2 million.

For all the hype and half measures, salespeople in the Nineties can make the world a better marketplace. Any inefficiencies wholesalers and retailers squeeze out of the supply chain will benefit consumers by keeping a lid on prices. And smart solutions from any corner have a far-reaching payoff. At the very least, the new ethos may herald the decline of in-your-face salesmen who sell things people don't want, don't need, and can't afford.

© 1994 Time Inc. All rights reserved.

66

Sales Support:
An Automated Approach

By Betsy Spethmann

When AlliedSignal Automotive Aftermarket gave laptop computers to its 200-plus sales force last year, it gave them a whole library, too.

The Power Point Library and its hundreds of photos of FRAM air filters, Autolite spark plugs and Bendix brakes lets sales reps customize presentations. That's a big advantage when sales calls run the gamut from more sophisticated buyers at major warehouse chains, to local mechanics. It's also cutting-edge for the $110 billion auto aftermarket industry.

"This lets our sales force respond to customer needs more professionally and in less time," said Sandra Iannone, manager of sales force automation and telesales operations. "They come across as much more knowledgeable and professional."

With about $800 million in North America sales, AlliedSignal has three of the top replacement-part brands, with FRAM and Autolite topsellers to do-it-yourself backyard mechanics, and Bendix a popular brand among professional mechanics. The industry has been slow to automate because it costs so much to give a computer to each sales rep. "And the return on that investment isn't always in hard dollars, do it's difficult to judge how much you're getting on your investment," Iannone said.

When AlliedSignal designed its computer software, it created a standard presentation for each brand, then added a template for customized presentations. Reps can cut and paste to their heart's content, even putting a customer's name in the illustrations and mixing products, depending on each customer's wish list. That customized pitch then shows up on the computer's slick main menu.

"They used to try to put slides together, and it was so disorganized," said Karen Borger, AlliedSignal marketing communications manager. "This gives them lots of tools to be creative, with the kinds of information they used to have to call and ask for, right at their fingertips."

The library resides on each laptop's hard drive. AlliedSignal can update it so that when each rep calls in for a daily dose of order forms and e-mail, a new version of the library overlays the old version. The company already has updated the full library twice this year.

Another standard presentation on the software uses the laptop's multi-media capabilities to pitch AlliedSignal's value-added programs, including its motorsport sponsorships, advertising and point-of-purchase support. The company worked with multi-media specialist Warm Boot, Chicago, to design the software and library.

"One of the biggest appeals of the program isn't the information, it's the image," said Christy Means, Warm Boot vp. "This sets them apart, makes them a slick, sophisticated supplier."

How slick? An AlliedSignal rep recently manned a customer's booth at a trade show, took orders on his laptop and filled them by the end of the day. Competitors were almost more impressed than clients. "All the other reps from other booths came by to see how we did it," Iannone laughed.

© 1995 ASM Communications, inc. Used with permission from *Brandweek* magazine.

Price

Cheaper PCs Start to Attract New Customers

By JIM CARLTON

Staff Reporter of THE WALL STREET JOURNAL

The personal-computer industry now has some concrete evidence that the new category of sub-$1,000 machines is expanding the penetration of PCs into U.S. households rather than just cannibalizing sales.

Demand for ultracheap PCs, once considered a niche market at best, exploded early last year as tumbling component costs allowed manufacturers to offer more power and features for under $1,000. Some PC makers and distributors feared people who would have bought $2,000 machines would gravitate to the low end, while consumers who had resisted buying PCs would continue to stay out of the market.

But in a just-completed survey, Dataquest, a widely followed San Jose, Calif., market researcher, found that U.S. unit shipments jumped 18.5% in the fourth quarter, resulting in a booming 20.9% growth rate for the entire year. Earlier last year, Dataquest had forecast that PC shipments in the U.S. would grow 17.5% in the quarter and 16% for 1997. The year ended with a unit growth rate more than 30% above Dataquest's expectations, mainly because of the sub-$1000 PC, its researchers said.

"That price point stimulated the hell out of the market," said Bill Schaub, research vice president for Dataquest, unit of **Gartner Group** Inc.

Because of the popularity of sub-$1000 models, unit growth in the U.S. was much stronger than world-wide growth, which was hurt by a big 13% drop in unit shipments to the troubled Japanese market, according to another leading research firm, International Data Corp. Other Asian markets, especially China, did surprisingly well. A sharp recovery in Europe also helped sales. Dataquest estimated a world-wide growth rate of 13.7% for the quarter and 15.8% for the year.

IDC estimated lower U.S. growth than Dataquest, projecting a 16% jump in the U.S. in the last period and 19% for all of 1997. Its world-wide estimate was 14% for the quarter and 15% for the year, close to Dataquest's estimates.

IDC said sub-$1000 PC sales helped make up for continuing market-share losses among smaller PC makers. Indeed, both firms' figures showed continuing huge market-share gains by four giant PC makers — world leader **Compaq Computer** Corp., **Hewlett-Packard** Co. and direct-order companies **Dell Computer** Corp. and **Gateway 2000** Inc.

Manufacturers and retail stores also confirmed the growing importance of sub-$1,000 models.

H-P, for instance, attributed part of its blistering 76% world growth during the fourth quarter, based on Dataquest's calculations, to its sub-$1,000 line of Pavilion computers. H-P officials said Pavilion sales more than doubled in the quarter compared with a year earlier.

"The sub-$1,000 has clearly been the fuel for the engine of our Pavilion business," said Jim McDonnell, group marketing manager for H-P's PC group. "They are just flying off the shelves."

And, according to a survey of 46 retailers around the country by **ARS** Inc., a market-research firm in Irving, Texas, 73% reported that the sub-$1,000s expanded the market of buyers during the quarter as compared with a year before. Only 18% reported any cannibalization. In that same survey, 68% reported that the computers are profitable to sell — despite profit margins of between 7% and 9%, compared with 13% and 15% for the traditionally priced desktops. Analysts say this is because the increased store traffic is resulting in a surge in sales of ancillary computer devices, such as digital cameras, scanners and printers.

"These peripherals are flying out the door," said Mike Hagan, an ARS vice president.

This trend augurs well for the big, established players in the industry but not for weaker ones who are getting squeezed out. A handful of vendors, led by Compaq and H-P, are generating enough volume to make up for the lower prices and profit margins on the inexpensive machines, but most PC makers aren't.

Packard Bell-NEC Inc., for example, saw a 28% decline in world-wide market share, to 4.3%, for the quarter. IDC said world-wide shipments for Apple Computer Inc. continued to decline, falling to 3% in the fourth quarter, compared with the year-earlier period.

"These guys at the top are taking things away from the guys below," said John Brown, an analyst in charge of the quarterly PC report by IDC, which is based in Framingham, Mass. "You can't afford a slip-up in this industry. If you get behind the eight ball once, there's no coming out."

But for consumers, these are the best of times. For about $800, they can buy a computer that includes Intel Corp.'s latest 200-megahertz Pentium chip with MMX technology, **Microsoft** Corp.'s Windows 95 operating system and loads of features, including storage drives for more than two gigabytes of data, and speedy modems and CD-ROM drives. In just the past year, as component and manufacturing costs have fallen precipitously, prices on home computers have dropped to between $700 and $1,400 from $1,200 and $2,300.

"I don't think there are premium prices in the market anymore," said Steve Huey, marketing vice president for Compaq, referring to big manufacturers' former practice of pricing several hundred dollars more than smaller rivals such as Packard Bell.

Many people in the industry expect those entry prices to drop even further, to $600, later this year. About 35% to 40% of the nation's households currently own a PC, but some analysts expect the penetration rate to exceed 50% within several years because of this phenomenon. Already, the sub-$1,000 computers have exploded to account for about 40% of the market for retail PCs in the U.S. from just 7.2% in January 1997, when they first started hitting the market in a big way, according to a survey by Computer Intelligence, a market-research firm in La Jolla, Calif.

"They have been very good for the market and I think it will continue to be," said Matt Sargent, a Computer Intelligence analyst.

Further stoking overall demand, many analysts predict, will be a gradual expansion of the sub-$1,000 computer into the corporate market. Already, mail-order giant Gateway 2000 is scheduled to unveil Monday a $999 computer aimed at the office market. H-P has also recently begun selling some sub-$1,000s into the small to medium-sized office market.

"Businesses are not stupid," says ARS's Mr. Hagan. "They will either buy a computer at retail for under $1,000, or force their system providers to provide a product at that level."

Reprinted by permission of *The Wall Street Journal*, © 1998 Dow Jones & Company, Inc. All Rights Reserved Worldwide.

Value-minded consumers call the shots

By Bruce Horovitz
USA TODAY

Stuff is getting cheaper.

Not just because of weekend sales. Or temporary promotions. But honest-to-goodness price cuts.

All major brand cereal makers have lowered prices the past few months. So have several luxury car makers and personal computer makers. Nothing to sneeze at — even facial tissue prices are dropping fast.

'Every product. Every brand. Every price is under review.'

No longer is a strong economy an easy excuse for raising prices. Competition — domestically and globally is too great. The perceived difference between major brands and store brands is too small. And technological improvements have cut manufacturing costs, eliminating a prime justification for higher prices.

"Competition is coming from so many different angles that any company sitting fat and happy will get killed in this economy," says Joe Wilke, executive vice president of The Bases Group, a marketing consultant. "The rallying cry of American industry is to drive unnecessary costs out of the system and return them to the consumers."

American shoppers will save at least $17 billion over the next three years as a result of price cuts on packaged-good products such as cereal, frozen foods and toilet paper, estimates Meridian Consulting Group, a marketing consultancy. The trend is unmistakable:

▲ Post Raisin Bran has dropped to $2.99 from $4.13 for a 20-ounce box.

▲ Cheer, Era, Gain and Tide detergents will be an average 6.5% cheaper, effective Oct. 14.

▲ Bounty paper towel prices have been cut an average 4.8% from last year.

▲ Sprint's off-peak, long-distance telephone calls that averaged 15.4 cents a minute two years ago now cost 10 cents a minute.

▲ Burger King's Whopper — priced at 99 cents as an occasional promotion in some cities — will remain at that price in some highly competitive cities, including Tampa, Phoenix and San Diego.

▲ Toyota is cutting the base price of its redesigned 1997 Camry by $610. Its top-of-the-line XLE with a V-6 engine will be priced $1,745 less than a comparably equipped '96.

Why the price cuts? Industry experts say there is just one sure formula for sales success in 1996: lower prices.

"Consumers will no longer pay more than a product's worth," says Jeffrey Hill, managing director of Meridian Consulting Group. "Brand loyalty today means you stick with a brand only until you find a better deal."

Some predict lower prices will extend to virtually every product category in drugstores and supermarkets.

"This may be a consumer's dream," says Michael Silverstein, senior vice president of marketing consultant Boston Consulting Group. "But it's a plague for anybody on the business side."

From cereals to cars, many products that once routinely went up in price each year are instead heading down. The trend has been gaining momentum for several years.

In the face of an economy that many experts say is going gangbusters, price cuts might not seem to make much sense.

"Brand loyalty today means you stick with a brand only until you find a better deal."
— Jeffrey Hill
Meridian Consulting Group

After all, in good economic times, prices often tend to go up — not down — partially because of inflation and partially because consumers are in more of a spending mood.

By most measures, these are very good economic times. Consumer confidence hit a six-year high in August. The nation's unemployment rate plunged to a seven-year low of 5.1% last month. And July factory orders zoomed 1.8% to the highest level on record. Meanwhile, the consumer price index has been rising less than 3% annually since 1992.

Of course, not all prices are coming down. Air-

(Cont.)

lines, for example, raised fares about 2.5% last week, the second price increase in a month. And most medical-related costs still are on the rise.

But economists say the trend toward lower prices is very real. It's a new economic world.

Some say the consumer product giants are simply responding to the price pressures from makers of private-label goods. Sales of private label and store-brand products exceeded $37 billion the past year, estimates John Pierce, senior editor of the trade magazine, *Private Label*. That's a hefty increase of 5.2% from the year before, he says.

"Every category with a strong private-label presence will see prices drop," says Meridian's Jeff Hill.

That's one big reason consumer-product giants such as Procter & Gamble, Unilever and Kimberly-Clark reduced prices on some of their most popular consumer goods.

Some trace the price-slashing trend to the late 1980s, when fast-food giant Taco Bell began slashing menu prices. All major fast-food rivals eventually followed suit.

But bigger price-cutting tremors were felt in 1992, when Procter & Gamble started to kill its marginal brands, cut product lines and shave prices. Since then, P&G spokeswoman Elizabeth Moore says, the company has saved consumers about $2 billion by lowering its overall prices domestically by 6%.

P&G took aggressive moves to cut costs internally. It consolidated suppliers. And it eliminated dozens of slow-selling items. Its number of product variations fell to 2,200 this year from a peak of 3,300 in 1991.

P&G also cut way back on costly promotions like couponing. Right now, it's testing a program in Rochester, N.Y., that, if adopted nationally, could eliminate its coupons entirely.

Once P&G cut prices, Kimberly-Clark and Colgate-Palmolive were forced to follow. But it didn't stop there. An economic wave began to take shape that cut across American industries. Experts say this wave has a long way to go before cresting.

"It's a different mind-set now," says Katherine Kobe, vice-president of the Joel Popkin & Co. forecasting firm in Washington. "You just have to be prepared to compete, be the low-price producer."

Philip Morris sent unexpected smoke signals through the tobacco industry in April 1993, when it suddenly dropped the price of its premium cigarette brands — including the world's top-selling brand, Marlboro — by 40 cents a pack.

Reason: Value-conscious consumers were leaving Marlboro in droves. Some generic brands were selling for $1 less a pack than Marlboro. Executives at Philip Morris feared the brand would have lost five market share points in 1993 if prices were not cut substantially. "For the first time ever, Marlboro was losing market share to the price value segment," says spokeswoman Ellen Merlo.

Since 1993, Marlboro has added nearly 10 market share points. Although it has twice increased cigarette prices, each was limited to the cost of inflation — or about 3 cents a pack.

After years of rising prices, this reality finally hit the cereal aisles. "Consumers were fed up with the high prices on the shelf, " says Mark Leckie, president of Post Cereal, a unit of Philip Morris. "They learned to only buy cereal on sale."

Post lowered cereal prices 20% across the board in April. Kellogg quickly lowered many cereal prices, too. General Mills, which previously lowered prices on many cereal brands in 1995, again lowered prices after the action by Post.

Some consumer product makers have bucked the trend. But they probably won't for much longer, experts say. Among them, the makers of health and beauty-care products are likely to soon feel the pinch from private-label makers.

"In my 22-year career, I've never seen anything like this," says Hill. "Every product. Every brand. Every price is under review. And that's the way it should be."

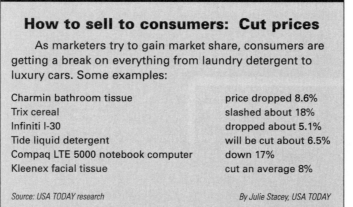

How to sell to consumers: Cut prices

As marketers try to gain market share, consumers are getting a break on everything from laundry detergent to luxury cars. Some examples:

Charmin bathroom tissue	price dropped 8.6%
Trix cereal	slashed about 18%
Infiniti I-30	dropped about 5.1%
Tide liquid detergent	will be cut about 6.5%
Compaq LTE 5000 notebook computer	down 17%
Kleenex facial tissue	cut an average 8%

Source: USA TODAY research   *By Julie Stacey, USA TODAY*

CONTRIBUTING: *Del Jones*

Copyright 1996, *USA Today*. Reprinted with permission.

69

Haggling in Cyberspace Transforms Car Sales

BY REBECCA BLUMENSTEIN

Staff Reporter of THE WALL STREET JOURNAL

MASSILLON, Ohio — Standing in his oak-paneled Honda showroom, Doug Waikem says he has seen the future of auto retailing — and it is on-line.

Since becoming one of the first dealers in Ohio to plug into the Internet three years ago, Mr. Waikem has watched in amazement as hundreds of customers have driven hours, from as far away as Pennsylvania, to buy his cars and trucks. Most are buying sight-unseen. But their journeys are sweetened by the conviction that they have saved hundreds — or thousands — of dollars. Because he pays less for advertising and commissions, Mr. Waikem can sell cars for less on-line, to the chagrin of competitors and even his own showroom salespeople.

"On the Internet, price is the only issue," says Mr. Waikem, whose on-line sales will exceed 400 vehicles by the end of the year, or 10% of his dealerships' total sales.

Forget all the buzz over no-haggle car pricing and stiff competition from auto-superstore chains. A real revolution in auto retailing is slowly starting to happen online, and it is changing everything about buying and selling cars.

Auto-By-Tel Corp., the on-line car-buying service that Mr. Waikem pays $2,160 a month for referrals, is processing 80,000 purchase orders a month that it forwards on to dealers. The service says it has served one million customers since it started in 1995.

Edmund's, one of the largest services of them all, gets an estimated 50,000 hits a day. Within four years, **Chrysler** Corp. predicts one in four customers will buy a car via the Internet. Chrysler's own studies show 70% of new-car buyers have access to a computer, and 45% say they will consult the Internet the next time they buy a car, compared with about 15% who do so now.

On-line car-buyers are a savvy bunch and are privy to information never before available to them. "In a very short period of time, the last stupid customer is going to walk through our dealership doors," says Richard W. Everett, director of strategic technologies for Chrysler's sales and marketing operations.

Chrysler was the first auto maker to launch its own Web site in 1995 and could soon go national with a program that allows consumers in Maryland and California to haggle with dealers on-line.

Just about every auto maker has joined Chrysler on-line, with extensive Web sites that compete with a growing list of independent buying services like Auto-By-Tel. On the West Coast, **General Motors** Corp. recently introduced an on-line service called GMBuyPower that lets consumers compare prices on GM and rival vehicles, search dealer inventories and get a dealer's best price — with the help of a 24-hour 800 number and bilingual operators if needed.

Buying a car isn't ever likely to be quite as easy as ordering a book on Amazon.com. Most people still like to feel the leather, sit behind the wheel and test drive what for most is still a big-ticket, emotional purchase. But more and more, buyers are visiting their local dealer to kick the tires — and then hopping on the Internet to hunt for the best buy.

Wired dealers like Mr. Waikem fret about the potential dislocations of the Internet revolution, such as fraying customer bonds and dwindling business for their high-margin service operations.

"What's going to happen to loyalty?" Mr. Waikem says. "The Internet knows no boundaries. It doesn't have state lines or franchise territories."

Internet searches will tell consumers what their dealer paid for the car (commonly known as the "invoice price"), what customer and dealer incentives are available and how much their old car is worth. On-line shoppers can figure out a list price for a given make and model by adding in the options they want and using independent agencies to tell them how much the new car should actually cost.

At no charge, services like Auto-By-Tel let consumers put in purchase orders that dealers like Mr. Waikem respond to, usually by telephone, with their best offers. Most services say they supply such a wealth of information that customers needn't haggle over prices. Consumers can also get financing and insurance by comparing rates on-line, eliminating other sources of potential dealer profit.

Mr. Waikem says his Internet customers are among the best-informed he deals with and often know exactly what they want. Typically they are well-educated and have sterling credit; only one so far has been denied financing.

Mr. Waikem and his two brothers operate probably the biggest auto-retailing outlet be-

KICKING THE VIRTUAL WHEELS

A list of some major Web sites for car shopping on the Internet.

- **http://www.edmunds.com**
  Known as the granddaddy of auto Web sites. Gets about 50,000 hits a day, provides comparative prices.

- **http://www.autobytel.com**
  One of the first independent sites, started in 1995, this service links customers to dealers in their geographic area.

- **http://www.autoweb.com**
  Autoweb is linked to Yahoo and is similar to Auto-By-Tel.

- **http://carpoint.msn.com**
  Carpoint, Microsoft Corp.'s high-tech automotive site, also refers customers to dealers.

- **http://www.autovantage.com**
  AutoVantage, America On-Line's automotive site. Also has an 800 number, 1-800-AUTOVANTAGE.

- **http://www.kbb.com**
  Kelley Blue Book's site. Provides pricing information similar to Edmund's.

- **http://www.priceautooutlet.com**
  Price Auto Outlet's site, which lists Oxford Financial's portfolio of cars coming off lease.

Virtually all the auto makers also have Web sites including **http://www.gm.com,** **http://www.ford.com** and **http://www.honda.com**

Source: Marketec Systems, Inc.

tween Columbus and Cleveland, with $100 million in annual sales and 12 franchises ranging from Buick and GMC to Audi and Chrysler. He says he can sell cars for less over the Internet because his costs are less.

For his monthly dues, Auto-By-Tel guarantees he will be the exclusive dealer for his brands in his region. Mr. Waikem figures he paid $63 in dues for each vehicle he has sold on-line so far this year. That compares with typical advertising costs of slightly under $300 per vehicle sold conventionally. "I put a full-page ad in the paper on Sunday that cost me $3,000. That's as much as the Internet costs me a month," Mr. Waikem says.

He runs the Internet operation with two employees who are paid salaries instead of commissions, to avoid an incentive to sell the vehicle for top dollar. And he has trained them to avoid high-pressure tactics. After they get a purchase order, one of Mr. Waikem's employees usually calls or e-mails the customer to confirm exactly what features they want. Later, the employee calls back with a price.

On-line, Mr. Waikem starts with the in-voice, or dealer price, instead of the sticker price used by his showroom salesmen. In a recent Internet sale, for example, he sold a four-cylinder Honda Accord with power doors and a CD player for $19,139, compared with the $20,070 price on his own showroom floor. The base sticker price without options was $19,485, compared with an invoice price of $17,263. The differences are even larger on older models.

Mr. Waikem acknowledges that the price gap has created some tension within his own dealerships. "Other sales people say, 'You just sold that Accord for $2,000 off, and you wouldn't let me sell it yesterday for $1,500 off,'" he says. "But I saved on advertising and commission."

One customer noticed the difference immediately. Tony Enerva, a professor of business management who lives a two-hour drive away in Chardon, Ohio, recently purchased a GMC Suburban from Mr. Waikem after finding him on the Internet. He figures he paid $6,000 less than his local dealer's best offer.

"We visited several Chevy and GMC dealerships, and they would never give us the dealer price, only the MSRP [sticker price]," Mr. Enerva says. When he showed other dealers his list of dealer prices obtained on the Internet, he says "they were really shocked that I had the information."

Mr. Waikem's dealer cost for the Suburban, he adds, was exactly the same as the one he had calculated on-line. This was Mr. Enerva's first Internet purchase, and, he says: "I doubt we will ever do it the traditional way again."

Mr. Waikem says he sees the impact of such stories starting to snowball. "This month was the best month we ever had on the Internet and the worst in the showroom," he says.

He concedes to some reservations. Most of his Internet customers will never use his service department, which accounts for 50% of his dealerships' profits. Still, as the computer beeps with another order, he smiles as he watches an employee respond. "For now," he says, "it's all gravy."

Reprinted by permission of *The Wall Street Journal*, © 1997 Dow Jones & Company, Inc. All Rights Reserved Worldwide.

70

Bitter Pill

Drug Makers Set to Pay $600 Million to Settle Lawsuit by Pharmacies

Retailers Object to Practice of Granting Discounts to HMOs but Not Them

Eight Defendants to Fight On

BY LAURIE P. COHEN AND ELYSE TANOUYE
Staff Reporters of THE WALL STREET JOURNAL

Call it the revenge of the mom-and-pops.

Independent pharmacies stand to collect close to $600 million in a tentative settlement of a lawsuit against 13 big drug makers, which the pharmacies accuse of a conspiracy to overcharge them for drugs, people familiar with the deal say. If approved by a judge and by all the companies involved, this would be among the biggest antitrust settlements ever.

The preliminary agreement stems from a class-action lawsuit by some 40,000 pharmacy owners who object to manufacturers' practice of offering big discounts to bulk buyers such as health-maintenance organizations and pharmaceutical mail-order firms. Such discounting, which began in the late 1980s, has hurt the pharmacy business — and critics charge that it has been particularly hard on those elderly people on Medicare who pay for medication out of their own pockets.

Far From Over

Significantly, the planned settlement includes no requirement that the pharmaceutical companies cease charging retailers more than they charge managed-care organizations, raising the question of whether the two-tier pricing system will change in the future. The absence of any such injunction, even though it was sought in the retailers' complaint, appears to weaken the impact of the settlement. But the private litigation, consolidated in federal court in Chicago, has caught the attention of federal antitrust regulators in Washington, who may push for pricing reforms, according to people familiar with the case.

Moreover, despite the preliminary accord,

the case is far from over—and defendants including Pfizer Inc., Merck & Co. and Bristol-Myers Squibb Co. could possibly have to cough up millions more by the time it is finished. While the proposed settlement includes more mom-and-pop drugstores, it doesn't involve any pharmacies belonging to such powerful retail chains as Rite Aid Corp., Albertson's Inc., Kroger Co. and Safeway Inc.

Attorneys for these well-heeled public companies say that they intend to continue pursuing their own lawsuits against the drug makers and that they haven't begun to discuss a possible settlement. Complicating the case further is the decision of eight large manufacturers — including Johnson & Johnson and Pharmacia & Upjohn Inc. — not to join the settlement with independent pharmacists but to fight all the antitrust allegations in court.

Denials From Defendants

None of the companies involved in the settlement would comment officially on any aspect of the proposed deal yesterday, although all the defendants contacted vehemently denied the charges in the lawsuits. The fact that a tentative settlement of roughly $600 million had been reached was confirmed, though, by lawyers involved in the negotiations. As part of the deal, defendants wouldn't be required to admit any wrongdoing.

A spokesman for SmithKline Beecham Pharmaceuticals Co., one of the companies believed to be part of the proposed settlement, said, "We do not comment on pending litigation, but we wish to make clear that SmithKline Beecham has never engaged in any conspiracy with its competitors on matters affecting its pricing." The company is a unit of SmithKline Beecham PLC.

Attorneys for participants in the planned settlement appeared in court in Chicago yesterday to inform Judge Charles P. Kocoras that negotiations were progressing and that they hoped to finish by next week. Some wholesalers that were also named as defendants aren't involved in these talks.

How Discounting Developed

Discounting to managed-care organizations is a relatively recent practice. In the past, drug companies generally had a one-price policy for all customers, with the exception of some volume-based discounts to big buyers. But in the 1980s, some institutional customers, such as hospitals and managed-care concerns, began to develop powerful techniques to extract deep discounts from drug companies.

Managed-care organizations developed "formularies," or lists of preferred drugs for use by doctors in their networks, and drug companies were given the chance to buy their way onto those lists by granting deep discounts.

Managed-care groups could threaten to exclude drugs that weren't discounted enough, because many classes of drugs include several products that are chemically

different but work similarly. For example, all seven ACE-inhibitor drugs lower blood pressure, allowing managed-care groups to select the cheapest to include on their formularies. They then urge—and sometimes require—their physicians to prescribe only the drugs on the formularies.

Fearful of losing market share, drug companies grudgingly acceded to managed-care companies' demands, and ultimately tried to outdo their competitors in discounting. Discounting contributed to the sharp slowdown in recent years in the industry's revenue growth, which precipitated heavy cost-cutting and tens of thousands of job losses.

Through it all, however, retail pharmacies were left out of the discounting frenzy, in part because they didn't have managed-care organizations' negotiating clout and the ability to shift market share from one drug to another. In general, retail pharmacies must carry all drugs that physicians in their area might prescribe; they can't threaten to exclude any drug. Because retail pharmacies must carry their products, drug manufacturers have little incentive to grant discounts to them.

Retail pharmacies, however, began to fight back a few years ago, in part by suing the drug companies. They also vigorously, but unsuccessfully, pursued the issue legislatively during the debate on overhauling the health-care system.

Critics of the drug industry contend that the discounting has led to cost-shifting, rather than lower costs overall, with retail pharmacies and their customers paying more because managed-care customers pay less. Retail pharmacies themselves have been further battered in recent years by the extensive changes in the health-care industry, including the rise of cost-containment efforts centered in managed care.

For several years, individual pharmacies and groups of retailers filed dozens of separate lawsuits in several cities across the nation. Finally, these were brought together in a federal court in Chicago in February 1994. Since then, armies of lawyers for both plaintiffs and defendants have filed hundreds of motions in the case, virtually all of them under seal.

Available court documents did reveal, however, that three top economists were paid by plaintiffs' lawyers to study the evidence for an alleged manufacturers' conspiracy. The trio, which includes Robert E. Lucas Jr., a University of Chicago economist who just won the Nobel Prize alleged the existence of a "cartel," according to one of the few court filings not under seal.

"It is my opinion that the defendant manufacturers and the defendant wholesalers in the brand-name prescription-drug market have been involved in ongoing price collusion to deny discounts to retail pharmacies at least since the 1980s," Prof. Lucas wrote. "The pattern of agreements and practices in the brand-name drug market are, in my judgment, consistent with no other conclusion."

(Cont.)

Highlights of drug retailers' class-action lawsuit and proposed settlement, as described by people familiar with it

DEFENDANTS:

Tentatively Agreed to Settle: Abbott Laboratories, American Home Products Corp., Glaxo Wellcome PLC., Bristol-Myers Squibb Co., Ciba-Geigy Corp. (a unit of Ciba-Geigy Ltd.), Eli Lilly & Co., Knoll Pharmaceuticals Co., Pfizer Inc., Schering-Plough Corp., Merck & Co., Smithkline Beecham Pharmaceuticals Co. (a unit of SmithKline Beecham PLC), Warner-Lambert Co., Zeneca Inc.

Not Part of Settlement: Forest Laboratories Inc., Johnson & Johnson, Marion Merrell Dow Inc. (now part of Hoescht AG), Rhone-Poulenc Rorer Inc., Sandoz Pharmaceuticals Corp. (a unit of Monsanto Co.), Hoffman-La Roche Inc. (a unit of Roche Holding Ltd.), Pharmacia & Upjohn Inc.

PLAINTIFFS

40,000 retail pharmacies

ALLEGATIONS

Manufacturers have discounted prescription brand-name drugs to mail-order pharmacies and managed-care programs and have conspired to charge retail pharmacies and drugstore chains much higher prices for the same drugs.

TENTATIVE SETTLEMENT

Almost $600 million

UNRESOLVED

Similar claims by 4,000 other pharmacies, including those belonging to Rite Aid Corp., Albertson's Inc., Safeway Inc., Kroger Co. and other chain stores, alleging price-fixing and price discrimination by the brand-name prescription-drug manufacturers.

There doesn't appear to be any allegation in the case that drug makers actually met to plot a cartel, however. Rather, the charges seem to involve complex analyses of how cartels behave.

Split Among Defendants

In response to the allegations, a lawyer for Rhone-Poulenc Rorer Inc., which isn't involved in settlement negotiations, said: "We've made the decision not to settle because we've never participated in a conspiracy, nor do we believe any conspiracy ever occurred."

Defense lawyers say the companies had initially entered into a joint-defense agreement and decided that if there were any settlement at all, it must cover all the plaintiffs, rather than just some.

The current split among defendants in the case reflects a sharp division over whether the drug makers would win at trial. One industry official said the companies that are settling "view this as insurance. Who knows what a jury would do?" But a lawyer for one company that won't participate said the settlement was "poorly timed and will end up costing everyone more."

It isn't clear what impact, if any, a settlement by some defendants would have on the remaining eight manufacturers that are fighting the charges (the trial is set for April 1). A lawyer for one of them said he hoped that with only eight defendants, "the case will be far more manageable."

But he said that news of any settlement could have a negative effect on jurors, who may assume that "with numbers like that, they must be guilty."

In contrast, attorneys representing the big retail chains and other pharmacies that had opted out of the class action and were still pursuing their case were elated. In light of the settlement by the mom-and-pops, some of the chains' attorneys say they now believe that $600 million is the minimum they will receive.

Mary Boies, an attorney representing the more than 4,000 retail pharmacies, including chains, that aren't settling, said that the bad blood between the various defendants was inevitable. "That's what happens when you depend on a cartel to further your interests," she said.

Effect on Consumer

There is disagreement in the industry about how any settlement would affect prices. Some industry officials and attorneys representing the defendants say the litigation will sharply raise the prices being paid by the estimated 50% of Americans who purchase drugs through managed-care organizations, while lowering prices for those who patronize retail pharmacies. "There will be a leveling out here," an industry official says.

Others say everyone could end up paying the higher prices as pharmaceutical manufacturers seek to recoup the costs of this settlement.

Attorneys involved in the negotiations stress that the proposed settlement is still days away from being signed. Defense lawyers are still insisting that the draft contain language emphasizing that they don't believe a conspiracy to fix prices ever existed. And the judge must still rule on the fairness of the pact. Plaintiffs attorneys also point out that if additional defendants join the settlement, the figure of nearly $600 million could rise.

Among plaintiffs, the big disagreement is over whether drug makers should be required to stop two-tier pricing in the future. Joseph Alioto, the San Francisco lawyer who filed the first suit on behalf of pharmacies in August 1993, is one who still opposes the deal, though he will have to accept it if the judge approves it.

"Our main beef isn't money," said Mr. Alioto, the former San Francisco mayor. His goal, he said, is "an injunction that will stop us from having to pay $100 for a prescription drug that others pay $10 for."

Reprinted by permission of *The Wall Street Journal,* © 1996 Dow Jones & Company, Inc. All Rights Reserved Worldwide.

71

CHEAPER EXPORTS?
NOT SO FAST
Manufacturers face soaring materials and financing costs

When East Asia's currencies started crashing last summer, Vigor International President Wang Yu-len smelled opportunity. Like many Asian middlemen who export garments and handicrafts to big retailers in the U.S., Taipei-based Vigor had been relying heavily on low-cost factories in China. With the Indonesian rupiah, Thai baht, Malaysian ringgit, and Philippines peso all suddenly trading at less than half their old values against the dollar—while China's renminbi remained stable—Wang figured Southeast Asia would be awash with bargains.

It seemed like a no-brainer. But after a swing through the region in early January, Wang returned empty-handed. Why? Most Southeast Asian manufacturers were hungry for foreign orders but so strapped for cash that they couldn't buy the imported materials needed to fill them. "Suppliers face a very embarrassing situation," says Wang.

TOUGH SLOG. To officials in Asia's most battered economies, the situation is downright depressing. They had hoped that cheaper currencies would translate into a major boost in export competitiveness in everything from toys to computer chips, allowing their countries to emerge quickly from the crisis. But for many, this silver lining is proving to be a mirage. That's because the fuel needed to

of computer components report surging sales, while South Korean conglomerates such as Samsung, Daewoo, and Hyundai are canceling plans to expand in the U.S. and Europe and are shifting production of some electronics goods back home in order to capitalize on the cheaper won. Factories that are either owned or financed by multinationals also stand to benefit.

But for most exporters, it will be a tough slog. Judging from the problems Asian traders and manufacturers are having so far, it seems doubtful that the increase will be enough to enable Korea, Thailand, and Indonesia to export themselves back to health. World markets for cars, chemicals, and many electronics components already are glutted. China, with its vast base of suppliers and efficient infrastructure, remains a ferocious competitor in many industries. And the new advantage of devalued wage rates in Korea and Southeast Asia is more than offset by higher import costs. Most Southeast Asian producers buy most of their raw materials and components from abroad.

Financing costs are also soaring. Interest rates in some countries have tripled, to around 30%, as panicked central bankers try to stabilize currencies. The area's currency devaluations may hurt Asian exporters much more than they help, says Toby Brown, managing director of General Oriental Investments (HK) Ltd. "The tidal wave of cheap exports isn't going to happen," Brown predicts.

Yet buyers for big stores in the U.S. have heard so much about the collapse of Asian currencies that they are already counting on huge price cuts of 35% to 75%. Manufacturers say they can't afford much more than a 10% cut. A Nike spokesperson notes that because 65% of the materials of shoes made in Indonesia are imported, prices on U.S. retail shelves won't change much. "Customers don't understand," says Lydia Hsu, a sales manager at Fairtrade Co., a Taiwan company that exports luggage and handbags made in the Philippines and China. Hsu says one of her big U.S. retail customers wants to renegotiate contracts that were struck a few months ago, hoping to get a better deal. But inflation of raw-materials costs makes that impossible, she says.

The gyrations in the currency markets are adding to the problem. Some Indonesian fabric suppliers, for example, have become so nervous about another dive in the rupiah that

Why Asia's "Export Boom" May Fizzle

Even though sharp falls in currencies will lower labor costs, producers must pay more for imported raw materials, components, and debt service.

The region's financial systems are so squeezed that many manufacturers can't get financing to fill export orders. Key suppliers, meanwhile, are going bankrupt.

Many Southeast Asian countries still lack the infrastructure and efficient network of local suppliers to compete with Taiwan, Japan, or China in many industries.

Data: Business Week

CASH CRUNCH
Many suppliers no longer accept the Indonesian rupiah, so manufacturers can't buy fabric

power these export machines—dollars—is in short supply. Whether they are small Indonesian shoemakers or South Korea's largest conglomerates, the region's manufacturers are having a hard time raising the cash to buy raw materials. Skittish foreign banks and overstretched domestic lenders are refusing to extend letters of credit. Local suppliers, fearful of further currency devaluations, are demanding dollars up front—or are bankrupt themselves.

To be sure, Asia's exporters will register gains as the months roll on. Thai producers

they won't quote prices for their products. "Every day, the prices from the mill are changing without notice," says Flor Cayanan, a merchandise manager for Hong Kong trading house Swire Maclaine, which buys garments in Indonesia. The 70% plunge in the rupiah has actually pushed up the price of Indonesian fabric by 20%, Cayanan says, because of the higher costs for financing and imported yarn. And suppliers no longer accept rupiah.

Meanwhile, banks are pulling back on credit, adding to the paralysis. For many normally sound manufacturers, getting export financing from shell-shocked Asian banks is nearly impossible. A manager at a trading arm of an elite Korean conglomerate says his company is facing difficulty in all export areas, including textiles, electronics, cars, and machinery. Moon Kye Ho, assistant manager at furniture maker Fursys Inc., says he hasn't been able to buy any imported raw materials since December. To fill export or-

(Cont.)

ders, he has been drawing down inventories. "If the situation continues for one more month, exports will be hard hit," Moon says. **LENDING FREEZE.** For Asia's export logjam to ease, its currencies must stabilize, and governments must make progress in cleaning up bad debts. Then they can start lowering interest rates and inject liquidity back into the system. But relief won't come soon. Many of the region's indebted banks simply can't lend because they remain far short of the 8% capital-adequacy ratios required by the International Monetary Fund as part of bailout packages. "If we don't meet the requirements, we get shuttered," explains a Korean bank exec.

Some Asian manufacturers are so starved for finances that Hong Kong trading giant Li

NO BARGAINS
U.S. retailers expecting 35% to 75% discounts will be sorely disappointed

Fung Ltd., which buys garments and other goods from vendors across the region, says it may have to take on the burden of buying raw materials itself and delivering them to factories. "We may have to do business in a totally different way," says Managing Director William K. Fung.

Not that less-than-expected export growth in Asia will be bad news for everyone. Predictions that a flood of cheap imports will push the U.S. trade deficit to $300 billion this year may turn out to be far overblown. And China could be under less pressure to devalue the renminbi if its competitors falter. A Chinese devaluation would shake financial markets worldwide. But for many Asian exporters that are barely hanging on, time is running out.

By Jonathan Moore in Taipei, with Moon Ihlwan in Seoul

Reprinted from February 2, 1998 issue of *Business Week* by special permission, copyright © 1998 by McGraw-Hill, Inc.

72

HDTV Sets: Too Pricey, Too Late?

BY KYLE POPE AND EVAN RAMSTAD
Staff Reporters of THE WALL STREET JOURNAL

The coming-out party for high-definition television begins today. But most of the debutantes will be unfashionably late.

Tens of thousands of home-electronics dealers, descending on Las Vegas for the industry's biggest convention, will see the first HDTV models from all the major TV makers, using souped-up digital technology long touted as the biggest thing to hit TV since color. But most will be merely prototypes, and nobody is willing to specify a rollout date.

In fact, no HDTV sets are expected in stores any sooner than Labor Day and some not until the holiday season. Samsung Electronics America Inc, for one, plans to showcase its new high-definition big-screen set. But it concedes that engineering and detail designs, including the actual appearance of the box itself, are incomplete. "Everybody's sitting back and waiting to see where it's all going to pan out," says Frank Romeo, a Samsung business product manager.

For now, HDTV's caught in a classic chicken-and-egg standoff. Broadcasters haven't decided when to offer high-definition programs — which will require special digital transmitters and, eventually, upgraded cameras — because they don't know how many viewers will have the necessary sets.

Meanwhile, TV makers haven't decided when to launch the sets, uncertain when programming for them will begin. And, because the first HDTV sets will be expensive — some selling for as much as $10,000 — there are doubts about whether they will have an appeal broad enough to get the market rolling.

Some form of digital TV is coming this year, thanks to a congressional requirement that stations in the nation's 10 biggest cities begin broadcasting a digital signal by the end of 1998. While that should be a boon to HDTV, the fact is that cable companies and some broadcasters are already more interested

in other benefits of digital-TV, such as the extra channels it allows.

Stations have some flexibility about how they use the extra capacity the government's giving them to handle digital signals. They can broadcast their current signal in super-clear, or high-definition, resolution — or they can break that capacity into several channels of less-clear programming.

Undercutting the need for consumers to buy new HDTV sets to enjoy digital technology, manufacturers are designing set-top boxes that will attach to existing TVs and act as receivers for digital programs. Such accessories will sell for several hundred dollars, but cable and satellite companies are also likely to distribute them at no cost.

With all this going on, the outlook for the HDTV set becoming a living-room staple is, at best, blurred. "It's sort of bleak," NBC President Robert Wright said at an investment conference in New York last month. "It's not looking as through we're talking about a huge revolution in buying."

That view particularly frustrates dealers like Mitchell Klein, president of **Media Systems** Inc., a Boston company that designs and installs custom electronics systems. Media Systems has equipped all its cus-

tomers in the past two years to convert to digital TV, and one client designed his home theater to be quickly altered for the new equipment and wider screen of HDTV — seven years ago.

"We're no longer interested in potential and concept products," says Mr. Klein. "We're beyond impatient at this point."

Still, some remain optimistic — particularly retailers and manufacturers, which have the most to gain from widespread replacement of existing sets with high-dollar, high-margin HDTV sets.

Brad Anderson, president of the retail chain **Best Buy** Co., says he is convinced HDTV is "probably the most exciting video product ever" and is going to the Consumer Electronics Show hoping to learn how his company will need to revamp its 285 stores to sell it. "I don't know what the TV sets are going to look like, what it's going to take to receive the programming, how many sets we're going to have to make room to sell," Mr. Anderson says.

Not too many in the near future, it would seem. The first digital TV sets with a high-definition picture will cost $5,000 to $10,000 and be aimed at videophiles or consumers with big home-entertainment centers. While

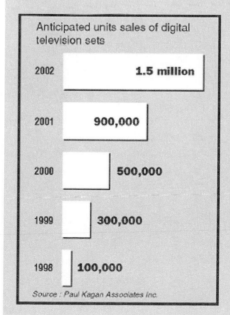

OFF TO A SLOW START

Anticipated units of digital television sets

Anticipated units sales of digital television sets

2002	1.5 million
2001	900,000
2000	500,000
1999	300,000
1998	100,000

Source : Paul Kagan Associates Inc.

Product showings expected at this week's Consumer Electronics Show in Las Vegas

- **Hitachi Ltd. and Thomson Consumer Electronics Inc.**
  Introducing a 61-inch, rear-projection HDTV

- **Samsung Electronics America Inc.**
  Demonstrating a prototype 55-inch, rear-projection HDTV

- **Sony Electronics Inc.**
  Demonstrating digital-TV broadcast cameras, editing, effects and transmission equipment and several prototypes of consumer HDTVs

- **Zenith Electronics Corp.**
  Demonstrating a digital converter box that will work with an existing Zenith projection television; introducing a 64-inch, rear-projection HDTV, available later this year though no firm date set

Source: Company reports

(Cont.)

this market is expected to account for fewer than one million sets by the turn of the century (compared with about 24 million conventional sets sold annually now), industry experts expect the cost to drop if volume picks up.

TV makers are especially eager for quick sales of HDTV sets because sales of current TVs have been declining since their peak year in 1994. Price discounting only worsened matters. For example, standard 27-inch TVs that sold for $500 three years ago now run about $350. At the same time, though, the manufacturers acknowledge that HDTV sales could eventually cut into their thriving big-screen TV business, the only segment of the TV market that is growing.

Thrown into the mix is the economic turmoil in Asia, which already forced Samsung to shut plants and cut back workers. Citing the same troubles, **Zenith Electronics** Corp. yesterday said it's hiring a turnaround expert. Zenith is now offering consumers the opportunity to apply the price of big-screen TVs toward the purchase of HDTV sets in the future.

Research being released tomorrow by the Consumer Electronics Manufacturers Association, a trade group, shows that consumers who have seen demonstrations of HDTVs strongly prefer them to lower-resolution sets, even those equipped with the extra services made possible by digital signals.

But Brent M. Magid, president of domestic television at Frank N. Magid Associates Inc., a TV consulting firm, says he is advising TV stations not to expect a big audience for ultraclear pictures. " HDTV holds very little or no appeal," he says. "For consumers, there's very little interest. For manufacturers and broadcasters, that's a big problem."

Reprinted by permission of *The Wall Street Journal,* © 1998 Dow Jones & Company, Inc. All Rights Reserved Worldwide.

Marketing Strategies: Planning, Implementation and Control

GILLETTE'S EDGE
The secret of a great innovation machine? Never relax

Amid airtight security, workers at the Gillette Co.'s World Shaving Headquarters in South Boston are putting the finishing touches on the long-awaited successor to Sensor, the world's most successful razor. The stakes are high: To maintain Gillette's double-digit growth, the new razor must top Sensor, sold as "the best a man can get." Developing a new razor might seem like child's play for Gillette, which has dominated shaving for decades. But it has been a tortured, six-year marathon, involving thousands of shaving tests and design modifications.

But even as Gillette's marketers gear up for their biggest product launch ever —the new razor is expected to hit stores this spring along with a multimillion dollar global marketing blitz —a team of Ph.D scientists is using the latest high-tech equipment to burrow even deeper into the mysteries of shaving. There's high-speed video that can capture the act of a blade cutting a single whisker and even a microscope capable of examining a blade at atomic level. The mission is to create the next shaving breakthrough. Expected debut: 2006.

In coming months, the launch will get all the attention. But it's in labs like these that the more significant Gillette story is unfolding. They are at the heart of one of the consumer world's great innovation machines—a machine dedicated not just to churning out new products but to inventing entirely new ways of making them.

Now, Chief Executive Alfred M. Zeien wants to throw this machine into overdrive across Gillette's entire family of consumer products—from its Oral-B toothbrushes and Braun appliances to recently acquired Duracell batteries. He predicts that 50% of Gillette's sales will soon come from products introduced within the past five years, up from 41% in 1996 and twice the level of innovation at the average consumer-products company. But his ultimate aim is even more audacious. "If I can't make the next five years better than the last five," when Gillette net earnings grew at a sterling 17% annual clip, vows Zeien, "I wouldn't think I was doing a good job."

It's an especially tall order for a mass marketer like Gillette. Indeed, a recent Mercer Management Consulting study of 50 top consumer packaged-goods companies—including Coca-Cola, Procter & Gamble, and Johnson & Johnson—found that only 17 managed to achieve above-industry-average growth in both sales and profits from 1985 to 1990. More tellingly, just 7 of these 17 maintained this excellence during the following five years. True, Gillette—along with J&J and P&G—was among the stellar seven. But the study's sobering suggestion is that most of these seven are doomed to fall over the coming five years, if only because of the sheer difficulty of continually finding new products and markets that can excel.

OUT OF STEAM? The odds seem even steeper in this era of low inflation, which makes it all but impossible to pass along cost increases. The supposed global cornucopia also has become more elusive, given the strong dollar and Asian flu. No wonder investors are edgy. It was bad enough that Gillette's sales grew just 3% in the first nine months of 1997—a far cry from the 9% pace of the past five years. But after Gillette advised analysts to modestly downgrade their 1997 estimates— from 17% to a 15% earnings increase— Gillette's stock plunged 24% below its July peak of $106. Investors worried that Gillette's steady growth machine was finally running out of steam —making it far harder to justify the sky-high price/earnings ratio of 41 times expected 1997 profits that its stock was then commanding. "Gillette took the 'p' out of predictable," says Morgan Stanley Co. analyst Brenda Lee Landry, "and made people worry about the long term."

In part, that's because slow sales in Germany and Japan at its Braun division raised questions about Gillette's dependence on foreign markets to keep up its growth. Yet Gillette's problems in 1997 may prove less of a harbinger than first feared. Earnings were also hurt because it was a transition year in which the company absorbed Duracell even as it slowed shipments of its old razor products in anticipation of the launch this year. "People overreacted" to last summer's earnings revision, argues Landry. With many major investors still bullish, the stock has since recovered almost fully, to $100. "Their prospects are spectacular," says Jay Freedman of institutional shareholder Lincoln Capital.

Zeien's strategy is built on Gillette's three great strengths. He's planning the most ambitious rollout of products in company history, with the razor just the beginning. It will be followed by a radically new toothbrush from Oral-B and a line of female-friendly razors designed to more than double that $250 million business. In time, he also hopes for battery breakthroughs that will leave the Energizer bunny in the dust.

Second, to ensure that earnings continue

Gillette Has Big Plans for the Next Five Years...

Continued double-digit annual growth, matching the heady 17% rate of the past five years.

Expansion of global markets in Asia, Russia, and Latin America.

Increased emphasis on new products will include rolling out a new premium razor and inventions in oral care and batteries.

But Also Faces a Host of Challenges

CEO Al Zeien may retire soon. His contract expires in February, capping three one-year extensions. Heir apparent Michael Hawley is largely unknown outside Gillette.

Lines such as Braun and the pen business continue to lag as researchers struggle to invent a "home-run" product like Sensor.

Global currency jitters threaten international growth strategy.

---

to outstrip revenue growth, Zeien plans to continue cutting manufacturing costs a full 4% annually, giving Gillette a huge edge in an era of low inflation. Third, Zeien is counting on Gillette's global strengths to produce growth overseas. True, those gains may be temporarily slowed by turmoil in Asia and the strong dollar. But longer term, few com-

(Cont.)

panies are better positioned. Some 1.2 billion people around the world now use at least one Gillette product daily, up from 800 million in 1990. With many of them now buying the cheapest products Gillette sells, Zeien figures over time the company can induce them to trade up.

Gillette's future hinges on a process its execs call "Gillettifying" a business. The model is Sensor, introduced at a time when even some Gillette executives feared blades were about to become a commodity, dominated by cheap disposables. Sensor reversed that trend by proving consumers could be induced to pay a premium for a high-tech shaving system delivering superior performance. Since 1990, Sensor and Sensor Excel have grabbed a leading 27% share of the U.S. market. The lessons: spend whatever it takes to gain technology supremacy in a category, and then produce innovative products that will capture consumers, even at premium prices.

To fulfill this promise, Gillette must overcome major challenges. Since King C. Gillette invented the safety razor early in the 20th century, the simple act of shaving has powered Gillette. But after the acquisition of Duracell International Inc., only 29% of sales and 52% of operating profits come from blades, the lowest levels ever. Now, at least half of Gillette's growth must come from other businesses—like batteries, toothbrushes, and toiletries—in which it faces far fiercer competition and has been far less successful in generating profits.

At the same time, Gillette faces a major transition. Zeien, 67, is nearing the end of the third one-year extension of his employment contract. Zeien refuses to be pinned down on when he'll step aside, saying only that it's "up to the board." But he is carefully grooming his No.2, President Michael C. Hawley, 59, for the top job. When Zeien retires, Gillette will suddenly be in the hands of a man who, while highly regarded internally, is largely unknown outside.

And Zeien's leadership has been a crucial element of Gillette's success. By 1985, profits were flat, and sales had increased hardly at all since 1980. "There seemed to be little sense of urgency... to stretch, set tough goals, and make strong moves to reassure restless shareholders," writes Gorden McKibben in a new history of Gillette to be published by Harvard Business School Press on Jan. 25. Highly vulnerable, Gillette faced a takeover bid from Ronald O. Perelman in 1986, and then a 1988 proxy fight.

Those narrowly won battles were a "wake-up call," says Zeien, who took over in early 1991 determined to shake things up. He insisted that Gillette must be the world leader, or have a plan to become leader, in all of its core businesses. He further decreed that at least 50 cents of every dollar in operating profit be plowed back into three growth drivers: research and development, capital spending, and advertising.

The results? Gillette is now the world leader in 13 product categories, accounting for 81% of its 1996 sales—up from just 50% in 1991. Although driven in part by acquisitions, sales have more than doubled since 1991, to 1996's $9.7 billion, while net earnings soared 189%, to $1.2 billion. All told, it has posted 29 quarters of double-digit earnings gains. This has pushed Gillette's market value to $56 billion, 14 times what raider Perelman offered in 1986.

ENGLISH BORN. The new razor will be the first major test of whether Gillette can keep it up. To increase sales in the mature shaving market, Gillette must persuade men to pay a huge premium for the new razor—probably 15% to 25% over the current $5.25 U.S. retail price for a five-pack of Sensor Excels.

To meet such product-development challenges, Gillette religiously devotes 2.2% of its annual sales, or over $200 million, to R&D, roughly twice the average for con-

sumer products. The company then uses a highly disciplined process to perfect its ideas. The original concept for Sensor, for instance, emerged all the way back in 1979. Gillette then developed seven different versions under the code name Flag. The winner incorporated many ideas from the six losers and 22 patentable innovations on top of the original idea. In similar fashion, Gillette set up three competing teams to produce what would be its breakthrough clear-gel deodorant, a product that has propelled that business to 21.5% of the U.S. market, its highest level in two decades. And the prototype for the new razor—which emerged from the company's lab in Reading, Britain in the early '90s—had to compete against two or three other contenders. Along the way, the razor was subjected to more than 15,000 shave tests.

To be sure, innovation is a goal of all major consumer-products companies. But the difference Gillette's approach can make is perhaps best illustrated by Oral-B, which Gillette acquired in 1984. At the time, "there wasn't a single person in R&D, and a new toothbrush hadn't been introduced since 1957," says Jacques Legarde, the executive vice-president who oversees Oral-B. Today, Gillette has a team of 150 researching manual plaque removal, "more than any other company in the world," he brags.

It has already produced a stream of new products—from a floss made with a proprietary fiber, to its top-of-the-line Advantage toothbrush, which retails for $3.49, compared with 99 cents for the brush Oral-B sold in 1984. This has pushed sales at Oral-B to $548 million, up from $110 million in 1984.

But Oral-B is just half the story. In 1989, Legarde ordered researchers at Braun, the German consumer-appliance giant Gillette acquired in 1967, to marry their expertise with Oral-B's bristles to create an electric toothbrush. The result —the Braun Oral-B Plaque Remover —is now the world leader,

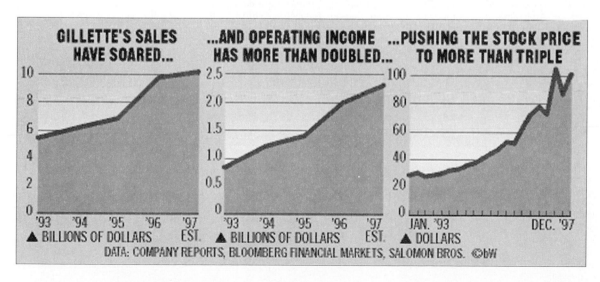

GILLETTE'S SALES HAVE SOARED...
▲ BILLIONS OF DOLLARS

...AND OPERATING INCOME HAS MORE THAN DOUBLED...
▲ BILLIONS OF DOLLARS

...PUSHING THE STOCK PRICE TO MORE THAN TRIPLE
▲ DOLLARS

DATA: COMPANY REPORTS, BLOOMBERG FINANCIAL MARKETS, SALOMON BROS. ©bw

(Cont.)

with over $400 million in annual sales. And with that market still tiny, Legarde figures Gillette can double its overall oral-care business to $2 billion in five years by marketing to aging baby boomers.

"TWO DWARFS." Because only the best ideas make it through Gillette's innovation process, "they're one of the few consumer-products companies that really pick their shots," says Suzanne Hogan, a senior partner at marketing consultants Lippincott Margulies Inc. Rather than "come out with a new razor every year," she adds, "they wait until they have something meaningful, and then go to the market with a bang."

But unlike Sensor in 1990, this time Gillette's new razor won't have the field to itself. Warner-Lambert Co.'s Schick—a distant second—soon will launch its largest ad campaign in history to promote its new Schick Protector shaving system. The bright-red Protector has blades wrapped with microfine wires to prevent nicks and cuts. Even so, "you're looking at Godzilla vs. the two dwarfs," Schick and Bic Corp., says Jack Trout, a Greenwich (Conn.) marketing consultant. Even Dick Jordan, Schick's vice-president of global business management, concedes Gillette "is a formidable competitor."

Yet Gillette is more than a new-products pipeline; it's equally expert at figuring out ways to make them more cheaply. To meet its annual 4% cost-cutting goal, engineers never stop searching for ways to run machinery faster and more efficiently. Such incremental gains have helped cut the cost of making Sensor by 30% since 1993, while slashing the costs of Oral-B's Advantage a huge 60%. Meanwhile, materials costs have been trimmed 10% to 15% by intensifying competition between suppliers.

But the truly big manufacturing gains come when Gillette introduces products. Few companies "marry product and process innovation" to the same degree as Gillette, says Harvard Business School Professor Rosabeth Moss Kanter. After Zeien was told the new razor would be too expensive to produce with the setup Gillette has used to make cartridges since they were introduced in 1971, for example, he ordered the engineers to invent a new one. It was a staggering undertaking, requiring Gillette to "bring on 196 different pieces of equipment, each one essentially designed by us," says Executive Vice-President Robert G. King. The new system will spit out cartridges twice as fast as that used to make Sensor, enabling Gillette to roll out the razor in just over two years, half the time it took for Sensor.

Zeien hasn't managed to Gillettify everything. The biggest failure: an inability to gain a dominant edge in its nearly $1 billion writing-instrument business. Gillette achieved world leadership in pens by buying Parker for $458 million in 1993, creating a stable that included the low-priced Paper Mate and top-end Waterman pens. But it has yet to come up with a home-run product. "It's a much more challenging area" than shaving, admits Dr. John C. Terry, director of Gillette's Boston Rlab. Some critics believe it's time to exit the business, but Zeien insists new products will save the day.

Braun also continues to weigh down Gillette's performance. Despite some successes, it is still burdened by slow-moving products such as electric razors, a big factor in last summer's earnings downgrade. To fix this, Braun is looking increasingly to faster-growing products, such as the electric toothbrush and personal-diagnostic equipment.

Perhaps the most pressing challenge is Duracell, acquired for over $7 billion in stock in late 1996. Duracell is already the world's leading producer of alkaline batteries, with nearly 50% of the U.S. market. Now, Gillette is determined "to escalate growth above and beyond that," says Edward F. DeGraan, the executive vice-president who took charge in early 1997. It's tripling spending on alkaline battery R&D. The aim, says DeGraan, is to build batteries so superior that the Duracell name will gain the same potency as the "Intel inside" logo.

But that's a huge challenge in what's essentially a commodity market, and most outsiders are skeptical. "I don't foresee any breakthroughs," says Martin Hersch, a battery expert at consultants Freedonia Group. Even if he's right, Gillette can do a lot to power Duracell simply by distributing its products more globally. Duracell—which in 1996 got only 20% of its sales from beyond North America and Europe—"didn't have the international organization" to exploit this opening, says Zeien. But Gillette does. That's why one of Gillette's first moves was to fold Duracell's distributors into its global juggernaut.

To be sure, Gillette is hardly immune to global turmoil. "Our growth [in Asia] might be less than what it has been for the next one to two years," concedes Jurgen Wedel, the executive vice-president heading Gillette's International Group. But he argues that Gillette will be far less affected than most. Asia still accounts for less than 10% of Gillette's sales. And Gillette has had success managing through troubled times.

Consider the former Soviet Union, one of the world's most challenging markets. When Gillette first opened its St. Petersburg office in 1992, it was all but unknown to Russian consumers and managed sales of just $150,000 a month. Gillette soon caught consumers' attention with colorful ads on billboards and buses. They then took their "best a man can get" campaign to televised sports. Today, the Gillette name is recognized by some 80% of Russia's city-dwellers, and Gillette has a leading 50% share of the Russian blade market. Gillette is expanding its marketing focus to promote batteries, toiletries, and toothbrushes. As it does, Wedel predicts Russian sales should explode to $500 million within five years, up from $200 million now.

As it pushes into brave new markets, Hawley readily admits Gillette "will hit some bumps along the way." But most observers are convinced that it still has a long ways to roll. Wall Street analysts expect Gillette earnings to grow at an 18% clip over the next five years, "slightly more than double the rate for the S&P 500," says Charles Hill, director of research at First Call Corp. And most are recommending the stock.

Of course, there are no guarantees. If Gillette's management becomes overconfident and complacent, it will begin to slip up and miss opportunities, just as it did in the early '80s. But say this for Al Zeien: He has laid a solid foundation for continued excellence. Now it's up to Hawley and his successors to execute.

By William C. Symonds in Boston, with Carol Matlack in Moscow and bureau reports

Reprinted from January 19, 1998 issue of *Business Week* by special permission, copyright © 1998 by McGraw-Hill, Inc.

74

Just Doing It
Nike Plans to Swoosh Into Sports Equipment But It's a Tough Game

Firm's Design Teams Take the High-Tech Approach to Bats, Balls and Gloves

The Skate Wheels Crumbled

By Bill Richards

Staff Reporter of The Wall Street Journal

BEAVERTON, Ore. — Seated behind a table piled high with brown leather baseball gloves, John Schulte breaks out a strange-looking creation.

It resembles a white foam-rubber clamshell with a gauzy black glove attached to the back. Mr. Schulte hands it around the table to a group of Nike Inc. executives, who look it over warily. The clamshell, he explains, is a prototype baseball glove that Nike hopes to introduce in early 1999.

"An early prototype," he adds hastily, acknowledging that no pro baseball player, no matter how rich his Nike contract, is likely to wear a glove that seems designed for a space alien. "The final version might not look like this at all," he says. "It is evolving even as we speak."

On the Attack

Catch this: Nike, which dominates the sneaker and sports-apparel markets and has made its swoosh one of the most-recognized international signs short of SOS, is barreling into the sports-equipment business. Nike design teams are pondering the physics of equipment such as baseball gloves and bats, hockey sticks, footballs, golf balls and snow boards. They are borrowing principles from rocket science and materials from military aircraft. Their mission, they say, isn't just to make and sell equipment; it is to design something new and then throw Nike's awesome marketing muscle into convincing the world of its technical superiority.

Within several years, says Andrew Mooney, who heads Nike's equipment division, "we will be Nike's fastest-growing division." Mr. Mooney pledges that Nike

"won't go into anything where we can't innovate." At Sports Authority Inc., a Fort Lauderdale, Fla., company that is the nation's biggest full-line sports-equipment retailer and has close ties to Nike, Robert Timinski, senior vice president for merchandising, says Nike's plan "is to be the category leader in three to five years."

That's a brash plan. But Nike became a Goliath with sales running $9.2 billion a year by persuading consumers to pay hundreds of dollars for spruced-up tennis shoes. Even Mr. Mooney, a Nike marketing veteran, admits tough work lies ahead. "If anyone had told me three years ago I had to launch hockey, snow boards, baseball, softball, in-line skates and all the rest at once," he says, "I'd have said, 'You're crazy.'"

A Huge Market

Or certainly bold. The sports-equipment market is fragmented — and huge. At about $40 billion a year, it is larger even than the $20 billion athletic-shoe market and the $38 billion sports-apparel market.

And Nike is playing catch-up against its shoe and apparel rivals: Italy's Fila Holdings SpA has its own brand of in-line skates. Reebok International Ltd., of Stoughton, Mass., has soccer balls and licenses exercise equipment. Last September, Adidas AG of Germany bought Salomon SA, a big French outdoor-equipment maker, for $1.3 billion and now has about 22% of the ski and golf market.

In addition, entrenched sporting-goods giants such as Rawlings Sporting Goods Co., of Fenton, Mo., and the Wilson Sporting Goods unit of Amer Group Ltd. of Finland are spoiling for the fight. "Our customers want performance, not Michael Jordan," sniffs John Rangel, a senior vice president at K2 Inc., a Vashon Island, Wash., maker of winter-sports equipment and roller skates. He and others say Nike may strike out in the lower-margin world of sporting goods. "Selling a baseball glove is a lot different than selling a sneaker," says Sebastian Dicasoli, director of marketing services for the Sporting Goods Manufacturers Association, a trade group based in North Palm Beach, Fla. Sneaker markups, for example, can run to 50% or more, but the markup on a baseball glove is closer to 30%.

An Embarrassing Flop

Moreover, the wheels have fallen off some of Nike's early sporting-goods forays — literally. At the trade group's giant convention in Chicago last July, Nike executives set up shop in a Winnebago van parked outside the convention hall and dispatched a troupe of skaters to whiz around the parking lot to demonstrate Nike's new in-line roller skates. The triumphal unveiling quickly fell apart, however, when the wheels on the skates began to disintegrate. It was, Mr. Mooney says, "a piece of rapid learning for us."

Nike clearly can learn, however. It took about a decade to climb from its beginnings,

when Phil Knight, its founder and chairman, was peddling running shoes out of his car trunk, to leadership of the athletic-shoe business. Along the way, Nike revolutionized the way corporations deal with athletes and professional teams, angered human-rights activists with its low-wage manufacturing overseas and stirred criticism of its outsize impact on popular culture. When Nike launched its apparel line five years ago, critics scoffed-and then watched it grab much of that market, too.

Since then, Nike's stock has soared 18-fold — in New York Stock Exchange composite trading yesterday, it closed at $42.8125 a share, up $2.75 on the day — while its profits have grown rapidly. In several recent blockbuster quarters, earnings surged more than 70% from a year earlier. But that growth suddenly evaporated last month. Breaking a string of 12 consecutive quarterly gains, Nike reported a 20% profit drop to $141 million, or 48 cents a share, for the fiscal second quarter, ended Nov. 30. Moreover, Nike officials warn that sneaker and apparel sales will stay slack during much of 1998.

The downturn makes Nike's current push into sports equipment seem eerily prescient. Its executives say "hard goods" sales — the equipment — will become its "third engine," powering the flagging sneaker and apparel sales. The assault on the equipment business began in 1996 with hockey: Nike designed a new lightweight skate and also a new stick made of high-tech carbon composites and coated with a Velcro-like material that clung to similarly coated Nike hockey gloves.

Surprisingly Tough Game

But hockey hasn't turned out to be the easy slap shot Nike expected. Retailers such as Clay Keeney, manager of Johnny Mac's Sporting Goods in St. Louis, say customers have been returning Nike's new hockey sticks, complaining the blades split because of poor glue. And although Nike says more than three dozen National Hockey League players use its skates, several high-profile players have complained that they are poorly designed. Phoenix Coyotes star Jeremy Roenick says he passed up a six-figure endorsement deal with Nike after he tried on six pairs of its skates and none fit right.

Even Sergei Federov, the Detroit Red Wings hockey star who two years ago signed a highly publicized contract to promote Nike equipment, has quietly replaced the blades on his Nike hockey sticks with a competitor's less-fragile ones, a Red Wings spokeswoman says. Other NHL equipment managers say players simply plaster Nike's logo over someone else's product to fulfill their contract obligations with the sneaker giant. "They're still wearing the stuff they've been wearing for years. They just slap a swoosh on it," says one, whose West Coast NHL team has a licensing contract with Nike.

Mr. Mooney says Nike has strengthened the glue in its hockey sticks. Players, he says,

(Cont.)

are free to wear whatever skates they choose. And he says he isn't aware of players adding a swoosh to rival gear.

Nike also stumbled in its drive to crack the markets for basketball and football equipment. Two years ago, it hired Voit Sports Inc., a small equipment maker in Tulsa, Okla., to manufacture a line of footballs and basketballs carrying the swoosh logo. Part of Nike's plan for building a better basketball involved color: Most balls sold off the shelf are dull orange because they are coated to reduce smudging. Nike's uncoated basketballs, however, were loud orange, the color of game balls pros use so they show up on television.

But Nike's new balls got razzed when they arrived in stores in 1996. "Technically, they weren't up to standard," says Roger Bruce, who sells football gear to the Dallas Cowboys and has three stores in the Fort Worth, Texas, area. "We didn't even bother to try to sell the stuff," he adds.

Customers who did buy complained that the basketballs quickly smudged and looked dirty. Nike officials blame Voit.

But a former Voit executive says the idea for the bright-orange balls came from Nike. "One of their top basketball-shoe guys showed up at a marketing session with a game ball" from the National Basketball Association's Portland Trailblazers, the former executive says. "He told us to make a ball to game-ball specs, smudges be damned."

In any event, Nike canceled its contract with Voit last December and says it is redesigning its inflatables. "We were naive," Mr. Mooney says. "We thought these were commodity items, but they're not."

Mr. Mooney brushes off the early flops as simply growing pains. "We're still in the earliest embryonic stages of this sector," he says. "We had complaints about our footwear 25 years ago and our apparel five years ago. Wait till you see our equipment in five years."

Despite its big plans, Nike's expenditures on developing its hard-goods lines have been relatively modest so far compared with the big bucks being shelled out by competitors. Nike officials estimate, for example, that they will spend less than $500,000 to design the new baseball glove.

And gloves, Mr. Mooney says, are a $200-million-a-year global market ripe for capture. "Talk about sleepy categories," he says, chuckling. "Baseball gloves have always been brown and leather. Ours will be neither."

Nike's researchers began trying to overhaul the traditional glove about 18 months ago. They started by asking about 200 minor-league and college baseball players what was wrong with their regular glove. (Major leaguers are too set in their ways to provide much help, Mr. Schulte says.) Right away, the dimensions of the problem became apparent.

"Most of the guys told us, 'My glove works fine,'" says Robert Ball, a Nike product developer.

Industry experts say Nike couldn't have found a tougher challenge than the baseball glove. Except for the aluminum bat, baseball innovations tend to flop, including one Rawlings effort in the early 1990s to sell an inflatable fielder's glove. The glove, with a tiny pump in the back, was supposed to emulate the success of Reebok's pump-sneaker line. "It was a bust," says Chuck Malloy, a Rawlings executive. "Baseball players don't like gimmicks."

The game itself is famously tradition bound. "It's not an accident that they still play baseball with white baseballs," says Mr. Dicasoli, the manufacturers group's marketing director. And mitts — their feel, their smell, the way generations of kids lovingly oil and work them to form the perfect pocket — may be the game's most traditional element.

Seeking fresh perspective, Nike imported some outsiders to develop its glove. Mr. Schulte says Nike "wanted to innovate but respect baseball's traditions." The developers ended up calling their clamshell prototype a "docking station."

They did manage to find one possible weak spot in the traditional glove. "Ball players spend months breaking in their gloves because leather is too stiff," Mr. Ball says. "We decided that because ours wasn't going to be leather, it would have minimal break-in time and would be more flexible and lighter than regular gloves."

Nike's minimalist prototype weighs less than 10 ounces, compared with about a pound and a half for traditional fielders' mitts. Instead of laces, the glove is held together with plastic clips and wire straps. The foam clamshell feels as limber as a well-broken-in glove.

Mr. Schulte says Nike is still weighing whether to line the inside of the clamshell with leather. "Right now," he says, "it doesn't smell like the traditional leather glove. It smells like glue."

A New Bat on Deck

Nike also designed a high-performance aluminum bat, to be introduced next fall. Most aluminum bats are made from aerospace scrap, but Nike hired Pechiney SA, a French metal-alloy specialist, to come up with a material that gives its new bats greater recoil, or "trampoline effect," for longer hits. Mr. Mooney also contends that Nike's bats will outlast rival models.

Nike's ambitious grab for the baseball- and softball-gear market jolted Rawlings, the 110-year-old leader in that business. Rawlings was so stodgy that under its former owner, Cleveland-based Figgie International Corp., it didn't budge from its old-style football shoulder pads when competitors introduced lighter urethane-based pads in the mid-1980s. "The industry ran right by us," says Randy Black, Rawlings's marketing vice president.

Rawlings says it won't let that happen to its baseball business. It has come out swinging against Nike, deriding Nike's new bats as "rock knockers" and introducing its own line of high-tech aluminum bats. The company also has a new array of "personality" gloves — some New York Yankees will be wearing pinstripe models next spring. Rawlings hired Seattle Mariners' superstar Ken Griffey Jr. to design his own glove, which features a lightning bolt on each finger. (Mr. Griffey gets paid for wearing the glove, plus a royalty on each one sold.) That has to sting Nike: Mr. Griffey is one of its best-known shoe and apparel pitchmen.

Early next year, Rawlings will add more gadgetry to its lineup. It plans to begin selling a new baseball with a built-in microchip that calculates the time elapsed from when the ball leaves a pitcher's hand to when it smacks into the catcher's glove. The chip converts the time and distance to figure the speed at which the ball traveled. Players will be able to check the speed of the pitch on a liquid-crystal display built right into the baseball's skin.

"There's a fine line between tradition and gimmickry," Mr. Black concedes. "But that swoosh means something: If you get complacent, Nike will kill you."

Reprinted by permission of The Wall Street Journal, © 1998 Dow Jones & Company, Inc. All Rights Reserved Worldwide.

75

The challenge of building a billion dollar brand

by Laura Liebeck

The making of the Martha Stewart home fashions program into a $1 billion Kmart brand was a lot like creating a souffle involving carefully measured ingredients in specific proportions. The cooks worked hard, making sure the recipe was followed precisely. Anything less would destroy the creation.

So it has been with Kmart's turnaround, of which the Martha Stewart Everyday program continues to be a pivotal element.

Martha Stewart Everyday, the broad-based home fashions program at Kmart, created and produced under the loving care of Martha Stewart herself and her Martha Stewart Living Omnimedia organization, in partnership with Kmart's own merchandising and executive team, plus home furnishings manufacturers, has, by most accounts, delivered on its promise of offering high-quality goods at a fair price.

The line will produce sales of $450 million this year, according to Kmart chairman, president and chief executive officer Floyd Hall. In 1998, Martha Stewart Everyday will approach $1 billion in sales from such products as towels, sheets, tablecloths and bathrobes.

Clearly, the MSE program is on a roll.

Accolades come from most quarters, including other retailers, manufacturers, retail consultants and retail analysts.

"I envision the Martha Stewart line to be the next Laura Ashley," said Margaret Cannella, research director for Citicorp Securities, referring to the design panache of the label. "It's phenomenal. It has appealing, great colors, all coordinated for you so you don't have to think much."

That's the point.

Both Kmart and Martha Stewart Living Omnimedia are thinking big. The Martha Stewart Everyday line will grow from 30% of the retailer's domestics sales to 70% by year-end 1998. Making up the balance of Kmart's domestics program will be opening price point goods not appropriate for the MSE label, plus some licensed products, said Steve Ryman, divisional vice president, Martha Stewart Everyday brand director.

The success of the MSE program was carefully crafted.

"We designed the program from the core out," said Ryman, referring to product needs of Kmart's core customer. "We had a clear vision of what the customer wanted from Kmart," added Shawn Kahle, vice president of corporate communications. "We knew we wanted to hone in on what customers wanted and one of them was home. Martha Stewart Everyday is the result of creative forces coming together."

Already, MSE has become the No. 2 brand in America among discount store shoppers, according to results of this year's *Discount Store News* Consumer Brands report (Oct. 20).

During the original Kmart introduction of Martha Stewart-branded goods in 1987, the program was built for "the outer edges" of the retailer's market or "the fringe," Ryman said.

Things are different now.

"We started on the core, and we'll work out to find where the outer edge is. We'll build and build until the customer resists," Ryman said.

So far, that outer edge is not yet in sight, despite some low-level criticism that items within the MSE program are too high priced for conventional Kmart shoppers. One critic pointed to the bed sheet program where some sheets sell for about $40 each. Program supporters disregard that criticism, saying the sheets are more cheaply priced than at department stores.

All of the ingredients for success in MSE have been built into the program: the design, the star power and the marketing muscle to keep the name out in front of consumers nearly every day in one form of media or another. By now, certainly most consumers know that Martha Stewart is more than just a home fashions and entertainment guru; she has become an icon of the '90s for taste and business savvy through her books, magazine, TV show and assorted guest appearances on TV and radio. Last month, she was on the cover of *Business Week* magazine and was at the COMDEX consumer electronics show representing IBM.

This kind of exposure has certainly pumped Stewart's "Q" score among consumers, and it is having a positive impact on Kmart. As a result, MSE sales are likely to advance quickly beyond the $1 billion sales mark for Kmart in the near future as the association builds momentum for the recovering retail chain. Its other in-store

> **Most everything concerning the Martha Stewart merchandise program has changed since Kmart and Martha Stewart joined forces 10 years ago; only Stewart herself is still around.**

programs are likely to benefit, too, as the lessons learned from MSE are applied to other categories and product development efforts.

Activity within the store could further heat up for Kmart if Martha Stewart Living Omnimedia creates an upscale line of Martha Stewart-brand products for a department or specialty chain, further enhancing the cachet of the Martha Stewart name and association for Kmart.

The multi-year agreement between Martha Stewart Living Omnimedia — a product development, design and marketing company — and Kmart, is for everyday basics. MSLO can, without violating its agreement with Kmart, develop a high-end line of goods for another retail channel. No program is currently in the works, however, said Sharon Patrick, president and ceo of MSLO.

For Kmart, MSLO set its sights on bringing its designs to the mass market.

"Martha is about bringing her products to the widest possible audience," said Patrick, noting that approximately 70% of bed and bath is bought at discount. "That's where America shops." The goal is to evolve the program, said Patrick, noting that MSLO, Kmart and the manufacturers work closely together. "We understand the assortment Kmart needs and the price points. They make us understand the merchants' requirements, and we meet those with our program," she said.

The role of each player in the program is well defined. MSLO is in charge of product development, design, marketing, advertising and packaging. Kmart is in charge of the in-store operation, spearheading the manufacturing process, the merchandise flow and the in-store execution. Together, both work with the manufacturers to bring Stewart's designs to life. Stewart, too, is very involved in the process, meeting with both manufacturers and the Kmart team.

"We're about service," Patrick said. "All else follows. We're interested in bringing [shoppers] choice in product that really has features not previously available in a color pallet, in design features and in a collection that was previously unavailable to them with a good, better, best assortment.

Both parties are dedicated to evolving the program

and creating within the Kmart store a one-stop shop for home goods needs.

Window coverings, the next category slated for stores, is scheduled for spring 1998. The most recent addition was the Silver line of 100% Egyptian cotton towels and 230-count all-cotton sateen sheets, considered the 'best' offering. They were introduced in September.

New product categories will be added to the lineup to keep the program vibrant and growing, both on shelf and in consumers' minds. Not all of the upcoming additions will be in domestics. By spring 1999, Kmart will introduce Martha Stewart Everyday product in lawn & garden.

Currently, Kmart is now focused on its spring initiative when it is planning a major introduction in soft and hard window, plus decorative hardware, bathroom accessories (coordinates and matching shower curtains, ceramics, plasticware, hampers and waste baskets), Ryman said. Another major introduction is slated for fall 1998, he said, declining to identify the category of goods.

The floor space will remain the same as the program builds, about 4,500 sq. ft. Sku count will rise, however, from nearly 1,500 items today to about 3,000 in home textiles by the end of next year. Vendor counts will rise from 17 to between 20 and 25 in this same period. Sales, he said, "will grow proportionately."

Neither MSLO nor Kmart would divulge specific details on new products or categories to come. They are dedicated to keeping a tight lid of new introductions, making sure that both the products and the launch are timed correctly and accompanied with the right promotion.

These elements were missing from the 1987 Kmart/Martha Stewart partnership.

Most everything concerning the Martha Stewart merchandise program has changed since Kmart and Martha Stewart joined forces 10 years ago; only Stewart herself is still around.

Over that time, Patrick said, "Martha evolved and Kmart changed.

"With the buyback of the company, Martha Stewart Living now has a whole company working together. All resources are brought to bear on this program. Martha has a different organization in place to support this effort," Patrick said.

The key difference this time for Kmart lies in the details. This time, Kmart laid out a plan, got the appropriate people and companies on board and then started executing according to that plan.

Kmart didn't have much of a commitment to the earlier Martha Stewart program, said Sid Doolittle, partner in

McMillan/Doolittle, Chicago-based retail consultants. "They didn't realize what they had." This time, Kmart scored big. "They got a brand before it was a brand," Doolittle said, and as a result, the program is making Kmart a destination store for shoppers.

"How do you build a brand? You treat it like a favorite child. You give it a lot of space; add the skus — which they are doing — and you give it a disproportionate amount of energy and you make it a flagship symbol of the turnaround of Kmart," said George Rosenbaum, president of Leo J. Shapiro Associates, Chicago.

Rosenbaum feels that if Kmart succeeds with the Martha Stewart Everyday program, as it appears it is, the retailer will have built one of the largest private label brands ever and certainly the largest in soft goods. MSE's company: Sears' Kenmore, Craftsman and DieHard labels — all hard lines.

"Kmart succeeded with Martha Stewart because it thought big," Rosenbaum said. "Back in the '80s, no one thought in terms of $450 million or $1 billion in sales. Once you have the vision, you commit the space, merchandise the space in the store and advertise you have a recipe for success."

Rosenbaum added that because Kmart has committed such huge resources to the program, customers are paying attention.

At times, this has seemed an understatement.

Available in mass only since March, the MSE program has met with huge success — but also with a little frustration and angst by both consumers and manufacturers. At first, demand seemed to outstrip supply, causing out-of-stocks within the program and elsewhere in the domestics industry, according to sources. Most of that has been addressed, and manufacturers are now looking for ways to further support and grow the program they know is a major retail success story.

Bob Gehm, president of mass brands at Westpoint Stevens, which produces product for the Blue label towel and bedding program, plus some Silver line bedding, said that from the beginning Kmart was very specific about its long-term goals for Martha Stewart Everyday and its vendor requirements for program participation.

The retailer was determined to make MSE one of the largest domestics programs in the country, and it was willing to invest time and money in seeing it succeed. The biggest aspect of the success of MSE, he said, was getting store associates on board with the efforts.

"Floyd [Hall] and Warren [Flick, retiring president and COO] laid it all out to us. Kmart believed this time that it would work," said Gehm, noting that MSE has met and exceeded Westpoint Stevens' expectations. He feels that Martha Stewart's personal involvement has been instrumental in the program's success.

Steve Puckett, divisional vp and business development manager for Fieldcrest Cannon, which produces product for the Blue Label, echoed Gehm's sentiments, adding that Kmart outlined the parameters of the program so that everyone knew their part in the effort. Each product in the line is reviewed and interpreted for their appropriateness for consumers, he said. "They brought us in to strategic alliance meetings with other vendors to discuss and explain just what Martha Stewart would mean to Kmart and how large it was going to be," Puckett said.

These strategic meetings still occur frequently. Puckett said he meets with Kmart executives once per month to discuss inventories and production schedules.

MSLO also is monitoring the progress of the program. Associates there shop the stores to be sure the goods are on shelf in sufficient quantities, that the stores are clean, neat, properly signed and that associates are helpful. They also shop the stores for merchandise to be sure that the product is produced according to spec.

This time around, nothing is left to chance.

Reprinted with permission from the December 8, 1997 issue of *Discount Store News*. Copyright Lebhar-Friedman, Inc., 425 Park Avenue, New York, NY 10022.

MAKE IT SIMPLE
That's P&G's new marketing mantra—and it's spreading

Does the world really need 31 varieties of Head & Shoulders shampoo? Or 52 versions of Crest? Procter & Gamble Co., the world's preeminent marketer, has decided that the answer is no. After decades of spinning out new-and-improved this, lemon-freshened that, and extra-jumbo-size the other thing, P&G has decided that it sells too many different kinds of stuff. Now, it has started doing the unthinkable: It's cutting back. Procter's U.S. product roster is a third shorter today than it was at the start of the decade. In hair care alone, it has slashed the number of items almost in half. Fewer shapes, sizes, packages, and formulas mean less choice for consumers. So sales went down, right? Wrong. Market share in hair care grew by nearly five points, to 36.5%, over the past five years. P&G's overall sales, powered by international expansion, have grown by a third in the same period.

P&G's drive to trim its product list is just one piece of a larger strategy of simplification. The company is now taking an ax to many of its marketing practices, hacking away at layers of complexity in a drive to cut costs, serve customers better, and expand globally. Besides just saying no to runaway product proliferation, it's standardizing formulas and packaging worldwide, selling marginal brands, cutting inefficient promotions, and curbing new-product launches. It's even putting its sacrosanct ad budget under the microscope to help shrink overall marketing costs to 20% of revenues by 2000, from 25% now.

Sure, these moves are saving Procter money—lots of it. And those savings are giving P&G the leeway to propel sales with lower prices, while increasing margins. But although the drive to simplicity began as an exercise in old fashioned cost-cutting, P&G is looking for other benefits. It knows the thousands of supermarket products leave shoppers staggering down aisles in sensory overload, increasingly immune to marketing messages, indifferent to brands, and suspicious of pricing. Since so many of the 30,000 items in a typical supermarket offer niggling differences from each other, shoppers face numbing selection—but little in the way of real variety. "There's this vast array of products," says Shelby Reyes, a 58-year-old Cleveland bookkeeper. "A lot of times I end up getting what's on sale...or I say the hell with it." Concedes P&G's president, Durk I. Jager: "It's mind-boggling how difficult we've made it for them over the years."

LESS IS MORE. The upshot: Stores have become crammed with things that people never buy. Here are the startling statistics of that waste: Almost a quarter of the products in a typical supermarket sell fewer than one unit a month, according to research by consulting firm Kurt Salmon Associates Inc. On the other hand, just 7.6% of all personal-care and household products account for 84.5% of sales, according to PaineWebber Inc. analyst Andrew Shore. A lot of the rest go almost unnoticed by consumers. A 1993 study by Willard Bishop Consulting Ltd. and market researcher Information Resources Inc. found that when duplicative items were removed, 80% of consumers saw no difference—and 16% actually thought there was more variety. "Most cosmetic and household product companies need an in-house Dr. Kevorkian," Shore says.

> "It's mind-boggling how difficult we've made it for consumers over the years"
>
> *— Durk Jager*
> *P&G President and*
> *Chief Operating Officer*

Complicated product lines and pricing cause worse problems for the retailer, who has to struggle amid the specials, rebates, and discounts to figure out the invoice. Often he fails. An astonishing 38% of all grocery invoices end up with errors requiring costly special handling to fix, according to a study by Andersen Consulting. "We created a whole plethora of allowances and deals and conditions which were just simply confusing and added cost to the system," Jager says.

Five years ago, Procter led the way to more stable pricing by vastly reducing the array of supermarket specials in favor of lower list prices. At first, retailers, stung by the loss of their discounts and special deals, slowed purchases, and P&G's sales stalled. But by May of this year, its overall volume market-share had either held steady or increased for 38 months in a row.

Though Procter's drive to make it simple has been gathering force for years, it gained momentum with the ascent of Chairman John E. Pepper and Jager to their posts a year ago. Pepper sees enormous opportunities in simplification, and Jager is ramming the program through. The goal is to make the best choice for the consumer crystal clear, something Jager calls transparency. A case in point: With much fanfare eight years ago, P&G launched separate disposable diapers for boys and girls. Now, it's eliminating them, claiming its diapers have become so absorbent that such, well, anatomical targeting isn't necessary anymore. More to the point, a parent of a baby girl won't rummage through the boy Pampers, give up, and buy Kimberly-Clark Corp.'s Huggies instead.

As usual, P&G is something of a bellwether for the packaged-goods industry. The Cincinnati-based company is leading a broad movement among marketers as executives realize complexity alienates consumers and generates expensive and error-prone operations. "Complex processes are the work of the devil," in the words of reengineering guru Michael Hammer.

CORPULENT SYSTEMS. Now, some of America's biggest consumer-products companies are exorcising deviltry from their product lists, pricing, promotions, and ads. Nabisco Inc., acknowledging it let brand extensions get out of hand, is cutting new-product launches by 20% and taking some 15% of existing items out of production. Cereal makers have all vastly cut their once ubiquitous weekly promotions in favor of simplicity, stability, and lower list pricing

And the urge to simplify isn't limited to packaged-goods companies. Toyota has simplified car design by stripping out needless or redundant parts. Showtime Networks Inc. has made its bills easier to figure out, cutting the error rate dramatically. Instead of custom-designing model branches in each market, Citibank took a successful design in Chile, refined it in Greece, and reapplied it around the world. And Sun Co. is reducing the number of grades of Sunoco gasoline in the Northeast from five to four. "In an effort to give you more, we gave you more choices than you wanted," its ads confess. "So now, at Sunoco, we've simplified."

There's some debate over how far the simplification drive will go. After all, it wasn't long ago that companies were waving the banner of micromarketing, aiming carefully calibrated products and messages at ever-smaller consumer segments—selling spicier canned soup in the Southwest, for example. And John D. Bowlin, CEO of Kraft Foods International, continues to argue that Procter's variety-reduction kick is ill suited to food companies, which depend on new offerings to drive sales.

Still, there's no denying that the corpulent packaged-goods marketing system that grew up in the 1970s and 1980s needs to slim down. Consumer-product companies are launching more than 20,000 new items each year, according to *New Product News*, a trade publication. But the death rate is high: Barely more than a quarter of new products, excluding line extensions, introduced by the nation's largest advertisers maintain national distribution for more than two years, says market researcher IRI.

P&G's push to cut complexity began in manufacturing, amid the 1980s' Total Quality movement. Procter realized big savings by cutting the number of specifications, consolidating suppliers, and streamlining plants. Incredibly, P&G once had 61 different kinds of cover sheets on the back of Always sanitary pads. Now it has 13. Such moves, together with a 1993 restructuring that claimed 13,000 jobs and 30 plants, have helped the company cut its annual production and distribution costs by $1.6 billion, or about 8% over the past five years. It thinks it can remove $2 billion more by the end of the decade. "The world is moving faster. That makes it even more important to simplify," says Pepper.

Meanwhile, the rise of supermerchants such as Wal-Mart Stores Inc. also spurred simplification. The hyperefficient retailer has become one of Procter's biggest trade customers, and it has increasingly demanded simplified pricing and shipping from its vendors. Learning from Wal-Mart, P&G created a leaner approach to logistics. More than 40% of P&G's orders are now shipped automatically, based on withdrawals from customers' warehouses, cutting reams of paperwork and sharply reducing inventory costs. "I think they've been making moves that are absolutely essential for the industry," says Wal-Mart CEO David D. Glass. Indeed, Procter's system has become a model for other manufacturers.

While the industry has made considerable progress streamlining how goods are made and moved, the task of eliminating extraneous items has just begun. Procter again has been out front. One of the biggest cuts came in its U.S. hair-care business. P&G sold its Lilt home permanents in 1990, and minor brands such as Prell and Ivory shampoo were cut way back. Even the mighty Head & Shoulders line was pared in half, to 15 variations. The moves met some resistance from P&G's brand honchos, who thought, "Oh my God, we're going to lose sales because we're going to have fewer items," says U.S. hair-care chief Robert S. Matteucci. "There's a huge skepticism that this is the right thing to do, and that it's doable."

INDUSTRY SHOCKER. But simplification quickly paid off: Sales per item in hair care more than doubled. In Japan, P&G cut the number of its Max Factor cosmetic items from 1,385 in June, 1995, to 828 nine months later. Sales have since climbed 6%.

Such payoffs have caught the eye of many top consumer-products companies. H. John Greenius, CEO of new-product star Nabisco, estimates that the company's 77 new products last year were about 20% too many. More than a quarter of a $428 million pretax re-

structuring charge it took in June will be used to eliminate more than 300 of the items it now carries, such as single-serving sizes of Lorna Doones and king-size packages of Nutter Butter cookies. Longer term, it plans to reduce the 8,000 items it carries worldwide by 15%.

Manufacturers that refuse to trim may find retailers doing it for them. Wegmans Food Markets Inc., a Rochester (N.Y.) supermarket chain, says it has culled redundant items from its shelves for greater variety. For instance, it dropped Bristol Myers-Squibb's slow-selling Nuprin, which is like other ibuprofens, for some herbal products. Instead of carrying four different sizes of the same brand of toilet paper, it's stocking only two, but added one with baking soda, one that's recycled, another that's free of dyes, and a fourth with a print.

only is Procter shucking unproductive items and brands, but it is also practicing what Jager calls birth control for new products, by charging managers' budgets when they launch new items. "There is a real push in the company to do fewer, bigger things," one P&G executive says.

Procter has also taken strides to cut through the chaos and expense of special deals offered to retailers and distributors. Such deals are another costly and confusing form of marketing complexity. They cause shelf prices to bounce weekly and train consumers to buy on price instead of perceived brand superiority. A forthcoming study by Andersen Consulting will report manufacturers spent a staggering $49 billion, or 11% of sales, on such promotions in 1994, up from $15 billion, or 5%, in 1978. Yet half the time

---

How Procter & Gamble Is Paring Down

STANDARDIZING product formulas and packages. P&G now uses just two basic packages for shampoo in the U.S., saving $25 million a year.

REDUCING trade promotions. P&G gives stores fewer discounts and rebates, and it bases them on sales volume. That means more stable prices.

EASING UP ON coupons. With redemption rates falling, Procter is issuing fewer coupons—and going cold turkey in an upstate New York test.

GETTING RID OF marginal brands. Selling off second-tier brands such as Bain de Soleil sun-care products lets P&G concentrate on its market leaders.

CUTTING product lines. Axing extraneous sizes, flavors, and other variants makes it easier for consumers to find what they're looking for.

REAPPLYING strategies that work. Always sanitary pads uses the same ads worldwide. A distribution system developed in Eastern Europe is being exported to Asia.

TRIMMING new-product launches. Only items with a strong chance of making the top half or third of their category in unit sales get the green light.

Weeding out the losers doesn't stop with product extensions. To instill greater financial discipline—and measure results based on the contribution of each business to shareholder return—P&G has tossed out brands that aren't leaders. Since last year, it has gotten rid of 11 brands, from Lestoil household cleaner to Lava soap.

In June, the company shocked the industry when it bailed out of a joint venture selling the painkiller Aleve, upon which P&G had lavished a $100 million product launch two years earlier. Unable to extend Aleve globally and renegotiate the financial terms of its agreement with partner Roche Holding Ltd., P&G sold its 50% stake for a $120 million aftertax gain. It was hardly the sort of move associated with a company that has long pursued its strategic goals almost regardless of the financial consequences. Not

consumers buy an item on special, they don't even realize it, says Andersen partner Victor J. Orler.

The endless trade promotions don't confuse just the consumer; they also bewilder stores trying to navigate the discounts and rebates as they compute their bills. And since one-time-only deals cause wholesalers and retailers to stock up while the price is low, factories constantly cope with artificial surges in demand.

In a gutsy move five years ago, Procter cut sharply into the endless round of discounts it offered to retailers and instead lowered list prices on most of its products. The strategy, explains Pepper, was "directed at trying to avoid pricing patterns that discourage loyalty through ups and downs." By cutting down on the special deals, P&G has sliced the proportion of invoices on which it

The Rest of the World Goes Simple

How other companies are streamlining

NABISCO plans to trim its product line by 15% and cut new-product launches by 20%

TOYOTA is slashing by 20% the development costs of its 1997 Camry by taking out unnecessary content

---

CITIBANK is replicating model branches developed in Chile and Greece around the world, instead of reinventing them in each market

---

CLOROX simplified its trade promotions and trimmed the number of items it sells

---

GENERAL MOTORS has reduced the number of U.S. car models from 53 to 44 since 1994 and combined its Pontiac and GMC divisions to simplify marketing

---

COLGATE-PALMOLIVE consolidated worldwide advertising under a single agency to move winning ads around the world fast

---

KRAFT this spring led a cereal-industry move toward lower, more stable list prices

DATA: BUSINESS WEEK

needs to make manual corrections to 6% from 31% two years ago. It's now applying the same concept in Europe.

P&G is taking the ax to consumer coupons, too. With redemption rates down to 2% from 4% in 1980, coupons are a less and less efficient way to draw new customers. "Over time, they've lost a lot of their effectiveness," says ad chief Robert L. Wehling. Instead, Procter is putting the money into lower prices and other promotions such as sampling and in-store demonstrations. So far, it has cut its use of coupons by half, and it may go much further. Since February, Procter has been testing total elimination of coupons in upstate New York. Wegmans, which operates in that test region, says sales of P&G products are up at its stores.

VULNERABLE AD BUDGET. Procter's value pricing is helping to spark a major change in U.S. trade promotions. Few have made the outright cuts that P&G has, but marketers from Quaker Oats Co. to Colgate-Palmolive have overhauled their systems. After a debilitating price war using endless coupons and buy-one-get-one-free offers, General Mills Inc. and Kellogg Co. started the move to simplified cereal pricing in 1994. And these days, when Kraft's Post distributes coupons, they're good on any cereal that it makes.

As a global marketer, Procter has another reason to peel away complexity: Whenever it can apply an existing package, product formula, or ad campaign to a new market, it saves big money and can move faster. "Reapplication is very, very important. A good reapplication is as good as a creation," says Herbert Schmitz, P&G's head of Central and Eastern Europe operations. In Eastern Europe, packages of Ariel detergent are printed in 14 languages, from Latvian to Lithuanian. Vidal Sassoon shampoos and conditioners now contain a single fragrance worldwide, with variations only in the amount; less in Japan, where subtle scents are preferred, and more in Europe.

P&G, the world's largest advertiser, is even rethinking how much it spends on advertising—a major break with tradition. Even in its 1993 restructuring, advertising remained off-limits. "For the first time, Procter is not afraid to touch that sacred marketing budget, " says Smith Barney Inc. analyst Holly Becker. Advertising spending will probably still grow from last year's $3.3 billion, but at a slower rate. "The main thing is to look at inefficient practices," says Pepper. The company has saved millions by consolidating most of its U.S. media-buying at one agency. And it has reduced TV production costs by 25% by using fewer production houses and shooting commercials for several countries at one location.

AUTO MAKERS SIMPLIFY. It's also looking to spread good campaigns around the world. Procter had to step up its production recently of Pringles potato chips to keep up with global demand, thanks to a successful advertising campaign used around the world. Nearly everything in one ad—the rap-music theme, the young people dancing around, the tag line, "Once you pop, you can't stop"—was the same in Germany as in the U.S.

Colgate wanted to achieve much the same thing when it consolidated its $550 million in yearly ad spending at a single agency late last year. It's seeking more efficiencies like the savings it reaped when it replaced 20 separate local campaigns for laundry detergent with a series of successful commercials developed in France—a campaign that ran in 30 countries.

Outside packaged goods, the attack on complexity is gathering force in the auto industry. The Japanese, pressed earlier this decade by a soaring yen, are simplifying the way cars are built by reducing the number of parts. Toyota, for example, set a goal of slashing development costs by 20% on the 1997 Camry coming out this fall. General Motors Corp., meanwhile, is working to comb out overlapping products and marketing efforts. It combined its Pontiac and GMC divisions in February and pruned the number of car models it sells in the U.S. from 53 in 1994 to 44 in the coming model year.

Not everyone embraces P&G's less-is-more credo, though. Kraft's Bowlin argues that the food industry is simply a different breed from Procter's household products. "Variety is important," he declares. "Look at ice cream. Vanillas and chocolates make up the majority of your buying, but how often will you go back to a shop if all they have is vanilla and chocolate?" And rival Kimberly-Clark scoffs at Procter's move back to unisex diapers. "Three out of four parents tell us they prefer boy and girl diapers," says a Kimberly spokesperson. "Our strategy is to offer parents a choice."

But it's hard to argue with P&G's overall results. Earnings excluding extraordinary items for the fiscal year ended June 30 were up 12%, to $3.03 billion, even though sales were up just 5%, to $35.3 billion. At 8.6%, margins were the highest in more than 45 years. Big leaps in overseas markets helped—unit volume growth in China was more than 50%—but those hefty margins are a testament to the power of simplicity.

Yet simplification doesn't guarantee double-digit earnings gains; in the current quarter, Procter's growth will slow, as lagging over-the-counter drug and toothpaste businesses take a toll. And P&G's struggle with Crest toothpaste shows it still sometimes falls off the simplicity wagon when the going gets tough. Battered by Unilever PLC's Mentadent and other rivals, Crest will soon offer a buy-one-get-one-free promotion—a move P&G acknowledges "isn't in line with the overall direction we're taking." Even for Procter, making it simple is no simple matter.

By Zachary Schiller in Cincinnati, with Greg Burns in Chicago, Karen Lowry Miller in Brussels, and bureau reports

Reprinted from September 9, 1996 issue of *Business Week* by special permission, copyright © 1996 by McGraw-Hill, Inc.

77

INVOICE? WHAT'S AN INVOICE?
Electronic commerce will soon radically alter the way business buys and sells

Ever since Wal-Mart Stores Inc. revolutionized retailing by linking its computers to those of suppliers, executives in every other industry have been dreaming of doing the same. They've seen how Wal-Mart's pioneering use of computer networks to conduct business electronically squeezed costs and time out of clunky supply chains and helped it outgun just about all of its rivals.

Well, hang on. Electronic commerce, once little more than a management buzzword, is about to radically alter how all companies sell to and buy from each other. The techniques that Wal-Mart and giants such as General Motors, Eastman Kodak, and Baxter International have been perfecting on private networks for the past decade are evolving and are now about to move to the wide-open Internet.

SIZZLE. U.S. companies already buy $500 billion worth of goods electronically each year, reckons Torrey K. Byles, a director at market researcher Giga Information Group. That's a small fraction of their total purchases, but it shows why Internet experts believe that business-to-business links—rather than glitzy online malls—will be the first form of Web commerce to pay off. Doing business on the Net is "a cost-reduction and efficiency-improvement play," says Jim Sha, vice-president, new ventures at Netscape Communications Corp., the sizzling Web software maker.

E-commerce could have profound effects on efficiency. As more transactions move from the numbing pace of paper to the lightning speed of electrons, economists predict that a new era of nearly friction-free markets will arrive. Companies that don't move quickly to the new technology risk being left behind. "Electronic commerce will happen," says Brad Wheeler, professor of information systems at the University of Maryland. "People can't stick their head in the sand or they'll be dealt right out."

Take something as simple as a purchase order (table). Even though manufacturing giants such as GM have used a scheme called electronic data interchange (EDI) to order parts automatically from suppliers since the concept was proposed in the early 1970s, most business-to-business sales still are done with paper forms—a reminder, in triplicate, of outdated methods. If you eliminate paper, you spend less time and money re-keying information into different computers and correcting the resulting errors. By some estimates, E-commerce could slash the cost of processing a purchase order from $150 to as little as $25.

Once the software—and security measures—are available, the Internet's World Wide Web will become the global infrastructure for electronic commerce. IBM, General Electric Information Services (GEIS), Dun & Bradstreet, Microsoft, and a raft of others are scurrying to build what's needed—everything from software for securing payments and building electronic catalogs to services that authenticate a new trading partner's electronic identity. One company, Industry.Net Corp., headed by former Lotus Development Corp. CEO Jim P. Manzi, is developing a sort of industrial mall to help companies find customers and suppliers in cyberspace.

EARLY BIRDS. "I really see the Internet as an explosion of electronic commerce," says Hellene S. Runtagh, president and chief executive of GEIS. That company is rushing to extend its EDI services, currently delivered over a private network, out to the Internet so it can reach thousands of new businesses. By putting global markets at virtually anyone's fingertips, Runtagh says, the Net should trigger the creation of a multitude of new companies worldwide. "This is the most exciting sea change to hit commerce globally in the last 100 years," she says.

In the meantime, some companies are already rigging E-commerce systems on the Net. Fruit of the Loom Inc., until recently a self-confessed technology laggard, is using the Net to make up for lost time. Led by computer executives hired away from Federal Express Corp. and elsewhere, the apparelmaker is using the Web to one-up Hanes Cos. and other brands in the market for blank T-shirts and other items sold through novelty stores and at special events.

Fruit depends on some 50 wholesalers nationwide to ship its goods in bulk to thousands of silk-screen printers, embroidery shops, and similar outfits. And now, it's offering to put those wholesalers on the Web, at virtually no charge to them. Fruit's plan is to give each one a complete computer system, called Activewear Online, that's programmed to display colorful catalogs, process electronic orders 24 hours a day, and manage inventories.

One of Fruit's major goals is to avoid losing customers when a wholesaler is out of stock. If, for instance, a silk screener needs 1,000 black T-shirts in a hurry for a Megadeth concert and the wholesaler is low, Fruit's central warehouse can be notified to ship the shirts directly to the customer. "We'll make Fruit's inventory a virtual inventory for our wholesalers," says Charles M. Kirk, Fruit's chief information officer.

Until now, it would have taken years to

Less Paper, More Electrons

1. Browsing an electronic catalog, the customer clicks on items to purchase. A computer sends the order directly to the merchant's machine.

2. The merchant's computer checks the customer's credit and determines that the goods wanted are indeed available.

3. The warehouse and shipping departments are notified and goods readied for delivery.

4. The accounting department bills the customer electronically.

---

build such a rich E-commerce system—even if it were possible on the closed, mainframe-based EDI networks run by companies such as GE and IBM. But for Fruit of the Loom, Connect Inc.'s software, called OneServer, and a catalog program from Snickleways Interactive helped it get online in just a few months. And its retailers need only an ordinary PC with a modem and Web-browsing software.

Along with Connect, players such as TradeWave, TSI International, OpenMarket, Netscape Communications, and Microsoft are chasing a Web commerce software market that should hit $750 million in 1999, according to Forrester Research Inc. New software from Premenos, GE, and Sterling Commerce, meanwhile, is starting to move traditional EDI traffic over the Internet, too—at a fraction of the cost that the private EDI nets currently charge.

For large-scale E-commerce initiatives, however, the private EDI setups still have the edge for now. Campbell Soup Co., for instance, has just spent $30 million to redesign its order-processing system around EDI. Called Compass, the new setup is scheduled to go live in August. One goal: Double the portion of paperless orders that the food

(Cont.)

company receives to 80%, whether from salespeople's laptop computers or the "continuous replenishment" systems that companies such as Flemings Cos. use to automatically restock warehouses.

Compass should reduce Campbell's costs by $18 million a year and speed deliveries, says Ronald W. Ferner, vice-president for low-cost business systems. Just cutting out the errors would be a boon. Mistakes now creep into 60% of the orders that Campbell gets by fax and phone. The result: Sales-people spend 40% of their time straightening out problems instead of selling. Compass, which relies on software from Industri-Matematick, a Swedish firm, and an IBM SPsuperscript/2 computer, will turn around orders within 18 hours, down from 48 now. It will even book space on delivery trucks and reserve time at customers' loading docks. Says Ferner: "Even the trees are happy. We're not chopping them down to make paper."

BIG SAVINGS. As impressive as that is, the Web promises to take E-commerce much farther. AMP Inc., for instance, has put up a multilingual catalog of more than 40,000 connectors and other electronic parts on the Web. Eventually, the Web site may take orders, but for now that's being left to distributors. But CEO William J. Hudson Jr. says the catalog is already saving money compared with the $8 million a year it costs to print and mail paper catalogs. And the Web catalog's fresher data should generate more orders.

Ultimately, E-commerce will take place in virtual marketplaces. These trading posts will allow buyers and sellers who may not know one another to meet electronically and trade in goods and services without the aid—or cost—of traditional agents and brokers. Industry. Net now collects fees from more than 4,000 makers of all kinds of industrial gear in return for listing their products and services in a large electronic catalog. Purchasing agents and engineers from all over the world browse the data for next to nothing. Now, purchases continue to go through local distributors. But CEO Manzi wants Industry. Net to process orders and transfer payments, too—for a service fee on each transaction. To develop a system capable of handling thousands of transactions hourly, he hired Mark Teflian, a computer expert who helped to design United Airlines Inc.'s reservation system.

Meanwhile, a consortium that includes D&B, AT&T, Digital Equipment, and SHL Systemhouse has created International Business Exchange, or IBEX. It's a sort of electronic bulletin board on which companies in any country can list goods they want to buy or sell. The system lets them negotiate anonymously and, if a deal gets far enough, helps them initiate credit checks, arrange financing, and get legal and customs paperwork completed by local companies. "Electronic commerce is really a massive information management job," says Mady Jalinous, president and CEO of Global Business Alliance, IBEX' major investor.

The Web is seeing all sorts of specialty markets sprout up, too. EarthCycle Inc. in Woodland Hills, Calif., runs one that deals in chemicals recycled from industrial waste. In September, an online market for buying and selling electricity is to go online. Sponsored by a consortium of 170 utilities and cooperatives, it's intended to help meet a federal mandate to increase competition in the wholesale power market and smooth out price imbalances across the nation. The system is being designed to support futures contracts and other sophisticated commodity trading.

As powerful as the E-commerce concept is, it won't spread evenly across the economy. "People who are powerful sellers may be able to delay the development of electronic markets," says Thomas Malone, head of the coordination science department at Massachusetts Institute of Technology's Sloan School. After all, despite NASDAQ, a vast electronic market, the New York and American stock exchanges rely on humans and paper, and they're still entrenched. But, warns Malone: "Those who try to delay it will be fighting a losing battle. In the long term, buyers migrate to the market that's better for them." Get ready, there's an electronic market coming to a screen near you.

By John W. Verity in New York

Reprinted from June 10, 1996 issue of *Business Week* by special permission, copyright © 1996 by McGraw-Hill, Inc.

78

Are you as good *as* you think *you are?*

There's only one way to know for sure. Compare yourself with the fastest, smartest, most flexible, and efficient companies around. ■ *by Justin Martin*

When it comes to executing management concepts like speed, mass customization, learning organizations, and supplier relations, some companies have the right stuff. Chrysler, for instance, has saved billions by getting its huge and far-flung network of vendors to work as a team. Applying state-of-the-art computer design technology, Andersen Windows can now give customers anything they want, whether it's a 20-foot-high Gothic window or a 20-inch screen. Fast-growing credit card issuer MBNA relies on a 15-point measurement system to provide lightning-quick service. The nod goes to Chevron when it comes to knowledge management, a practice that involves breaking down barriers to sharing information within an organization.

What all four of these companies have in common is that they're known as management meccas, places where people come to learn how the best do it. Scores of companies—big names like Boeing and AT&T—have sent out teams to tour the facilities of these best practitioners, chat with their executives, basically figure out how they do what they do. Typically, there's no charge for benchmarking visits. The idea is to foster a free exchange of information—it's the business-world equivalent of doctors' sharing their findings with the medical community at large. Of course, this enlightened attitude doesn't generally extend to competitors. But they have their own sneaky ways of finding out about a company's practices—one flew over a rival's new factory, snapping spy pictures.

Not surprisingly, all this attention has become something of a distraction. It's at the point now where these companies are starting to turn away benchmarkers. Andersen Windows, for example, will agree to only mutually beneficial arrangements, in which the benchmarker can provide useful information in return.

Even so, all four of these companies allowed FORTUNE to soak up their secrets. So

here, then, is a unique opportunity to get a whirlwind benchmarking session with four masters. Learning about their best practices may give you ideas that can be applied to your own company. But beware. Seeing the ways in which your own company fails to stack up may be a bit off-putting. That's no reason to despair, though. As Robert Hiebeler, partner in charge of Arthur Andersen's global best-practices group, says, "The goal of identifying best practices is to disturb yourself in a positive way."

ANDERSEN WINDOWS

LEGEND HAS IT that when Hans Jacob Andersen arrived in the U.S. from Denmark in 1870, the first English phrase he learned was: "All together, boys." He set out for the timber-rich Midwest, where he opened a retail lumberyard, but soon moved into window-frame making. In 1904 he set up an assembly line in his factory, beating Henry Ford to the mass-production punch by nine years. All together, boys. Today Andersen Windows, of Bayport, Minnesota, has grown into a $1 billion private company. What's helped its rapid growth is something called mass customization—the use of mass-production techniques to assemble items uniquely tailored to the demands of individual customers.

As recently as 1980, Andersen was essentially a mass producer, making a range of standard windows in large batches. "But the market kept asking for more and more unique things," says Mike Tremblay, manager of business systems at Andersen. "People didn't want their windows to look like their neighbor's windows, or anyone else's in the world for that matter."

Andersen did its best to keep up with the custom options the market demanded. It rolled out various embellishments, like hardware and muntins that could make a window

look prairie-style, Gothic-style, you name it. When homeowners or contractors visited a retailer, however, they were left to make sense of a mind-boggling array of choices laid out in an ever-thickening set of catalogues. Calculating a price quote for windows could take several hours, and it could be 15 pages long. In the case of something truly complicated—an arched window, say—a working knowledge of trigonometry was necessary.

The net effect of all this complexity was a growing error rate that threatened to damage the company's sterling reputation. From 1985 to 1991 the number of different products offered by Andersen grew from 28,000 to 86,000. By 1991, 20% of truckloads of Andersen windows contained at least one order discrepancy, double the number in 1985. "When our accuracy numbers suffered," says Tremblay, "it brought a sense of urgency."

Andersen responded in the early Nineties by selling its retailers and distributors what is

> CUSTOMERS, *while in the store, can now use a computer to design their own windows. Their creations are then built to spec in Andersen's Minnesota factory.*

essentially an interactive, computerized version of its catalogue. Using this tool, a salesperson can help customers add, change, and strip away features until they've designed a window they're pleased with. It's akin to playing with building blocks. The computer automatically checks the window specs for structural soundness, and then generates a price quote.

The system requires a Macintosh computer, an Oracle database, and some proprietary software. The whole package can be had for about $4,000. Currently 650 of them are installed at various distributors and retailers around the country. David Steele, president of the Window Gallery, which has three locations in the Southeast, reports that he can now do a customer's window specs five times faster. Sales of Andersen products at his stores have nearly tripled in the past five years. "It's a terrific tool," he says. "It does things that would drive me crazy when I used to have to do them by hand."

Of course, if the new project was to work, Andersen had to link the showroom with the factory. The retailer's computer transmits each order to a company database. Each window is then assigned a unique "license plate number," which can be tracked in real time, using bar-code technology, from the assembly line through to the warehouse. This helps ensure that what the customer orders is what gets built and ultimately what gets shipped. The new system has ended errors as Andersen knew them: Last year the company offered a whopping 188,000 different products, yet fewer than one in 200 van loads contained an order discrepancy.

The next frontier in mass customization for Andersen is what is termed batch-of-one manufacturing, which would dramatically reduce the company's inventory of finished window parts. Currently Andersen makes its custom windows using some standard parts, like sashes and muntins, which it must keep in stock. But with batch-of-one, everything is entirely made to order.

The perfect venue for this technique is the window-replacement market. When it comes time to replace windows, homeowners often can't determine who had made them. Most have to settle for a rough approximation of the originals, made by one of the legions of vinyl window makers, many of them fly-by-night.

Lured by a market estimated at roughly $15 billion a year in the U.S. alone, and confident that it can trounce the fly-by-nights, Andersen has just started a pilot program it calls "renewal." A key to the program is Fibrex, a new, patented composite of wood and vinyl. It's tougher than vinyl and doesn't age like wood. The advantage, when it comes to mass-customization, is that Fibrex can easily be cut to match almost any old window.

Andersen's pilot Fibrex plant is in suburban St. Paul. Everything is made to order; practically no inventory is kept on hand—all that's in the warehouse is raw Fibrex and some hardware. Only a month is required between receiving an order and installing a finished custom window.

In the near future, when a customer's old window is removed, the wood will be ground up to make more Fibrex. Hence renewal. The company hopes to take the program national within five years. And after that, who knows? "You can't go and get all enamored of where

you've been," says Tremblay. "We're on a journey toward purer and purer mass customization."

CHRYSLER

CHRYSLER DOESN'T EXACTLY make cars from scratch. Fully two-thirds of the components the company uses in manufacturing—everything from lug nuts to wiper blades—come from outside sources. All told, Chrysler purchases 60,000 different items from 1,140 different suppliers, arrayed in an awesomely complicated chain. And no one manages that chain more efficiently than the carmaker—so much so that AT&T;and Harley Davidson as well as the Department of Energy have been out to Chrysler's Auburn Hills, Michigan, facilities to see how the company does it.

It's surprising that an automaker has achieved best-practitioner status in supply-chain management. Traditionally the industry has made a practice of jerking its supply chains, often encouraging wild bidding wars. José Ignacio López de Arriortúa, GM's notorious former purchasing head, even canceled supply contracts outright.

But Chrysler has seen advantage in forming less adversarial relations with its vendors. The company shares most of its 150 major suppliers with Ford and GM. Since it hasn't as much purchasing clout as the two Detroit giants, Chrysler figures the only way to get an edge with suppliers, sappy as it sounds, is to be easier to work with.

One thing the company does is to involve suppliers earlier in the car design process, soliciting their ideas on cost savings and technological innovation. As a consequence, Chrysler often finds out about new materials, parts, and other technologies before the other automakers. "When it comes to new technology, Chrysler winds up getting a peek under the tent early," says Richard Schultz, director of worldwide automotive products for Alcoa. "None of the other car companies we work with are as accessible or willing to take advice from suppliers."

In 1989, Chrysler took a giant step forward in supplier relations when it initiated a program called Score, an acronym for "supplier cost-reduction effort." The notion is simple: Where auto companies have tended to hold down costs by squeezing suppliers' margins, Chrysler decided instead to work with its suppliers on dreaming up ideas for cost cutting. The arrangement is mutually beneficial in that the supplier can save money and Chrysler gets cheaper parts. Of course, the company doesn't want suppliers to capriciously cut corners—quality may suffer. So it asks them to submit ideas for approval first; the goal is for each supplier to identify cost-cutting opportunities equal to 5% of its annual billings to Chrysler.

The ideas can be quite small. One supplier named Sur-Flo Plastics & Engineering reduced the thickness of the splash shield (a sheet of plastic that covers the wheel well) on the 1995 minivan, for a paltry savings of $72,500. But in aggregate, Score has been a huge success. Lately, ideas have been rolling in at a rate of more than 100 a week; 16,000 have been received so far, for a total savings of $2.5 billion to Chrysler. The company estimates that suppliers have received a similar windfall from the program. It's only natural that the demand for savings winds up rolling down the chain, with suppliers in turn asking their suppliers to be more cost-conscious.

The unprecedented back-and-forth with vendors has given Chrysler an unusual grasp of the complexity of its supply chain. "In the old days we didn't even know where the bolts came from," admits Thomas Stallkamp, Chrysler's head of procurement and supply. But these days Chrysler has actually undertaken the laborious task of mapping out some of the chains. The company discovered, for instance, that even a simple-looking item like a roller lifter—a $3 engine part—required 35 separate suppliers.

Chrysler has also been rigorously pruning its family of suppliers. For example, the number of vendors that supply fasteners has been cut from 350 to 92; the goal is 42 by 1998. The total supplier base is down 36% in the past five years, and will drop another 25% by the turn of the century. Who will survive? One clue: Any supplier that fails to generate sufficient Score savings risks being out of a job.

To get those who do survive working more in sync, Chrysler assigns a particular supplier to act as a team leader. Its job is to oversee other suppliers in the design and manufacture of a component such as a seat. Time was, Chrysler workers had to assemble seats themselves, right on the line, with components from 150 vendors. Today the company buys fully assembled seats directly from suppliers such as Johnson Controls, Lear, and Magna International. This approach eliminates inventory costs for Chrysler, saving millions.

All of Chrysler's cutting-edge supply-chain management techniques come together in the Plymouth Prowler, a kind of test bed for the practice. The Prowler is a 1930s-style roadster (pricetag: around $35,000) and will be produced in a limited run of roughly 3,000 cars annually, starting in 1997. With the Prowler, many key vendors were involved from day one in the design process, and several were willing to give Chrysler dibs on their newest offerings. For example, thanks to a new, sturdier alloy developed by Alcoa, the Prowler will be the first car built in North America with an all-aluminum body. The company saved money, too, by making a supplier named the Becker Group a team leader that worked closely with both Chrysler and

(Cont.)

other suppliers in designing and assembling the car's interior. Says Chrysler's Stallkamp: "In the end this business is driven by emotions and relationships and how people feel about you."

MBNA

MBNA IS TRULY a speed freak. The Wilmington, Delaware, credit card company has a near-religious devotion to serving its customers swiftly and then measuring how it's doing. But make no mistake. This is no fad of the moment that MBNA is caught up in. Neither has the company fallen under the sway of some swami of speed, parceling out choice bits of theory while collecting a fat retainer. Far from it. MBNA, first among its peers to make service reps available to customers 24 hours a day, way back in 1986, has been on this kick for a long time. Speed of service is vital to the highly profitable niche the company has fashioned for itself.

While many credit card issuers blanket the nation with cold calls and junk mail, MBNA focuses on an eminently desirable customer base—affinity groups. Currently the company produces Visas and MasterCards for 4,300 of them, including the National Education Association, Georgetown University, and Ringling Brothers. Custom cards with everything from the Dallas Cowboys logo to personal pet photos, in the case of a new program with Ralston Purina, are available from MBNA. Its cardholders, meanwhile, tend to have family incomes that are 20% above the national average and carry balances of roughly $3,000, vs. an industry average of $1,073. Warmed, presumably, by a sense of affinity, they're a loyal lot too. MBNA is able to retain an enviable 98% of its profitable customers.

But premium customers are very demanding. They want good service, and they want it now. MBNA continually takes stock of its performance according to 15 measures, many of them relating directly to speed. Customer address changes must be processed in one day, for instance; the telephone must be picked up within two rings; calls coming into the switchboard must be transferred to the appropriate party within 21 seconds.

Where measuring such processes has traditionally been a soft science at best among service companies, the folks at MBNA are sticklers for hard numbers. They measure everything perpetually and down to tenths of 1%. At any given moment on any given day, it's possible to get a reading that shows, for example, that employees are achieving "two-ring pickup" 98.4% of the time, 1.2% above average, but representing a full 1% falloff from the previous day. The net effect: "If you're an MBNA employee and you go to a store or restaurant and hear a phone ring more

than twice, it drives you nuts," says Janine Marrone, a division head.

To track such nuttiness-provoking standards as "two-ring pickup," MBNA relies heavily on technology. Take the example of a customer wanting to increase his credit line. The company's standard is to provide an answer within half an hour for a basic customer, 15 minutes for a so-called platinum customer. As soon as a request is received, service representatives pass it along to the credit department, in the process triggering an electronic time-stamp mechanism that's part of a proprietary PC-based system. Now the clock is ticking. Managers in the credit department can access the system to see how requests are queued up and to determine the amount of time elapsed on any given one. This makes it possible, if necessary, to shift the requests around to MBNA's various credit analysts in an effort to meet deadlines and keep customers happy.

Results for the 15 standards are posted daily on roughly 60 scoreboards at MBNA facilities around the country. The company has a target rate for the 15 standards, which it just happened to raise from 98% to 98.5%. What this means: The companywide goal is for the phone to be answered within two rings 98.5% of the time, for responses to credit-line questions to be forthcoming in half an hour 98.5% of the time, and so forth. Ten years ago the standard was 90%. "We've had to keep raising the bar over time as customer expectations have risen," says Marrone.

So what keeps employees scrambling like mad, even when faced with a new 98.5% hurdle? The company is fond of telling curious visitors that a thoroughgoing concern for customers permeates the organization. Above every doorway at MBNA's headquarters are signs that read THINK OF YOURSELF AS A CUSTOMER. Employee paychecks come with the reminder BROUGHT TO YOU BY THE CUSTOMER. The company has even taken the step of placing "the customer" at the head of its organizational chart.

But incentives help too, no doubt. Every day in which the 98.5% standard is met or broken, money is thrown into a pool for nonofficers. The pool is designed so that if the company were perfect, hitting the 98.5% target every single day, each employee would get a bonus of about $1,000 at the end of the year. Fat chance of that. But if employees meet the goal, say, 75% of the time, they each get a bonus of around $750.

Of course, MBNA doesn't want to simply encourage the mindless pursuit of raw speed. Thus, all employees are also on individual incentive plans, overseen by their direct managers. These plans stress achieving quality goals over being speedy. Says Marrone: "You can be the fastest, but if you don't drive quality too, it's not worth much."

Overall, even if MBNA has a rather Orwellian corporate culture, it's hard to argue with the company's results. Since going public in 1991, total return on the common stock has climbed 602%, compared with 216% for the S&P 500. It's proof, in MBNA's case at least, that speed does not kill.

CHEVRON

SOME COMPANIES are so big that they could potentially build a better mousetrap in one division, cure the common cold in another, and grasp the meaning of life in a third. Yet because of poor communication, nobody outside the various divisions would ever even know that each of these solutions existed under one roof.

That's where knowledge management comes in. This is a practice that centers on identifying and transferring best practices within a company. Chevron is a pro at knowledge management, no cakewalk for a $32 billion enterprise that operates in more than 100 countries.

Chevron's U.S. refineries have posed a particular challenge. There are six of them, and they all do roughly the same thing—refine crude oil into gasoline and other petroleum products. But they are spread out all over the map, everywhere from Pascagoula, Mississippi, to Honolulu. Getting them to share information can be quite a task.

Chevron's solution, dreamed up in 1992, was to create a new full-time job known as process master. The duty of a process master is to oversee different processes across all six refineries. There's one, for example, dedicated to staying abreast of the process for getting more gasoline out of each barrel of crude, and figuring out which techniques can be transferred from one refinery to another.

Process masters tend to be company veterans of roughly 20 years, with both operating and technical experience. In filling these positions, Chevron looks for natural leaders possessed of good communication skills. Although the process masters don't have any official authority per se, their breadth of experience generally commands respect. As with Zen masters, people tend to heed their advice.

Currently there are masters for 25 processes, and among them is Billy Williams, second-generation oilman and 18-year company veteran. He has helped transfer several inno-

---

CREDIT CARD *issuer MBNA sets up scoreboards in its various offices to keep employees up to speed on how quickly they're serving customers.*

(Cont.)

> The next frontier in mass-customization for Andersen is called "batch of one" manufacturing, an approach that would virtually eliminate inventory.

vations among the refineries, for considerable savings. His bailiwick is the company's crude units, which are like giant pressure cookers that, as an initial step in refining, separate oil into heavy and light components. Every four years or so it's time for "turnaround," when the big units must be cleaned. Removing caked-on coke from the pipes is the tough part. Typically it has to be burned out, and the furnaces must be cranked way up high, at considerable cost.

But during a turnaround in 1994, the Richmond, California, refinery tried out a new device, known as "the pig," to remove coke from the crude unit. The pig is a hard rubber cylinder with little abrasive nubs on it and can be propelled through the pipes with a jet of water. It scrapes off the coke and saves about $1 million every time a refinery needs cleaning. Thanks to the process master system, Williams and his team were able to pass the pig on down the pike to the El Segundo, California, refinery. Now Salt Lake City's new crude unit is being designed for easy pigging. Says Williams: "The big powerhouse in this whole process is communication." Chevron hopes that projects like the pig will eventually wend their way into its other operations with the promise of additional savings.

Convinced that there must be other hidden repositories of knowledge throughout the company, Chevron's corporate quality department formed a so-called best-practices discovery team in 1994. It consisted of ten quality-improvement managers and computer experts representing a cross section of the company, including oil production, chemicals, and refining.

The team uncovered numerous examples of people sharing best practices, many of which Greta Lydecker, a consultant to the corporate quality staff, calls grassroots networks. Within Chevron there turned out to be quite a few groups dedicated to discussing everything from safety to saving money. Some of the groups communicate regularly via E-mail; others use groupware such as Lotus Notes; still others hold periodic meetings, conferences, or forums. What they all had in common was that they were trying, often in very modest ways, to share knowledge.

The discovery team gave them a big boost. Last year it published a "best-practice resource map," which was distributed to 5,000 Chevron employees. It's like a bona fide foldup road map and contains brief descriptions of the various official and grassroots groups, along with directions on how to contact them. "You can think of this as a yellow pages," says Lydecker. "It helps connect people working on very diverse things across our very diverse company."

Since the map was published, new groups, such as one devoted to competitor intelligence, have formed. And everyone at Chevron has a useful new resource. Recently, when the strategic-planning department needed to develop a departmental safety procedure, it located a discussion group known as SafeNet on the best-practices map and had some new ideas within hours. Chevron wants to be in the oil business, after all, not the wheel-reinvention business.

It's one thing, of course, to read this article, get a feel for the practices of four class-act companies, and be disturbed in a positive way. The next challenge is figuring out how to apply the lessons to your own company. That can be tough. As Arun Maira, a vice president at Arthur D. Little, says, "You can't just impose a best practice. It has to be adapted to your company's own style." Yes, that's a challenge, but not an impossible one. And given the stakes, surely well worth the effort, especially if it means making it to the head of the class.

REPORTER ASSOCIATE *Joyce E. Davis*

© 1996 Time Inc. All rights reserved.

DETROIT TO SUPPLIERS:
QUALITY OR ELSE

"Brutal," says one parts maker of the QS-9000 standard the auto companies have set. But the ordeal of complying may be worth it. ■ *by Stuart F. Brown*

Thousands of companies that supply parts to the Big Three automakers are facing an ultimatum they can't ignore: Implement a comprehensive quality standard called QS-9000, or risk losing these gigantic customers. The mandate is making lots of people nervous. In all, about 10,000 North American companies fall into the category of Tier 1 suppliers to Detroit, and so far fewer than 300 have won certification that they pass the QS-9000 test. That leaves the vast horde of auto parts makers scrambling to meet deadlines set by the car companies.

Suppliers that want to get or keep Chrysler's business are supposed to get on board QS-9000 by July 31, 1997. GM suppliers have until December 31, 1997, to comply. Ford, which participated in developing the standard and expects its suppliers to conform to the intent of QS-9000, isn't forcing its suppliers to get formal certification—at least not yet.

QS-9000 is an expanded version, with requirements tailored to the automotive industry, of the ISO 9000 group of quality standards being adopted by a growing number of companies worldwide. A visitor arriving at Detroit's Metro Airport is struck by evidence that the locals are taking QS-9000 seriously. Ads tout consultants offering help with achieving the sought-after certification, as well as some of the 40-odd "registrars," or firms accredited to bestow QS-9000 certification. Earning the right to hang a QS-9000 plaque in the company lobby isn't easy; a year or more can easily be spent overhauling a company's procedures and quality documentation to the point where they're prepared to survive scrutiny by auditors dispatched by a registrar.

What sets QS-9000 and its ISO 9000 cousins apart from previous quality programs pushed by the automakers is that they dictate "surveillance" checkups to make sure that previously identified shortcomings in a supplier's quality system have been corrected.

"With mandatory audits at least every six months, you can't drift too far, or you will lose your certification," says Tripp Martin, director of quality at Peterson Spring, whose parts go into airliners as well as cars. "There's a discipline to this system."

Does this begin to sound like another trendy, time-wasting management fad concocted by the Big Three to torture suppliers? ISO 9000 has already been the butt of Dilbert cartoons; does its souped-up Detroit version call for even more skepticism?

QS-9000 has plenty of defenders, notably Thomas Stallkamp, Chrysler's executive VP for procurement and supply. Stallkamp says his company is asking parts makers to jump through no more hoops than it is willing to jump through itself. "I decided that if we're putting our suppliers through this, we should do it too," Stallkamp says. "Our whole procurement activity is working right now to be registered by the deadline we've asked our suppliers to meet. And it is a lot of work."

"The way you get quality," Stallkamp maintains, "is by standardizing a job and then doing it the same way each time—whether it's on an assembly line or in an office. That's the intent of QS-9000." So far, 5% of Chrysler's 650 Tier 1 suppliers have been certified, with another 40% now going through the process. The company has a rating system for suppliers that awards bonus points—and more business—to those who get up to snuff early, and subtracts points for those that miss next July's deadline. "By then," Stallkamp says, "I expect we'll see that half our suppliers are registered, and the rest will be working on it."

ISO 9000, which forms the core of QS-9000, is designed to remove a big obstacle to global sales. It gives companies a way to document their quality procedures according to internationally recognized standards. Its intent is to assure customers that their suppliers have effective quality systems in place, without having to conduct expensive and time-

consuming audits at each plant. The procedures include establishing a document-management system for keeping track of policies, and work instructions that describe in detail how a company operates and who is responsible for quality at every step of the way. To get certified, a company must satisfy auditors (1) that its documentation says what the company does; (2) that the company actually does what it says it does; and (3) that there's a paper trail to prove it.

Ironically, QS-9000 is a Big Three response to supplier complaints. It got its start at a 1988 workshop organized by the American Society for Quality Control's automotive division. As Big Three representatives listened, the parts makers vented their frustrations at having to comply with three different—but similar—sets of quality rules in order to win business.

Out of this came a task force chartered by the Big Three's purchasing and supply vice presidents to harmonize their supplier-quality systems: GM's Targets for Excellence, Chrysler's Supplier Quality Assurance Manual, and Ford's Q-101 Quality System Standard. To the 20 requirements of ISO 9000, the task force added more than 100 items important to the way automakers work. Among these is continuous quality improvement, which ISO 9000 doesn't prescribe. The Big Three unveiled QS-9000 to their North American suppliers in August 1994.

To find out the travails and rewards of going through the QS-9000 wringer, FORTUNE visited five auto-industry supply firms that have won or are close to winning certification. It also looked in on a nonautomotive company, workstation maker Sun Microsystems, that has accommodated itself to the older ISO 9000. Conversations with the parts makers yield these nuggets of insight:

■ QS-9000 is a big undertaking. "A brutal phenomenon is a pretty accurate description of what QS-9000 actually is," says Jackie Parkhurst, director of quality assurance at

Federal-Mogul, an engine parts maker in Southfield, Michigan.

■ Getting certified is merely the beginning. Unlike passing management fads, QS-9000 commits a company to an eternal process of continuous improvement.

■ But the pains can yield gains. Some of the companies already certified report that QS-9000—often referred to simply as QS—helped them get their houses in order in unexpected ways.

Cases in point: At Aetna Industries of Center Line, Michigan, defects have been cut in half for each of the past three years and profitability has improved. Reductions in work-in-process inventory freed up enough room for a two-story engineering office. And thanks to the QS cachet, a new prospective customer, Mitsubishi Motor Manufacturing of America, needed only a brief onsite assessment to certify Aetna as a supplier, according to quality assurance VP Ed Lawson.

A private, 1,500-employee welding, stamping, and roll-forming company with sales of about $200 million, Aetna supplies major underbody assemblies and bumpers to Chrysler and GM. The company has nine plants in the Detroit area, all QS certified. The wood-paneled conference room where visitors from Aetna's suppliers recently got briefed on the company's quality system shook mightily as gigantic stamping presses elsewhere in the building bent sheet steel into contoured shapes that will end up in Jeeps and minivans.

An inquiry several years ago from Volvo's truck-manufacturing operation in the U.S., which requires suppliers to be ISO 9000 certified, first drew Aetna's attention to the issue of emerging global quality standards. Going through a preliminary assessment with a Volvo auditor was an eye opener. "We felt at that time that the quality system we had in place already met the ISO requirement, so we were a bit arrogant and thought we were ready," Lawson recalls. "But we weren't able to demonstrate that we were actually complying with all the procedures we had in our quality manuals."

By way of example, Lawson says that if a coil of steel with the wrong specifications was sitting next to a machine tool, "there was a risk that somebody could inadvertently use it to make parts. It should have been clearly labeled as nonconforming, and moved elsewhere." Once Aetna became aware of such careless practices, "we started to look at ISO 9000 as being of value to our business, and not just a requirement." By early 1994, Aetna had achieved ISO 9000 registration at all of its plants. A year later they had the QS-9000 badge.

Despite his enthusiasm for QS-9000, Lawson finds one aspect objectionable: nitpicking over operational details. "I'm a big proponent

of ISO 9000 because it tells you what you should do, but doesn't tell you how to do it. It doesn't presume to know your business. There's nothing bad about anything QS-9000 says a supplier should do, but it's very prescriptive. To me, if your business focus is on improvement and developing your internal system, then someone else shouldn't presume to tell you how to do that. You should decide for yourself because you understand the benefits."

At Federal-Mogul, says quality boss Parkhurst, the big lesson of QS-9000 is that "there's no way to implement it without involving everyone in a plant, from the manager to the person who sweeps the floor. They all need to be aware of their job description and where their work instructions are, and be able to tell you—at least in their own words—what the corporate quality policy is." A maker of such parts as pistons, bearings, gaskets, and oil seals, with 1995 sales of $2 billion, Federal-Mogul has learned what it takes to meet the new quality requirements at the 25 plants it is certifying under ISO 9000, QS-9000, or both. To date, five plants in Ohio, Indiana, Virginia, and Mexico have made it through QS-9000.

"The way that we approached getting all these plants certified," Parkhurst relates, "was to set up four teams drawn from all our factories, which wrote an 80-page ISO and QS survey. We called it the survey from hell. It takes me several trips into each facility to explain what all the questions mean, and about a year to complete the assessment. The upside of this is that if a plant fully complies with this internal survey, it can go on to the final audit without having a registrar's initial preassessment, which saves us about $15,000."

The QS-9000 ordeal has already produced payoffs. At Federal-Mogul's engine-and transmission-bearing plant in Blacksburg, Virginia, setup and tooling costs have been reduced through improved training and by documenting successful shop-floor procedures. "They have found ways to take the art out of setup and changing dies," Parkhurst says. "That results in consistently getting quicker setups. And people can be taught to do a specific task in less time."

Parkhurst's thinking about QS-9000 has gradually shifted. "The first year I was working on this, I thought it was just a quality audit. Now I see it as a complete business system. Anybody who embraces it can save money. Complaints will go down and the cost of quality will go down."

Peterson Spring, also of Springfield, Michigan, found itself pleasantly surprised by QS-9000 in one important way. "If you're used to audits where the guy from the big car company is beating you up about how to do things," says quality director Martin, the QS-9000 registrar comes across as reasonable

and nonthreatening. "He's here as a third-party auditor to scrutinize you—to give you a firm and fair assessment against the requirements, nothing more."

A private company with $100 million in annual sales, Peterson makes a dizzying array of springs, from exotic titanium ones that are part of a DC-9 airliner's braking system to springs that close engine valves, return throttle pedals, and perform hundreds of other jobs in cars and trucks.

Peterson invested a lot of effort in selecting a QS-9000 registrar from a list of 14 candidates. One criterion was that the firm should click with the company's culture, which is roll-up-your-shirt sleeves rather than button-down. "We wanted somebody who talks our language and isn't coming in with a hammer or a report card," Martin explains.

The first recommendation Peterson's registrar made was not to twist the company into a pretzel to meet perceived QS requirements. Rather, says Martin, the advice was to "document what works for you. Then we'll tell you what needs to change. You are already doing things 90% right. We need to get the last 10% to meet the Big Three's requirement."

For companies that are too loosely run, on the other hand, QS-9000 can introduce some needed structure. That's what happened at J.B. Tool & Machine in Wapakoneta, Ohio. A producer of stamped-metal television components, "landing gear" that supports parked semitrailers, and motor and transmission mounts for vehicles, J.B. Tool keeps 450 workers at three plants busy, often on a three-shift schedule.

CEO William Petty says his company realized about six years ago that the good-old-boy way of doing business in the stamping industry was going to be replaced by comprehensive quality-control systems to keep increasingly demanding customers satisfied. "When I started this company 38 years ago with $500, I got things done by doing it right now, and if something wasn't right, we'd make it right," he says. "But I can't be everywhere at once now. We realized that quality is what's going to sell, and that ISO 9000 and QS are a necessity to do business. Eventually you're not going to be on the bid list if you don't get on board."

Richard Busch II, J.B. Tool's TQM manager, says that "when we started the certification process, this was a job shop. It took orders and gave orders verbally, and documentation hardly existed. It's been painful to change the culture of this company, but now everyone has been through training and understands our process controls and record keeping."

Still, a concerted effort was made to keep paperwork to a minimum. Repeated editing trimmed the binder that holds the quality manual, procedures, and work instructions for all three plants down to three-quarters of

(Cont.)

an inch thick. Investments in training and consultants raised J.B. Tool's costs during the preparation for final auditing, but the investment has more than paid off. "At the end of the day, this is a cost-reduction system that weeds out scrap and pleases the customer," Busch says. "Six years ago we were only a $10 million company. Now we're a $50 million-plus company."

And then there's the company that used ISO 9000 and QS-9000 as a manual for completely rebuilding itself. Laser Specialists of Fraser, Michigan, is a small firm with 25 employees that uses sophisticated multi-axis laser machines to cut prototype car chassis parts from sheet metal. After owner Thomas Paquin was killed in a horse-riding mishap in mid-1993, Daniel Henry Jr. went from being the company's lawyer to its president. The situation he stepped into needed improving: Only 55% of finished work was delivered to customers on time, and in 1993 the scrap rate

was an unacceptable 10% to 15%.

Although the Big Three mandate QS-9000 compliance only for suppliers of production components, Henry sought certification anyway because he saw it as a good way to get better organized. It took 36 months and about $250,000—including staff time—to bring the company up to snuff. "We recouped the investment in three months," the ebullient Henry says, "by landing business with a company that had a parent in Germany and wanted its suppliers to be certified."

Many things changed at Laser Specialists. In the past, jobs were always being juggled, and salesmen would pressure the manufacturing people to give their customers' jobs priority. "That's why we had 55% on-time delivery," Henry says. "Now only manufacturing can set delivery time, and all our deliveries are on time or early."

Over the past 18 months, careful new documentation has also helped cut the scrap rate

to almost nil. Today, a laser machine operator won't start cutting a pile of metal sheets unless a quality person has signed off that it's the right material and the right machine, running the correct computer program. Sometimes two jobs involve parts that are the same shape but made from slightly different alloys. In the past this could cause mix-ups and scrap-page, but no more.

All of which has turned Henry into an evangelist. "I'm a very strong advocate of QS-9000 as a management tool," he wants you to know. "Forget that the Big Three are shoving it down your throat. It's a perfect management tool, because it creates objective standards and makes everything traceable." Skeptics, take note.

REPORTER ASSOCIATE *Alicia Hills Moore*

© 1996 Time Inc. All rights reserved.

165

Ethical Marketing in a Consumer-Oriented World: Appraisal and Challenges

80

SELLING DRUGS

Doctors might not be crazy about the idea, but patients are walking into their offices asking for specific drugs. They have heard about them on TV or read about them in magazines.

by Patricia Braus

A skier travels blissfully down a mountain of ragweed, his skis in perfect position as pollen scatters across a parched mountain landscape. Quick — is this an advertisement for weed killer, a new type of skiing, or an allergy drug?

Unless you've stayed away from magazines and TV this year, you probably know this is an ad for Allegra, an allergy drug manufactured by Hoechst Marion Roussel, Inc. The caption reads: "This allergy season, live with ahhhbandon. Ahhh! Allegra!"

The Allegra print campaign is one of a multitude of highly visible prescription-drug advertisements aimed directly at the public. Ever since federal regulations changed laws governing the advertising of prescription

> *Where's the line between effective and tasteless? How much hype is acceptable?*

drugs in the 1980s, such advertising efforts have taken off. Manufacturers spent $137 million on direct-to-consumer drug advertising on television alone in 1996, according to IMS America and Nielsen Media Research. Advertising is also extensive in most major consumer magazines. "They're spending a ton of money," says Jack Trout, a marketing expert based in Greenwich, Connecticut, and author of *The New Positioning: The Latest on the World's Number 1 Business Strategy.* "They're keeping these magazines afloat."

But the increasing presence of such ads has also raised questions about what works best — and what doesn't work — in advertisements selling prescription drugs. The personal and graphic nature of products addressing problems like cracked toenails and sexually transmitted herpes brings up a host of questions. Where's the line between effective and tasteless? How much hype is acceptable? Above all, what is most effective in persuading consumers to request products from their doctors?

The answers are increasingly important to manufacturers of pharmaceutical products, as direct-to-consumer ads claim a greater share of the marketing budget. It is no coincidence that Premarin, one of the best-selling drugs in the country, depends heavily on advertising directly to consumers. How did it get there? How does a new product achieve brand-name recognition? There is no simple formula, but experts suggest that consumers are looking for specific things in a drug ad.

THE KNOWLEDGEABLE CONSUMER

Twenty years ago, patients who thought they might have an allergy problem went to their doctor, discussed their symptoms, and heard about what was available from the doctor. They were unlikely to know what drugs were available for allergies and took their doctor's word. Direct-to-consumer drug ads were considered unethical, reflecting the widely held societal belief that doctors were the only ones qualified to make judgments about something as important as prescription drugs.

The rules have changed. Consumers have become more involved with their health care. And once they became the target of advertising for prescription drugs, they had a new way to find out about what might be wrong with them and how to treat it. In particular, the ads have changed the way doctors and patients talk about medicine, says Mickey Smith, Barnard Distinguished Professor of Pharmacy Administration at the University of Mississippi in Oxford. "For the first time, people are coming into their physician's office knowing what they want. A lot of the mystery is gone."

Many physicians dislike the ads. "Information is given to people in a limited form," says Gillian Shepherd, clinical associate professor of medicine at New York Hospital-Cornell Medical Center and past president of the New York Allergy Society. "People don't know how to incorporate it. Patients are being manipulated. Everything is being presented to them as a wonder drug."

Ads for allergy medicine are particularly dramatic, offering drug users visions of happiness and serenity. One ad for Claritin from Schering features a woman gazing beatifically at a surreal blue and pink sky. Patients often ask for the drug by name, says Shepherd. "They say Claritin. Nothing else. The way the ads are presented to the public, it's like any ad. It's brand recognition."

The best ads incorporate the basics of good advertising. First and foremost, they establish brand recognition in the eyes of the public. Good consumer drug ads also include solid information, clarity, powerful visual images, and a convincing message. But the complicated nature of health care forces advertisers to be extra careful. A major force in drug advertising is federal regulation, which limits the types of messages released to the general public. Drug advertisers typically show their ads to the Food and Drug Administration before broadcasting them on TV to make sure the agency will not consider them false and misleading. The agency also

(Cont.)

requires that print and TV ads provide information about product risks. Recent guidelines allow TV commercials to provide some of this information in alternate forms, such as Web sites and brochures in pharmacies.

This means drugs cannot be hyped the way other products are. At the same time, it is clear that many drugs within particular classes don't significantly differ. This is definitely the case with allergy drugs. "There isn't a big difference between them" says Shepherd. This makes the advertising effort especially challenging.

Advertisers must also be careful to attract interest in medical problems and products without fearmongering. "People are vulnerable when it comes to their health," says Yank Coble, a Jacksonville, Florida, endocrinologist and member of the American Medical Association board of trustees. "People can easily be made overanxious." Advertisements that do this risk public criticism.

DOS AND DON'TS

Experts agree that developing direct-to-consumer drug advertising involves a multitude of pitfalls. The most commonly perceived problems are ads that oversell products and ads that are too vague or confusing.

For example, treating heart disease is complex. It's no surprise that some are critical of the information provided in ads for heart-related medications. In one way, they've provided Americans with information, says endocrinologist Coble. "Making people aware of this has been very positive." On the other hand, Coble believes the ads don't have enough information about reducing the risk of heart disease through good diet and regular exercise. Instead, he claims, they promote the erroneous mentality that taking a pill can provide good health.

One thing on which marketers and physicians agree is that drug advertising should offer good information. "Theoretically, what works is an ad that helps the consumer to determine they might have the problem," says Smith of the University of Mississippi. Many serious medical conditions remain undiagnosed because Americans don't know about the symptoms or don't regularly see a physician. For example, only half of the estimated 16 million Americans with diabetes know they have the disease.

Providing information about health issues shouldn't be the sole goal, though. A meandering text ad by Eli Lilly and Company discussing the pros and cons of hormone therapy annoys Lisa Cox, director of programs and policy for the National Women's Health Network in Washington, D.C. "If estrogen is the answer, why are there so many questions?" the ad asks. Cox criticizes the ad for not getting to the point. It has no product information, but encourages women to call a toll-free number for the "latest information on post-menopausal health." Readers are left with no concrete idea of what the company is promoting.

A good ad, says Smith, convinces the consumer that something may help them, and that the something is your product. Smith thinks the Allegra ads with their vivid visual images are memorable and effective. But these same ads frustrate marketing consultant Jack Trout. The message could be clearer, he says. Indeed, a skier or surfer navigating through weeds does not necessarily make the immediate link to allergy medication.

Trout prefers straightforward ads, such as one for Merck Company Incorporated's Proscar product, a drug for men with prostate disease. The ad offers a clear message, that prostate disease can be treated without surgery. Such directness is the foundation for the best direct-to-consumer drug ads, says Trout. "You should almost play these like public service announcements," he says.

From this viewpoint, graphic images are appropriate, Trout says, adding that federal regulations limit just how graphic they can be, anyway. Do consumers recoil from detailed descriptions and images? Not really, says physician Coble. "I think if things are explicit but honest, we can handle it."

While Smith worries about how graphic things could get, he appreciates current ads showing rotten toenails. "If I look at those toenails, I know they're ugly." This makes the ad a good one, says Smith, because it demonstrates that ugly toenails can benefit from treatment. Some observers are less concerned about ugly pictures than about ads that make light of health problems. Trout thinks "cutesy" ads seem out of place when it comes to health care and advises drug marketers to tread carefully.

In spite of inevitable missteps, the future of direct-to-consumer drug advertising looks bright. Supporters suggest the ads are reshaping health care for the better. "It pushes intelligent people to take control of their own health," says Smith.

Even those who don't see the ads as a positive force see their influence as profound. "I'm sure it's going to escalate," says Richard Honsinger, an allergist who practices in Los Alamos, New Mexico, and is a clinical professor at the University of New Mexico. "Brand awareness is a big deal in allergies now." The cost and benefits of that brand awareness will determine the future of prescription drug advertising.

PATRICIA BRAUS IS A CONTRIBUTING EDITOR OF AMERICAN DEMOGRAPHICS AND AUTHOR OF MARKETING HEALTH CARE TO WOMEN (AMERICAN DEMOGRAPHICS BOOKS, 1997).

Reprinted from American Demographics magazine with permission. © 1998, Cowles Business Media, Ithaca, New York.

TERRIBLE TIMING

When you're rolling along on the Convenience Trend Wagon, watch out for potholes.

by Robert M. McMath

There used to be more time to develop and introduce products. But as competition has heated up, timing has become more critical. When the Trend Wagon is rolling, you have to catch it before it passes by. The New Products Showcase is stuffed with products that tried to catch the wagon as it pulled away from the stop.

Campbell's Souper Combo is a good case in point. It was a combination frozen soup and sandwich. It was intended for people with microwaves at the office, or for kids on their own at home. Super convenient, thought the Campbell people.

The product apparently did well in tests. Campbell rolled it out nationally, whereupon it flopped. The company reportedly spent $10 million in marketing support during its last 12 months. In spite of that, sales kept falling. People tried it out of curiosity, but they didn't come back for more. Why?

> **Some versions of Souper Combo had as many as 11 pieces of packaging.**

We are constantly being berated to recycle, use less packaging, and withhold our dollars from environmentally unfriendly products. Some versions of Souper Combo had as many as 11 pieces of packaging. At the time of its release, the magazine *Garbage* awarded the line its "Worst Product of the Month" award. Because the magazine was new and had an unusual name, it got a lot of national attention, and so did Souper Combo's unwanted "award." The timing might have been dumb luck, but it should not have taken a magazine editor to realize that 11 pieces of packaging were excessive.

Excess packaging wasn't the product's only flaw. It was convenient to prepare and eat, but it wasn't necessarily convenient to transport. Even a neatly self-contained frozen meal can't sit in a briefcase or other carrier for many hours without beginning to defrost. This flaw needn't have been fatal, though. After all, many offices with microwaves also have freezers, as well as well-established protocols about lunchroom etiquette (i.e., don't eat other people's food). So the potential storage problem didn't do in the product, either.

Taste may have played a role. Fresh sandwiches taste better than nuked ones. There's also the possibility that some were put off by the idea of frozen soup. Even latchkey children turned out to be an inappropriate target — not because they couldn't prepare the products, but because they'd undoubtedly choose to microwave something other than a nutritious soup-and-sandwich meal if left to their own devices.

In the final analysis, it's possible that the product's biggest flaw was also its key benefit. Campbell thought it was giving consumers a product that would save time. But it tried to improve on what was already a pretty convenient meal. Consumers can heat up a bowl of canned soup and make a sandwich just about as easily as they could prepare Souper Combos. Timing is everything, so they say. In this case, it seems to have been off.

ROBERT M. MCMATH IS DIRECTOR OF THE NEW PRODUCTS SHOWCASE & LEARNING CENTER IN ITHACA, NEW YORK, A COLLECTION OF MORE THAN 60,000 ONCE-NEW CONSUMER PRODUCTS, MOST OF WHICH ARE NO LONGER SOLD.

Reprinted with permission. © 1998 *American Demographics*, Ithaca, New York.

Out of Ideas? Give a Goat or a Seaweed Body Wrap

Charities Adopt Savvy Tactics Of Catalogs

BY JOSHUA HARRIS PRAGER
Staff Reporter of THE WALL STREET JOURNAL

Betty Lindner opens a slick new gift catalog, flips through pictures of smiling boys and girls and dials an 800 number for some holiday shopping. For her two grandchildren, she sends a rabbit and two chicks to a Rwandan family. For her brother, she stocks a Bangladesh pond with fish. For her daughter, she provides prenatal care to women in Bangladesh. And for her husband, the 73-year-old Cincinnati resident gives a $250 business loan to a Haitian woman.

This is clearly not your ordinary catalog. It's the "Global Gift Guide," created by World Concern, a nonprofit Christian organization based in Seattle. It's one of a handful of charities seizing the tools of state-of-the-art catalog marketing to connect with donors who are bleary-eyed from too many philanthropic pitches.

This year, Heifer Project International, another nonprofit relief organization that markets "gifts" through catalogs, even purchased mail-order lists from J. Crew and other merchandisers to expand its outreach. It sent out one million catalogs, up from 70,000 in 1990.

The results are impressive. "Ay caramba!" says Tom Peterson, HPI's communications director, when asked how the holiday catalogs have done. "They have become our most successful mailing by a long shot." HPI, based in Little Rock, Ark., was founded in 1944 and today boasts a $12.5 million budget. Its catalog raised $1.4 million last year, up from $400,000 in 1993.

The relief groups are unabashed about their marketing tactics. "Nonprofits are just that, but they have to think like a business," says HPI president Jo Luck. A former executive director of Arkansas parks and tourism, Ms. Luck became well acquainted with Bill Clinton and has attracted celebrity support for HPI. In October, actress Mary Steenburgen "gave" Hillary Clinton an HPI goat for her 50th birthday. Last month, Susan Sarandon presented a llama to Rosie O'Donnell on her talk show.

World Concern, founded in 1955, has no celebrity pitchmen, but this year, it enlisted professional marketing help, and early returns on its catalog are good. Last year's World Concern catalog brought in $85,000, up from $30,000 the year before, though still a fraction of its total $16 million budget. (Donated supplies, federal grants and church donations comprise the bulk of its funds.)

A large part of the catalogs' appeal is the notion of giving something tangible and personal, not just a lump sum. "You can wrap your hands around it and say 'I'm giving *this* goat to Uncle Harry,'" says Christy Gardener, World Concern's communications director. HPI's Ms. Luck agrees. "My friend was telling everyone there was a water buffalo somewhere in the world named Jennifer."

By issuing the catalogs at Christmastime, the charities also tap the season's gift-giving sentiment, says Leonard Brown of Gold Bar, Wash. Last Christmas, friends of Mr. Brown sent a pig in his name to Cambodia through World Concern. "It's better than getting a pair of socks," says the 48-year-old building contractor.

The catalogs smartly display animals and services available to donate, along with prices, descriptions and photographs. For example, in the HPI catalog a llama runs $150 ($20 for a share). The catalog explains that llamas provide Bolivian families with transportation, income and wool used to weave blankets, ponchos, carpet and rope.

HPI's catalog is also peppered with headline quips like "Sheep: Shear Profit" and such heartwarming stories as "A Boy and His Buffalo" — the tale of nine-year-old Parmatma Prashad in northern India, who rises at dawn from the burlap-covered bed of hay he shares with his father and grandmother to milk the family's precious animal.

Making donations to HPI is "a nonpatronizing way to help people break the cycle of poverty," says Ms. Sarandon. The actress is giving a goat, some sheep, chicks and a heifer to people on her list this Christmas. Ms. Sarandon is a staunch supporter of HPI, in part because of its modest overhead. "I'm leery of projects where you don't know where the money is going," she says.

Where donor dollars go varies with the charity. "We factor the cost of care for an animal into its price," says Ms. Luck, explaining why it costs $120 to give a pig through HPI, and only $25 for two through World Concern.

What if there's a surfeit of donors who want to give, say, honeybees over rabbits? The fine print in the HPI catalog informs donors that their dollars go into a general livestock pot and are not actually earmarked for individual animals, despite what the donor cards say. "It's symbolic," says Mr. Peterson.

World Concern, on the other hand, notifies donors when programs are already glutted, like reforestation in Bolivia and dental examinations in Cambodia, and suggests alternate programs instead.

These aren't the perfect gift for everyone. Two Christmases ago, Ruth Coburn, 76, of Wimberley, Texas, "gave" her four grandsons, aged 19 to 27, a heifer. "I don't think they were as impressed as I was," she says.

Ms. Sarandon raises one more concern: "I try not to give an animal that might be taken the wrong way, like a pig."

Reprinted by permission of *The Wall Street Journal,* © 1997 Dow Jones & Company, Inc. All Rights Reserved Worldwide.

Why the Veterinarian Really Recommends That 'Designer' Chow

Colgate Gives Doctors Treats For Plugging Its Brands, And Sees Sales Surge

Offering a Fat-Cat Bounty

By Tara Parker-Pope

Staff Reporter of The Wall Street Journal

NEW YORK — Shopping at a pet store here, Meredith Kane grabs a 4-pound bag of Hill's Science Diet. At $9, it is nearly double the price of cat food sold in supermarkets. But Ms. Kane is unswerving in her devotion to this "designer" brand for her cats, Cecily, Oscar, Kit Kat and A.J.

Why?

"My vet recommends it," she says.

Every year, millions of people spend a total of $9.4 billion on pet food — and many, like Ms. Kane, choose brands solely on a veterinarian's recommendation. Over examining tables across the country, more pet doctors lately are trashing trusted brand names like Purina and Kal-Kan, calling them "junk food," and directing people to shell out an extra $20 or so for a month's supply of super-premium "high science" foods.

The biggest beneficiaries: Hill's Science Diet lines, made by toothpaste giant Colgate-Palmolive Co., and Eukanuba and Iams brands from Iams Co. of Dayton, Ohio. Sold only through pet stores and veterinary clinics, the designer brands pack more calories per bite and promise higher-quality ingredients based on "pioneering research in animal nutrition" tailored to a pet's "life stage," or age.

The result: Vet suggestions ringing in their ears, many pet owners have switched brands — and the life-stage category has amassed a Doberman-sized $2 billion chunk of the market.

But few pet owners know just how far premium-market-leader Hill's has gone to sew up the vet endorsements.

'Vets Trust Them'

Borrowing a page from pharmaceuticals companies, which routinely woo doctors to prescribe their drugs, Hill's has spent a generation cultivating its professional following. It spends hundreds of thousands of dollars a year funding university research and nutri-

tion courses at every one of the 27 U.S. veterinary colleges. Once in practice, vets who sell Science Diet and other premium foods directly from their offices pocket profits of as much as 40%.

"Vets trust them," says Jana Norris, a fresh graduate of the School of Veterinary Medicine at the University of California, Davis. While she was in school, a Hill's program allowed the struggling student to pay just $3 a bag for a special prescription brand for her cat, Buffalo Jean. A bag normally runs about $25. She also received a small stipend, courtesy of the Hill's program, to study orthopedic surgery with a Los Angeles vet. "Hill's was just always around," she adds.

A little too much, perhaps, for makers of supermarket brands. During the past five years, Hill's sales have surged more than 20%, and now make up an 8% share of the market — half that of No. 1 Ralston Purina Co., according to Davenport Co. in Richmond, Va. For the same period, sales at pet-food giant Ralston grew 11% but its market share fell one percentage point; sales at Mars Inc.'s Kal-Kan unit tumbled 28% and its share slipped three percentage points.

Nabbing Tabby Early

Hill's marketing strategy is especially potent since pets are among the world's most loyal consumers. Nabbing Tabby early is critical: Once a pet takes to a particular brand, a later switch can sometimes cause gastrointestinal troubles; and because a lot of felines are finicky about the look of their vittles, many brands come in distinct shapes, like X's and triangles. Since almost everyone asks their vets what to start feeding a new pet, Hill's cleverly has managed to steer billions its way with that all-important early recommendation.

By chasing after the nation's 126 million cats and dogs through the backdoor of vet offices, Hill's has emerged as a crown jewel at Colgate. Hill's sales — which last year were nearly $900 million, up from $40 million 15 years ago — reflect the power of word-of-mouth marketing. While some competitors spent between $40 million and $90 million each to advertise last year, according to Davenport, Hill's paid $1.9 million. Chicken feed.

Part of the Family

"The bulk of our expenditure goes to the veterinary community," says John Steel, who just retired as Colgate's senior vice president of global marketing and sales. The company won't reveal its marketing and promotions budget. He adds: "It's just like taking drugs: You go to the doctor and he prescribes something for you and you don't much question what the doctor says. It's the same with animals." Pet-food marketers also say the rise of high-science vittles has to do with American consumers' obsession with their own health. "People think of pets as an extension of the family," says Robert C. Wheeler, Hill's chief executive.

But the reliance on vet endorsements has

its critics. "Consumers think they're getting a better product because veterinarians are recommending it," says Ann Martin, author of a new book, "Foods Pets Die For." She notes that many pet doctors are "brainwashed into thinking they have to recommend these commercial foods," having been so heavily exposed to them in vet schools.

Adds Francis Kallfelz, professor of nutrition at Cornell University's School of Veterinary Medicine in Ithaca, N.Y., "I've never seen any research to prove animals fed premium products all their lives have fared better than animals fed standard products." More definitive research would require "a lot of animals and a lot of time," he says, and it is too early to say there is "one best pet food." Despite that, he feeds his golden retriever Hill's Prescription Diet.

Science and Sales

Pet-food marketers insist it is science, not salesmanship, that ultimately sways many of the estimated 36,000 small-animal veterinarians in the U.S.

At the Hill's research center in Topeka, Kan., scientists proudly point to Cocoa and Brandy, two 18-month-old Labrador retrievers. Since she was a pup, Cocoa has munched only Hill's products, while Brandy ate a Brand X food that Hill's won't name. Brandy is fat and has a dull coat. Cocoa is bright-eyed and slim, with a lustrous coat. "The products do what we say they do," Mr. Wheeler says. "We're not selling dog food. We're selling nutrition."

Makers of supermarket pet foods disagree. Ralston Purina, which now sells two premium lines and is reaching out more to veterinarians, says even its lower-priced foods such as Dog Chow and Puppy Chow provide the same basic nutrients as the super-premium brands. "What you're hearing from veterinarians might be colored somewhat by the products they have for sale," says Larry McDaniel, a vet himself, and Ralston's director of veterinary marketing.

But Hill's has a long history with the veterinary community. Hill's Pet Nutrition was founded in 1948 by Kansas veterinarian Mark Morris, who, in his own kitchen, cooked up a special diet for treating kidney problems in dogs; 20 years later the company introduced its Science Diet brand, touted as a healthier alternative than the table scraps commonly used or low-priced foods sold in supermarkets.

The company — which never was more than a niche player in pet food and began to diversify into other pet products, such as flea shampoos and sprays — was acquired by Colgate in 1976, when Hill's was part of Houston-based Riviana Foods. Several years later when Colgate, of New York, decided to shed all non-core business and put Hill's on the block, a senior executive named Reuben Mark, who would later become Colgate's chairman, argued to keep the fledgling company.

"I was struck by the similarity of our world-wide toothpaste business, with the endorsement of the dentists being so important," Mr. Mark says. "I knew if we did the same thing with Hill's, it could be an enormous global brand."

So, similar to Colgate's spadework in dental schools, Hill's now funds a nutrition professorship in nearly half of the nation's vet schools. Hill's employees wrote a widely used textbook on small-animal nutrition that is distributed for free to students. Hill's also sends practicing veterinarians to seminars on wringing more profit from clinics and offers the only formal nutrition-certification program for clinic technicians. In a savvy marketing coup now being copied by other pet-food companies, Hill's each year donates tons of free food for the pets of cash-strapped veterinary students.

Hill's also beefed up its sales force, which has grown to more than 500 people from just 16 in the early 1980s, including many who are vets. Outside universities, Hill's is believed to be the country's single largest employer of veterinarians.

One is Tony Rumschlag, a territory manager for Hill's in Indianapolis. Last month, he arrived at the Post Pet Hospital armed with framed posters to hang on walls, post-it notes for the reception desk and free samples of Hill's dog treats for the clientele.

Weight Watchers

"Dr. Tony" headed for Exam Room Three, where he met with hospital veterinarian Scot Harbin to talk about recommending Hill's diet foods for the fat cats and pudgy dogs that visit the clinic. Today, Hill's is launching a special two-month promotion to pay the clinic $3 per animal it puts on a diet. "We're offering a bounty to get pets on a weight-management program," Dr. Rumschlag says.

Dr. Harbin likes the idea, and sets a goal of putting one dog and one cat on a diet each day. The money raised might be used to host a pizza party or even dinner at a fancy restaurant for the staff, he says.

Later, Dr. Harbin concedes that for years Hill's "sort of had a lock on the veterinary market." But now, he says, competition has increased. "At 12:30, the Eukanuba rep is coming in to give her spiel," he says.

Dr. Rumschlag moves on to the Broad Ripple Animal Clinic, where he hands over 200 custom-printed coupons for pet owners to receive a discount on Hill's food. He also pledges about $1,200 worth of free puppy and kitten food, about 175 bags, to dole out to new pet owners who visit. Not only will the perquisites help the clinic sell more food, but the coupons could help get pet owners back into the clinic for a checkup, he figures.

David Brunner, who owns the hospital, says the marketing push sometimes makes him uneasy and adds that he is careful to tell clients they can always find the same foods at the pet store. "I don't want to be perceived as a food salesman," he says. "We don't want it to enter clients' minds that 'Oh, you're just trying to sell me dog food.'"

Junk-Food Diet

Yet he and other vets say they are convinced premium foods are far better than cheaper brands. One doctor compared using cheaper supermarket pet foods to feeding a child potato chips and pizza every day. Dr. Kallfelz of Cornell says the basic ingredients in most pet foods are the same, but the difference lies in the amount, quality and concentration of ingredients. In general, he says, standard foods have a higher concentration of vegetable proteins, while premium foods have a higher concentration of animal proteins. Premium foods are generally the same from bag to bag, while the formulation of standard foods can change, depending on market prices for ingredients.

But Dr. Brunner says his trust in Hill's products stems mainly from the success he has had in treating animals with urinary-tract infections, kidney disease and other problems with the specially blended Hill's Prescription Diet foods. The diets can only be prescribed by veterinarians and are more than twice the price of supermarket foods.

Other pet-food makers that have launched their own premium brands, including Purina's Pro-Plan and Mars's Waltham brand, have also tailored their products to tempt vets. Ralston Purina, for instance, offers 13 "therapeutic" diets, which can only be prescribed by vets, to compete with Hill's popular Prescription Diet brand. The company also now has free food programs at a handful of U.S. veterinary colleges, and this year "significantly increased" its veterinary-marketing budget to provide coupons for vet students to receive big discounts on Purina foods.

To compete with Hill's stature in vet schools, Purina last year announced a $550,000 endowment for a professorship in small-animal nutrition at the University of Missouri-Columbia College of Veterinary Medicine. The company also provided a $175,000 grant to the American College of Veterinary Nutrition to develop a "noncommercial" nutrition curriculum for all vet schools to follow.

'Share of Mind'

"We feel strongly if the playing field is leveled in the veterinary colleges, it will go a long way toward unbiased education, and it will only benefit us," says Purina's Dr. Mc-Daniel. "We feel we're making significant inroads into 'share of mind' of the veterinarian."

Not to leave anything to chance, the company is hoping to grab a share of consumers' minds. In new ads for a blend of Purina One, a dog visiting a neighbor's house prefers the Purina One food served up there. The reason? The main ingredient is lamb, the ad says, tastier than the corn in that "designer dog food."

For its part, Mars has hired a public-relations firm to tout its Waltham pet-nutrition-research center in England, and is running ads saying its foods are "developed by vets" at the research facility. Last year, Mars spent $50 million on advertising, a 50% jump from 1995, according to Davenport.

The rivals are clearly nipping on Hill's heels. New York vet Harold Zweighaft says a sales call from a Purina representative persuaded him to start stocking Purina food along with Hill's. "Now I have as much Purina as I do Hill's," he says. When New York interior designer Christiane Lemieux got her frisky Labrador pup Jake six months ago, she was all too happy to snap up some Eukanuba Lamb Rice, on her vet's recommendation. "It has coat enhancers," she says, stroking Jake's smooth amber fur. "My vet says it's the highest-quality brand."

Reprinted by permission of *The Wall Street Journal,* © 1997 Dow Jones & Company, Inc. All Rights Reserved Worldwide.

IT'S NOT EASY BEING GREEN

Are Environmentally Committed Companies Hitting the Wall?

Outdoor clothing company Patagonia Inc. has worked hard to be one of the greenest businesses around. It was the first apparel maker to sell synthetic fleece sweaters and warm-up pants made from recycled soda bottles. Last year, it switched to organic cotton for shirts and trouser—and ate half of the 20% markup that organic production added to the garments' cost. Its glossy catalog, printed on recycled paper that is 50% chlorine-free, uses pictures of adventurers in wild places to promote environmental causes.

But Patagonia still has a troubled conscience. In a surprisingly public mea culpa, the company's fall catalog opens with a letter to customers that is a stark critique of Patagonia's reliance on waterproof coating such as Gore-Tex, which contains chemical toxins, and bright dyes based on strip-mined metals. It is only by using such "dirty" manufacturing processes, the company confesses, that it

---

PATAGONIA
The bright colors customers love come from strip-mined metals, and waterproof coatings require toxic solvents

---

can offer the "bombproof" outdoor gear and striking colors that customers love. As the letter laments: "The production of our clothing takes a significant toll on the earth."

Turns out it's not easy being green. Patagonia and a handful of other companies that have made protection of the environment a central tenet of their businesses are running into a new wave of polluting problems that require tougher trade-offs than those of the past. Whether it's Ben & Jerry's Homemade coping with massive amounts of high-fat dairy waste, Stonyfield Farm searching for an affordable way to convert to organic fruit for its yogurt, or Orvis, the fishing-gear maker, trying to build a new headquarters that won't threaten bear habitats, green pioneers are struggling for ways to balance environmental principles with profit goals.

None are backing off their commitment to the environment. Instead, the greenest companies are testing the limits of what can be done cleanly. "We want it all," Yvon Chouinard, Patagonia's president, told a meeting of the company's suppliers last year. "The best quality and the lowest environmental impact." But it's getting tougher to push the green envelope without compromising business goals. "Our whole system of commerce is not designed to be ecologically sustainable," says Matthew Arnold, director of Washington-based Management Institute for Environment & Business. "These guys are showing the limits of the system to respond."

FEWER OPTIONS. Patagonia has worked the system well so far. When the company decided in 1994 to switch to organic cotton, it bypassed conventional growers that use fertilizers, pesticides, and heavy watering, and ordered cotton grown organically in California, Texas, Arizona, and Turkey. Patagonia has pressed Nike and Levi Strauss to purchase organic cotton as well—crucial support for a fledgling industry.

But Chief Executive Officer Dave Olsen says the options are fewer when it comes to solvent-based coatings for clothing meant to fend off harsh weather. Patagonia wants to use water-based coatings, which release fewer volatile compounds in the manufacturing process, but they aren't durable enough to stay waterproof. "For now, the market's owned by Gore-Tex," Olsen says. And customers have made it clear that quality comes first, even if it means passing up the chance to have less impact on the environment. Patagonia surveys show that just 20% of its customers buy from the company because they believe in its environmental mission.

ENDLESS GLOP. Like Patagonia, Ben & Jerry's has also made much of its environmental do-goodism. Still, it hasn't been able to come up with a satisfactory solution to the high-fat dairy waste that is a byproduct of making ice cream. The company's oldest plant, in Waterbury, Vt., relies on a series of lagoons, where microorganisms break down milk solids before they enter the local waste-water-treatment plant. But the remaining fat can still overwhelm the sewage system, so

---

BEN & JERRY'S
Every other day, a tanker truck hauls away 3,500 gallons of high-fat dairy waste

---

the company uses giant paddle wheels to scoop out 60% of the waste. Every other day, the glop fills a 3,500-gallon tanker truck, which hauls it off to compost pits.

In 1995, Ben & Jerry's built a new ice-cream manufacturing plant in St. Albans, in northern Vermont, in part because it was one of only two communities in the state that could handle untreated dairy waste. Ben & Jerry's managed to reduce the amount of dairy waste at the St. Albans plant by 53% in 1996 and an additional 35% so far this year, but it's still not satisfied. "It remains a perennial top item on our agenda, along with reducing solid waste," says Andrea Ashe, natural resources manager for Ben & Jerry's. An overhaul of the Waterbury plant this winter will include a new pipe-cleaning system that should help cut waste even further, Ashe says, but the company has yet to come up with a waste-free way to make ice cream.

One reason Patagonia and Ben & Jerry's agonize publicly about their shortcomings is that their environmental commitment is equally public. After all, though both Nike and Levi Strauss are using organic cotton, it amounts to less than 3% of their cotton total—with no public hand-wringing. Still, continued efforts by green pioneers set the standards for others to follow. "Unless these companies are the vanguard, we're going nowhere," says think-tank director Arnold. Good thing they remain true believers.

By Paul C. Judge in Boston

Reprinted from November 24, 1997 issue of *Business Week* by special permission, copyright © 1997 by McGraw-Hill, Inc.

Greasing Wheels

How U.S. Concerns Compete in Countries Where Bribes Flourish

Foreign Travel, Donations and Use of Middlemen Help Them Win Business

Paying for Reporters' Cabs

Percy Chubb III is spending a million dollars trying to make friends.

The vice chairman of Chubb Corp., of Warren, N.J., wants a license from Chinese officials to tap that country's potentially huge insurance market. So the company has set up a $1 million program to teach insurance at a Shanghai university—and named as board members some of the officials who will decide if and when Chubb gets its license. "You try to show them this is a two-way street," explains Mr. Chubb, who says his company has spent "millions" on similar projects to improve its prospects overseas.

Mr. Chubb's philanthropy stands in contrast to the outright graft and bribery still common in much of the world, especially in big, fast-developing countries: Aggressive European and Asian companies commonly use payoffs to gain access to new markets; some countries even consider bribes tax-deductible business expenses. Virtually alone among major economies, the U.S. forbids its companies from paying bribes to win international business, regardless of what rivals do.

And so, to compete, U.S. companies have found new ways to make friends, influence people and win contracts. Some take foreign officials on junkets to Disney World. Others hire middlemen who—known to them or not—do the dirty work. And most multinationals do make small "facilitation" payments to hasten building inspections, telephone installations and customs clearances.

U.S. laws have "teeth, big teeth," including hefty fines and prison sentences, says an attorney for a U.S. power-generation company that just lost a $230 million contract to a Japanese company in the Middle East. The reason: The American company walked away after government officials demanded a $3 million bribe.

There are still those who violate the law. Take the case of Lockheed Corp., the aero-space company whose bribery of Japanese politicians two decades ago brought down Tokyo's government and inspired the 1977 Foreign Corrupt Practices Act, which barred U.S. companies from paying bribes to win business. Just this year, the company—since merged with Martin Marietta Co. into Lockheed-Martin Corp. of Bethesda, Md.—pleaded guilty to making payments of $1.5 million to an Egyptian government official who helped it to win a contract for three C-130H aircraft. Lockheed paid $24 million in fines, more than twice the profits from the sale.

Fewer Yes Men

In 1989, Goodyear Tire & Rubber Co., of Akron, Ohio, pleaded guilty to offering bribes or "commissions," to an Iraqi trading company, saying the payments were for marketing studies and advertising. The company paid a $250,000 fine. The same year, Napco International Inc., of Hopkins, Minn., paid a $1 million fine after admitting it paid bribes to officials in Niger to help secure a contract to maintain government planes.

On the whole, though, says Peter B. Clark, who heads the Justice Department's enforcement of the anticorruption law, U.S. companies "are much cleaner than they were before" the law was enacted. In some cases, bribery is becoming less of an obstacle because of the current "privatization, free-trade mania," says John Cavanagh, a fellow at the Institute for Policy Studies in Washington. "There are fewer corrupt dictators with an entourage of yes men you have to get through to get the contract." More vital are benefits such as low-interest loans and promises to shift production to the country that grants a contract.

But in Eastern Europe, Africa, the Mideast and parts of Asia, which are just now throwing open their doors to foreign investment, the pressure for handouts remains. In Indonesia, businesspeople complain that a bribe of $100 is almost always necessary just to get a driver's license. Speedily extending an expatriate's work permit can cost $1,800 or more.

Pressing for Business

In India, corruption remains so pervasive that the biggest foreign investment in the country to date, a $2.8 billion power-plant project led by Enron Corp. of Houston, was canceled after several hundred million dollars had been spent. The state government that scrapped the project cited environmental and cost concerns. But privately, officials said the project was canceled, in large part, because, when they came into office, they just couldn't believe their predecessors and political rivals hadn't taken bribes. (Indian courts and government reviews have supported Enron's statements that there was no corruption involved.)

In Hong Kong, famous for its stern anticorruption laws, a survey by Political & Economic Risk Consulting Ltd. recently found that 57% of businesses there fear a rise in corruption as the territory's scheduled 1997 reversion to China nears. "With Asia emerging as a market, the opportunity for corruption is probably greater than it's ever been," says the consulting firm's founder, Robert C. Broadfoot. But he adds, "multinationals, especially from the U.S., do it more in petty, small, everyday things to build relationships."

Sometimes companies just cave in to local custom. Hewlett-Packard Co. offers Chinese journalists the equivalent of $12 to attend its news conferences. The company says the money is for taxi fares — which could cost that much — but it is equal to a week's pay for some journalists. "It's not a bribe," a spokeswoman says. "It's a Chinese local practice." The practice of companies paying reporters is so rampant that several big U.S. public-relations firms have drawn up guidelines, discouraging their clients from doling out any more cash for coverage.

One of the most widely bestowed favors by U.S. companies is the foreign trip. "Those trips provide an excellent opportunity to build relations with customers," says William Warwick, chairman of China operations for AT&T Corp., which like some other big U.S. companies treats Chinese decision makers to U.S. and sometimes European trips.

When Union Texas Petroleum Holdings Inc., of Houston, formed a petroleum joint venture with Pakistan's government, the company said it would spend more than $200,000 a year training government personnel. "Some portion of the training," it told the Justice Department, "will more readily be accomplished . . . in the U.S. and Europe." Union Texas said it would pay "necessary and reasonable" expenses.

Slots of Fun

Once in the U.S., visiting officials or executives spend at least part of their time seeing factories and training facilities or meeting with leaders of the U.S. companies—necessary under the law for the trips to qualify as a business expense. But side forays are virtually required, executives say.

"You'd think Disney World was a training site," says a person with the U.S.-China Business Council, an industry-funded group. Las Vegas and Atlantic City also are regular pit stops; Dow Jones & Co., the publisher of this newspaper, arranged an Atlantic City trip for one delegation from China. At Atlantic City, casinos often will give the visitors $20 or $25 to play at the slot machines. That may seem like small change, but for many Chinese officials, that is the equivalent of a week's salary.

The huge wealth gap makes trips to the U.S. generous fillips for developing-country visitors. For Chinese officials, the daily allowances given them by American companies over two weeks can equal a year's pay. U.S. companies say it isn't uncommon for Chinese delegations to arrive in the U.S. with no luggage, expecting their hosts to buy them clothing.

One U.S. electronics company operating in China pays allowances of $125 a day for visitors to its California headquarters. That money is so tempting, the company's Beijing representative says, that Chinese visitors often cram four people into a room. "We have to find a hotel that will accept that, and issue four receipts," he says.

"But is it corruption?" the executive asks. "I mean, if someone came up to me and offered me something worth 18 months' salary, it would certainly get my attention."

The U.S. government doesn't object to paid travel. Sometimes, it even lends a hand. A U.S. diplomat in Eastern Europe says that sometimes the U.S. government itself will pay for a ministry head to visit America before a U.S. company bids on a big contract.

Other enticements include scholarships for family members of officials that U.S. companies want to do business with, and help getting a visa to the U.S. "I spend a fair amount of time developing relations with people at the U.S. Embassy," an American Chamber of Commerce official in Beijing says. "If someone recommends a visa because it's good for U.S. business, it usually gets approved." A U.S. Embassy spokeswoman in Beijing says each visa application is considered individually.

Like Chubb, the insurance company, some U.S. companies just pour money into legal channels and hope for the best. Boeing Co. is spending more than $100 million to train Chinese workers how to use its technology. When International Business Machines Corp. Chairman Louis V. Gerstner visited Beijing in March, the company donated $25 million in hardware and software to 20 Chinese universities. It also funds scholarship programs.

But many small, privately held companies are now venturing overseas for the first time and can't afford such expensive means of buying goodwill. Small companies are also often less accountable to shareholders and the public, and can't complain to foreign leaders if low-level bureaucrats are demanding bribes. In one recent case, Vitusa Corp. of New Jersey paid a "service fee" of $50,000 to a government official in the Dominican Republic so Vitusa could get the final payment on its $3 million milk-powder contract. Vitusa pleaded guilty to a violation of U.S. law, and paid a $20,000 fine.

Local Agents

Another possible source of corruption: multinationals are becoming more decentralized, preferring to operate as a network of joint ventures and licensing arrangements. In Greece, for example, "there is a change of mentality of American companies," says Symeon G. Tsomokos of the American-Hellenic Chamber of Commerce. "They find a local consultant or agent and offer certain things through them. You cannot tell who is doing what."

Though some companies go to great lengths to make sure they are using reputable agents, such arrangements often invite corruption. Donald Zarin, a lawyer for U.S. companies with Dechert Price & Rhoads in Washington, says it is a "common occurrence" for an American company to discover that its agent is paying a bribe. Kroll Associates, a New York investigations firm, says it finds a dozen such cases a year in China. One U.S. consumer-products company found that its Chinese partner paid kickbacks to government officials when the Americans left the room. "If a U.S. company legitimately didn't know, it would not be liable," he says, as long as it fired the agent after finding out.

A less frequently reported problem revolves around what is known as an "inter-vening purchaser." Such a person or company gets a contract from a government— possibly by using bribes—and then sells the contract to a U.S. company. In such cases, it's "virtually impossible to prove" wrongdoing by the U.S. firm, the Justice Department's Mr. Clark says. "It's something we're concerned about."

High Toll

The U.S. law gives companies some flexibility in doling out money to cover payments necessary to keep a business going. Such "grease" payments are the most common, "sort of accepted practice, a tip," says a U.S. diplomat in Romania, where one U.S. joint venture was recently discovered paying a customs official $2,000 to get its trucks across the border. Mr. Clark says his "heart rate isn't going to jump if you pay the inspector a couple of hundred bucks to look at your plant." Even so, these grease payments can verge on outright bribery. Mr. Zarin, the Washington lawyer, says one of his clients was asked to pay $100,000 to get a company plane through an airport.

Refusing to give bribes can be costly. When Loy Veal, who heads Bucharest-based De Vealle Corporate Services, went to get approval for a building the company wanted to construct there, an official demanded a 1% commission to hasten the approval. Mr. Veal said no. "I don't play that way," he says. "I resent it."

The approval process, normally 90 days, stretched over a year, and his company lost the contract. A local company then took over the project and won approval, he says, "in hours."

Reprinted by permission of *The Wall Street Journal,* © 1995 Dow Jones & Company, Inc. All Rights Reserved Worldwide.